THE BEST OF THE
GOLD COUNTRY

*A complete, witty and remarkably useful
guide to California's Sierra foothills
and historic Sacramento*

By Don W. Martin and Betty Woo Martin

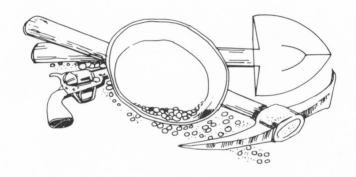

Pine Cone Press • Columbia, California

BOOKS BY DON & BETTY MARTIN

THE BEST OF THE GOLD COUNTRY • Pine Cone Press (First printing, 1987; second printing, 1990; revised 1992)

THE BEST OF THE WINE COUNTRY • Pine Cone Press (1991)

INSIDE SAN FRANCISCO • Pine Cone Press (1991)

COMING TO ARIZONA • Pine Cone Press (1991)

THE BEST OF ARIZONA • Pine Cone Press (1990)

THE BEST OF SAN FRANCISCO • Chronicle Books (1986; revised 1990)

SAN FRANCISCO'S ULTIMATE DINING GUIDE • Pine Cone Press (1988)

Library of Congress Cataloging-in-Publication Data
Martin, Don and Betty—
The Best of the Gold Country.
Includes index.
1. Northern California—Description and Travel (California Gold Country); 2. Northern California—History (California Gold Rush) 917.944
ISBN 0-942053-11-7
Library of Congress card catalog number 91-66845

Chapter illustrations & Golden Chain map • **Charles L. Beucher, Jr.**
Cartography • **Dianne Shannon,** Columbine Type and Design, Sonora, Calif.
Photography • **Don W. Martin**

The cover • This giant "tailing wheel" was used at the turn of the century to remove excess rock and dirt from the Kennedy Mine near Jackson.

CONTENTS

This book is dedicated...

...to the people who have made it their business to preserve the story of California and the Gold Rush: the men and women of the state parks of the Gold Country and historic Sacramento, and the volunteers of the state park associations.

With each passing year, there is more to discover, uncover and preserve in the California Gold Country. Yet each year, less money is available to protect that which can never be replaced, less money to teach ourselves and our children the priceless lessons of history. To close the gap between what is needed and what is available, concerned citizens have formed non-profit associations to help these and other California state parks. We salute these folks for their good works.

You can help by contacting one of these groups and offering your time, your skills or a financial contribution:

Chaw'se Indian Grinding Rock Association
Indian Grinding Rock State Historic Park
14881 Pine Grove-Volcano Road
Pine Grove, CA 95665
(209) 296-7488

Columbia Docent Association
Columbia State Historic Park
P.O. Box 367
Columbia, CA 95310
(209) 532-4301

Empire Mine Park Association
Empire Mine State Historic Park
10787 E. Empire Street
Grass Valley, CA 95945
(916) 273-8522

Gold Discovery Park Assn.
Marshall Gold Discovery State Historic Park
P.O. Box 265
Coloma, CA 95613
(916) 622-3470

Malakoff Diggins Park Assn.
Malakoff Diggins State Historic Park
23579 North Bloomfield Road
Nevada City, CA 95959
(916) 265-2740

Plumas Eureka Park Assn.
Plumas-Eureka State Park
310 Johnsville Road
Blairsden, CA 96103
(916) 836-2380

Railtown Docents Association
Railtown 1897 State Historic Park
P.O. Box 1250
Jamestown, CA 95327
(209) 984-3953

Sacramento State Parks Docent Association
111 I Street
Sacramento, CA 95814
(916) 323-9278

Sutter's Fort Docent Association
2701 L Street
Sacramento, CA 95814
(916) 445-4422

Wassama Round House Assn.
Wassama State Historic Park
P.O. Box 328
Ahwahnee, CA 93601
(209) 683-8869

FOREWORD

By the time you've reached this page, there's a good chance that you are not just thumbing a fresh copy into a slightly used one at a bookstall but have actually bought, borrowed or been given this book.

Don and Betty will be particularly glad if you bought it, and if you'll pick up another dozen copies to use as gifts. The reasons I am glad that you have it, and have it *open*, can be summed up in a presently out-of-favor word: *discrimination*. Don't confuse that with selectivity, a voguish sissy word about picking and choosing. Dis- crimination is knowing what to throw away.

One of the frustrating things about touring the California Gold Country is that there is so much of it, you will never be able to "do" it all. You had better find out ahead of time what to discard in today's somewhat tarnished Eldorado, lest you waste time there. So here you have The *Best* of the Gold Country, not omitting the worst, which it enables you to shun; or the mediocre, which it lets you ignore.

My Cornish grandfather and my Devon-born grandmother—a "direct" descendant of King Canute, we were always told—moved from Grass Valley to San Francisco's Twin Peaks in time for my mother, as a twelve-year-old, to store up vivid memories of days and nights spent looking down over the burning city. But all those images took second place to cherished remembrances of times in the Gold Country, when population had thinned and (even then) the ravaged earth was healing. It seemed I could hear the heavenly choirs of hardrock Cornish miners *a capella,* and the hell-shaking din of the stamp mills. I did not have to conjure up the aromas or the flavor of pasties, because as long as Grandma was alive, we occasionally were stuffed with them at home.

The Gold Rush came and went in a decade, before the Civil War. Then the placers petered out, hydraulic mining was outlawed and from the turn of the century through two world wars most of the Gold Country merely aged and mellowed, with a few huge dredges eking diminishing returns out of lowland stream beds. Most gold production was dependent on corporate mining of lodes as far under the surface as two miles, straight down to bedrock. The Depression put marginal operations out of business; the law requiring that all mined gold be turned over to the government at $35 per ounce pretty well wiped out the rest. All the while, the Gold Country grew more tranquil and beautiful. Even thirty-five years ago, when I last wrote anything of presumed substance about the region, the lovely towns weren't split by freeways, parking was easy, few mobile-home "parks" jarred the senses, and there wasn't much that wasn't genuinely quaint.

And I don't remember encountering one bed & breakfast. Think of that.

The new Gold Rush—not as dusty, perhaps not as ugly, not as visibly inspired by greed, and promising to be a lot more permanent than the first one—has changed the relative worth of sights to see and places to be. Many enterprises compete for your custom, and not all of them deserve it, by any means. How to avoid or dispel confusion, how to come away contented, how to feel enriched by the experience, how to *discriminate:* Don and Betty found the answers and assembled them here.

To be as complete as it has to be, this book must be reasonably thick. At the same time, it is one of the rarest of things: a how-to-do-it, where-to-find-it, what-you'll-pay guidebook that is fun to read.

It is, of course, better suited to studying piecemeal than to skimming all the way through at once—unless you're toying with the idea of doing all of Highway 49 in one bite (madness). Savor the apt chapters when you plan; use the references for making reservations when you need them. Then keep up with—and a little ahead of—your progress along the way by checking through these pages as Don and Betty take you by the hand.

Come to think of it, it will have to be both hands.

Martin Litton
Sequoia Forest Alliance

"In the beginning, cupidity may have strongly motivated the gold seekers, but courage and ardor sustained them through ceaseless toil in sandy river bed and stony gulch, over icy trail and burning desert. Their capital was pick and shovel, pan and cradle, grub and grit. They settled at various diggings along the Sierra foothills, in that strip of country known as the Mother Lode."
— From *Coulterville Chronicle* by Catherine Coffin Phillips, 1942

INTRODUCTION TO THE REVISED EDITION

We have a special reason for our love affair with California's Gold Country; we live in the gold rush town of Columbia, now a state historic park.

When we wrote the first edition of **The Best of the Gold Country** in 1987, we were San Francisco Bay Area residents, and we commuted to do our research. We have since made these history-ridden foothills our home.

Through the years, we have visited every slope, crevice and corner of California's Sierra Nevada foothills, where argonauts once probed every corner, slope and crevice in search of glitter. We've clunked along boardwalks of towns alive with yesterday memories, we've prowled every museum, poked about ancient headframes, enjoyed the nostalgia and hospitality of Victorian bed and breakfast inns, and shared an occasional beer with the good old boys in saloons that seem right out of a Western movie set.

We know the California Gold Country like our own back yard.

Because it is.

And now, on the pages to follow, we're going to tell you about our home territory—what it is and how it got to be this way.

The California Gold Rush spurred the greatest human migration in history. By the hundreds of thousands they came, abandoning their hardware stores in Illinois, their worked-out rice paddies in Canton and their ships in San Francisco Bay. Within months, a foothill wilderness became a tent camp suburbia of hastily assembled mining towns. California's 1848 population of 15,000—not counting native Americans—exploded to 225,000 in four years.

The 49ers had hardly swirled their first pan of gold-bearing gravel before tourists began poking around the place. Some likely were lured to the area by two early travel writers—Bret Harte and Mark Twain. Close on the heels of the curious came hoteliers, restaurateurs and (good grief) even tour guides. By 1874, the Yosemite Stage and Turnpike Company was running escorted tours from the gold camps into nearby Yosemite National Park.

At the peak of the Gold Rush in the 1850s, several hundred thousand miners were sloshing through the rivers and hacking at the hills of this region the Spanish called *La Veta Madre*—the Mother Lode. Soon the streams were panned out, so the relentless fortune hunters began burrowing into the earth, sometimes more than a mile, seeking elusive veins of gold-bearing quartz. Many streams were turned inside out as dredges sifted through the gravel. Men aimed high-powered hoses at hillsides, blasting away topsoil to reach the gold-bearing gravel beneath. This hydraulic mining was outlawed in 1884; hardrock mining continued but dwindled to almost nothing by the 1940s. Then, many of the streams were dammed to bring water and power to booming postwar California.

Thus, after decades of abuse by man, the Gold Country was good for nothing but tourism.

We're kidding, of course. Mother Nature has healed most of *La Veta Madre's* wounds, and this is one of the most scenic as well as historic areas in America. It offers a wealth of lures for the visitor, from sleepy old mining camps to vibrant towns proud of their heritage, from white water rafting to quiet swimming holes, from silent forests to noisy Gold Rush celebrations, and from hiking trails to ski trails. And yes, you can roar your speedboats above drowned mining camps on those reservoirs.

Tourism, in fact, is the leading industry for most of the Gold Country's eleven counties. Figures released by the Tuolumne County Visitors Bureau, for instance, indicated that visitors spent $60 million dollars, thousands of motel nights and three million "camping days" in the county in 1991. That's quite an economic impact for a county of less than 50,000 residents.

The Gold Country stretches for about 300 miles through east central California—a handsome foothill region of oak groves and golden meadows, bull pine forests and narrow river canyons. Above all this rise the bold granite spires that the Spanish named *Sierra Nevada*—the snowy peaks. A millennia of winter snows and spring rains leached gold from the stubborn granite of the Sierra and washed it down to the foothills, where it awaited discovery by James Marshall.

State Highway 49 twists through the area like a stepped-on snake, offering awesome ridgeline views and plunging dizzily into river canyons. It dips into lowlands that sizzle like a miner's skillet in summer and it traverses mountain passes dusted by winter snows.

Ironically, it's sometimes difficult to find a gold mine in the Gold Country. Most are on private property, and many abandoned shafts have been filled for safety's sake. A few mines have been re-activated in recent years, but folks grubbing around for gold aren't particularly hospitable. However, on the pages ahead, we will find you a few mine sites to explore.

To compile the original edition, we spent several months touring the Gold Country in Ickybod, our 1979 Volkswagen camper. We hurried Ick along foothill highways, bumped him over dusty side roads and made him climb—over his panting objections—to its highest vista points. We explored the Gold Country's towns, sampled its foods, toured its historic parks and poked through its boutiques. We talked to the people of the Mother Lode, and we read its books, trying to learn the way it was and the way it is.

We retraced our steps to do the revised edition, to determine what was new, what was changed and what was still old and interesting.

Then we sorted through all this, and saved the best for you.

Incidentally, we've cleverly edged this section with a black border, so you can thumb quickly back to it.

THE WAY THINGS WORK

Gold Country dining

Our intent here is to provide a selective dining sampler, not a complete list. In Gold Country towns suffering suburban sprawls, such as Placerville and Auburn, we focus more on restaurants in and about the historic districts.

We used several methods to select cafe candidates for possible inclusion: Inquiry among locals, suggestions from friends and our own experiences. Comments are based more on overviews of food and service, not on the proper doneness of a specific pork chop.

One has to be careful about recommending restaurants. Obviously, people's tastes differ, and it's difficult to judge a cafe by a single meal. Your well-done fish is someone else's artgum eraser. The chef might have a bad night, or a waitress might be recovering from one. Thus, your dining experience may be quite different from ours.

We graded the restaurants with one to four little wedges, for food quality, service and ambiance.

△ **Adequate**—A clean cafe with basic but edible grub.

△△ **Good**—A well-run place offering a fine meal and good service.

△△△ **Very good**—Substantially above average; excellent fare, served with a smile in a fine dining atmosphere.

△△△△ **Excellent**—We've found heaven, and it has a good wine list!

Price ranges are based on the tab for an average dinner, including soup or salad (but not drinks or dessert). Obviously, places serving only breakfast and/or lunch are priced accordingly.

$—Average dinner for one is $9 or less

$$—$10 to $14

$$$—$15 to $24

$$$$—$25 to $34

$$$$$—$35 and beyond

Ø—Non-Smoking section available in dining room. Double symbol means entire dining room is smoke-free.

Incidentally, if you love fresh seafood, don't expect miracles here. The Gold Country is a long way from the nearest ocean and most places get their orders only once or twice a week. So if the menu boasts that the catch of the day has never been frozen, perhaps it should have been.

A final culinary note: bedtime comes early for many Gold Country cooks. Some more contemporary restaurants in Nevada City, Sutter Creek and Sonora may keep later hours, but don't plan on chicken fried steak much past 9 p.m. in Mariposa or Volcano.

Gold Country lodgings

We checked most lodgings to insure that they're reasonably neat, clean and well run. We often rely on the judgment of the California State Automobile Association (AAA) because we respect its high standards. We also include some budget places that may fall short of Triple A ideals but still offer a clean room for a fair price. Of course we can't anticipate changes in management or the maid's day off, but hopefully your surprises will be good ones.

Some of California's earliest bed and breakfast inns were established in the Gold country's rich trove of Victorian and early American homes. We offer a good selection of them in each chapter. We list only true B&Bs, not merely family homes with an extra room because the oldest son is out panning for paydirt. With few exceptions, we've selected B&Bs with three or more units.

Generally, we list lodgings that are in or near the historic districts, not those in ordinary neighborhoods. This time, we use little Monopoly® style houses to rate them:

⌂ **Adequate**—Clean and basic; don't expect anything fancy.

⌂⌂ **Good**—A well-run establishment with comfortable beds and most essentials.

⌂⌂⌂ **Very good**—Substantially above average, generally with facilities such as a pool and spa.

⌂⌂⌂⌂ **Excellent**—An exceptional lodging with beautifully-appointed rooms, often with a restaurant and extensive amenities.

Ø—**Non-Smoking rooms** available. Double symbol means the entire facility is smoke-free (common with bed & breakfast inns).

Most bed & breakfast inns do not allow pets, so it is wise to inquire when you make reservations so your poor pooch doesn't have to spend the night in the back seat of your car.

Price ranges are listed for rooms during the most popular visitor months, which is summer in the Gold Country. Of course, many places reduce their rates during slower periods. Bed & breakfast inns, for instance, often have lower weekday rates. Price codes below indicate the cost of a standard room for two during high season. All prices were furnished to us by the establishments.

$—a double for under $25

$$—$25 to $49

$$$—$50 to $74

$$$$—$75 to $99

$$$$$—$100 or more

It's always wise to make advance reservations, particularly during weekends and local celebrations (listed at the end of each chapter). If you don't like the place and you're staying more than a day, you can always shop around after the first night and—hopefully—exchange lodgings.

Miscellany

TIMES & PRICES ● Don't rely too much on times listed in this book because many places seem to change their hours more often than a dead-beat changes his address. Prices change, too—inevitably upward—so use those shown only as guidelines. Also, restaurants seem to suffer a rather high attrition rate, so don't be crushed if one that we recommended has become a laundromat by the time you get there.

CAMPING ● Of course, there are campgrounds and RV parks scattered throughout the Gold Country. You also should know that all county fairgrounds in the area offer RV and trailer sites, usually with electrical hookups and showers. You won't get much of a wilderness experience in these places, but if you're traveling through the area with an RV or trailer—as we were for several months—they'll come in mighty handy.

NUGGETS ● These are lesser known, often overlooked attractions, shops, monuments, wide places in the road and other things that we felt had special appeal.

RIVER RUNNING ● The Sierra foothills offer some of the finest whitewater stretches in America, and we touch upon a few of them. But, as an old river runner, I must stress that you should never tackle wild water without proper equipment, skill and advance scouting. Our brief mentions aren't sufficiently detailed to prepare you. The safest way to hit the rapids is to sign up with a good, reliable outfitter. If you feel confident enough to go without a pro, your best information source is Fryar Calhoun and Jim Cassady's excellent book, *California White Water.* If you can't find a copy at a bookstore or specialty outdoor store, send $19.95 plus $2.05 for postage and handling to: Pacific River Supply, 3675 San Pablo Dam Rd., El Sobrante, CA 94803; (510) 223-3675.

CLOSING INTRODUCTORY THOUGHTS

Nobody's perfect, but we try. This book contains thousands of facts and a few are probably wrong. If you catch an error, let us know. Also, drop us a note if you discover that an historical museum has become an auto repair shop or the other way around; or if a restaurant, motel, bed & breakfast inn or attraction has opened or closed.

All who provide useful information will earn a free copy of the revised edition of *The Best of the Gold Country* or one of our other publications. (See listing in the back of this book.)

Address your comments to:

Pine Cone Press
P.O. Box 1494 (11362 Yankee Hill Rd.)
Columbia, CA 95310

A BIT ABOUT THE AUTHORS

The husband and wife team of Don and Betty Martin has produced more than half a dozen "opinionated, witty and remarkably useful" guidebooks. *The Best of the Gold Country* revision was a fun project, since they live on land once trod by 49ers. Their home is within the boundaries of Columbia State Historic Park.

Don has been writing for a living since he was seventeen, starting with a weekly newspaper in Idaho. He served as a Marine correspondent in the Orient, worked for assorted California newspapers and functioned for several years as associate editor of the California State Automobile Association's travel magazine. He also contributes travel articles and photos to assorted magazines and newspapers.

Wife Betty, equipped with the curious credentials of a doctorate in pharmacy and a California real estate broker's license, does much of the research and editing for their travel books. Like her husband, she has sold articles and photos to various newspapers and magazines.

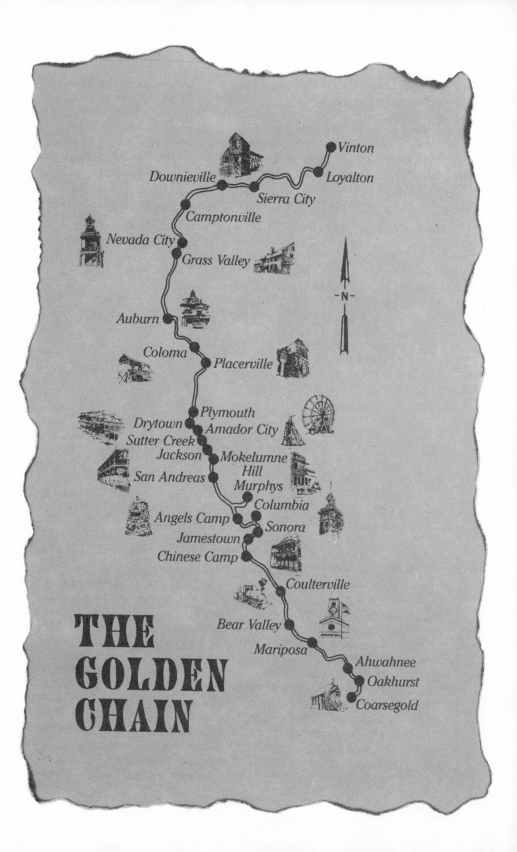

"There's thy gold, worse poison to men's souls."
—Shakespeare's *Romeo and Juliet*, Act V, Scene I

Chapter One
FOR THE LOVE OF GOLD
What it is; where to find it

In great and eager swarms they came—for the love, the lure and the lust of gold. Within months they catapulted a sleepy, remote American province—only recently snatched from Mexico—into world prominence.

"Gold! Gold in California!" Newspaper headlines shouted the news to a world that didn't even know what or where this place was.

Despite the state's Spanish heritage, it was gold that created California. Latino missionaries had ventured north from Mexico 80 years earlier to plant a string of missions along the coast and harass the native Americans into Christiandom. But their presence merely scratched the surface of what was to become the Golden State.

When California was ceded to the United States by the Treaty of Guadalupe Hidalgo in 1848, most of the Spanish-Mexican influence ended. What remained was a legacy of musical place names and a handful of Latinos who stayed on to become *Americanos*. Both are important parts of the state's fabric today.

The *real* California—the most populous, wealthiest, most racially mixed and sometimes wackiest state in the Union—is a bastard child of the Gold Rush. It attracted the sort of people who create a rich sociological stew: adventurers, opportunists, plutocrats, snake-oil peddlers, preachers, whores, noble men and women, highwaymen and thieves. And it lured them from the globe's farthest reaches.

One thing is for certain: the Gold Rush attracted damned few wimps.

"Every difficulty should be met with manly fortitude," gold-seeker Enos Christman wrote to his fiancèe back in Philadelphia. "My intention is to meet them in such a manner that I need never be ashamed. I now boldly turn my face toward the celebrated Sierra Nevada. What we may have to encounter I cannot anticipate; perhaps we shall have to engage with the native Indian in bloody conflict, or be hugged to death by the fierce and savage grizzly bear."

There is no record as to whether young Enos got rich, mugged by Indians or hugged by bears.

In early 1848, when itinerant handyman James Marshall had the dumb luck to find gold in the tailrace of a sawmill he was building for Swiss-German entrepreneur John Sutter, the United States ended at the Missouri border. All that lay beyond was a wilderness vaguely described as the Great Plains, with something called the Oregon Territory to the northwest.

In the mad dash to cash in on Marshall's discovery, argonauts overshot and ignored the great middle of America. When California became the thirty-first state in 1850, it was a socio-political island, tied to the rest of the nation only by thin, dusty wagon tracks. Communication with eastern America required months, via the uncertainties of ocean travel around Cape Horn, across the malaria-ridden isthmus of Panama or by Butterfield stage south through the New Mexico Territory. Early miners sent their laundry to China by clipper ship, for that was quicker that getting it back to Mom in Boston.

Thinkers in San Francisco and Washington saw the need to tie the fragile young nation—about to engage in a great civil war—together. The Gold Rush, then, became the reason for the Pony Express, the transcontinental telegraph and railroad. When the Civil War came, the south sought to lure California into the Confederacy. Skirmishes were fought between Union and Rebel sympathizers as far west as Arizona. Ironically, it was gold from California and silver from Nevada that helped defeat the Confederates.

That useless, precious prize

There are misconceptions about the people lured west by the discovery of gold in California. Most were not penniless drifters or idealistic dreamers. Records show that many—perhaps most—of the argonauts were educated. Many were doctors, lawyers, skilled craftsmen and artisans. Further, most of the gold-seekers were reasonably affluent—what we'd consider today as middle class or upper middle class. A substantial sum of money was required to buy wagon train or ship passage to California. The great majority were men in their early to mid- twenties. Women were a rarity in those first days, comprising about two percent of the Gold Country population.

What enticed so many educated young men on the threshold of useful lives to abandon everything and gallop into an uncertain wilderness? Gold had little practical use in the middle 19th century, except in the manufacture of false teeth and jewelry. However it has been, since man's earliest recording, the ultimate measure of wealth. In fact, loose gold—dust and nuggets—was used as legal tender in early California.

Although most argonauts were lured by the possibility of literally pulling money out of the ground, many of these sojourners struck out for Eldorado just for the adventure of it. They went to "see the elephant"—a popular expression of the day. For many, even those who returned with empty pockets—and the vast majority of them did—it was the experience of a lifetime.

All that glitters

Malleable, virtually indestructible, with a lustrous and sensual beauty, gold is the stuff of which dreams are made and wars are fought. Archeologists say it was one of the first metals used by man since—unlike most other ores—it often occurs in a near pure state. Thus, it can be worked without smelting or refining.

Tomb inscriptions reveal that Egyptians, using panning techniques similar to those of the 49ers, were washing for gold 50 centuries ago. With slaves to do their mining, Egyptian royalty amassed great quantities of the stuff—perhaps as much as five million pounds! Most of it was buried with these ancients, and most of that was taken through the centuries by tomb-robbers. The crypt the child king Tutankhamen, with its golden death mask and 224- pound golden coffin, is one of the few Egyptian burial sites left untouched until modern times.

After the Egyptian empire crumbled, Greeks and Romans accumulated vast quantities of gold, most of it through conquest. In the third century B.C., Alexander the Great snatched two million pounds of gold and silver ingots and half a million pounds of golden coins from the Persian city of Susa. Later, Roman Emperor Trajan relieved the province of Dancia—now Rumania—of half a million pounds of gold.

Romans also mined extensively, particularly in conquered Spain, where they sank deep shafts and shattered ore by heating it with fire, then dousing it with cold water.

Spain had her era of bloody golden glory as well. In 1532, Francisco Pizarro looted Peru's Incas of their gold, melting 20 centuries of fine craftsmanship into ingots for shipment back home. Later Spaniards raided Mexico's Mayan and Toltec temples. The greedy *conquistadores* were so thorough that only a handful of pre-Colombian icons remain from tons of objects thought to have existed. After conquering Mexico, Spain sent young Francisco Vasquez de Coronado into what is now the American southwest on a wild goose chase after the golden cities of Cibola. He found nothing but trouble, and returned empty-handed.

Little Portugal was no piker. During the 18th century, the tiny globe-girdling country hauled nearly *two million pounds* of gold dust from Brazilian mines.

Still mankind couldn't get enough of the stuff. During the Middle Ages, alchemists tried to create gold from a variety of substances, particularly lead. They never succeeded, but in the course of their efforts, they laid the foundations for modern chemistry.

Curiously, with all these hordes of gold gathered through the ages, there was never a true "gold rush" until James Marshall's discovery in California. It spurred the greatest movement of humanity up to that time, with estimates ranging anywhere from 300,000 to a million souls.

Few struck paydirt. In fact, more millionaires were created in the mercantiles than in the goldfields. During the peak of the fever in 1851 and 1852, butter and cheese commanded $6 a pound, eggs were sold for a dollar each and a bottle of ale would set you back $8. Even those who found gold didn't necessarily get rich. The market was so inundated during the early years of the rush that the price dropped from $20 to $9 an ounce.

An even bigger gold rush began in Australia in 1851 after an Aussie named E.H. Hargraves, prospecting in California, noted geological similarities to his homeland. Sprinting back to the land down under, he discovered vast deposits west of Sydney. Within four years, hundreds of thousands of eager argonauts swarmed over Australia; more than a million came from England alone.

Suddenly, avaricious men were looking everywhere for gold—and finding it. Strikes were made in British Columbia and Colorado in the 1850s, in

Reversal of fortunes? This sketch on the E Clampus Vitus "Wall of Comparative Ovations" at the Old Timers Museum in Murphys ponders the wisdom of the thousands who came seeking gold.

the Comstock Lode of Nevada (along with a lot of silver) in 1859, in Montana in the 1860s and in the Black Hills of South Dakota in 1875.

In the 40 years following Marshall's discovery, more gold poured from America and Australia than had been produced in the entire world in the previous four centuries.

Strikes were made around Nome, Alaska, and in Canada's Yukon as the twentieth century drew near. The celebrated Klondike Stampede began after three characters named George Carmack, Skookum Jim and Tagish Charlie found gold in a creek bed near Dawson City in 1897. By the time 50,000 "Ninety-Eighters" had trekked over tortuous Chilkoot Pass the following winter from Skagway, Alaska, most of the claims had been taken.

The Klondike, in fact, yielded more publicity than prosperity, generated by the writings of Jack London and poet Robert Service. *A single California mine*, the Empire near Grass Valley, yielded more glitter than entire Klondike Gold Rush—nearly three and a half million ounces between 1850 and 1928.

All of history's gold strikes pale when compared with the yield from the Witwatersrand area near Johannisberg, South Africa. Discovered in 1888 and still being worked today, the area has yielded 1.2 billion ounces of gold, nearly one third of the world's total supply. Ironically, there never was a rush to "The Rand." The gold is impregnated in the conglomerate rock of a sunken, landlocked reef and can be extracted only by heavy machinery. It has been a corporate venture since the beginning, when initial mining efforts were financed by Kimberly diamond mine millionaires.

Not surprisingly, South Africa is the world's leading gold producer, followed by Russia, Canada and the United States. These four countries provide 85 percent of the current supply. Nevada is America's largest gold-producing state, due to a 1980s resurgence of open-pit mining. Next in order are California, Colorado, South Dakota, Alaska, Utah, Montana and Arizona.

The fundamentals of gold

Did you ever, in a moment of love-smitten passion, say you wouldn't trade your sweetheart for all the gold in the world?

Just how much is that? According to F.W. McQuiston, Jr., author of *Gold: The Saga of the Empire Mine,* roughly four billion ounces of the stuff has been mined in the past 6,000 years; about three billion since Columbus discovered America.

Since gold is virtually indestructible and it's generally guarded rather jealously, a good part of that glitter is still around. The gold in a necklace you picked up in a Spanish curio shop may have come originally from an ingot melted down from the treasures of the Incas. Of course, a few of those treasure ships were sunk, so a fair amount of gold is lying at the bottom of the ocean, awaiting discovery and retrieval by aquatic treasure hunters. Other hordes have been hidden in jungles and caves to avoid theft, and lies forgotten by succeeding generations.

Let's say two-thirds of all the gold in the world still exists—about three billion troy ounces. You may know that troy weight is used to measure gold and *avoirdupois* is used for most everything else. There are 14.583 troy ounces in an avoirdupois pound, so the world"s gold supply weighs 102,859.49 tons. Half a ton measures about one cubic foot, so you could store all of the world's gold in a 65 by 65 foot room with a 12-foot ceiling.

Are you sure you don't want to re-consider that declaration to your sweetheart? You could store a good chunk of your treasure in the spare bedroom.

Just exactly what is this stuff, for which men sell their souls and governments plunder their neighbors?

Gold is one the naturally-occurring elements. Its scientific symbol is Au, from the Latin *aurum*. That, in turn, comes from the Greek word *Aurora,* the goddess of dawn, which is certainly appropriate.

Geologists think it formed eons ago as a blend of gases and liquids within the earth's molten core. In solution with silica, it gradually was forced toward the surface. Since gold has a relatively low melting point, 1,063 degrees Celsius, compared with iron's 1,530, it often liquefies and deposits itself in veins and pockets, particularly in areas with a history of volcanic activity. Quartz is a common golden host.

Gold is the most malleable and ductile (stretchable) of all metals. An ounce can be drawn into a thread 40 miles long; a cubic inch can be hammered over a 1,400 square-foot surface. It can be beaten to 1/300,000 of an inch thick without disintegrating. A gold layer as thin as one half millionth of an inch, applied through electroplating, is used on some satellites to reflect the sun's heat. It's also an excellent and tarnish-proof conductor of electricity, often used in micro-circuitry.

Chemically inactive, it's virtually corrosion free. Golden coins found in sunken ships still glitter after centuries of exposure to salt water. It can be altered only by the most caustic solutions, such as *aqua regia,* a blend of nitric and hydrochloric acid. Refineries use another potent brew, sodium or calcium cyanide—to dissolve pulverized ore in order to separate the gold from its host material.

Gold is one of the heaviest metals, with a specific gravity of 19.2, which means it's more than 19 times heavier than water. It's also six to seven times heavier than most other minerals, which is the key to its recovery by panning, which we will discuss shortly. Despite its weight, gold is as soft as your fingernail, rated on the Mohs' scale at 2.5, compared with 6 for iron and 7 for quartz. For this reason, most gold used in jewelry is alloyed with copper, nickel or other minerals.

Gold deposits are widely distributed throughout the world. The greatest cache, in fact, is in seawater. However, no one has devised a practical way to mine the big briny, since gold occurs in solution at six parts per one trillion parts of water. But don't dismay. The U.S. Bureau of Mines estimates that 20 million ounces of economically recoverable gold remain in American soil and bedrock. Most of it is concentrated in the Western and southern states. Worldwide, geologists guesstimate that only one 200,000th of one percent of the gold in the earth's crust has been recovered!

The Mother Lode

The Sierra Nevada offers ideal conditions for placer deposits. The surface of east-central California was uplifted and twisted by magma during the Jurrasic Period, about 160 million years ago. As it cooled, the igneous rock was shattered by cracks and fissures, where gold and other elements—in liquid form—gathered and congealed.

As the dinosaurs started biting the dust, during the late Cretacious and early Tertiary periods (70 to 130 million years ago), erosion began wearing down the "pre-Sierra Nevada" and exposing these gold-bearing veins. Streams gathered and concentrated the deposits. The Tertiary Sierran Uplift, which built the Sierra Nevada 70 million years ago, shifted stream flows from north-south to east-west. This cut into these deposits, loosened some of the gold and carried it downstream, there to await Jim Marshall's luck.

Gold deposits occupy narrow faulted bands, from a few hundred feet to a few miles wide. They extend nearly 300 miles from Sierra City in the north to Coarsegold in the south. The main cache is a broken fault line, tilted downward and jammed as much as a mile into the earth. Called the Mother Lode (from *La Veta Madre* in Spanish), it runs parallel to the Sierra Nevada, reaching from Georgetown above Placerville, 120 miles south to Mormon Bar, just southeast of Mariposa.

To the dismay of Gold Country residents and nitpicky geologists, chambers of commerce, tourist brochures and misinformed travel writers often call the entire Sierra Nevada foothills the Mother Lode. For general purposes, one should refer to the area south of Auburn as the Mother Lode and the region above as the Northern Mines district. Incidentally, James Marshall, in discovering gold at Sutter's Mill, missed *La Veta Madre* by about eight miles.

HOW & WHERE TO FIND GOLD

One of the pleasures of visiting California's Gold Country is to pan for the precious metal, in much the same manner as the 49ers did. Panning is akin to winnowing with water. Since gold is considerably heavier than its host material, the idea is to joggle and slosh a pan of sand and gravel to gradually work the glitter to the bottom.

It doesn't require a lot of equipment, preparation or even skill. You can become a latter-day 49er with these items:

1. A gold pan, available at stores and shops in the Gold Country.

2. "Crevice tools"—a small pick, thick-bladed knife or slot-bladed screwdriver and a spoon.

3. A shovel for loosening gravel and filling your pan.

4. A pair of tweezers to work particles out of crevices.

5. A magnifying glass (not needed if you intend to pan for large nuggets).

6. A magnet to remove black sand (iron ore) from the bottom of your pan.

7. A vial to hold your booty.

8. Optional items include rubber gloves for protection from cold water, waterproof shoes or water-resistant feet, liniment for your aching back and patience.

The best time to pan is during spring runoff, which may bring new gold downstream from the Sierra, or uncover existing deposits.

You can prospect for gold in streams on any public land that isn't posted, such as state park, state and national forest and Bureau of Land Management holdings. U.S. Forest Service offices often have maps showing likely panning areas, as do some Gold Country chambers of commerce. Many Sierra foothills motels, inns and resorts located on streams permit—yea—encourage panning. Bookstores, gift and curio shops and museums offer maps and books about gold and panning techniques.

Where to look

Working from south to north, here are some areas open to public panning in the Gold Country:

Mariposa County • Along the Merced River off Highway 140 in Sierra National Forest, between Savage Trading Post and El Portal.

Tuolumne County • South and middle forks of the Tuolumne River in Stanislaus National Forest, between Groveland and the Big Oak Flat entrance to Yosemite National Park. Also on the upper reaches of the Stanislaus River, reached via Italian Bar Road out of Columbia State Historic Park.

Calaveras County • On the north fork of the Stanislaus and its tributaries, around Calaveras Big Trees State Park.

Amador County • Along the various tributaries of the Cosumnes River in El Dorado National Forest, following North-South Road north from State Highway 88 above Jackson (turn off at Cooks Station).

El Dorado-Placer counties • Along the American River around Coloma, and on the north and middle forks of the American River in Auburn State Recreation Area.

Nevada County • South Yuba Recreation Area north of Nevada City, and around the hamlet of Washington, off Highway 20.

Sierra County • This area has more easily-accessible riverfront than any other in the Gold Country. Try the banks of the Yuba River as it follows Highway 49 between Camptonville and Sierra City, and the Downie River northeast of Downieville. Also, Downieville offers public panning areas.

Where does gold hide?

To begin, find a spot where gold is likely to be deposited in a stream bed. Look for places where the flow of water has been slowed, allowing it to drop any particles of gold and other heavier materials. Likely spots include:

1. An inside bend in the stream.
2. The upstream side of a tree root or other obstruction.
3. Grassy and mossy areas.
4. Downstream from rapids or fallen trees.
5. Under the downstream side of a boulder.
6. Cracks in the stream bottom or any crevice in the stream's course or bank. These grooves are good gold traps, and should be dug out with your crevice tools.

The panning technique

1. Fill your pan more than half full of gravel and sand, then discard the heavier stones and break up any clods. Give it several hard shakes and hit the rim with the heel of your hand to start the heavier material working toward the bottom.

2. Lower it into the stream, almost level but tilted slightly away from your body, and let it flood with water. Bring it to the surface, with the forward rim dipped into the stream. Jiggle and slosh it to encourage the mud, gravel and lighter sand to spill over the lip. Use a back-and-forth circular motion, with an occasional jerk or a tap on the rim of the pan with the heel of your hand. Level it occasionally and toss off lighter but larger pebbles that have worked to the surface.

3. Keep swirling and sloshing the pan from side to side, occasionally bucking it forward to let more material slough off, until you've reduced the material to black sand, *hematite* or *magnetite*, which are about three-fourths iron ore.

4. Continue working the sand—very carefully—until you've reduced your pan to hoped-for "color," or save it in a bucket and do your final pan-out later. Use the magnet to separate the last of the black sand from the gold dust.

We usually work the first two or three pans completely, to determine if there is any yield in the area. If it doesn't "pan out"—which is where that term originated—we move on to another spot.

What we're doing here is placer mining ("*a*" *as in cat*). We're seeking gold that has been leached from its "lode vein" by erosion, rainfall and other acts of nature.

Go with a pro?

Several outfits in the Gold Country can teach you gold-panning techniques and take you—for a fee—to some chosen spots. You'll find more detailed listings under Diversions in the chapters ahead. Among the gold-finding firms are:

Gold Prospecting Expeditions in Jamestown, (209) 984-4653; offering gold panning lessons at a trough out front, and expeditions ranging from a few hours to several days.

Jensen's Pick and Shovel in Vallecitos near Angels Camp, (209) 736-

THE CLAMPERS: WHERE DID THEY COME FROM?

E Clampus Vitus, the "secret society" created by high spirited miners as a parody of serious fraternal orders, was one of the more colorful and lighthearted by-products of the Gold Rush.

Service clubs were quite active in early California and virtually every foothill town has its surviving I.O.O.F. and Masonic hall—often the most substantial structures built. These sober institutions were tempting targets for the high living Clampers.

Curiously, no one is certain just where or when E Clampus Vitus was founded. "The trouble was," a member once explained, "during the meetings none of the brothers was in condition to keep any minutes, and afterwards nobody could remember what had taken place."

Some historians say the organization started in Sierra City in 1857. However, freelance writer and Gold Rush historian Pat Jones, whose husband is an active Clamper, traces its roots back further, possibly to San Francisco. She quotes from a September 28, 1852, *Sacramento Union* article: "Some of the San Francisco editors are puzzling their heads to know what can be the object or aim of a newly created secret society." The article called the group *E Clampsus Vitus.*

Clampers of the day insisted that their club, named for St. Vitus, was considerably older. Dating from 4004 B.C., it was established in the Garden of Eden, with Adam as the first Noble Grand Humbug.

The group's primary function was to recruit new members, charge them a large fee, then drink up the proceeds during a wild initiation ceremony. Typical of the procedures was to place the initiate on a large wet sponge in a wheelbarrow and run it over a stepladder laid on the ground.

Their avowed purpose was to assist widows and orphans—and particularly widows. Once members survived the initiation, they were given "titles of equal importance." The group met in the "Hall of Comparative Ovations", and their fraternal banner was a hoop skirt bearing the motto: "This is the flag we fight under."

Despite their lust for partying and their love of silliness in general, they sponsored many worthwhile services during the Gold Rush.

"They sat down and discussed whether the family of the preacher in the next town didn't perhaps need a benefit" or whether some other worthy cause needed serving, writes Joseph Henry Jackson in *Anybody's Gold*. "The newspapers of the Fifties are full of notices of charities being carried out by the society."

The order died out along with the Gold Rush, then it was re-activated in 1931 by historian Carl I. Wheat and author G. Ezra Dane. It still thrives, with chapters throughout California, and particularly in the Gold Country. Today's Clampers perform the valuable functions of compiling and preserving early California records and erecting monuments at historical sites.

E Clampus Vitus hasn't lost its love of partying. Expect to see members of local chapters parading and whooping it up at Gold Country celebrations, then adjourning to the nearest saloon to review the day's events over a wee dram of spirits.

0287; with panning supplies and gold-seeking trips.

Lor-E-L Mining in Mariposa at (209) 742-5255; gold panning lessons at a flume or at creekside and all-day mining excursions.

Roaring Camp near Pine Grove, (209) 296-4100; a hideaway streamside resort where gold panning is part of your vacation.

Doss Thornton's Gold Panning Tours in Grass Valley, c/o Holiday Lodge, (916) 273-4406; offering hourly or all-day gold panning.

Vista Gold Tours in Mariposa, (209) 966-5100; featuring three-hour panning trips, panning lessons and visits to a hardrock mine.

Mine tours and museums

California State Mining and Mineral Museum at the Mariposa County Fairgrounds, (209) 742-7625. The museum offers some fine gold and mineral exhibits, plus books on gold prospecting and panning and Gold Country history.

Hidden Treasure Mine Tour in Columbia State Historic Park, (209) 532-9693. The firm offers a salted panning trough in the park and excursions into a nearby hardrock mine.

Sonora Mining Company, offers tours of its Jamestown Mine every Thursday by reservation: (209) 984-4641. Don't expect a journey into the center of the earth. The Jamestown is an open pit mine and the gold is scooped up by giant earthmovers—at the ratio of about an ounce to a ton of rock—and trucked to a modern reduction and chemical smeltering plant.

To learn more...

California Division of Mines and Geology, P.O. Box 2980, Sacramento, CA 95812-2980, (916) 445-5716. This state agency can send you three very useful publications for $5 each: *Geology of Placer Deposits* (SP-34); *Basic Placer Mining* (SP-41); and *Placer Gold Recovery Methods* (SP-87). Price includes tax and shipping. Send a check or money order and designate which books you want by number and title, since the department has scores of publications.

Department of Conservation, 1416 Ninth St., Sacramento, CA 85814; (916) 322-7683. The agency can provide general information about gold prospecting and mining in California.

U.S. Bureau of Land Management, 2800 Cottage Way, Sacramento, CA 95825; (916) 978-4754. Should you want to get serious about gold mining, BLM can send you two publications at $4 each: *Discovery, Location, Recordation and Assessment Work for Mining Claims and Sites in California* and *Patenting Mining Claims and Mill Sites in California*. Enclose a check or money order, or you can order the publications by phone with a credit card number.

"This monument marks the southern terminus of Highway 49, which passes through 51 cities, towns and settlements and 11 counties in its 310-mile wandering route through some of the most scenic and mineral-rich area in all of the land." **— Marker Inscription in Oakhurst**

Chapter Two
OAKHURST & SURROUNDS
Have some
Madera, M'dear?

"LITTLE CHURCH ON THE HILL" IN OAKHURST

Our journey through the California Gold Country begins—curiously enough—in Madera County, generally regarded as a flatland farming area in the broad San Joaquin Valley.

Fortyniners never got this far south unless they were prospecting for salad vegetables. However, they did reach the county's hilly northeastern corner, below Yosemite National Park. Madera is Spanish for lumber, and the name applied to a wooden flume that carried water to the city of Madera, the county seat. Around the turn of the century, another flume carried timber to the railhead in that city from the Madera Sugar Pine Lumber Company's operation near Fish Camp.

(The name is coincidentally similar to Madeira, a sticky, sweet wine produced hereabouts and suitable only for dessert topping or nipping from bottles concealed in paper sacks.)

Starting in the city of Madera, follow State Highway 145 northeast through the county's flat agricultural land. After 14 miles, swing left onto Route 41. If you're approaching from the south, you can pick up Highway 41 in Fresno—a quick route since it's freeway through most of that city's suburban sprawl.

Soon, you begin climbing into brushy, scrub oak foothills, the forerunners of the Sierra Nevada, those granite peaks that give birth to the gold-bearing streams of the Mother Lode. However, during your Gold Country exploration, you rarely see those legendary spires; you're too close to the foothills to see the main range.

Your first stop is a hamlet with a name right out of a low budget Western movie—Coarsegold. You haven't yet reached Highway 49, the so-called "Golden Chain." That route begins eight miles to the north, in Oakhurst. But we're including Coarsegold in our Mother Lode exploration because it does figure in the history of the California Gold Rush. Besides, with a name like that, how could we resist?

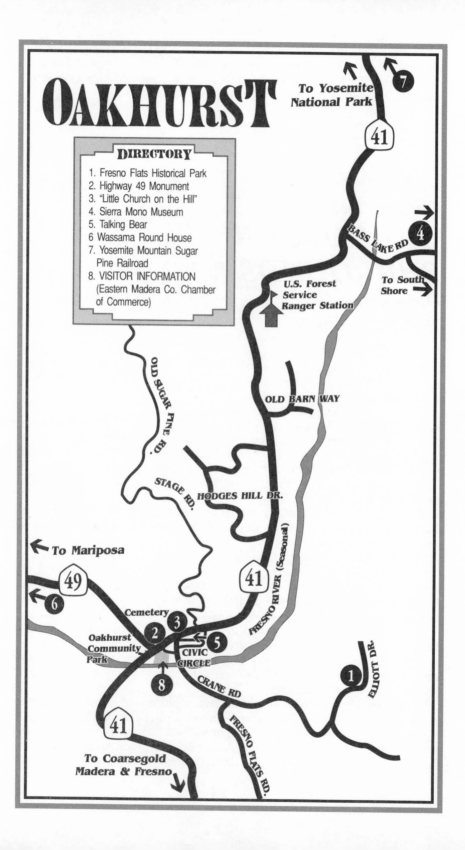

THE WAY IT WAS • The towns of Coarsegold and Oakhurst were late bloomers in the settling of the Gold Country. Although a few prospectors panned the Fresno River south of present day Oakhurst and seasonal creeks around Coarsegold as early as 1852, serious occupation of eastern Madera County didn't begin until about five years later.

Coarsegold, in name and in fact, was more of a mining town than Oakhurst. Around 1890, a single nugget worth $15,000 was discovered by four Texans working a supposedly worthless claim. Scores of other claims—nearly 70 by one historian's count—were being worked between the 1850s and the turn of the century. Most were hardrock mines, for the easy creek bed pickin's had long since been picked clean.

Oakhurst was primarily a lumbering and farming community, and the original settlement, across a dry creek bed from the present-day town, had a much more earthy name—Fresno Flats. And therein lies a tale.

It seems that around the turn of the century, some bad guys held up a stagecoach near town, and the son of a prominent local family was accused of taking part. Although he was cleared, he left town—and in doing so—left his wife. He returned a few years later with a brand new bride. The new Mrs. Somebody soon grew weary of hearing stories about the great Fresno Flats stagecoach robbery and her husband's suspected implication. So she petitioned—persistently and finally successfully—to have the name changed. In 1912, Fresno Flats became Oakhurst.

THE WAY IT IS • Today's Coarsegold, a tree-shaded hamlet of 1,365 souls, doesn't offer much to the visitor. Its primary lures, Coarsegold Inn and Pizza Joe's, burned down since we wrote the original edition of this book, and haven't been replaced.

About all that survives of tourist interest are the Coarsegold Saddleshop, offering Western wear, a few curios and veterinary supplies in an oldstyle false front building; and Yosemite Gallery, with an assortment of Indian crafts and jewelry and Western art.

Oakhurst is considerably larger, with a population topping 2,000, and a disjointed business district that stretches for several blocks in three directions. A few false front stores are scattered among the service stations and fast food places, but all are of recent origin. Little of the town's past has been preserved, except in Fresno Flats Historical Park, which we will discuss shortly.

Today's Oakhurst visitor sees a tidy, prosperous if poorly planned town experiencing a sudden growth surge. Refugees from the hot San Joaquin Valley below seek shelter in these cooler Sierra Nevada foothills. The town offers several motels and restaurants, supported more by tourists headed for nearby Yosemite National Park than by Gold Country explorers. The park's Big Trees entrance is less than 20 miles east on Highway 41. The popular Bass Lake recreation area and the Yosemite Mountain Sugar Pine Railroad are just up the highway as well.

The highway you seek, Route 49, begins in downtown Oakhurst. A monument, from which we quoted to open this chapter, is situated at the entrance to Raley's Shopping Center, near the junction of highways 41 and 49, under a Bank of America sign.

DISCOVERIES
The best attractions

Fresno Flats Historical Park ● *49777 Road 427, Oakhurst; (209) 683-6570. Wednesday-Saturday 1 to 3 and Sunday 1 to 4; weekends only from 1 to 4 the rest of the year. Adults $1, kids 50 cents. Picnic area.* Fresno Flats is a combined museum and outdoor historic park, where Oakhurst's history-conscious citizens have reassembled several structures dating back a century or more. Although hours are rather limited, the grounds are open and visitors can drop in any time to peer into the assorted historic buildings.

Among its structures are an unusual 1867 double log cabin with an open breezeway (called a "two-pen dog trot" in the Old South, where it originated), a cheerful yellow wood frame house dating from 1878, a blacksmith shop, several early-day wagons and buggies and an 1880 jail from Fresno Flats and another—built in 1890—from the nearby town of Raymond. Both were constructed by stacking two-by-six timbers on their sides. James Bond could probably make short work of these flimsy old structures, but they look sturdy enough to contain the survivors of Saturday night bar brawls. The main museum features some beautiful country quilts and lacework, plus assorted pioneer curious and photos of early-day eastern Madera County.

Here, we learned that the original Yosemite Sam wasn't a mustachioed character who gave Bugs Bunny a hard time. He was Samuel L. Clark, a ranger who earned his nickname by spending 40 years at Yosemite National Park. After he died in 1978, his family gave the museum his fine collection of guns, leather chaps and other Western regalia.

Yosemite Mountain Sugar Pine Railroad ● *Yosemite Mountain, Fish Camp, CA 93623; (209) 683-7273. Steam train rides $6.75 for adults and $3.75 for kids 3 to 12 ($4.75 and $2.75 in the Jenny railcar). Also special train ride/Western barbecue packages with live entertainment for $18.50 and $10.50. Train rides daily mid-April through October. Complex includes a museum, "Cookhouse" sandwich shop, gift shop with extensive railroading memorabilia and picnic area.*

Tucked into the pines about 15 miles above Oakhurst, Sugar Pine Railroad takes visitors on a four-mile run over the route of the old Madera Sugar Pine Lumber Company. This firm logged more than 30,000 acres from 1899 to 1931, sending the logs by a 34-mile flume to Madera.

Passengers ride behind a chuffing steam engine in open rail cars—some of them with seats fashioned from huge notched logs. The big trains operate weekends only. On alternate days, neat little Model-A powered Jenny rail cars offer 30-minute narrated trips over the same route. A restaurant and rooms are available at the next-door Narrow Gauge Inn; see Lodgings below.

The rest

The Little Church on the Hill ● *Crowning a hilltop above Highway 41, Oakhurst.* This typical New England style steepled church is open for special services only, or when the caretaker happens to be around. Built in 1892 as Christ Church in Fresno Flats, it was later moved to this hilltop site. Surrounding tombstones of Oakhill Cemetery tell some of the grim history of the settlement of the West. One is a monument to Lieutenant Skeane S.

This "two-pen dog trot" double log cabin with a breezeway is one of several early-day structures at Oakhurst's Fresno Flats Historical Park.

Skeenes, who was killed in an encounter with Indians near Ahwahnee, north of Oakhurst. The inscription doesn't indicate how many Indians were killed.

Sierra Mono Museum ● *Junction of roads 225, 228 and 274, North Fork; (209) 877-2115. Monday-Saturday 9 to 4; Adults $1, kids 75 cents.* Housed in an interesting cross-timbered stone-faced structure, it's operated by Mono Indians of the region, and contains a pleasantly undisciplined collection of everything from the usual reed baskets and grinding rocks to stuffed critters. We like beautiful examples of native American beadwork and a full sized bark wikiup outside, guarded by a pair of handsomely carved wooden cougars. What the museum lacks in consistency, it makes up for in variety.

Wassama Round House ● *Road 628 (five and a half miles north of Oakhurst), Ahwahnee; (209) 683-3631 or 683-8194. Daily 11 a.m. to 4 p.m. Admission 75 cents. Picnic area. Native American dances and demonstrations of basketry, acorn preparation and beadwork presented periodically; call for times.* Round houses were large shelters where Mi-Wuk Indians danced and sang to celebrate the harvest, communicate with their spirits and mourn the dead. The original structure on this site was built in 1860; it and several others were burned, usually as a ceremonial gesture upon the death of a chief.

The present round house was assembled in 1975 by area Indians with the help of several local and state agencies, and it's now a state historic park. Visitors can step into the cool, spacious interior, furnished only with a fire pit and a few low seats. Nearby are a model Indian compound with a sweat house, dance ring and three Mi-Wuk wikiups made from large sections of tree bark. The complex is shaded by a cluster of massive oaks. To find it, follow Highway 49 through Ahwahnee, then go right on Round House Road for half a mile.

Nuggets

Highway 49 Monument • *At the entrance to Golden Oak Village Shopping Center near its junction with Highway 41.* As we mentioned earlier, this marks the southern terminus of Highway 49. An interesting feature of this monument is that it's assembled from eleven different stones—each native to one of the eleven Mother Lode counties.

The Talking Bear • *At the corner of Highway 41 and Road 426 in downtown Oakhurst.* You may feel a little silly standing there, waiting for the statue of a grizzly to say something interesting. But the bear does talk, offering commentary on the history of the extinct California grizzly and telling you to be careful with fire in the forest. Smokey couldn't do better.

Chevron Service Station • *Downtown Coarsegold.* If service stations can be historic, this one is. It began life a century ago as a blacksmith shop, livery stable and Yosemite stage stop, then was converted to a Red Crown service station in 1920. It's now one of California's senior Chevron stations, dating back to 1940. Several photos of old Coarsegold are displayed inside.

DETOURS

Coarsegold to Raymond to Oakhurst • *A 43-mile loop trip.* This route takes you through the tawny wild oat foothills west of Coarsegold to an active granite quarry, an interesting granite church and past 100-year-old stone fences built by early Chinese immigrants.

From Coarsegold, follow Raymond Road west for about ten miles, then bend slightly left onto Road 606 to Knowles. Once a busy granite quarrying area, Knowles today is a tiny collection of oak shaded houses, with no business district. Note the unusual granite St. Anne's Catholic Chapel just east of the little town. In an area where most churches are classic New England clapboard, this solid stone chapel looks oddly misplaced, even a bit stern. Just beyond the church is the area's only active granite quarry. Stone quarried from here was used to rebuild much of San Francisco after the 1906 earthquake and fire.

Continue on Road 606 for about a mile until it hits Road 600, then swing right and drive north to Raymond. It's a quiet farming town that's lost all trace of its once active role as a quarrying center and minor Gold Rush town. Along Road 600, stone fences follow the lazy contours of this pleasant farm country. They were built more than a century ago by Chinese who came here after the gold mines had played out.

Road 600 eventually returns you to Highway 49 about five miles north of Oakhurst.

Oakhurst to Bass Lake • *A 35-mile loop from Oakhurst and back.* Bass Lake is basically a reservoir recreation area with the usual boating, swimming and fishing amenities, high in the Sierra foothills. It has little to do with the Gold Rush, but it's a nice woodsy place.

To begin, head north from Oakhurst on Highway 41, then turn right after 3.5 miles onto Road 222 at the Bass Lake sign. After four miles, take a left fork onto Road 274. This is an area rich in evergreen forests, but do not mistake it for a pristine wilderness. We counted nearly as many summer homes around Bass Lake as bull pines, and on a July weekend, the lake rivals Santa Cruz for bronzed bodies and busy activities.

Continuing south on Road 274 toward North Fork, you see the Sierra Mono Museum (list above) at the merger of three county roads. From here, turn right onto Road 222 and pass through the folksy little mountain town of North Fork. A few miles beyond, you can follow sign to the left Old Town, a made-to-look-old tourist attraction. This western-style town with shops, a saloon and restaurant was closed in the late 1980s, but it may have re-opened by the time you pass by.

Beyond Old Town, you'll merge onto Road 222 again, which twists into steep hills then winds downward and hugs the irregular south shoreline of Bass Lake. It passes several Forest Service campgrounds and offers frequent vistas of the busy blue surface, then rejoins Highway 41 for the return to Oakhurst.

DIVERSIONS

Apple munching • *Yosemite Apple Growers Association, P.O. Box 2687, Oakhurst, CA 93644; send for a free map of direct-to-consumer apple orchards.* More than 30 apple growers in the hills above Oakhurst invite U-pickers and sell apples and things made from apples, direct to consumers. Apple harvest generally is in October.

Excursion boat • *Bass Lake Queen II, (209) 642-2585. One-hour narrated cruises of Bass Lake daily mid-June through Memorial Day; adults $5, kids 12 and under 2.50.* This oldstyle paddlewheeler chugs about Bass Lake; voyagers can bring their own food and beverages or have food catered by Pines Resort. Breakfast, picnic, sunset and dessert cruises scheduled as well.

Hiking, backpacking and such • Sierra National Forest, east of Oakhurst, offers the usual assortment of high country trails, plus some alpine lakes and a ski area. To learn all about it, check the national forest headquarters listed at the end of this chapter.

Water sports of all sorts • Bass Lake is a popular water recreation area, offering fishing, swimming, water skiing and just about anything else one can do on water. For details, contact the Bass Lake and North Fork chambers of commerce; addresses are listed below.

GOLD COUNTRY DINING

Castillo's Mexican Food • Δ $

49215 Golden Oak Loop, Oakhurst, (209) 683-8000. Mexican; dinners $6.25 to $12; wine and beer. Daily 10 a.m. to 10 p.m. No reservations or credit cards. A basic smashed beans and rice place with specialties such as *machata* roast beef with egg, *fajitas* and chili verde. It's housed in a railway station-style structure with an old red Santa Fe caboose (courtesy of the former tenant, Oakhurst Station Restaurant). Wood-paneled interior with Mexican curios on a high shelf where model trains once ran.

Erna's Elderberry House • ΔΔΔΔ $$$$$ ØØ

Highway 41 and Victoria Lane, (P.O. Box 2413) Oakhurst; (209) 683-6800. Continental; prix fixe dinners $45; full bar service. Open daily except Tuesday with two dinner seatings at 5:30-6:15 and 8-8:30; Sunday brunch 11 to 1, lunch Wednesday-Friday 11:30 to 1. Reservations advised, essential on weekends; MC/VISA. Opulent restaurant housed in a Mediterranean villa in a wooded grove, on a hill overlooking Oakhurst. Beautifully appointed interior with chandeliers and European furnishings; tables set with damask linen, fresh flowers and leaded crystal. Daily-changing menu featuring European and California *nouveau* dishes; extensive wine list. Four smoke-free dining rooms; summer meal service on a terrace. Smoking permitted in the Wine Cellar bar.

The Old Barn • ΔΔΔ $$

41486 Old Barn Way, off Highway 41 just north of Oakhurst; (209) 683-BARN. Basic American menu; dinners $9 to $16; full bar service. Dinner daily starting at 5, Sunday brunch 10 to 2. Reservations accepted. MC/VISA. Housed in a barn that was hauled to this spot and reassembled as a country restaurant. Basic chops, chicken and fish, with hearty portions that'll send you waddling out the door. It's a fun place, with assorted down home doodads hanging from the walls and open rafters. Popular with locals.

Ol' Kettle Restaurant • ΔΔ $$ ∅

Highway 41 at Hodges Hill Road, next to Shiloh Inn; (209) 683-7505. American menu; dinners $6 to $15; full bar service. Monday-Saturday 6 a.m. to 9 p.m., Sunday 7 to 8. MC/VISA. Chicken and chops served in a pleasing early American environment with bay windows, lace curtains and print wallpaper. Comfortable booths or tables; attentive service and reliably tasty food in reasonable portions.

Pines Restaurant • ΔΔ $$

At The Pines Resorts, Bass Lake; (209) 642-3233. American; dinners $10 to $15; full bar service. Daily 7 a.m. to 9 p.m. (to 10 Friday and Saturday). Major credit cards. Attractive restaurant in the Pines Resort complex on the north shore of Bass Lake. Basic good ole' American fare such as babyback ribs, fried chicken, catch of the day and even chicken fried steak. Pleasantly woodsy interior with open beams, knotty pine walls and a view—over a parking lot—to the lake. Outdoor deck for summer dining.

Viewpoint Restaurant • ΔΔ $$

40530 Highway 41 (in the Best Western Yosemite Gateway Inn), Oakhurst; (209) 683-5200. American; dinners $8 to $14; full bar service. Daily 7 a.m. to 9:30 p.m. Major credit cards. Nicely decorated place offering a steak-seafood-fowl menu, a large salad bar and a picture window view of greater Oakhurst and its surrounding hills. The look is contemporary, with a hint of elegance: wood paneled walls, a planter room divider and large chandelier dominating the dining room. With specialties such as teriyaki chicken, hot mini-loaves of honey wheat bread and breakfast cinnamon rolls from the in-house bakery, it's a cut above the average motel coffee shop.

LODGINGS

Château du Sureau • ⌂⌂⌂⌂ $$$$$ ∅

Highway 41 at Victoria Lane (P.O. Box 577), Oakhurst, CA 93644. Doubles $250 to $400, including full European breakfast. MC/VISA. This opulent French country style chateau occupies a landscaped, wooded knoll above Erda's Elderberry House. Its nine rooms are furnished with antiques, Provencal fabrics, tapestries and European oils. Oversized canopied beds have goose down comforters; marble baths are finished in French tile. Each room offers a wood-burning fireplace and stereo center, with an extensive music selection from a CD library. TV and room phones are available on request. A decorative fountain, pool and even a small chapel grace the formal grounds.

Best Western Yosemite Gateway Inn • ⌂⌂ $$$ ∅

40530 Highway 41, Oakhurst, CA 93644; (209) 683-2378. Doubles and singles $64 to $74, kitchenettes $5 to $10 extra. Major credit cards. Attractive 92-unit motel with TV movies, room phones, some room refrigerators; outdoor and indoor pools and spas, fitness center. **Viewpoint Restaurant** listed above.

Days Inn • ⌂ $$$ ∅

40662 Highway 41 (Hodges Hill Road), Oakhurst, CA 93644; (800) 325-2525 or (209) 642-2525. Doubles $45 to $95, singles from $38. Major credit cards. New nicely-appointed motel with TV movies, room phones; swimming pool, free continental breakfast.

Ducey's on the Lake • ⌂⌂ $$$$

P.O. Box 329 (nine miles from Oakhurst on North Shore Drive), Bass Lake, CA 93604; (800) 350-7463 or (209) 642-3131. Doubles $80 to $150, suites $135 to $275. Major credit cards. New luxury resort built on the cite of the old Ducey's resort. Nicely appointed lakeview rooms and suites with full resort amenities, including tennis courts, sauna, spa, fitness room and water sports on the lake.

Narrow Gauge Inn • ⌂⌂ $$$

48571 Highway 42, Fish Camp, CA 93623; (209) 683-7720. Doubles $70 to $125, singles $70 to $115. Major credit cards. Pretty 27-room inn nestled in pines above Oakhurst with a blend of Western and European chalet architecture. Twenty-eight rooms with rural American decor, TV, some with forest-view balconies. Wooded grounds, saloon, lounge and gift shop. **Dining Hall Restaurant** with rustic Western look; American menu; dinners $8 to $14; full bar service. Breakfast 7:30 to 10:30, Sunday brunch 10:30 to 11, dinner nightly 5:30 to 9.

Oakhurst Lodge • ⌂ $$

P.O. Box 24 (Highway 41 at Road 426), Oakhurst, CA 93644; (209) 683-4417. From $35 for two. Major credit cards. Small motel in downtown area; TV, in-room coffee.

The Pines Resort • ⌂⌂ $$$$$ ∅

P.O. Box 329, Bass Lake, CA 93604; (800) 350-7463 or (209) 642-3121. Chalets with full kitchens, up to six people $125 to $160, suites $140 to $275. Major credit cards. Lakeside resort with rustic cabins, many with fireplaces and lake views. TV movies, kitchens; tennis courts, sauna, spa, fitness room and water sports on the lake. **Pines Restaurant** reviewed above, grocery store and gift shop.

Shiloh Inn • ⌂⌂ $$$$ ∅

40530 Highway 41 (Hodges Hill Road), Oakhurst, CA 93644; (800) 222-2244 or (209) 683-3555. Doubles $86 to $92, singles $79 to $85. Major credit cards. New 80-unit motel with attractive rooms; TV movies, room phones; continental breakfast, pool, spa, sauna and fitness center, laundromat.

Snowline Lodge • ⌂ $$

42150 Highway 41 (two miles north), Oakhurst, CA 93644; (209) 683-

5854. *Doubles from $37.50. MC/VISA.* Rustic cabin type units above Oakhurst. TV; restaurant and bar across the highway.

CAMPGROUNDS & RV PARKS

Ducey's Bass Lake Lodge • *P.O. Drawer A (on shores of Bass Lake), Bass Lake, CA 93604; (209) 642-3131. RV and tent sites; $11 for full hookups, $9 for water and electric.* Flush potties, water, showers, picnic tables and barbecues, swimming, fishing and boating. Reservations accepted. Open all year.

Sierra National Forest campgrounds • *Several campgrounds near Oakhurst and around Bass Lake with RV and tent sites. Varying fees; some free. Reservation in summers only for Bass Lake area sites; call (800) 283-CAMP; MC/VISA. For general Bass Lake information, call (209) 642-3212.* No hookups; most have pit potties, water; all have picnic tables and barbecues.

Is there life after dark?

Golden Chain Theater in Oakhurst offers both old fashioned melodramas and contemporary drama in a cabaret style theater at Snowline Lodge above Oakhurst; no-host cocktails and dinners optional. Tickets are $8 for adults $7 for seniors and $6 for kids 12 and under. Season is April through October with shows Thursday through Saturday at 8, with a 2 p.m. Sunday matinee; call (209) 683-7112 for information. **Wildwood Players** presents musical comedies and other theater fare at the Pines Resort at Bass Lake; tickets are generally $10, with curtain at 8:30 p.m. on weekends. Call (209) 683-2002.

The Old Barn offers country music Thursday through Saturday nights, with a piano bar Sunday through Wednesday.

ANNUAL EVENTS

Coarsegold Rodeo, early May at Coarsegold Rodeo Grounds on Road 415, P.O. Box 3, Coarsegold, CA 93614; (209) 683-8383.

Gathering of the Indian People, mid-July at the Wassama Round House, c/o Wassama Round House Association, P.O. Box 328, Ahwahnee, CA 93601, (209) 683-3631; traditional dances, Ibarbecue, arts and crafts.

Indian Fair Days, first weekend of August at Sierra Mono Indian Museum, North Forks, (209) 877-2115; Mono Indian dances, demonstrations, crafts and foods.

Mountain Peddlers' Flea Market and Craft Fair, Labor Day Weekend, P.O. Box 369, Oakhurst, CA 93644, (209) 683-7766 or 683-2537; one of the foothills' largest crafts fairs and flea markets

Mountain Apple Fest and Crafts Fair, late October, Yosemite Apple Growers Association, (209) 683-4796 or 683-8670; apple goodies, booths, cooking demonstrations.

Sierra Mountaineer Days, late September at Oakhurst Community Center, Road 425-B; (209) 683-8492; chili cookoff, foods, booths and such.

ON THE ROAD AGAIN—TO MARIPOSA

Heading north from Oakhurst, Highway 49 squiggles through handsome oak groves and meadows of the Sierra foothills, passing through towns with wonderful native American names like Ahwahnee and Nipinnawasee. Both are tiny places, little more than slight widenings in the road. Ahwahnee, named for the former Indian village of Awani, was a stage stop and active apple, peach and pear producing area in the late 1800s. Most of the old wooden homes of Nipinnawasee were burned in 1961, but the careful eye will discover a couple of weed-covered foundations.

You've been in oak foothills thus far on Highway 49, but as you approach Mariposa, you begin climbing toward pine forests. Before departing this area, remember to pause at the Wassama Round House which we discussed earlier; it's just beyond Ahwahnee. Wassama means "leaves falling," and that's a nice thought as we move on to the next chapter in our exploration of the Gold Country.

To learn more...

Eastern Madera County Chamber of Commerce, P.O. Box 369 (49074 Civic Circle), Oakhurst, CA 93644; (209) 683-7766. The chamber maintains a visitors information center in an A-frame near its office, open 9 to 4, daily in summer and weekdays the rest of the year.

Southern Yosemite Visitors Bureau, P.O. Box 1404, Oakhurst, CA 93644; (209) 683-INFO.

Bass Lake Chamber of Commerce, P.O. Box 126, Bass Lake, CA 93604; (209) 642-3676.

North Fork Chamber of Commerce, P.O. Box 426, North Fork, CA 93643; (209) 877-2410.

Sierra National Forest, 41969 Highway 41, Oakhurst, CA 93644-9435; (209) 683-4665. Send $2 for a forest service recreation map containing specifics on camping, picnicking, hiking and other Sierra National Forest pursuits.

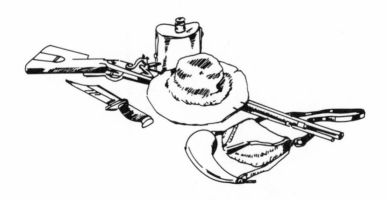

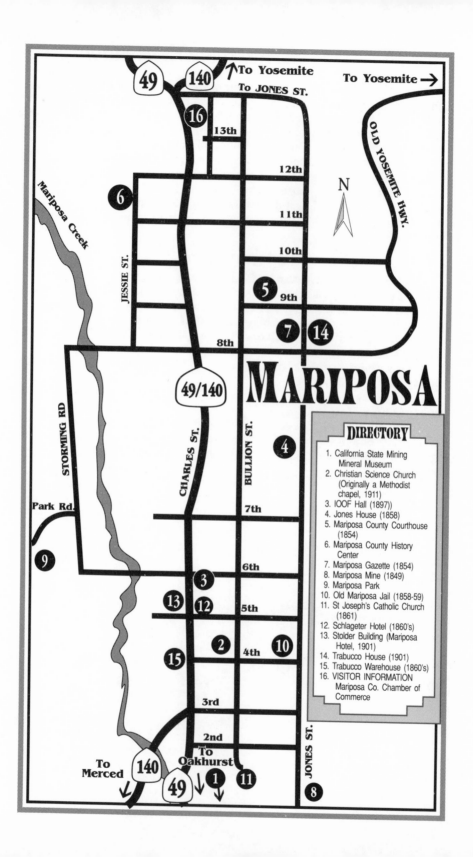

"In the month of June, 1807, a party of (Spanish) Californians pitched their tents on a stream at the foot of the Sierra Nevada, and whilst there, myriads of butterflies, of the most gorgeous and variegated colors, clustered on the surrounding trees...from which circumstance they gave the stream the appellation of Mariposa." — **from an 1850 California legislative report**

MARIPOSA COUNTY
COURTHOUSE CLOCKTOWER

Chapter Three
MARIPOSA & SURROUNDS
The little city in the "Mother of the Counties"

Driving along gently curved Highway 49 in downtown Mariposa, you begin to sense the presence of Mother Lode history that was missing in Oakhurst. Although much of the town has been modernized, several authentic relics of the Gold Rush survive.

The sturdy stone Trabucco warehouse and balconied Schlageter Hotel speak of an earlier time, and the 1901 Stolder building with its Greek revival false front stands in proud defiance of "progress." In the hills above town, the whitewashed glimmer of an old steepled church catches your eye, and beyond it, you may perceive the outbuildings and tailing dumps of a real gold mine.

THE WAY IT WAS • As quoted above, the town and county took their pretty name from *Arroyos de Las Mariposas*, a creek where a small expeditionary group from New Spain encountered great swarms of butterflies. They were so plentiful, according to a report, that one "had to be extricated from a soldier's ear."

It was not the Spanish, but statesman, soldier (and suspected land grabber) General John C. Frémont who put Mariposa on the map. In 1847, Frémont's agent Thomas Larkin bought a 45,000-acre Mexican land grant called The Mariposas for $3,000. Problem was, Larkin had been instructed to use the money for a nice parcel near Mission San Jose, southeast of San Francisco. Frémont was furious to discover that he owned instead several thousand acres of worthless dry foothill land. (It was near—but did not include—present day Mariposa.)

Then in 1849, the wily entrepreneur heard that gold had been discovered around the nearby settlement of Logtown, so he floated his boundaries to include that area, and he re-named the town Mariposa.

When California became a state in 1850, a massive 30,000-square-mile chunk—one-fifth of its total land area—was set aside as Mariposa County, with Mariposa as the seat. The town and its mines prospered, but absentee landlord Frémont did not. Most of the mining profits were invested in expansion or lost to employee theft and mismanagement, and squatters occupied much of the general's land.

He finally came to the area in 1857 and built a ranch home near Bear Valley, there to enjoy his fortune and while away his golden years. But high operating costs continued eating the profits of his mines and in 1863 he sold his massive holdings—at a tidy profit. This money he lost in railroad speculation, and he died in poverty in New York City in 1890.

Mariposa County's fortunes shrank, too. It unwillingly earned the title of "Mother of the Counties" as huge chunks were annexed from it. Its extensive boundaries, once reaching from the central Mother Lode to the Coast Range to the San Bernardino Mountains and Mojave Desert, yielded six new counties and pieces of five others. It eventually was whittled down to its present 1,455 square miles.

A fire razed the town of Mariposa in 1866 and output from the mines dwindled toward the end of the century. But it never became a ghost town. The popularity of nearby Yosemite National Park kept the tourists coming, as it does today.

THE WAY IT IS ● The most pleasing thing about Mariposa is its location in a wooded valley, with a crewcut fringe of evergreens on the ridges above. The town of about 2,000 citizens has a prosperous look. As a popular gateway to Yosemite National Park, it lures many visitors, and some return to settle in this pretty valley.

Unfortunately, some of the buildings in the oldstyle business district have been "modernized" through the decades. However, this mix of old and new architecture is not unpleasant. Downtown Mariposa was declared an historic district in 1990, and many of its 19th century structures were added to the National Register of Historic Places. Happily, this will curb future attempts at modernization. Several of these handsome old structures house assorted boutiques, curio shops, a couple of family restaurants and the new Mariposa Hotel Inn.

Incidentally, the weekly *Mariposa Gazette,* at Ninth and Jones streets, is the oldest continually-published newspaper in California, established in 1854. The building has been burned twice and has been modernized. However, you can see one of its old flatbed presses and other artifacts at the Mariposa County History Center.

Ironically, the "Mother of Counties" is today one of California's least populated, with about 15,000 people scattered through its upland pines and lowland oaks. It has no incorporated cities. All public business is conducted by a county board of supervisors, meeting in the same courthouse where their forbearers convened nearly 150 years ago. The county has no movie houses, shopping centers, bowling alleys, traffic lights, parking meters or video game parlors. Most of the residents think that's just dandy.

DISCOVERIES
The best attractions

California State Mining and Mineral Museum • *At the Mariposa County Fairgrounds, a mile and a half south of town; (209) 742-7625. Daily except Tuesday 10 to 6 from May through September; Wednesday-Sunday 10 to 4 the rest of the year. Adults $3.50, seniors 60 and up and teens $2.50, kids free.* The new state mineral museum is one of the finest exhibit centers in the Gold Country. Visitors receive a quick lesson in geology and mining as they view glittering exhibits of gold and other minerals, walk through a realistic mine tunnel mock-up, operate a mini-stamp mill and view scores of other displays.

There is no clutter here. Mineral specimens of California and the world sit in tidy display cases and gold nuggets glow sensuously under their personal spotlights. Graphics explain the origin of the three basic rock types—igneous, metamorphic and sedimentary. Other exhibits describe modern uses of minerals such as borax, quartz and gold. In the mine shaft—so believable you can smell its musty dust and hear the echoes of yesterday—you learn about timbering (shoring a newly-blasted area), mucking (removing the shattered ore) and tramming (carting it out of the mine).

You can buy your own personal trilobite pendant in a tidy little gift shop, along with mineral specimens, jewelry and books on minerals, Gold Rush history and other relevant subjects.

Originally displayed in the old San Francisco Ferry Building, the mineral museum was housed temporarily in a rented Mariposa motel room until its impressive new home was completed in the late 1980s.

Mariposa County History Center • *12th and Jessie streets, Mariposa; (209) 966-2924. Daily 10 to 4:30 April through October; weekends only 10 to 4:30 November, December, February and March; closed in January. Free admission, donations accepted.* The museum, which shares a low ranch style building with the town library, is another fine interpretive center. No disorganized collection of artifacts, this place offers a carefully assembled record of early Mariposa, from Native Americans to Spanish and Mexican explorers, through the Gold Rush to the turn of the century.

Each exhibit is a tableau, focusing on a particular element of the town's history. Entering the museum, you pause at the front counter of the Gagliardo General Store with its old coffee mill, tins of chawin' tobacco and patent medicines. Other exhibits contain selected artifacts from the Indians, Mexicans, Gringos and Chinese who called this valley their home. Peer into an old safe and you'll see examples of various kinds of gold unearthed in the Mariposa diggins.

After prowling the museum interior, step outside to see a full-sized stamp mill, still operational, along with a mule-powered *arrastra* used by Mexican miners to grind their ore (the same type they used to grind corn for tortillas). You can poke through a typical 19th century Indian village with its bark wikiups and sweat house.

Museum documents indicate that 15,000 miners once swarmed the hills around Mariposa. In the 1850s, one needed $250 to rent half a house and $20 for a pair of pants. Things haven't changed much.

The rest

Mariposa County Courthouse ● *Bullion Street between Ninth and Tenth, Mariposa; (209) 966-3222. Daily 8 to 5; free. Tours on weekends.* Visitors can stroll the hallways on weekdays and peek into the upstairs courtroom if it isn't in use. Built in 1854, this is the oldest continually-used seat of government west of the Rockies, and one of the finest examples of 19th century Greek revival architecture in the Mother Lode.

Constructed at cost of $9,000, the white pine courthouse hasn't missed a day of business since its doors first opened. Its clock tower, installed in 1866 because few people could afford watches, still bongs out the time on the quarter hour. This isn't a museum, although many of the furnishings within are certainly of museum quality. Some are more than a century old.

Note particularly the old fashioned pews in the courtroom. They appear to be rich oak, but closer inspection reveals simple pine, painted with simulated oak grain. So, what do you want for $9,000?

Historic Mariposa walking tour ● *Downtown area.* A map available from the Chamber of Commerce or from Mariposa Mercantile in the Mariposa Hotel Building will guide you past more than a dozen of the town's historic buildings.

Nuggets

Mariposa Hotel (W.B. Stolder building) ● *5029 Charles Street at Sixth, Mariposa.* The 1901 false-front Stolder Building has been carefully restored and now houses a new bed & breakfast inn (see listing below) upstairs and several curio shops on the ground floor and in the basement. It once served as a way station for the Mariposa and Le Grand Stage.

Mariposa Mine ● *On a hill behind St. Joseph's Church.* It's one of the few still intact mines in the area, but visitors are discouraged. Supposedly, it was founded by Kit Carson in 1848 or 1849 and purchased by Frèmont. Remarkably durable, it was worked off and on until the 1950s. Its main shaft is 1,550 feet deep.

Old Mariposa Jail ● *Jones Street between Fourth and Fifth.* It's about as inhospitable place as you'll see: a small, stern edifice of hewn granite with thick iron bars over tiny windows. But dealers of Mother Lode justice were not concerned with hospitality. During the construction of the new mineral museum, the jail's thick walls provided refuge for many of the collection's more valuable specimens.

St. Joseph's Catholic Church ● *On a hill at the east end of Bullion Street.* With its typical New England steeple, St. Joseph is one of the area's most familiar and photographed landmarks. It was built in 1863 and is still in use.

DETOURS

Mariposa to Hornitos and Bear Valley ● *A 40-mile loop trip.* Begin your detour to Hornitos by following Highway 49 north from Mariposa for about five miles, then turn left onto Old Toll Road just beyond the hamlet of Mount Bullion. It takes you through a land rich in foothill shadings—the dense green of oak groves, ruby-barked manzanita, and in springtime, flaming yellow mustard.

You soon begin losing altitude, descending into a hot lowland of tawny grasses and scrub oak as you approach Hornitos. It means "Little Ovens" and the name is appropriate. The thermometer nudged a hundred when we visited there in August. At 980 feet, it's one of the lowest towns of the Gold Country.

This is an intriguing place—a ghost town coming into being. Once one of the most hell-raising hamlets of *La Veta Madre* and reportedly the lair of bandito Joaquin Murieta, Hornitos has shriveled from a peak population of 15,000 to perhaps 50 or 60. And it's shrinking still; when we visited, the only surviving business was a small saloon.

"The old timers are dying," said an old timer, basking in the warm afternoon sun on the plaza. "And nobody else wants to come to take their places."

Hornitos was established around 1850 when Mexican miners were kicked out of nearby Quartzburg by their American brothers. But the Latinos had the final chuckle, because it became one of the most prosperous towns of the Mother Lode, while Quartzburg soon shrank to nothing. Legends say that Murieta robbed stage coaches by day, then slipped back into town after nightfall to spend his loot on wicked ladies in the wild fandango halls. A tunnel at the corner of High Street and Bear Valley Road supposedly was Murieta's escape route when the posse got too close.

However, some historians, more concerned with dull fact than fascinating fantasy, suggest it was only used for beer barrel storage. They suggest further that Murieta is the figment of early-day pulp magazine writers' imaginations.

The hamlet's Spanish heritage is still apparent; it's one of the few Mother Lode towns built around a plaza. The sleeping village is rich in relics of yesterday. A mean-looking granite block jail with two-foot-thick walls and one-foot-square windows survives—but on a hot Hornitos day, did its occupants? Nearby is the brick shell of D. Ghirardelli & Co., a general store established in 1859 by the founders of the still active Ghirardelli Chocolate Company of San Francisco.

After exploring the town, follow St. Catherine Street up to the 1862 St. Catherine's Church, a silent sentinel on a nearby hill. It's an unusual structure with wooden walls held in place by stone buttresses. A cemetery behind the church seems grim and forlorn, even in the bright sunlight.

As the wind mourned among the tombstones during our first visit, we wondered if the old church bell might soon toll the death knell for Hornitos. Perhaps not; on our last visit, we found a prim little green park with picnic table and play apparatus; several of the weathered-worn homes were still occupied.

Departing Hornitos, follow Bear Valley Road about 11 miles northeast to Highway 49 and the village of Bear Valley, Frèmont's base of operations.

There's more history than substance to this hamlet of a few hundred souls. Gone are Frèmont's home and the Oso House hotel he built to host visiting dignitaries. However, you can view a later version of the Oso House and the 1852 Odd Fellows Hall, now an antique shop. Also functioning are the Bon Ton restaurant, whose forerunner dates back to Frèmont's day, and a restored Victorian housing Granny's Garden Bed & Breakfast (both listed below).

Follow Highway 49 south toward Mariposa, then after six miles, veer to the right onto Mount Ophir Road.

We'd been told of a Gold Country ruin along here—the remnants of an old assay office of the town of Ophir. Generations of fallen leaves scrunched under our feet as we poked through an oak thicket, seeking our historic quarry. We came upon it suddenly, as jungle explorers might stumble across a Mayan ruin. Before us stood two decaying fieldstone walls huddled under sheltering oaks. We lingered for several moments before returning to Mariposa, enjoying the silence, listening for the whispers of history.

Mariposa to Yosemite National Park's doorstep ● *A 60-mile round trip north on Highway 140.* This trip will remind you that the Sierra Nevada's alpine beauty is never far from the Gold Country. From any point along Highway 49, a brief drive eastward takes you into evergreen slopes.

Leaving downtown Mariposa on Route 140, you'll climb quickly into a digger pine forest, passing through the scattered pieces of the mountain settlement of Midpines. Beyond, follow the winding course of the Merced River Canyon. Across the stream, matching the highway's route, you can see the abandoned right-of-way of the Yosemite Valley Railroad. It was built just after the turn of the century to haul tourists from Merced to El Portal, near Yosemite's entrance. The old rail bed makes a nice hiking trail.

The highway follows the river for about ten miles. As you approach Yosemite National Park, you encounter the settlement of El Portal and a piece of history called Savage's Trading Post.

Pioneer James Savage operated a series of trading posts in the area. He found it more profitable to barter with the Indians for gold than to dig for it himself. Before outsiders came, the Native Americans had little use for the mineral. But when they saw the newcomers working so diligently to get the stuff, they began mining themselves. They swapped their gold for things that made sense, like metal pots, blankets—and rifles to keep white men out of their women's wikiups.

Savage befriended the Native Americans and even had an Indian wife— or two. However, members of the hostile Yo Semite tribe that lived high in the Sierra Nevada attacked two of his trading posts. He organized the volunteer Mariposa Battalion and went in pursuit of the bad guys. One of their forays led them into Yosemite Valley. They thus became the first outsiders to witness the present-day park's stunning vistas.

That brings us back to the present. Today's version of the Savage Trading Post is a pleasantly rustic whole earth kind of general store, featuring crafts by local artists. A three-unit motel is adjacent.

For the record, our detour now reverses itself and heads back to Mariposa, perhaps after a picnic alongside the Merced River at nearby Indian Flat campground. However, you'll probably insist on driving on into Yosemite National Park.

DIVERSIONS

Carriage rides ● *Outings in a 19th century carriage are offered by Butterfly **Carriage and Stage Lines**, (209) 966-4441.* Twenty-minute history tours are $5; in the evening, the surrey serves as downtown a shuttle at $1 per ride.

Gold tours ● Two outfits offer gold panning lessons and trips to the source. **Vista Gold Tours,** (209) 966-5100, features panning lessons, creekside panning and trips to a hardrock mine, where visitors can study a quartz vein 220 feet into a mountain. **Lor-E-L Mining,** (209) 742-5255, offers panning lessons in a trough or at creekside and all-day trips to pan for gold and observe a gold dredge at work.

Hiking, backpacking, fishing and such ● The footloose set will find a host of hiking trails and an occasional alpine lake in Sierra National Forest above Mariposa. Hiking guides and a detailed area map are available from the Mariposa Ranger District office at the intersection of highways 49 South and 140 in Mariposa. Or you can spend $2 for the national forest recreation map (see the end of this chapter).

River running ● The Gold Country offers some of the finest whitewater excitement in California, since more than a dozen of the state's swiftest rivers and creeks drain the Sierra Nevada. Many of these have been dammed, also turning the Mother Lode into a flatwater boaters' haven (which we admit only grudgingly). However, some of the whitewater stretches survive.

The first "runnable" Gold Country river—coming from the south—is the Merced. Whitewater stretches range from novice to advanced, and it's essential that you inquire locally before sticking your raft, kayak or inflatable kayak into the enticing but icy current. Since the Merced issues from Yosemite National Park (and indeed helped shape Yosemite Valley, with a lot of assistance from glaciers), there are no upstream dams. Therefore the river is highly seasonal, with runnable levels generally from March through June. By fall, it's a poetic trickle.

Most river runners put in at Red Bud picnic area, 29 miles up Highway 140 from Mariposa. Some stretches are safe for canoeing, but others will have you for lunch. The folks of Sierra National Forest can be helpful, or refer to the *California White Water* book we recommended in the introduction. Also, call the State Flood Operations Center at (916) 322-3327 for river flow information.

Wine tasting ● Radanovich Winery tasting room in the Mariposa Hotel, weekdays 3 to 9, Saturdays 11 to 9 and Sundays 11 to 4. Tours of the nearby winery can be arranged by calling (209) 966-3187.

GOLD COUNTRY DINING

Bon Ton Cafe ● ΔΔ $$
7307 Highway 49 North, Bear Valley; (209) 377-8229. Mexican; dinners $6.50 to $14; wine and beer. Wednesday-Saturday 11 a.m. to 9 p.m.; Sunday brunch 8 to 2 and dinner 3 to 9. No credit cards. A former saloon dating to the 1800s; now a California-Mexican cafe. It's more interesting than typical smashed beans and rice places, with entrées such as *churrasco* (thinly sliced steak in herb butter) and garlic shrimp. High ceilings, cafe curtains and ancient stone walls give it a properly historic aura.

Charles Street Dinner House ● ΔΔΔ $$
Charles Street at Seventh, Mariposa; (209) 966-2366. American; dinners $7 to $15; wine and beer. Wednesday-Sunday 5 p.m. to 9 p.m. Reservations advised on weekends. MC/VISA. An attractive Western theme restaurant serving American fare, often innovatively prepared and spiced; a definite cut

above the average. The interior is a pleasant clutter of old photos, Tiffany type lamps and wagon wheel decor; waitresses in long gingham dresses scurry about, serving up good food and friendly smiles. The menu ranges from steaks to chops to chicken and occasional fresh seafood hurried in from the coast.

Country Pantry ● △ $$

5029 Charles St., Mariposa; (209) 966-4097. American; dinners $7 to $12; no alcohol but it can be brought in. Breakfast and lunch daily 5:30 a.m. to 2 p.m., dinners Friday-Monday until 10. No credit cards. Country-style cafe popular with locals, particularly early-risers. Varied menu, wandering from teriyaki chicken to steak to linguine with clam sauce. The simple interior is a mix of American folk and Formica.

The Red Fox ● △△ $$

Highway 140 and 12th Street, Mariposa; (209) 966-5707. American; dinners $6 to $12; wine and beer. Breakfast and lunch daily 7 to 2, dinner nightly except Thursday 5:30 to 9. MC/VISA. Essential American steaks, chicken, chops and seafood and an occasional pasta served in a pleasing setting. Print wallpaper, wainscoting and French windows. Ample portions, friendly and prompt service.

Sugar Pine Restaurant ● △ $$

5038 Main St. (Seventh), Mariposa, (209) 966-3818. American; dinners $6 to $12; no alcohol. Daily 6:30 a.m. to 10 p.m. MC/VISA, DISC. Family cafe serving generous portions of chops, chicken and steak. Simple rural decor with open beams and Naugahyde booths.

LODGINGS

Bed & breakfast inns

Boulder Creek Bed & Breakfast ● △△△ $$$ ØØ

4572 Ben Hur Rd., Mariposa, CA 95338; (209) 742-7729. Doubles $65 to $75, singles $60 to $70. Three units, one private, two shared baths. Full breakfast. Smoking on the patio. Major credit cards. This new European-style chalet, built in 1988 by innkeepers Michael and Mary Habermann, occupies a pretty wooded glen next to Boulder Creek, about two miles from Mariposa. Floor to ceiling windows add brightness to the modern home, which is furnished with a mix of contemporary and antiques. Amenities include a therapeutic spa and an A-frame living room with a wood burning stove and stereo. Gourmet breakfasts are prepared by Michael, a former chef/restaurateur.

Meadow Creek Ranch Bed & Breakfast Inn ● △△△ $$$$ ØØ

2669 Triangle Rd. at Highway 49 South, Mariposa, CA 95338; (209) 966-3843. Doubles $75 to $95. Three rooms with share bath and a cottage with private bath. Full country breakfast. Smoking on the front porch. MC/VISA, AMEX may be used to secure reservations. Bob and Carol Shockley have nicely refurbished this venerable ranch house, which dates back to 1857 and once served as a Wells Fargo stage stop. The rooms are furnished with early American and European antiques. We like this quiet ranch setting about 11 miles southeast of town, with its old water wheel, neatly groomed grounds and creek. You can sit and whittle on the front porch, and snuggle up beside the wood burning stove in the living room. Arriving guests are greeted with refreshments.

Granny's Garden Bed & Breakfast ● ⌂ $$$$ ∅∅

7333 Highway 49, Bear Valley, CA 95223; (209) 377-8342. Doubles $75. Two suites with private baths. Full breakfast. No smoking. MC/VISA. This small Victorian farmhouse was built in 1896 for Nancy (Granny) Trabucco, a member of one of Mariposa's oldest families. It's still family owned; B&B hosts are Dave and Dixie Trabucco. The yellow and white exterior is bright and cheerful; two large units are furnished with Victorian and early American antiques, some used by Granny herself. One room has an adjoining sitting room; the other features a private balcony. While not opulent, the old home offers a warm, comfortable atmosphere. Guests can enjoy complimentary wine in their rooms, stroll in the rose garden, talk to the animals in the oldstyle farmyard or relax in a spa.

Mariposa Hotel Inn ● ⌂⌂ $$$ ∅∅

5029 Charles St. (P.O. Box 745), Mariposa, CA 95338; (209) 966-4676. Doubles $64 to $74. Six rooms, all with private baths. Smoke-free rooms; smoking permitted on veranda. MC/VISA. Having started life as a stagecoach way station 90 years ago, this small downtown hotel has come full circle, with its recent restoration and opening as a cozy inn by Mac and Lyn Maccarone. The look is 19th century America with antique reproductions, oak wainscoting and trim, scalloped lace curtains and print wallpaper. Guests can sip coffee on a rear veranda and look out over the rooftops of old Mariposa. The hostelry served the past two decades as a senior citizens apartment complex, operated by Lyn's parents, Maurice and Helen Brown.

Oak Meadows, Too ● ⌂ $$$ ∅∅

5263 Highway 140, Mariposa, 95338; (209) 742-6161. Doubles $59 to $69. Six units with private baths. Expanded continental breakfast. No smoking. MC/VISA. This is a new facility in downtown Mariposa, built to be a B&B. It's an attractive structure, fashioned in a New England "salt box" style, painted gray with white trim. Although it's almost too modern for a bed and breakfast, it avoids a motel look with its early American decor and period furniture. Guests can gather around a massive river-stone fireplace in a large common room.

The Pelennor ● ⌂ $$ ∅∅

3871 Highway 49 South, Mariposa, CA 95338; (209) 966-2832. Doubles $40 to $45, singles $30 to $35. Three units with share baths. No credit cards. A rustic, modestly priced inn, the Pelennor occupies 15 wooded acres six miles south of Mariposa. Many of the furnishings in the small, comfortable rooms were handmade by innkeepers Dick and Gwen Foster. They have another interesting talent, and will demonstrate it on request: both are accomplished bagpipers. Amenities at this country-style B&B include a lap pool and spa.

Rockwood Gardens Bed & Breakfast ● ⌂ $$$ ∅∅

5155 Tip Top Rd. (half mile south of Highway 49), Mariposa, CA 95338; (209) 742-6817. Doubles $60 to $80, singles $55 to $70. Three units with one private and two share baths. Expanded continental breakfast. No credit cards.

Built in 1989, this modern ranch style home occupies a five-acre wooded knoll about 11 miles south of Mariposa. Rooms, furnished with a mix of American antique and country, open onto decks with small private gardens. Guests can gather in a large living room around a wood stove, or stroll in nearby wildflower meadows and oak and pine forests.

Schlageter House Bed & Breakfast • ⌂ $$$ ∅

5038 Bullion St. (P.O. Box 1202), Mariposa, CA 95338; (209) 966-2471. Doubles $70, singles $60. Three units, all with private baths. Full breakfast. Smoking outside and in parlor. No credit cards. Fifth-generation Mariposa residents Lee and Roger McElligott have carefully restored and renovated this 1856 Victorian and furnished it with comfortable, "homey" antiques. Guest rooms have queen or twin beds. Located in downtown Mariposa, the home is rimmed by gardens and patios.

Shangri-La • ⌂ $$ ∅∅

6316 Jerseydale Rd., Mariposa, CA 95338; (209) 966-2653. Doubles $40 to $60. Three units, one private and two shared baths; room phones. Full breakfast. No smoking. Unusual for a bed and breakfast—although appropriate to its name—this B&B is housed in an Oriental style structure with Asian furnishings, including Japanese style beds and a sunken bathroom in one of the units. A Japanese garden, fish pond and waterfall completes the Far Eastern setting. Shangri-La is nestled amidst 38 acres of pines, 12 miles north of Mariposa. Gazebos provide vistas of the surrounding forests. Arriving guests are offered—of course—a cup of tea and invited to enjoy the serenity of Japanese gardens.

Motels

Best Western Yosemite Way Station • ⌂ $$$ ∅

P.O. Box 1989 (4999 Highway 140), Mariposa, CA 95338; (209) 966-7545. Doubles $66 to $76, singles $56 to $66. Major credit cards. An attractive, modern 78-room motel in downtown Mariposa. TV, room phones; pool, spa. **Restaurant** adjacent.

Mariposa Lodge • ⌂ $$$

P.O. Box 733 (5052 Highway 140), Mariposa, CA 95338; (209) 966-3607. Doubles $65, singles $50. Major credit cards. A 37-unit motel with TV movies, pool, whirlpool. Modern, well maintained, downtown.

E.C. Yosemite Motel • ⌂ $$$

P.O. Box 399 (5180 Jones St.), Mariposa, CA 95338; (209) 742-6800. Doubles $55, singles $50. Major credit cards.. A 26-unit motel in downtown Mariposa; TV movies, room phones; pool and spa. **Coffee shop** adjacent.

Miners Inn • ⌂ $$$ ∅

P.O. Box 246 (Highways 49 and 140), Mariposa, CA 95338; (800) 237-7277 in California only or (209) 742-7777. Doubles $50 to $64, singles $40 to $44. Major credit cards. A 40-unit motel with TV, room phones, free coffee. **Restaurant** serves American fare; dinners $10 to $18; 6 a.m. to 10:30 p.m., full bar service.

Muir Lodge Motel • ⌂ $$$

P.O. Box 85 (Highway 140), Mariposa, CA 94345; (209) 966-2468. Dou-

bles $45 to $79. MC/VISA. Rustic lodge in woodsy setting, ten miles east of Mariposa, 25 miles from Yosemite. TV, nightly movies, coffee pots and microwaves in most rooms.

Sierra View Motel ● △ $$
Seventh and Bullion (P.O. Box 1467), Mariposa, CA 95338; (209) 966-5793. Doubles from $34.50. Major credit cards. Small motel in downtown Mariposa, half a block off Highway 140; TV movies; some suites.

CAMPGROUNDS & RV PARKS

Yosemite/Mariposa KOA ● *6323 Highway 140, Midpines, CA 95345; (209) 966-2201. Hookups $25, tent sites $18. MC/VISA.* Full hookups, flush potties, water, showers, picnic tables and barbecues, coin laundry, groceries, pool, rental boats and bikes, rec room, playground.

Bagby Recreation Area ● *On Lake McClure, off Highway 49 fifteen miles north of Mariposa, c/o Merced Irrigation District, 909 Lake McClure Rd., Snelling, CA 95369; (800) 468-8889. Camping $5.50, day use fee $3 per car and $3 per boat.* Twenty-five tent and RV sites, no hookups or showers. Flush potties, picnic and barbecue areas, store, marina, water sports. Open all year.

Mariposa County Fairgrounds campground ● *5007 Fairground Rd. (a mile and a half south of town on Highway 49), Mariposa, CA 95338; (209) 966-3686 or 966-2432. RV sites only, $12 per vehicle.* Hookups, flush potties, water, showers, picnic tables and barbecues, lawn area and playground; dump station. Open every day but Labor Day Weekend, when the county fair is in progress.

Sierra National Forest ● The forest offers an assortment of campgrounds. Most have RV and tent sites, with pit potties, water, picnic tables and barbecues; no hookups or showers. For the nearest national forest office, see the end of this chapter. Among the campgrounds in the foothills are Jerseydale, Indian Flat and Summit Camp. Indian Flat is on the Merced River with swimming and early season river running (see Diversions above); the other two are higher in the woods.

Is there life after dark?

The **Hull House** (966-2065) in downtown Mariposa is a busy saloon offering dancing and live entertainment Thursday through Saturday nights. **Hurricane Sally's Saloon** at the Miners Inn Motel and Restaurant on Highway 49 north offers live music Friday and Saturday night, usually country and western. That's about all we found in way of night life. You can't even go downtown and watch the traffic light change, because there isn't one.

ANNUAL EVENTS

Annual Storytelling Festival, early March at Mariposa County Fairgrounds, (209) 966-2456.

Butterfly Days, early June at Mariposa County Fairgrounds, (209) 966-3686; mountain ride, wagon train, dinner dance.

Mariposa County Fair, Labor Day weekend at the fairgrounds, (209) 966-3686; booths, exhibits, rodeo, demolition derby and such.

ON THE ROAD AGAIN—TO COULTERVILLE

The route north from Mariposa takes us through more of the now-familiar oak and pine foothill country. Then it plunges suddenly and dizzily into one of the greatest natural barriers of the Mother Lode—Merced River Canyon. It yielded its gold to the placer miners only reluctantly; the canyon was so steep—and so hot in summer—that argonauts called it Hell's Hollow.

This cleft divided southern and northern Mariposa County, isolating the county seat from a major mining center at Coulterville. Mrs. John Frèmont once said of this thousand-foot-deep chasm: "A fall into it was death." Much of the once beautiful canyon has been filled by McClure reservoir, one of those fake lakes created in case San Franciscans wanted to drink something besides dry martinis. It's a long, twisting drive down to the bridge crossing the reservoir, and an equally sinuous climb back up the other side.

McClure reservoir drowned the town of Bagby, once the home of Ridley's river ferry and a water-driven stamp mill built by General Frèmont. After inundating history, the lake-makers named the nearby Bagby Recreation Area after the town, which is either an honor or an insult, depending on one's point of view. The recreation area offers a boat launch, camping and picnicking.

After climbing the north slope of Hell's Hollow, Highway 49 heads for one of our favorite little towns in the Gold Country—Coulterville.

To learn more...

Mariposa County Chamber of Commerce, P.O. Box 425 (Ninth and Jones streets), Mariposa, CA 95338; (209) 966-2456. Office open weekdays 8 to 5 and Saturdays 9 to 4.

Southern Yosemite Visitors Bureau, P.O. Box 1404, Oakhurst, CA 93644; (209) 683-INFO.

Sierra National Forest, P.O. Box 747 (highways 49 South and 140), Mariposa, CA 95338; (209) 966-3638. Send $2 for a forest service map/brochure containing specifics on camping, picnicking, hiking in Sierra National Forest east of Mariposa.

"We have just two ailments in the mines, bellyache and headache. If a man works hard, he doesn't have the first. If he doesn't gamble, he doesn't have the second." — **George Coulter, quoted in Catherine Coffin Phillips'** *Coulterville Chronicle*

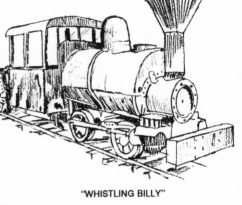

"WHISTLING BILLY"

Chapter Four
COULTERVILLE & SURROUNDS
Looking forward to yesterday

In Coulterville, we begin to believe in the Gold Rush, for the town radiates history. It hangs thick in the air, like heat waves shimmering from the nearby dry gulches, where miners worked and cursed and sweated on hot August afternoons.

This is a stubborn old man of a town, weathered and creased, but surviving. And it survives without gaudy gimmicks that most historic places use to lure tourists. There are no made-to-look-rustic shopping centers, no jewelry shops selling gold nugget earrings, no neon. Coulterville doesn't need signs and stone monuments to tell visitors of its past, because yesterday is still here. History is written in the sun-baked adobe of the Sun Sun Wo Store, in the embossed tin walls of the Jeffery Hotel and the silent gravestones on the hillside cemetery.

THE WAY IT WAS ● In the spring of 1850, merchant George W. Coulter set up shop near a seasonal stream (wet in winter and spring, dry as dust in summer) in northern Mariposa County. Most of the miners in the area were Mexicans, so he stuck an American flag above his tent store to remind folks where his sympathies lay. He treated the Latinos fairly; they liked this easy going, honest merchant and called his settlement *una tienda azul bajo un roble con una bandereta*—the blue tent under an oak with a small flag.

"Bandereta" would do for the moment. However Coulter nurtured the dream of founding a settlement bearing his name. Trouble was, George Maxwell, another merchant who had set up shop in the area, had the same idea. The two Georges discussed the problem one afternoon while sipping warm beer in Coulter's tent-store-bar.

In *Coulterville Chronicle*, Catherine Coffin Phillips records the historic confrontation: "Coulter considered a moment and then said, 'Let Jim here whittle two sticks. Whichever draws the longer one names this settlement. The other names the creek.' "

Ms. Phillips doesn't identify Jim—presumably somebody who stopped by for a drink—but Coulter drew the longest stick and Coulterville made the map. It followed a pattern typical of Mother Lode towns; within five years, it blossomed from a tent city into a boomtown of brick and adobe. Coulterville became an important regional supply center, with dozens of stores, ten hotels, 25 saloons and the Devil knows how many fallen women. With all these inducements to separate the miners from their gold pokes, the town prospered. Unfortunately, it also burned back to the dirt three times, oddly at 20-year intervals—1859, 1879 and 1899.

Three famous names are linked to Coulterville's past, either by fact or fancy. During the 1870s Nelson Cody, brother of Buffalo Bill, clerked and later managed a trading post in the Wells Fargo building, which still survives; he also served as the town's postmaster. Some historians insist that Teddy Roosevelt and Ralph Waldo Emerson slept at the Jeffery Hotel. Emerson's visit is fairly well documented but Teddy's is doubtful. The rough riding President did tour Yosemite National Park in 1909. But if he stayed at every hotel in the area that claims to have hosted him, he would have spent more time in the Gold Country than in the White House.

When mining dwindled, Coulterville survived into the 20th century as an important tourist route into the Yosemite Valley. Its Yosemite Turnpike toll road was opened in 1874 and served for more than a quarter of a century as the only vehicle access to the park. This trade sagged when better highways were built from Sonora above and Oakhurst below. But Coulterville, stubborn old man that it is, managed to hang on.

THE WAY IT IS • The town sits in a shallow valley at the junction of highways 49 and 132. It boasts 115 citizens, a pair of saloons, a wonderfully funky antique shop, two restaurants, the grand old tin-walled Jeffery Hotel and a service station and general store built into a former blacksmith shop. It's a neat old town, with shaded boardwalks and wisteria vines climbing weathered stone walls.

Coulterville is so rich in history, so unblemished by progress that the entire town has been designated a state historic landmark, and Main Street is listed on the National Register of Historic Places.

Hardly a ghost town, it is seeing new life with the re-opening recently of the Jeffery Hotel and the addition of an RV park to encourage visitors to hang around a bit. The north county office of the Mariposa County Chamber of Commerce offers a guide to steer them past history-rich buildings and sites. Copies are available at the chamber office at 5007 Main Street, just up from the hotel (open daily 10 to 4), and from local merchants. For the most part, however, the town is being left alone, without gimmick shopping centers or fussy boutiques.

"Coulterville isn't a pretty town, or one that's been restored to death," Mariposa County columnist Forrest Barringer once wrote.

DISCOVERIES
The best attraction
Northern Mariposa County History Center • *Corner of highways 49 and 132, Coulterville, CA 95311; (209) 878-3015. Tuesday-Sunday 10 to 4*

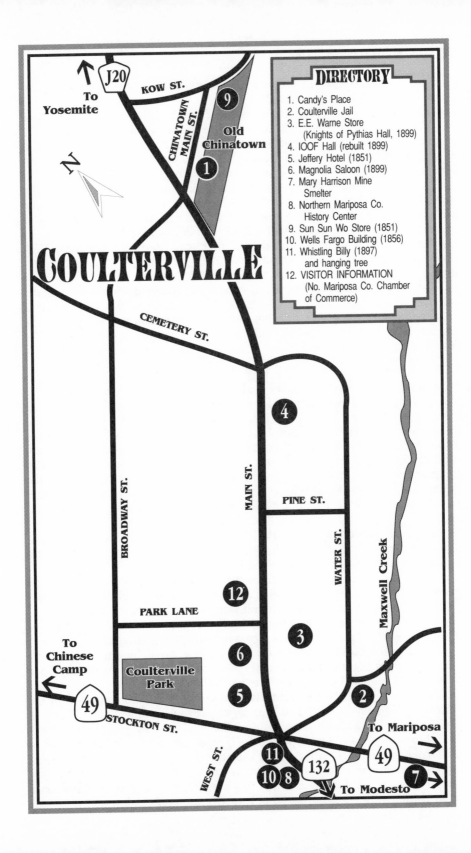

COULTERVILLE

To Yosemite

J20

KOW ST.

CHINATOWN MAIN ST.

old Chinatown

9

1

N

CEMETERY ST.

BROADWAY ST.

MAIN ST.

4

PINE ST.

WATER ST.

Maxwell Creek

12

PARK LANE

3

To Chinese Camp

Coulterville Park

6

49

5

STOCKTON ST.

2

To Mariposa

WEST ST.

11

10 8

132

49

7

To Modesto

DIRECTORY

1. Candy's Place
2. Coulterville Jail
3. E.E. Warne Store
   (Knights of Pythias Hall, 1899)
4. IOOF Hall (rebuilt 1899)
5. Jeffery Hotel (1851)
6. Magnolia Saloon (1899)
7. Mary Harrison Mine
   Smelter
8. Northern Mariposa Co.
   History Center
9. Sun Sun Wo Store (1851)
10. Wells Fargo Building (1856)
11. Whistling Billy (1897)
    and hanging tree
12. VISITOR INFORMATION
    (No. Mariposa Co. Chamber
    of Commerce)

April through September 1; weekends and school holidays the rest of the year. Admission free; donations accepted.

This small museum occupies portions of two buildings that date back to the 1850s, although the exact age of these venerable fieldstone and brick structures isn't known. They served variously as a drug store, post office and as the Wells Fargo office and trading post managed by Nelson Cody. One section housed a hotel run by one of Coulter's sons.

Today, it is Coulterville's memory vault. Exhibits include a scale model stamp mill that clanks merrily at the push of a button, an 1890 Victorian living room complete with love seat and an Edison talking machine, and a model drug store where shelves brim with elixirs and medicines. Our favorite exhibit is a Studebaker buckboard that was used in the movie, *High Noon*. Remember the scene where Grace Kelly sat primly in the seat, ignoring Coop's pleas to stay until he'd faced the bad guys?

The most cheerful part of the museum is its courtyard entrance—actually the shell of a collapsed building—where neatly-tended sunflowers, petunias, daisies and marigolds add splashes of color. On a summer afternoon, the garden with its iron grillwork and cool stone provides a pleasant respite from the heat.

The rest

Jeffery Hotel • *Highways 49 and 132 opposite the museum.* This beige and green-trimmed two-story structure with its distinctive embossed tin siding was built in the late 1840s. First used as a store, with a Mexican fandango hall upstairs, it was purchased by the Jeffery family and converted into a hotel in 1852. Rebuilt after the 1899 fire, it thrived well into this century, closed down for several years, then was refurbished in the late 1980s. So travelers again can dine and snooze in the place that hosted Ralph Waldo Emerson and maybe even Teddy. (See listings below.) It's still owned by descendants of the Jeffery family, which may be a Gold Country longevity record.

Magnolia Saloon • *Next to the Jeffery Hotel on Main Street; (209) 878-3186.* As we pushed through the batwing doors, we stepped further into Coulterville's yesterday. If one overlooks the jukebox and electric lights, the Magnolia Saloon seems little changed from its Gold Rush days. Not a tourist gimmick but a real tavern, it's a rich repository of Coulterville lore, with old-timey photos, display cases of mineral samples and Chinese fans, a pot bellied stove and the requisite wooden Indian. A register from the next-door hotel advises that "guests without baggage must pay in advance."

Towels once hung from the century-old bar, used by patrons to wipe beer foam from beards and mustaches. They were changed once a day. As a bewhiskered author, I can appreciate that little touch.

Moccasin Power House and Fish Hatchery • *Eleven miles north at the junction of highways 49 and 120. Hatchery open to visitors weekdays 7 a.m. to 3:45 p.m.* Heading north from Coulterville on Highway 49, you'll see the 1925 Moccasin Power House on your right, a classic of early 20th century California architecture with its pink stucco walls and tile roof. Small matching cottages in the adjacent "company town" still house employees. Visitors can stroll around the grounds of the fish hatchery just beyond, and peer into tanks shimmering with thousands of future frying pan candidates.

E.E. Warne Building (Sherlock's Americana Antiques) • *5006 Main St.; (209) 878-3621.* This two-story structure is a classic of Gold Country architecture, with side walls of quarried stone and a wooden false front and balcony. The original was built in the 1860s to house Warne's General Store, with a Knights of Pythias Hall upstairs. Rebuilt after the 1899 fire, the hall was used by the fraternity until the 1920s, and it has earned a spot on the National Register of Historic Places. The main floor store is a busy, glittering clutter of antiques, glassware, Venetian glass jewelry and sundry doodads. A bed & breakfast functions upstairs. (See listing below.)

NUGGETS

Mary Harrison Mine smelter • *A mile and a half south of Coulterville, just off Highway 49.* Fragments of a brick wall are all that remain of the Mary Harrison, one of the oldest and richest mines in the area. Hardrock miners sunk a shaft 3,000 feet deep, from which branched 15 miles of tunnels at 15 different levels. The company's dogged search for the elusive *Veta Madre* was quite successful. The mine produced $1.5 million in gold before it closed in 1904. And that was at an average price of $20 an ounce! To see the smelter remnants, drive 1.4 miles south of Coulterville on Highway 49, then turn right at a refuse site sign. Fortunately, you reach the mine ruins before the dump...

Sun Sun Wo Store and Candy's • *Chinatown Main Street at Kow Street.* One of the Mother Lode's largest Chinatowns once thrived in Coulterville, with a population of 1,500. Its lone remnant is Sun Sun Wo store, an 1851 adobe; it was one of the few buildings to survive the town's various fires. Next door, looking properly ancient and shored up by new timbers, is Candy's Place, once a busy bordello. An antique shop now functions in Sun Sun Wo; Candy's is a privately-owned home.

History seems to have misplaced Candy's last name, but oldtimers say she disappeared with one of the town's more prominent citizens.

Whistling Billy and Hanging Tree • *In front of the museum.* When we visited Coulterville, several youngsters were playing engineer on Whistling Billy, a cute steam engine that pulled ore cars four miles from the Mary Harrison Mine to the stamp mills. It was a steep, twisting climb, one of several California train routes that earned the title of the "crookedest Railway in the world." The engine sits in the shade of a giant oak that once functioned as the town's official hanging tree.

DETOUR

Coulterville via Greeley Hill to Yosemite National Park • *A 60-mile loop trip.* Thus far in our trek up Highway 49, Yosemite has remained temptingly close. This route into the park is winding and difficult, but it's perhaps the most scenic. Head northeast on Main Street, which becomes County Road J-20. It soon begins a steep climb, so you may want to pull into a turnout to give your panting machine a rest. You'll be rewarded with an impressive view of the foothills below and the broad, hazy farmlands of the distant San Joaquin Valley.

The route continues its climb, taking you from the familiar foothill oaks to pines. Shortly, you'll arrive in the mountain village of Greeley Hill, named for Horace Greeley's cousin Cyrus, an early settler who obviously took his more famous relative's advice.

From here, Old Yosemite Road leads into the park. As we said, it's very scenic but winding. And don't even think of attempting it in winter. For an easier route into Yosemite, stay on J-20, which swings north beyond Greeley Hill and intersects with Highway 120. Either way, you'll pass beneath the pristine pines of Stanislaus National Forest.

DIVERSIONS

Hiking, backpacking and other high country pursuits • Stanislaus National Forest, reached by Highway 132 above Coulterville, offers the usual Sierra Nevada outdoor activities. See the end of this chapter for addresses of the nearest district ranger stations.

Water sports • *C/o Merced Irrigation District Parks Department, 9090 Lake McClure Rd., Snelling, CA 95369; (209) 378-2520. Contact the department for a brochure.* Boating, swimming, camping and fishing are available along the irregular shorelines of Lake McClure and Lake McSwain, two reservoirs on the Merced River just below Coulterville. The nearest recreation area is Horseshoe Bend, three miles west, off Highway 132, with boating, water skiing and camping. Barrett Cove, McClure Point and Lake McSwain recreation areas are tucked into other sections of the twin lake shoreline, and we passed Bagby Recreation Area driving up from Mariposa.

GOLD COUNTRY DINING

Yosemite Sam's • ∆ $
5012 Main St., Coulterville; (209) 878-9911. Basic American; meals $5 to $10; beer and wine. Daily 9 a.m. to 9 p.m. No credit cards. Sam's is a funky old storefront saloon and restaurant that starts serving breakfast at 7, then turns into a pizza and burger parlor. Food service ends at 9; pool-shooting and good ole boy drinkin' and hollerin' continues well beyond.

The Banderita Restaurant ∆∆ $$
In the Jeffery Hotel; (209) 878-0228. American; dinners $8 to $13; full bar service. Monday-Thursday 7 a.m. to 9 p.m., Friday-Sunday 7 to 10. Reservations accepted. MC/VISA. Attractively refurbished oldstyle restaurant off the hotel lobby; print wallpaper, historic photos, other early-day lore. Basic American menu.

LODGINGS

Jeffery Hotel • ⌂ $$$
One Main St. (P.O. Box 440-B), Coulterville, CA 95311; (800) 464-3471 or (209) 878-3471. Doubles $54 to $68 with private bath, $43 to $58 with shared bath; rates include continental breakfast. MC/VISA. While not luxurious, the newly-restored Jeffery offers comfortable rooms with oldstyle brass beds and other yesterday furnishings. Wainscoting, rare pressed tin walls and ceiling fans help transport guests back to Coulterville's yesterdays.

Sherlock's Holmes' Bed & Breakfast • ⌂ $$$
5006 Main St., Coulterville, CA 95311; (209) 878-3915. Doubles $65 to $75; three rooms. Full breakfast. Neal and Mary Sherlock rescued the 1899

Sun Sun Wo store is the lone survivor of Coulterville's once-bustling China-town.

E.E. Warne building from oblivion in 1972, and opened an antique store on the ground floor. They later remodeled the old upstairs Knights of Pythias Hall for their residence. In 1990, they converted their apartment into a cozy B&B, furnished with a mix of Victorian and early American antiques. Wine and cheese are offered to guests in the afternoon.

Yosemite Americana Inn ● △ $$

10407 Highway 49 (P.O. Box 265), Coulterville, CA 95311; (209) 878-3407. Doubles from $37. MC/VISA. Nine-room motel with TV, free in-room coffee and tea; just north of town.

CAMPGROUNDS

Coulterville RV Park ● *Highway 49, just north of Jeffery Hotel (P.O. Box 96), Coulterville, CA 95311; (209) 878-3988. RV sites $10 with full hook-ups, campsites $7.* A new RV park with picnic tables, flush potties, showers, groceries, coin laundry and Propane; dump station.

Lake McClure and Lake McSwain ● *Several tent and RV sites on the shores of these two reservoirs, with and without hookups. From $10 to $13, plus a $4 reservation fee. Call (800) 468-8889 for reservations.* The nearest camping area to Coulterville is at Horseshoe Bend, three miles west on Highway 132. Others are at McClure Point, Barrett Cove, Bagby and Lake McSwain recreation areas.

Yosemite Americana Inn ● The inn (listed above) has several RV sites with full hookups, and tent sites; $10.

Is there life after dark?

Well, not like in the old days. Only two saloons survive—**Yosemite Sam** and the **Magnolia**. The Magnolia Bar has live music on Saturday nights and things sometimes get rather lively around Sam's pool tables. **Candy's Place** hasn't hosted gentlemen callers since Candy shocked the town by running off with a prominent citizen a century ago.

ANNUAL EVENTS

Coulterville Coyote Howl in mid-May, (209) 878-3074; adult and children's coyote howling contest, arts and crafts, entertainment and food booths.

Western Gunfighters Rendezvous in late September, (209) 878-3074; quick-draw artists, shoot-outs, arts and crafts, antiques, food booths and such.

On the road again...to Chinese Camp & Jimtown

Continuing north on Highway 49, you'll drive through typical Mother Lode foothills—a mix of oak and tawny grasslands, with pines in the higher slopes. Climbing a steep ridge, you leave butterfly land and cross into Tuolumne County, then spiral gently down into a scenic valley. As you cross Moccasin Creek bridge, you'll see a good example of a stream turned inside out. Mounded heaps of gravel remain from dredging more than a century ago. The route takes you past a dam and powerhouse of the Hetch Hetchy project at Moccasin (listed under Nuggets above). It delivers kilowatts and water to San Francisco.

Highway 49 merges into 120 and skims the western shoreline of Don Pedro Reservoir which—in early autumn—shows its reddish bathtub ring of a lowered water level. At a turnout, a sign advises you that the reservoir drowned the mining town of Jacksonville, settled by Julian Smart and named for a Colonel Jackson. Then, you'll round a bend and hit Chinese Camp which, unlike Jacksonville, is still alive.

More or less.

We'll explore Chinese Camp more thoroughly in Chapter 5, since it is a neighbor of Jimtown, our next stopover.

To learn more...

North County Office, Mariposa County Chamber of Commerce, 5007 Main St. (P.O. Box 333), Coulterville, CA 95311; (209) 878-3002. Office open daily 10 to 4.

Forest Supervisor's Office, 9777 Greenley Rd., Sonora, CA 95370; (209) 532-3671. Send $2 for a Stanislaus National Forest recreation map. Nearest office to Coulterville is: **Groveland Ranger District,** Highway 120 (P.O. Box 709), Groveland, CA 95321; (209) 962-7825.

Such was life in the Golden State:
Gold dusted all we drank and ate,
And I was one of the children told
We all must eat our peck of gold.
— **Robert Lee Frost**

Chapter Five
JAMESTOWN &
SURROUNDS
There's still gold
in those hills

EMPORIUM ON
JIMTOWN'S MAIN STREET

It's called the Lulu's Saloon and it sits on Jamestown's Main Street, where its forerunners sat nearly a century and a half ago. Inside, yesterday and today mingle in noisy camaraderie. A jukebox alternately issues twanging country music and blasts out rock.

Most of the patrons are locals, bearded good old boys who look like they just emerged from the mines. I almost expect them to pay for their bottles of Bud with a pinch of gold dust. Some resemble losers from a Charlie Daniels look-alike contest. As I perch on my bar stool, self-consciously sipping at a glass of red wine and waving away the smoky blue haze, it occurs to me that the surgeon general's report never made it to Lulu's.

The barkeep is a young lady, long and lithe, wearing snug faded jeans and glistening brown hair that cascades down her back. The good old boys lean over their drinks to grin and flirt; her smile is warm but she keeps them at bay. Maybe that grizzly of a man at the end of the bar is her boyfriend.

As the hours pass and more bottles of Bud are emptied, Friday night in Jimtown gains intensity. By midnight, the Buggy Wheel is a cheerful bedlam of jukebox music, husky laughter and feminine squeals. As I leave, someone is dancing with his dog. I don't think the pooch cares much for the cowboy two-step.

Jimtown hasn't returned to the past. Like Coulterville, it never left it.

THE WAY IT WAS ● Jamestown is one of the Mother Lode's senior citizens, founded in 1848 by a shyster lawyer from San Francisco named Colonel George James. He became involved in an assortment of land schemes and other shady dealings, and departed after a year, owing most of the miners money. It's not clear whether he was ordered out of town or left just ahead of a lynch mob.

The folks who chased him away weren't exactly angels, either. In a fit of bigoted patriotism, they evicted innocent Mexican miners from their diggins' and re-named the settlement American Camp. But Jamestown had a better ring to it, and it became official when a post office was established in 1853. Through the years, it has become simply Jimtown to locals.

Argonauts hurried to the area in herds when word got out that a 75-pound nugget had been found in Woods Creek near the present Main Street. Population peaked at around 6,000, then declined with the dwindling gold.

THE WAY IT IS ● Limited mining continues in the nearby creeks and hills today, and a giant open pit mine operates a few miles south. This is one of the most active placer mining areas in the Gold Country. Its streams are popular with weekend prospectors, and townsfolk exchange secretive gossip about recent "finds."

The last "strike" occurred on October 12, 1984, when some small nuggets were uncovered while a construction crew was laying a sewer line. Within 15 minutes, every gold pan in town was sold, and contemporary prospectors began carrying off the dirt faster than the crew could refill the trench.

If we liked Coulterville for its quiet sense of history, we enjoyed Jimtown for its high spirits. It's a bit larger, with just under a thousand souls, but like Coulterville, its Main Street belongs to yesterday. The place enjoys flaunting its storied past with handsomely restored hotels, raucous old saloons and tourist-oriented gold prospecting tours. Here, you can really pretend that you're part of the Gold Rush.

With no neon to mar its 19th century look, Jamestown's false-front stores with their wooden balconies and boardwalks often attract film companies. Look carefully, and you'll recognize scenes from *High Noon* and *Butch Cassidy and the Sundance Kid*. Rolling stock from the town's Sierra Railroad (now a state historic park) starred regularly on the old *Petticoat Junction* TV series; the trains still make frequent movie and TV appearances.

Jimtown's Main Street is off Highway 49 and therefore free of traffic— except for visitors looking for parking places. Main also is something of a restaurant row for Tuolumne County, exhibiting some of the area's better dining spots.

DISCOVERIES
The main attraction

Railtown 1897 State Historic Park ● *P.O. Box 1250 (just above Main Street on Fifth Avenue), Jamestown, CA 95327; (209) 984-3953. Grounds and gift shop open daily; various hours. One-hour "Mother Lode Cannonball" stream train rides several times daily in summer and weekends only the rest of the year; adults $9, kids $4.50. Extended two-hour "Keystone Special" tour to Keystone and return; adults $17.50, kids $11. "Twilight Limited" two-hour tour with snacks and beverages on the train, followed by a barbecue with live entertainment at Railtown; adults $34.50, kids $19.50. Roundhouse tours daily May through September and weekends the rest of the year; adults $2.50, kids $1.50.*

If you're haunted by lonely train whistles and fascinated by old steam engines, you'll love this place. Railtown preserves memories and much of the equipment of the Sierra Railroad, established in 1897 to haul freight from the San Joaquin Valley into the Sierra foothills. You can explore a fine collection of old-timey railroad cars, tour the original roundhouse and work sheds and take a ride through the foothills on the "Mother Lode Cannon-ball," star of scores of movies and TV shows.

A trip through the Sierra Nevada foothills behind a chuffing steam train is a trip into the past—or perhaps a journey to the local movie house. You'll recognize places where the bad guys ambushed the train, were yelling Native Americans gave futile pursuit to the strange iron horse. One of Railtown's steamers appeared in the recent Home Box Office film about Ishi, California's last "primitive" Indian.

Back at the depot, you can browse through an excellent collection of railroading memorabilia and books in the gift shop and fetch a cooling drink from an ice-filled clawfoot tub.

Nuggets

Antiques and boutiques • Main Street brims with boutiques and antique shops. You'll find a good collection at **Jamestown Mercantile Too** at Main and Donovan streets. A large antique gallery occupies the **Emporium** on Main Street, a two-story classic with a full balcony and green and cream gingerbready trim.

Gold nugget jewelry stores • Of all the Sierra foothills towns, Jimtown seems most preoccupied with gold. Some shops will fashion original jewelry for you—either from your own lucky pannings or from their stock. Stop by **Jamestown Gold Nugget Jewelry** at 18223 Main St. (984-4441) or **Woods Creek Jewelry Company** at 18148 Main (984-4482).

Jamestown Park • *Main Street.* This little postage stamp of a park in the middle of town is a pleasant place to sit and watch Jimtown happen around you. An octagonal gazebo, comfortable benches, public potties, an ore cart and ore bucket comprise the park's simple furnishings.

Marengo Courtyard • *Located within and behind the 1854 brick and wooden Marengo Building.* The Courtyard offers a collection of shops with such intrigues as dolls and teddies, wine tasting, hand painted goblets, collectors' china and cloisonne vases. Betty was fascinated by the teddy collection at **Bear Essentials** while I—of course—lingered at the **Chestnut Wine and Gift Shop**, which offers samples of wines from a variety of Gold Country vintners.

DETOURS

Jimtown to Chinese Camp and Groveland • *A loop trip of about 45 miles.* Seven miles south of Jamestown on Highway 49, you'll encounter a former Asian gold camp that once exceeded San Francisco's Chinatown in size. However, no Orientals are in evidence as you walk the streets of Chinese Camp today. Their descendants probably own half of Chinatown by now. To honor its former residents, the county built a so-called Chinese style school house—a temple-like thing with turned-up eaves that looks absolutely ridiculous.

Once one of the liveliest burgs of the Mother Lode, it is today a weather-worn village of 150 souls. It dozes quietly in the shade of the spike-leaf Tree of Heaven, which its Asian citizens planted more than a century before. Among its scatter of buildings—some weed-grown, some neatly tended—are a few notable landmarks, including an iron door post office that was used until 1984, stone-walled ruins of a Wells Fargo Express office and the 1855 St. Xavier Catholic Church, on a lonely hill across the highway, surrounded by lonely graves.

The post office now serves as a tourist information center for the Tuolumne County Visitors Bureau. It's open Monday-Friday 9 to 5, Saturday 10 to 5 and Sunday 10 to 3 (closed Sundays during the off-season).

The town was founded in 1849 by a group of Englishmen who employed Chinese as miners. Later, more Chinese began settling here, banished from other diggins by whites. By working tirelessly, as is their proclivity, they discovered several major veins. By the mid-1850s, the population had swelled to 5,000. It was the largest Asian settlement outside the Orient, and the scene of the one of the wildest and strangest brawls in the Gold Country.

The town's two major tongs, Sam Yap and Yan Woo, didn't get along too well. In 1856, tempers hit the boiling point, apparently over conflicting mining rights. One story says the fuss started when a group of Chinese miners accidentally rolled a heavy stone toward another. Whatever the reason, the two tongs decided to settle their differences on the field of battle. They kept every blacksmith in the area busy for weeks, making weapons.

Blacksmiths, like barbers, are terrible gossips. So when a thousand men from each tong gathered for combat on October 25, 1856, rowdy rooting sections of other miners were crowding both sides of the field of honor, like eager spectators before the kickoff. Most likely, they were taking bets on the outcome. The two groups went at it hammer and—well—tong. Fortunately, the local militia also had been tipped off, and it broke up the brawl before too many casualties occurred. Reports vary from one to four killed, with a few dozen wounded.

After exploring Chinese Camp, continue south on Highways 49/120, then take the 120 fork east toward Yosemite National Park. (Are you getting the impression that all roads lead to Yosemite?) The highway winds steeply up five-and-a-half-mile Priest Grade, taking you from oak foothills into cool, green pine forests.

Pause to prowl about Big Oak Flat, a rich placer mining area discovered in 1849 by Yosemite founder James Savage. It's now little more than a slight widening in the road, although two sturdy stone and adobe iron-shuttered buildings survive. Another monument to yesterday—a rather curious one—marks the site of a 13-foot-thick oak tree that gave the town its name. It toppled over when eager miners undermined its roots in their fevered quest for gold.

Continuing up Highway 120, you shortly encounter pine-shaded Groveland. It's one of our favorite upper Sierra foothill towns—a friendly, handsome hamlet with a handful of sturdy false-front stores hugging the narrow highway to Yosemite.

Of Groveland's surviving Gold Rush relics, the most intriguing is the Iron Door Saloon, built in 1852 and boasting that it's California's oldest drinking establishment. It is indeed a page out of the past—a rough stone building with a long polished bar, open beam ceilings, and farm implements and hunting trophies hung from weathered walls. Note the elaborate Gold Rush mural on the facade.

Two vintage roadhouses are interesting as well—the 1849 Groveland Hotel, one of the oldest structures in the upper foothills, and the cute Victorian

Hotel Charlotte (see lodgings below).

Groveland's original name was Garotte, inspired by the hanging of a either a horse thief or two Mexican gold thieves (depending on which history book you read). Should you wonder, *garotte* is the French word for strangulation. The town enjoyed a brief gold rush after Jim Savage set up a trading post in neighboring Big Oak Flat in 1849, but its population of 2,000 had fizzled to 100 by 1875. However, it is by no means a ghost town. Its ancient buildings are well-tended and several flatlanders are building summer homes in the area.

Just up the road from Groveland is Pine Mountain Lake, a popular planned mountain community offering golf, swimming, tennis, boating, fishing, a restaurant and an airport.

Groveland is the turn-around point on this detour, and you have two choices for your return to Jimtown. To sharpen your driving skills—while terrifying your passengers—follow a winding, twisting and sometime hair-raising route through the back country north of Don Pedro Reservoir. It challenged the stability and abilities of Ickybod, our sturdy little VW camper. If you're game to try it, take the first right off Highway 120 just below Groveland, then go right again onto Wards Ferry Road. You'll twist and wind through a beautiful wooded wilderness, spiral dizzily down to a crossing of the north fork of the Tuolumne River. You then pass through rolling ranch lands before landing back in Jamestown. (Wards Ferry becomes Algerine Road which leads directly into town.)

For the more cautious drivers, we suggest continuing down 120, swinging north on Highway 49 then turning right on Jacksonville Road at the Moccasin Point Recreation Area. This route takes you through pretty grasslands and past the two unmarked settlements of Stent and Quartz, once minor luminaries in the Gold Country spotlight. An ancient cemetery and weathered old red schoolhouse at Stent are worth a pause. Gold-seekers here apparently didn't do very well; Stent's original name was Poverty Hill.

Jimtown to Knights Ferry and return ● *A loop trip of about 30 miles.* Like Coulterville, grizzled old Knights Ferry has been designated an historic district. There are few modern structures among its ancient brick and wood frame buildings along the banks of the Stanislaus River. When we visited in the fall, early morning light danced off the water and yellow aspen leaves shimmered in a soft breeze; what a tranquil place it was!

It gets busy in summer, when refugees from valley heat come to swim and picnic in the river and camp along its banks. The Stanislaus River Parks along the stream offer stretches of calm and white water for boaters; see Diversions listing below.

To reach Knights Ferry, head south from Jamestown on Highway 108/49, staying with 108 when it separates from Route 49. You'll encounter the Knights Ferry turnoff after a dozen or so miles.

The town's most noted landmark is an 1863 covered bridge, the longest in the United States and supposedly designed by General U.S. Grant. An excellent visitors center and museum, completed in 1986 by the Army Corps of Engineers, occupies a sleek stone and metal-sided building near the bridge.

The settlement was started by William Knight in 1848. He built a ferry at this site to take advantage of the traffic hurrying into the Gold Country above. He got himself killed in a gunfight a year later and brothers John and

Lewis Dent took over his operation. They built a toll bridge in 1857 but it had "quite a sag in the center," according to the *Stockton Record,* and a flood took it out five years later. So along came U.S. Grant—who happened to be the Dents' brother-in-law—and designed a bridge that stands to this day.

DIVERSIONS

Bingo • *The Chicken Ranch, 16929 Chicken Ranch Rd. (P.O. Box 1699), Jamestown, CA 95327; (800) 75-BINGO or (209) 984-3000. Thursday through Saturday from 7 p.m., Sunday from 2:30 p.m. MC/VISA.* Did we say bingo? That's right. Federal law allows big-stakes bingo games on Indian land, and one of the largest in California is at the Chicken Ranch on a Mi-Wuk reservation. It's a couple of miles southwest of Jamestown, just off Highway 49/108. If you regard bingo as a quiet little pastime in a church basement where a few folks get together for coffee, gossip and a five-dollar game, check out the energy level of the Native American version when the prize gets up around $50,000!

Gold mine tour • *Jamestown Mine, c/o Sonora Mining Corp., 17400 High School Rd., Jamestown, CA 95327; (209) 984-4641.* One-hour tours every Wednesday at 1:30; free, reservations required. (See box.)

Gold panning tours • It's often difficult to find a place to pan for gold in the Gold Country because many of the streams are on private property and folks don't cotton to claim jumpers. However, two outfits in Jamestown will take you to streams where you can pan in peace. Both also offer an extensive line of panning and prospecting equipment.

Gold Prospecting Expeditions, *P.O. Box 974 (18170 Main St.), Jamestown, CA 95327; (209) 984-GOLD.* At Ralph Shock's place in an old livery stable, you can practice in a horse trough out front (if you don't mind standing under a dummy hanging victim, swinging from an overhead rafter). Or you can join one of a variety of gold panning excursions. Programs include half-hour panning sessions ($20 per person or $35 per family), half-day or full-day treks to nearby streams, gold dredging outings and five-day helicopter trips into the wilds.

Columbia Mining and Equipment, *P.O. Box 34 (18169 Main St.), Jamestown, CA 95327; (209) 984-3893.* This firm across the street also offers one-hour trough panning, at $20 a person or $30 per family. Longer outings include all-day panning trips to nearby streams for $60 per person or $110 a family, plus hiking, swimming and gold dredging trips.

Hiking, backpacking and other high country pursuits • Stanislaus National Forest offers the usual Sierra Nevada outdoor activities. See the end of this chapter for the addresses of the nearest ranger district.

Water sports of all sorts • The Stanislaus River and Don Pedro Reservoir offer the full menu of soggy fun—swimming, whitewater and flatwater boating, fishing, houseboating and rock skipping (find your own rocks). Here are the places to play:

Stanislaus River Parks, *P.O. Box 1229, Oakdale, CA 95361; (209) 881-3517.* The Army Corps of Engineers operate a series of river parks along the Stanislaus between Knights Ferry and Escalon, with bankside picnicking, fishing and river stretches designated for white-water rafting and gentle-water canoeing.

ALL THAT GLITTERS...

To experience the seductive lure that drew hundreds of thousands to the Sierra foothills, you need to hunker down over a stream with a gold pan in your hand.

Proper panning procedure takes a little practice, and of course, you need to know where to go. We decided to seek professional help and signed up for one of Ralph Shock's Gold Prospecting Expeditions, panning a creek just outside of Jimtown.

We learned to swirl and slosh our designer plastic gold pans properly. ("Make sure all that material is moving," said our guide). Then we dribbled the excess rocks, gravel and mud slowly over the lip until only tiny pebbles and then black sand remained. Gold, weighing 19 times as much as water, would surely find its way to the bottom.

A final slosh, tip, dribble and swish and, omygawd, there it was! Three tiny grains gleamed dully in the bottom of my pan. Once you have seen gold *au natural,* you will never mistake it for pyrite or any other metal. The appearance is distinctive: gently rounded, softly lustrous, an almost feminine look. Staring at my seven cents worth of glitter, I wondered if gold's sensuous curved shape and soft sheen intrigued those 49ers as much as the wealth it could bring. Perhaps it reminded them of the women they'd left behind.

Aided by our guide, we dug more dirt and gravel from the edge of the bank, where spring runoff had embedded bits of gold. Hours passed as we swirled, sloshed, tipped and dribbled pan after pan of muddy gravel. Our efforts yielded mostly fine dust, a pinch of which would buy a drink 130 years ago. But one of my pans surrendered an actual nugget, slender and rounded, perhaps a quarter of an inch long. It was beautiful, lying in its bed of fine iron sand. Eagerly, we attacked the area where our guide had dislodged that pan of material. I began to understand what gold fever was all about.

At day's end, we were weary, our backs ached and Betty's manicure was destroyed, but we were a bit richer. Not with gold, but with memories of a sunny afternoon on a shady creek bank, re-living one of the most intriguing chapters of American history.

Don Pedro Lake, c/o Don Pedro Recreation Agency, 31 Bonds Flat Rd., La Grange, CA 95329; (209) 852-2396. This reservoir on the Tuolumne River just south of Jamestown offers several marinas and lakeside parks with the usual boating, camping, picnicking facilities, plus houseboating. The facility nearest Jimtown is **Moccasin Point Marina,** 11405 Jacksonville Rd., Jamestown, CA 95327; (209) 989-2383.

GOLD COUNTRY DINING

Boomer's ∆∆ **$**

18141 Main St. (Donovan), Jamestown; (209) 984-5000. American graffiti; meals $7 to $9; no alcohol. Sunday, Monday, Wednesday, Thursday 11 to 9, Friday-Saturday 11 to 10, closed Tuesday. MC/VISA, DISC. Neat 1950s style diner with Wurlitzer jukebox, black and white checkered floor, Marilyn Monroe photos and a vintage Mercury poking from an upper wall. Essential bobbysox fare such as Boomer Burgers, fries and sodas, plus light entreès like shrimp fry and barbecued chicken.

The Hotel Charlotte ● △△△ $$

Highway 120, Groveland; (209) 962-7872. American-Italian; dinners $9 to $15; wine and beer. Dinner daily except Tuesday 5 to 9, Sunday brunch 9 to 2. Reservations accepted. MC/VISA, AMEX. Charming Victorian style restaurant with print wallpaper, lacy curtains, pink nappery and polished woods. Excellent prime rib, chicken and chops, plus Italian entreès such as veal piccata and scaloppine and chicken primadonna.

Jamestown Hotel Restaurant and Saloon ● △△△ $$

Main Street, Jamestown; (209) 984-3902. American-continental; dinners $12 to $18; full bar service. Lunch 11:30 to 2:30, dinner 5 to 10, Sunday champagne brunch 11 to 3. Reservations accepted, essential on summer weekends. MC/VISA, AMEX. Elegant yesterday atmosphere in one of the area's most appealing restaurants. Diners choose between a nicely appointed 19th century dining room with cozy booths, etched mirrors and glass flower-petal lamps or a cheerful screened porch. The menu is rather pedestrian—a conventional selection of steak, London broil, barbecued spare ribs and country fried chicken. Adjoining Gold Rush style saloon.

Kamm's ● △△ $ ØØ

18208 Main St., Jamestown; (209) 984-3105. Chinese; dinners $6 to $10; wine and beer. Lunch Monday-Friday 11:30 to 2, dinner Monday-Thursday 4 to 9 and Friday-Saturday 4 to 9:30. MC/VISA. Newly remodeled and redecorated restaurant in one of Jimtown's Gold Rush buildings; a pleasing mix of China and oldstyle Americana, with distinctive floral wainscoting. Menu is a mix of mild Cantonese and spicy northern China dishes such as Mongolian beef and Kung Pao chicken; also hamburgers and fries for those who must. Smoke-free dining room.

Michelangelo ● △△△ $$ ØØ

18228 Main St., Jamestown; (209) 984-4830. Italian; dinners $7.50 to $14.50; full bar service and espresso bar. Dinner Monday-Saturday 5 to 10, Sunday 4 to 9, closed Tuesday. Reservations accepted. MC/VISA. Attractive new restaurant in one of Jimtown's vintage buildings; a pleasing blend of modern Italian black and white decor against oldstyle pressed tin walls and ceilings. Walls decorated with Michelangelo reproductions. Large Italian menu with the usual pizzas, pastas and piccata, plus *griglia* (grilled) steak, fish and chicken. Two dining rooms, one smoke-free.

National Hotel Restaurant ● △△△ $$ Ø

P.O. Box 502 (Main Street), Jamestown; (209) 984-3446. American-continental; dinners $11 to $18; full bar service. Lunch 11 to 4:30, dinner 5 to 10. Reservations accepted, essential on weekends. MC/VISA. Excellent fare with a small but versatile menu ranging from chicken Chelsea to lamb chops to New York steak. Served in a pleasant 19th century setting of polished woods, wainscoting, tulip glass and wafting ceiling fans. Non-smoking tables. Oldstyle bar adjacent.

The Smoke Cafe • ∆∆∆ $$ ØØ

Main Street, Jamestown; (209) 984-3733. Mexican; dinners $8 to $15; full bar service. Tuesday-Saturday 5 to 10, Sunday 4 to 9; closed Monday. No credit cards, checks accepted. Stylish place in an oldstyle building with a Southwest decor of beige, salmon and turquoise; dining rooms open to the street in summer. Typical Mexican fare is rather ordinary, but some of the specials are excellent. A favorite is carne asada—seared beef strips topped with fried onions and mild chilies, with a guacamole and homemade refried beans on the side. Flautas are quite tasty as well. The Smoke, in pleasing contradiction to its name, has a smoke-free dining room. A second room, adjacent to the bar, accommodates puffers.

Willow Restaurant and Saloon • ∆∆∆ $$

Main Street at Willow, Jamestown; (209) 984-3998. American-continental; moderate; full bar service. Lunch Monday-Friday 11:30 to 2:30, dinner nightly from 5, Sunday brunch 10:30 to 2:30. Reservations accepted, advised on summer weekends. MC/VISA. Housed in an 1862 hotel with a decor to match its heritage—simple but classic 19th century with walnut wainscoting, print wallpaper, lace curtains and impressive high-backed Victorian booths. Consistently good fare; a local dining-out favorite. Versatile menu ranges from chicken Kiev to veal to country fried chicken; dinners served with a tasty cheese fondue.

Is there life after dark?

The **Rawhide Saloon** on the edge of town on Highway 49/108, near the former gold camp of Rawhide, offers Friday and Saturday night dancing music with a definite Western tilt. We knew it was a classy place because of all the pickups in the gravel parking lot. The interior is cheerfully Western, with the usual quota of wagon wheels and hunting trophies. And the floor is covered with sawdust.

"Shucks," grinned one of the good old boy patrons, "that's just yesterday's furniture."

Other lively spots are the **Iron Door Saloon** in Groveland (962-8904), which imports live music on Friday and Saturday nights; **Hotel Charlotte** (962-7872), featuring live piano music on weekends; **Jamestown Hotel** (984-3902) offering live bands Friday and Saturday nights; and the **National Hotel** (984-3446) with live entertainers on some Friday and Saturday eves.

LODGINGS

Historic hotels and B&Bs

Jamestown Hotel • ⌂⌂⌂ $$$

P.O. Box 539 (18153 Main St.), Jamestown, CA 95327; (209) 984-3902. Doubles $55 to 86. Eight rooms, all with private baths. Continental breakfast. Smoking OK. MC/VISA, AMEX. Handsomely furnished rooms in a sturdy brick, false-front hotel building that steps right out of the Gold Rush. Furnishings—predictably—are Victorian, with floral prints and brass beds, yet accommodations are modern. Restaurant (listed above) and elegant Gold Rush bar.

Groveland Hotel • ⌂ $$$ ∅∅

P.O. Box 289 (18767 Main St.), Groveland, CA 95321; (209) 962-4000. Doubles $45 to $55 with share bath, $55 to $65 with private bath, suite $80, two-bedroom family unit $110. Continental breakfast; no smoking. Major credit cards. One of the Mother Lode's oldest hotels, dating from 1849. The adobe and wood frame structure was renovated and re-opened in 1986; a restaurant, bar and conference center were added in 1992. The small rooms aren't posh, although they're cozy, with simple and comfortable oldstyle furnishings.

The Palm Hotel • ⌂ $$$ ∅∅

P.O. Box 515 (10382 Willow St., just up from Main), Jamestown, CA 95327; (209) 984-3429. Doubles $60 with shared bath, $80 with private bath, suites $90 and $110. Nine units; five private baths, four share. Expanded continental breakfast. No smoking. MC/VISA, AMEX. Despite its "hotel" designation, it's more of a bed & breakfast inn, occupying a restored blue-gray and white trimmed turn-of-the-century Victorian. Step inside and you're in the retreat of a world traveler—a virtual museum of antiques, artifacts and curios from around the globe. The collection includes items from the South Pacific, China and Europe. Tucked among the *objets de musee* are attractive pieces of antique furniture.

National Hotel • ⌂ $$$

P.O. Box 502 (Main Street), Jamestown, CA 95327; (209) 984-3446. Doubles $65 to $75. Eleven units, five private baths, six share. Continental breakfast. MC/VISA. One of the oldest continually functioning hotels in the Gold Country, dating from 1859. Authentically restored with some of the original furnishings, including brass beds and pull chain toilets. The small, neat rooms aren't opulent but they're clean and comfortable. **Dining room** reviewed above.

Royal Hotel • ⌂⌂ $$$

Main Street, Jamestown, CA 95327; (209) 984-5271. Doubles $50 with share bath and $64 to $70 with private bath, suites $75 to $80. Nineteen units, including restored hotel rooms and cottages, most with private baths. Continental breakfast. Smoking OK. MC/VISA, AMEX. Restored 1922 hotel with turn of the century and Gold Rush furnishings—lace curtains, print wallpaper and other frills. Guests can sip herb tea and other refreshments in the inviting parlor. Communal kitchen, picnic facilities and gas barbecue on the patio. Laundry facilities and RV parking available. The attractive Nostalgic Bookshoppe opposite the lobby specializes in Westerns and Hollywood books and collectibles.

The Hotel Charlotte • ⌂ $$$

P.O. Box 787, Groveland, CA 95321; (209) 962-6455. Doubles $48.60 with share baths, $59.40 with private bath, singles $37.80 and $48.60, suites $91.80 to $102.60. Continental breakfast; smoking OK. MC/VISA, AMEX. Simply furnished but neat and tidy rooms done in the Gold Rush style, with iron beds, lace curtains, wainscoting and print wallpaper. The Charlotte was built in 1921, although its column-supported balcony and lacy gingerbread give it a Victorian look.

MOTELS

Sonora Country Inn ● ⌂⌂ $$$ Ø

18755 Charbroullian Lane, Jamestown, CA 95327; (209) 984-0315. Doubles $64, singles $54, suites $105; non-smoking rooms. Major credit cards. TV, swimming pool, whirlpool. Rooms in this modern new facility are simple but spotless and comfortable. Although it's close to town, the motel sits a bit off Highway 49, in a quiet area.

Buck Meadows Lodge ● ⌂⌂ $$$

7647 Highway 120, Groveland, CA 95321; (209) 962-6366 or (800) 332-6300. Doubles from $55; MC/VISA, AMEX. Rustic and modern motel units in a wooded setting near the Big Oak Flat entrance to Yosemite National Park. Near popular hiking and rafting areas.

GOLD MINING IN THE MODERN MANNER

Want to see a *real* gold mining operation? Sign up for the Wednesday afternoon tour of Sonora Mining Corporation's Jamestown Mine. It's free but you'll need reservations by calling (209) 984-4641. (Details under Diversions.)

There's no sluicing or cool, dim mine tunnels in this operation. It's large-scale, state-of-the-art mining, using monster trucks to carry 100-ton loads of ore from the huge Harvard open pit. The operation started here in 1986, although mining began in this area in 1850, in nearby Woods Creek.

Like the great copper pits of Arizona, the Jamestown Mine is a huge terraced spiral, being dug ever deeper by blasts of ammonium nitrate and fuel oil. You're escorted by bus to the open pit's edge, from where the massive trucks look like Tonka toys. They're loaded by giant shovels that scoop up the ore in hungry 12-cubic-yard bites. How large a shovelful is 12 cubic yards? That's twice as much as a *full load* typically carried by big highway trucks.

These Tonka titans haul their heavy cargo to the reduction complex—which is your next stop. From a catwalk within these huge pea soup-colored buildings, you watch an array of noisy, efficient machinery hammer and grind all that rock and dirt. Jaw crushers, cone crushers, rod crushers and ball mills reduce it to powder and finally to a foamy slurry resembling a bubbling gray witch's brew.

But where's the gold? Everything is gray and dusty. Final extraction isn't done here. The slurry is hauled by truck to a processing plant in Yearington, Nevada. And don't bother to hijack one; it wouldn't be worth your while.

Sonora Mining officials figure they're having a good day if they extract less than .7 ounces of gold per *ton* of ore! However, since they process up to 7,200 tons a day, they'll get about 350 to 400 ounces, along with a bonus of 100 ounces of silver.

Railtown Motel • ⌂ $$$

P.O. Box 1129 (Willow at Main Street), Jamestown, CA 95327; (209) 984-3332. Doubles $55 to $80, singles $50. Major credit cards. Small nicely-maintained motel near historic area; TV, swimming pool and spa. In-room spas in eight units.

Sugar Pine Ranch • ⌂ $$

Highway 120, Groveland, CA 95321; (209) 962-7823. From $30 for two. MC/VISA. Comfortable, rustic rooms on an 1860s ranch, four miles east of Groveland.

CAMPING

Don Pedro Lake • *c/o Don Pedro Recreation Agency, 31 Bonds Flat Rd., La Grange, CA 95329; (209) 852-2396.* Camping is available at Moccasin Point, Fleming Meadows and Blue Oaks. All three have tent and RV sites and hookups. Activities include swimming, fishing and other water sports.

ANNUAL EVENTS

Gunfighters' Rendezvous, early July in downtown Jamestown, (209) 984-3851; western celebration with quick-draw artists, shoot-outs and such.

Wild West Days, last weekend of September in downtown Jamestown, (209) 984-3851; quick-draw artists, old West dress-up, antique show and other things Western.

ON THE ROAD AGAIN...TO SONORA

It's woodsy, but it isn't much of a trip, since Sonora is only four miles up the road. We've been gaining altitude since Coulterville and as we approach the seat of Tuolumne County, cool green pine forests begin to mingle with the familiar oak groves.

At the new Sonora cutoff just above Jamestown, remember to bear right and swing under the overpass, staying on Highway 49. The bypass (Highway 108) will deliver you to Sonora's main shopping area, including a large complex called The Junction, and ultimately to Twain Harte and the high Sierra country of Sonora Pass.

To learn more...

Tuolumne County Visitors Bureau, P.O. Box 4020, Sonora, CA 95370; (800) 446-1333, locally (209) 533-4420. or 984-INFO. The bureau operates a visitor center in the old Wells Fargo building on Main Street in Chinese Camp, open weekdays 9 to 4, Saturdays 10 to 4 and Sundays (summers only) 10 to 3. The main visitor center is in Sonora; see end of the next chapter for location and hours.

Stanislaus National Forest, Groveland Ranger District, P.O. Box 709 (on Highway 120), Groveland, CA 95321; (209) 962-7825.

"This was a gambling scrape in which T. Smith the monte deeler shot and wounded Felipe Vega. After heering witnesses on both sides, I ajeudged Smith guilty of shooting and fined him 10 dolars, and Vega guilty of attempting to steele 5 ounces (of gold). I therefore fined him 100 dolars..."

— **Entry from Sonora Justice R.C. Barry's court proceedings**

Chapter Six

SONORA & SURROUNDS

Tourism and Tuolumne history

TUOLUMNE
COUNTY
COURTHOUSE

Sonora occupies one of the prettier settings in the Gold Country, terraced into the thickly wooded slopes of an attractive valley. Its main thoroughfare, Washington Street, crawls through a shallow ravine at the base.

Although early fires and later progress erased many of its Gold Rush relics, it retains a special charm. Busy Washington Street is a virtual architectural museum. You'll see everything from iron door Gold Rush to Victorian to 1930s Art Deco—and one quasi-Byzantine dome. With its neatly scrubbed, prosperous look, Sonora boasts one of the most appealing downtown areas in all of the Gold Country.

THE WAY IT WAS ● The town inherited its pretty name from Mexican miners who came here from Sonora, Mexico, in 1848. They discovered rich placer diggins and built one of the liveliest, largest mining camps in the Mother Lode, called by some the *Queen of the Southern Mines*. But things got ugly in pretty Sonorian Camp when greedy gringos tried to crowd out the Mexicans.

Violence flared in the scenic valley. Forced off their claims, some of the Mexicans turned outlaw, and Sonora became one of the wildest towns of the Sierra foothills. Supposedly, this was yet another lair of the Mother Lode's most famous *bandito*, Joaquin Murieta. Some say he was a Sonoran who swore vengeance against the Yankees after being abused and chased out of town. Many modern historians question Murieta's existence, however. More than one Latino bandito may have used that name. Murieta exploits later were glamorized and distorted by pulp magazines and eventually by Hollywood.

67

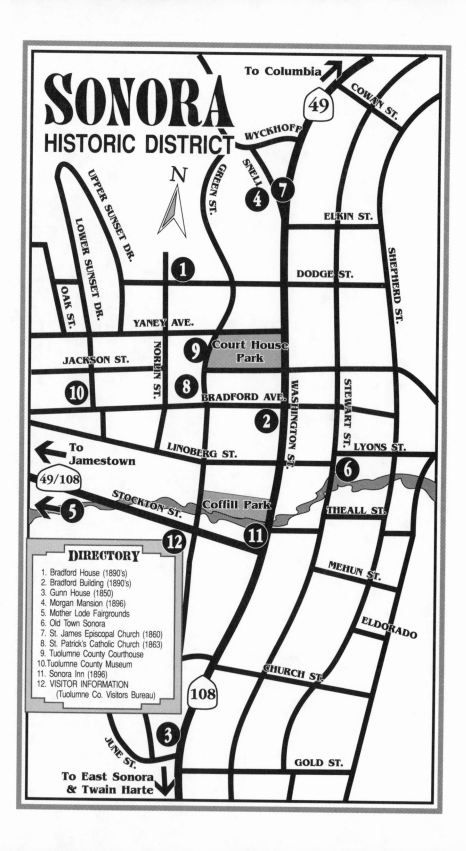

SONORA
HISTORIC DISTRICT

N

To Columbia

49

COWAN ST.

WYCKHOFF

UPPER SUNSET DR.

LOWER SUNSET DR.

OAK ST.

GREEN ST.

SNELL

4   7

ELKIN ST.

SHEPHERD ST.

1

DODGE ST.

YANEY AVE.

NORLIN ST.

9   Court House Park

JACKSON ST.

8   BRADFORD AVE.

10

2

WASHINGTON ST.

STEWART ST.

LYONS ST.

LINOBERG ST.

To Jamestown

49/108

6

STOCKTON ST.

Coffill Park

THEALL ST.

5

11

12

MEHUN ST.

ELDORADO

108

CHURCH ST.

3

JUNE ST.

GOLD ST.

To East Sonora & Twain Harte

DIRECTORY

1. Bradford House (1890's)
2. Bradford Building (1890's)
3. Gunn House (1850)
4. Morgan Mansion (1896)
5. Mother Lode Fairgrounds
6. Old Town Sonora
7. St. James Episcopal Church (1860)
8. St. Patrick's Catholic Church (1863)
9. Tuolumne County Courthouse
10. Tuolumne County Museum
11. Sonora Inn (1896)
12. VISITOR INFORMATION
    (Tuolumne Co. Visitors Bureau)

Although Sonorian Camp's rich placer fields were soon panned out, hard rock mines yielded modest rewards for decades, particularly in nearby Soulsbyville. In fact, mining continues in the area to this day.

Lumber, cattle ranching, agriculture and tourism supplanted the dwindling mineral resources. Sonora survived the usual Gold Rush fires and recessions to become an important provisioning and commercial center—a role it still plays. It's the seat of Tuolumne County.

THE WAY IT IS ● Sonora's location in a narrow valley is a scenic blessing and a vehicular curse, since all traffic is funneled down Washington Street. This is one of the largest, busiest and most popular towns of *La Veta Madre*, so it naturally draws quite a bundle of visitors. Others pass through on their way to the alpine recreation area of Sonora Pass to the east. The recent completion of the Sonora Bypass has eased that congestion somewhat.

Washington Street is tightly packed with shops, cafes and boutiques. Many are in century old buildings that have taken on an assortment of latter day facades, from Depression era Art Deco to California Fifties. The Sonora Inn at Washington and Stockton is a textbook example of Spanish California architecture with tile roof, whitewashed walls and an arched colonnade. Another worthy is the 1852 City Hotel building, across Washington and just to the north; this cut stone and brick edifice now houses professional offices and stores.

As the seat of government and marketing center of Tuolumne County, this is one of the Mother Lode's most prosperous cities. It's currently experiencing a modest growth boom, with a population topping 5,000. Actually, there are two Sonoras. Most of the growth is in East Sonora, a busy corridor of shopping centers and subdivisions extending toward the mountains along Mono Way (an extension of Washington Street). Downtown, with an active, preservation-minded merchants' association, is thus able retain its compact, oldstyle charm.

DISCOVERIES
The best attractions

Historic Sonora ● *Downtown and the surrounding neighborhoods with their Victorian homes are attractions unto themselves. Two guides will help you find your way. Pick up a copy of the* Heritage Home Tour *for a small fee at the Tuolumne County Museum, 158 W. Bradford Ave. To explore the commercial area along Washington Street, get a copy of* The Life and Times of Historic Sonora, *an oldstyle newspaper free at most downtown stores.*

Old Sonora is a park and walk place. Most of the historic structures—and their attendant boutiques, galleries and specialty shops—are along Washington between Stockton (Highway 49) and Elkin, a stretch of about six blocks. Parking is free but sometimes scarce on Washington, so try any of the side streets, or the public parking structure near the upper end.

The area's focal point is the red St. James Episcopal Church with an unusual conical spire, at Washington and Snell streets (listed below under Nuggets). Across the way, the Queen Anne style 1896 Street-Morgan Mansion is painted a matching red. It rivals the most elaborate San Francisco Victorians with its filigree, decorated balconies and gables.

Looking curiously stern amidst all this architectural whimsy is the ponderous three-story, Roman style yellow brick Tuolumne County Courthouse, built in 1898. But it isn't *too* serious a structure; it's topped by a Byzantine-domed clock tower that keeps watch over the town. The courthouse is fronted by a pretty little park shaded by huge conifers, on Washington between Yaney Avenue and Jackson Street.

Tuolumne County Museum and History Center • *158 W. Bradford Ave. (P.O. Box 299), Sonora, CA 95370; (209) 532-1317. Monday, Wednesday and Friday 9 to 4:30, Tuesday, Thursday and Saturday 10 to 3:30 all year; plus Sundays 10 to 3:30 during the summer. Free admission, donations accepted.*

The most intriguing thing about the museum is its location, in the former Tuolumne County Jail. It incarcerated bad guys and Sonora's Saturday night rowdies for more than a century, from 1857 until 1960. Several of the cells are used for exhibits; one houses a typical high-country bunk house and another contains a gunsmith shop.

The museum's main attraction is a glittering display of gold and quartz from Sonora County's mining days, with graphics on the county's three gold rushes: 1849, the 1890s and the currently active Jamestown open pit mine. Other displays include a fine series of historic county photos and an excellent collection of *Cowboys on Canvas* paintings by Bill West. These oils capture in vivid realism the energy and vitality of the working cowboys and critters of the Western frontier.

A term in the county jail was no picnic in bygone days, but it can be now. The former inmates' exercise yard has been converted into a picnic area.

Nuggets

Foster's Prospector Park • *Bradford Avenue at Stockton Street, Sonora.* This tiny park just downhill from the museum offers a nice little picnic retreat and few gold mining relics.

Main Street Shop • *134 S. Washington St., Sonora.* A large G-gauge German electric train chugs around a Bavarian village, with a cable car in the background, in the shop's charmingly busy window display. The shop itself offers a collection of gifts, toys and photography equipment.

Old Town Sonora • *Stewart and Lyon street, Sonora.* This large yellow building, housing several shops, boutiques and businesses, looks like a survivor of the 1890s. However, it's actually a clever imitation, built into the framework of a defunct Purity supermarket. Particularly interesting is an elevated patio where patrons can relax in the Sonoran sun, several feet above the street.

St. James Episcopal Church and History Room • *North Washington and Snell streets, Sonora; (209) 532-7644. History room open weekdays 9 to 5.* This famous dark red edifice, one of the most photographed structures in the Gold Country, was built in 1860; it's the second oldest wood frame Episcopal edifice in the state. Stained glass windows and unusual barrel arch window eaves accent this distinctive structure. A history room in the rectory offers exhibits tracing the background of the "Red Church."

St. Patrick's Catholic Church • *127 W. Jackson St., Sonora.* It's not as

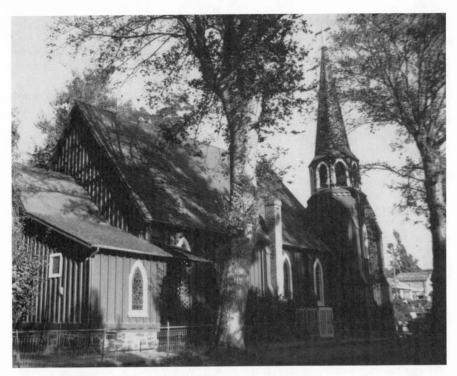

"The red church," St. James Episcopal, is one of Sonora's most famous and most-photographed landmarks.

well known as the Red Church, but St. Patrick's is one of the Mother Lode's more imposing worship parlors, with elaborate biblical scenes in stained glass and a lofty spire visible throughout the town. It was built in 1863.

Servente Grocery Liquor • *64 S. Washington St., Sonora.* This iron and brick store, dating from 1856, is the only iron-front building in the county. Check out the unusual detail in the brick facade and the ornate ironwork.

Sonka's Apple Ranch • *19200 Cherokee Rd., Tuolumne; (209) 928-4689. Open daily 8 to 5:30.* If you believe in that apple-a-day business, stop in at Sonka's, about half a mile north of Tuolumne Road. Browse through the selection of apple specialties, from fresh picked apples (in season) to pies and other fresh-baked goods, preserves and jams, along with country gift items. Take your goodies along or enjoy them at a shady picnic area.

Steam locomotive • *At the Mother Lode Fairgrounds entrance, 220 Southgate Drive on Highway 49 southwest of Sonora.* This bold black cog-driven steam engine is a favorite jungle gym for youngsters, who can climb up into the engineer's seat and pretend they're hauling a load of ore from the mines. The 19th century chuffer carried wood products on the Westside and Cherry Valley Railroad for Tuolumne City's Pickering Lumber Company.

DETOUR

Sonora to Twain Harte via Tuolumne • *A 30-mile loop trip from gold fields to evergreens.* Head northeast out of Sonora on Highway 108, and hang a right onto Tuolumne Road just short of the large Junction Shopping Center. It's the county's largest, and a good provisioning place.

Follow Tuolumne Road about seven miles toward the town of the same name. About a mile short of Tuolumne, you might want to swing left onto Cherokee Road for a pause at Sonka's Apple Ranch (listed above).

Continue into Tuolumne, a quietly rustic little collection of old homes beneath shady maples. If you turn right at the stop sign in downtown Tuolumne and drive three blocks, you'll find the Tuolumne Memorial Museum at 18663 Carter Street, on your left. This rather scruffy little exhibit center in a brown wooden cottage is open Saturday and Sunday from 1 to 4; phone (209) 536-1253 or 928-4029. Therein, assuming you arrive on a weekend afternoon, you'll learn of the town's yesterdays.

Tuolumne began life as Summerville when gold was discovered in the 1850s. It prospered until the mines ran out, then lumbering arrived at the turn of the century to keep it on the map. Unfortunately, a 1918 fire consumed much of its past; most of its buildings are of early 20th century vintage.

Reverse your route on Carter, which becomes North Tuolumne Road, follow it about a mile and turn right onto Mi Wu Road. This takes you to the small Tuolumne Mi-Wuk Rancheria (reservation), site of a typical Indian Round House. This shingled, conical meeting hall is still in active use. The Mi-Wuks conduct an annual Acorn Festival here in September to perpetuate their centuries-old traditions.

From Mi-Wuk, Tuolumne Road climbs steeply into lush evergreen forests and rejoins Highway 108 at Twain Harte. To enter this mountain village, continue straight across the highway onto Twain Harte drive.

With a name like Twain Harte, it's an historic Gold Rush town, right? Wrong. It's an attractive little alpine hamlet with a deliberately rustic shopping center and chalet type homes tucked among the pines. Developers merely borrowed the names of the Mother Lode's most famous publicists to give their planned community a Gold Country flavor.

We're now in pine cone and squirrel country, the luxuriant alpine forests of the Sierra Nevada. From Twain Harte, route 108 passes through more woodsy villages with pleasant names like Sugar Pine, Strawberry and Pinecrest. It eventually leads over Sonora Pass, one of the Sierra's most spectacularly scenic crossings.

The downhill return to Sonora is brisk, since Highway 108 is four-lane through most of this area. En route, pause to visit two more old-timey towns. Four and a half miles below Twain Harte, turn left onto Soulsbyville Road for a short drive into the town of that name.

Soulsbyville was settled in 1851 by Ben Soulsby, who was interested in lumbering and farming, not gold. But his 12-year-old son, Ben Jr., literally tripped over a nugget while walking the family cow home one day. Little Ben wasn't old enough to file a claim so Big Ben took care of the paper work and began digging one of the first hardrock mines in Tuolumne County. He also was one of the first to employ Cornish miners, who were skilled at deep-pit copper and tin mining back in England.

Today's Soulsbyville is a neat and prim little community of well-tended homes, many with shiny tin roofs. Among its yesterday survivors are the white United Methodist Church with a squared witch's hat tower, dating from 1860 and still in use; and the rusting conical sawdust burner and scattered machinery of an old mill. They're across the road from one another, each standing behind monuments that describe the town's early days.

Drive another pair of miles down Route 108, then turn left again onto Standard Road. You'll shortly encounter Standard, a classic old company town built by the Pickering Lumber Company in the 1920s. It's now part of the Fibreboard Corporation complex, Tuolumne County's largest single employer. Not much of the original town remains, although you'll see some early 20th century California-style stucco buildings, a couple of false front stores and an old fashioned railway depot.

From here, you can cross over to Tuolumne Road or backtrack to Highway 108 to complete your return to Sonora.

DIVERSIONS

Whitewater rafting • The Tuolumne River is one of the most popular rafting streams in California, with two stretches that pass through spectacular Sierra scenery. Neither run is for the novice, however. The Upper Tuolumne is a nine-mile stretch from Cherry Creek to Meral's Pool, for expert rafters and kayakers only, with white water up to Class V. The lower Tuolumne offers an 18-mile run from Meral's Pool to Ward's Ferry bridge, also rough but not quite as wild.

Permits are required for either stretch, and may be obtained from the District Ranger, Stanislaus National Forest, Groveland Ranger District, P.O. Box 709, Groveland, CA 95321; (209) 962-7825.

Several commercial operators offer whitewater trips on the Tuolumne and other Sierra Nevada streams. Among those based in the area are **Ahwahnee Whitewater Expeditions**, P.O. Box 1161, Columbia, CA 95310, (800) 359-9790 or (209) 533-4101; **American River Touring Assn.**, 24000 Casa Loma Rd., Groveland, CA 95321, 962-7873; **OARS,** P.O. Box 67, Angels Camp, CA 95222, 736-4677; **Sierra Mac River Trips,** P.O. Box 366, Sonora, CA 95370, 532-1327; and **Zephyr River Expeditions,** P.O. Box 510, Columbia, CA 95310, 532-6249.

Flatwater boating • Boating, water skiing, fishing and swimming are available on two large reservoirs—Tulloch Lake and New Melones Lake—and several smaller ones. Check the visitors' bureau for specifics. Pinecrest Lake in Stanislaus National Forest offers fishing, sailing and windsurfing, and the Forest Service operates a marina and launching facilities. Another Forest Service launching ramp has been built at Beardsley Lake.

Hiking and the like • "Dwarf trees, delicate wildflowers, gargoyle-like rock formations, aquamarine lakes and streams...await hikers and nature lovers in the Stanislaus National Forest." So says the Forest Service hiking trails leaflet. Popular trailheads are at Leavitt and Kennedy meadows, Cherry Lake, Gianelli Cabin and Hetch Hetchy. For details, contact the ranger station listed at the end of this chapter.

GOLD COUNTRY DINING

Barron's Restaurant • ∆∆ $ ∅∅

In the Sonora Inn at 160 S. Washington St. (Stockton), Sonora; (209) 532-0566. Mexican-American; dinners $7 to $11.75; wine and beer. Breakfast and lunch weekends 8 to 2, lunch Wednesday-Friday 11 to 2, dinner Sunday-Thursday 5 to 8 and Friday-Saturday 5 to 10. MC/VISA. Housed in the refurbished

1896 Sonora Inn, with a cheerful Spanish decor to compliment the inn's mission-style architecture. Menu features typical Mexican items plus Garlic chicken, fresh fish and steaks on the American side. Separate non-smoking section.

Good Heavens • ∆∆ $$

49 N. Washington St., Sonora; (209) 532-3663. Contemporary American; meals $5 to $12; wine and beer. Daily 11 to 3 and Sunday champagne brunch from 10 to 2. No credit cards. Cute boutique cafe set in the 1858 Yo semite Hotel in Sonora's historic district, with early Americana decor and yesteryear paintings. Changing menu features crepes, pastas, unusual—and tasty—broiled sandwiches, plus elaborate homestyle desserts and jams.

Hemingway's Cafe Restaurant • ∆∆∆ $$$ ∅∅

362 Steward St., Sonora; (209) 532-4900. Contemporary cuisine, dinners $15 to $20; wine and beer. Open Tuesday-Saturday, lunch 11:30 to 2:30, dinner from 5. Reservations recommended. MC/VISA, AMEX. One of the area's better restaurants. Eclectic menu wanders from Norwegian gravlox and "California stir fry" to fajitas and elegant full-course dinners. In a charming ranch style house set in a garden-like atmosphere. French windows and floral print wallpaper provide an old European cafe look, although the cuisine is contemporary. Live music on weekends. A smoke-free restaurant.

Ristorante LaTorre • ∆∆∆∆ $$$ ∅∅

39 N. Washington St., Sonora; (209) 533-9181. Italian-Continental; dinners $9.50 to $17; full bar service. Lunch weekdays 11:30 to 3, dinner Monday-Saturday 4:30 to closing and Sunday 3 to 9. Reservations accepted. MC/VISA, AMEX. Strikingly handsome second-floor restaurant in an 1889 brick and masonry building. Elegant Victorian decor with cozy high-back booths, lots of polished wood, brass and glass, old time photos and vertical striped wallpaper. Easily one of the Gold Country's most striking dining salons. Small, versatile menu ranges from Chateau Briand and tournedos to *cannelloni della casa, fettuccini Alfredo* and grilled chicken. Equally attractive bar adjacent with imposing carved-wood mirrored backbar. Smoke-free dining room.

The Wagon Wheel • ∆∆ $$

126 S. Washington St., Sonora; (209) 532-1266. American with an Italian tilt; dinners $9 to $14; full bar service. Lunch 11 to 2:30 weekdays; dinner 5 to 9:30 weekdays and 4:30 to 9 weekends, closed Wednesday. Reservations accepted. MC/VISA. Typical small town family restaurant and a long-time local favorite. It's a curious blend of the old West and the 1950s, with wagon wheel chandeliers, woodgrain paneling and comfortable plush vinyl booths. Chicken, chops, steaks and several Italian dishes. It's in a cozy spot, downstairs along the concrete banks of Sonora Creek. An itimate—if rather smoky—brick and wood cocktail lounge with batwing doors is adjacent.

Is there life after dark?

The Sonora-Columbia area is surprisingly rich in cultural offerings, with two on-going theater groups and a new performing arts showcase.

Sierra Repertory Theatre, *2113 Mono Way (P.O. Box 3030), Sonora, CA 95370; (209) 532-3120.* Fine professional troupe, critically acclaimed statewide, offers a year-around mix of dramas, comedies and musicals. Equity performers are drawn from across the country to appear in productions directed by Dennis Jones.

Dream West Theatre for the Performing Arts, *#6 Washington St., Sonora, CA 95370; (209) 532-5000.* At press time, a downtown showcase for musical talent was being created by Musical producer Stephen M. Rangel, formerly with the San Francisco Bay Area's Concord Pavilion.

Columbia Actors Repertory, *See listing in next chapter.*

Here's a partial list of restaurants, pubs and clubs offering live entertainment: **The Brass Rail** at 131 S. Washington Street (532-4830) offers live or jukebox music for dancing nightly; **Eproson House** on Twain Harte Drive in Twain Harte (586-5600) has live country and Western music Friday and Saturday nights; the **Gunn House's** Josephine Room at 286 S. Washington has live entertainers on weekends; **Hemingway's** at 362 S. Stewart Street in Sonora (532-4900) features live music of the Gershwin, Rogers & Hammerstein and Cole Porter era on weekends; **Sullivan Creek Restaurant and Bar** (532-6767) provides live music Friday and Saturday from 9 to 1:30.

LODGINGS

Bed & breakfast inns

Barretta Gardens Inn • ⌂⌂⌂ $$$$ ØØ

700 S. Barretta St., Sonora, CA 95370; (209) 532-6039. Doubles $80 to $95. Five units, all with private baths. Full breakfast. Smoking on front porch only. MC/VISA, AMEX. This elegantly appointed Victorian built in 1904 overlooks Sonora from its hilltop above terraced gardens. Rooms are furnished with antiques and those frilly extras that create an authentic Victorian atmosphere. Particularly impressive is the Periwinkle Room, with a 12-foot ceiling; its focal point is a floor-to-ceiling beveled mirror in an ornate frame. A wrap-around porch has been converted into a sunny sitting room, where guests can relax and enjoy vistas of the town.

Llamahall Guest Ranch • ⌂⌂⌂ $$$$ ØØ

18170 Wards Ferry Rd., Sonora, CA 95370; (209) 532-7264. Doubles $85. Two units with private baths. Full breakfast. No smoking; no credit cards. This ranch style country inn sits in a woodsy grove in a peaceful rural setting southeast of Sonora. Why the odd name? It's a working llama farm and guests and their children are invited to pet and even ride these furry, gentle critters. Rooms are comfortably furnished and sprinkled with antiques. Life at Llamahall can be hedonistic, with a hot tub, sauna and a glass of wine with music before a large stone fireplace.

Lavender Hill Bed and Breakfast • ⌂⌂⌂ $$$ ØØ

683 Barretta St. (off Highway 108), Sonora, CA 95370; (209) 532-9024. Doubles $60 to $70. Four units, two with private bath, two share. Full breakfast. No smoking; no credit cards. Built around 1900, this Victorian mansion offers a peek into Sonora's past, with several original antiques mixed with reproductions and contemporary furnishings. It's a tasteful blend of Victorian frills and modern plumbing; the overall effect is warm and homey. The inn sits amidst neatly manicured grounds in downtown Sonora.

Oak Hill Ranch Bed and Breakfast Inn • ⌂⌂⌂ ØØ

P.O. Box 307 (18550 Connally Lane), Tuolumne, CA 95379; (209) 928-4717. Doubles from $65. Five units including a private cottage, three private, two share baths. Full breakfast. No smoking; no credit cards. This appears to be an elegantly appointed Victorian from yesterday, but it was built in 1980, designed by the owners' architect son. Sanford and Jane Grover collected Victorian artifacts and materials for 25 years to equip their appealing "country Victorian." Rooms are furnished in Classic Eastlake antiques and other family heirlooms. The home sits on a knoll in an 1850s homestead, surrounded by a landscaped garden, with views of the distant Sierra Nevada. Each morning, the hosts dress in Victorian finery to serve lavish breakfasts in a formal dining room.

The Ryan House Bed & Breakfast ⌂⌂⌂ $$$$ ØØ

153 S. Shepherd St. (Theall), Sonora, CA 95370; (209) 533-3445. Doubles $75 to $80, singles $70. Three rooms, all with private baths; TV available on request. Full breakfast. No smoking. Major credit cards. Nancy and Guy Hoffman refurbished this 1855 Gold Rush home in downtown Sonora and styled it with a nice mix of early American and Victorian furnishings. Handmade quilts cover comfortable queen-sized beds. Surrounded by rose gardens, the home is within walking distance of Sonora's historic Washington Street shops and restaurants.

Serenity • ⌂⌂⌂ $$$$ ØØ

P.O. Box 3484 (15305 Bear Cub Drive off Phoenix Lake Road east of town), Sonora, CA 95370; (209) 533-1441. Doubles from $75. Four units with private baths. Full breakfast. Smoking on veranda only. Major credit cards. Rebuilt after a 1988 fire, this handsome inn is fashioned in a "Mother Lode Colonial" style, offering a blend of yesterday atmosphere and modern conveniences. Rooms are furnished appropriate to the period in a bright floral motif, with antiques, reproductions and needlework art. Guests can try their board game skills in a well-equipped game room or relax in the sun on a wrap-around veranda. The home is tucked into six wooded acres near Stanislaus National Forest. Afternoon refreshments.

Via Serena Ranch • ⌂⌂ $$$ ØØ

18007 Via Serena Dr., Sonora, CA 95370; (209) 532-5307. Doubles $60. Three units with shared baths. Full breakfast. Smoking outside only. No credit cards. This modern white stucco ranch style home in Sonora's wooded Questa Serena development is rimmed by a large deck. Visitors can enjoy the countryside view, or become a part of it, since hiking and fishing areas are nearby. Rooms are decorated with an English country theme.

Willow Springs Bed and Breakfast • ⌂⌂ $$$ ØØ

20599 Kings Court, Soulsbyville, CA 95372; (209) 533-2030. Doubles $50 to $80, singles $45 to $75. Five units, two with private baths, three share. Full breakfast. No smoking. No credit cards; personal checks accepted. None other than Ben Soulsby built this Victorian ranch house around 1881. Although not elegant, the rooms are comfortable and nicely furnished with a mix of contemporary and antique. Amenities include a hot tub and barbecue area; guests have access to next-door tennis courts, horse shoe pits and shuffleboard courts. Guests are welcome to use the kitchen to prepare light meals.

Motels and inns

Best Western Sonora Oaks Motor Hotel ● ⌂⌂⌂ $$$ ∅

19551 Hess Ave. (at Highway 108), Sonora, CA 95370; (800) 528-1234 or (209) 533-4400. Doubles $61 to $75, singles $57 to $65. Major credit cards. Attractive 70-unit in East Sonora, in a quiet setting away from traffic. TV movies, room phones; pool, spa; **coffeeshop** adjacent.

The Gunn House ● ⌂⌂ $$

286 S. Washington St., Sonora, CA 95370; (209) 532-3421. Doubles $40 to $70. All rooms with private baths and TV; small pets and smoking OK. MC/VISA, AMEX. Sonora's most historic lodging, occupying a picturesque two-story Spanish adobe once owned by one of Sonora's leading citizens, dating from 1850. Comfortable rooms with rather eclectic furnishings; the place could use a good interior decorator. It's a charmingly weathered inn, with landscaped grounds, a heated pool and a stone and wrought iron patio.

Miner's Motel ● ⌂ $$

18740 Highway 49 (P.O. Box 1), Sonora, CA 95370; (209) 532- 7850. Rooms $40 to $65. Major credit cards. Small motel with TV movies, in-room coffee; pool, picnic area, boat parking. Between Sonora and Jamestown.

Sonora Gold Lodge ● ⌂⌂ $$ ∅

480 W. Stockton St. (Highway 49/108), Sonora, CA 95370; (209) 532-3952. Doubles $48 to $62, singles $46 to $48. MC/VISA, AMEX. A 42-unit motel opposite Mother Lode Fairgrounds. TV, room phones, free coffee; pool, wooded grounds.

Sonora Inn ● ⌂⌂ $$ ∅

106 S. Washington St., Sonora, CA 95370; (800) 321-5261 or (209) 532-7468. Doubles $45 to $55, singles $32 to $50. Major credit cards. Refurbished rooms—not elegant but clean and comfortable—in Sonora's landmark Spanish-style inn, dating back to 1896. TV, swimming pool, bar and **Barron's Restaurant** (listed above); some non-smoking rooms.

Sonora Towne House Motel ● ⌂⌂⌂ $$$

350 S. Washington St., Sonora, CA 95370; (800) 251-1538 or (209) 532-3633. Doubles $50 to $65, singles $45 to $60; Major credit cards. A 112-unit motel in downtown Sonora. TV, room phones, wet bars; pool and spa.

CAMPGROUNDS & RV PARKS

Mother Lode Fairgrounds ● *220 Southgate Drive (off Highway 49 just south of town), Sonora, CA 95370; (209) 532-7428. RV sites only, $11. Reservations accepted, recommended on weekends.* Water and electrical hookups, flush toilets, a few picnic tables. Open all year.

New Melones Reservoir ● *(984-5248) Two campgrounds—at Glory Hole (144 sites) and Tuttletown (89 sites). RV and tent camping, $10; w/Golden Age or Golden Access card, $5.* Showers and flush potties; no hookups. Fishing and various water sports. Campsites have lake views but many are exposed to the sun, so they can get toasty in summer. Open all year.

River Ranch Campground ● *P.O. Box 1268 (off Buchanan Road northeast of Tuolumne City), Tuolumne, CA 95379; (209) 928-3708. Fifty tent or*

RV sites, $14 per vehicle. Reservations accepted. Barbecues and tables, showers and flush potties, no hookups. Rustic campground on 100 wooded acres with swimming, fishing and gold panning in adjacent Tuolumne River. Some campsites at riverside. Open March 1 to October 31.

Stanislaus National Forest ● *More than 40 campgrounds available in a variety of areas. RV and tent sites.* No hookups or showers; pit toilets; most sites have barbecues or fire pits and picnic tables. For a map and list of campgrounds, contact the forest service office listed at the end of this chapter.

ANNUAL EVENTS

Celtic Celebration first weekend of March at Mother Lode Fairgrounds, (209) 533-3473; Irish, Scottish, Cornish and Welsh crafts, customs and foods.

Mother Lode Roundup, second weekend of May at Mother Lode Fairgrounds, (209) 532-8394; professional rodeo and parade.

Strawberry Spring Music Festival, in late March at Camp Mather, Yosemite, (209) 533-0191; outdoor classic and contemporary music.

High Sierra Music Festival over Fourth of July weekend at Leland Meadows, 39 miles east of Sonora on Highway 108, (800) 273-8813 or (209) 533-2851; popular and Western music, crafts fair, environmental booths.

Mother Lode Fair, in mid-July at Mother Lode Fairgrounds, (209) 532-7428; fair exhibits, carnival, parade, booths.

Strawberry Fall Music Festival in mid-September at Camp Mather, Yosemite, (209) 533-0191; classic and contemporary music.

Mi-Wuk Indian Acorn Festival in mid-September at Tuolumne Rancheria, Tuolumne, (209) 928-3475; Indian dances, arts, crafts and foods.

Tuolumne County Wild West Filmfest and Rodeo, last weekend of September at Dreamwest and Memory Bank theaters downtown, (800) 446-1333 or (209) 533-4420; Western films and in-person guest stars; professional rodeo, barn dance and barbecue at Mother Lode Fairgrounds.

Christmas crafts fair, parade and open house, last weekend of November at Mother Lode Fairgrounds and downtown Sonora; (209) 533-3473 and 532-4820; arts, crafts, music, merchants' open house, Yule parade.

ON THE ROAD AGAIN...TO COLUMBIA

It's another short drive; about three miles north on Highway 49, then right onto Parrots Ferry Road. Our destination is Columbia, where preservation, restoration and a little show biz keep the California Gold Rush very much alive.

To learn more...

Tuolumne County Visitors Bureau, P.O. Box 4020, Sonora, CA 95370; (800) 446-1333, locally (209) 533-4420. The bureau operates a visitor center at 55 W. Stockton Rd. (Highway 49), a block below Washington Street. It's open weekdays 9 to 5:30, Saturdays 10 to 4 and Sundays (summers only) 10 to 3. The Chinese Camp office in the old Wells Fargo building (984-INFO) is open weekdays 9 to 4, Saturdays 10 to 4 and Sundays (summers only) 10 to 3.

Tuolumne City Merchants Association, P.O. Box 1291, Tuolumne, CA 95379; (209) 928-4297.

Twain Harte Chamber of Commerce, P.O. Box 404 (22984 Joaquin Gully Rd.), Twain Harte, CA 95383; (209) 586-4482.

Forest Supervisor's Office, Stanislaus National Forest, 19777 Greenley Rd., Sonora, CA 95370; (209) 532-3671. Send $2 for a national forest map listing campsites and other recreational facilities.

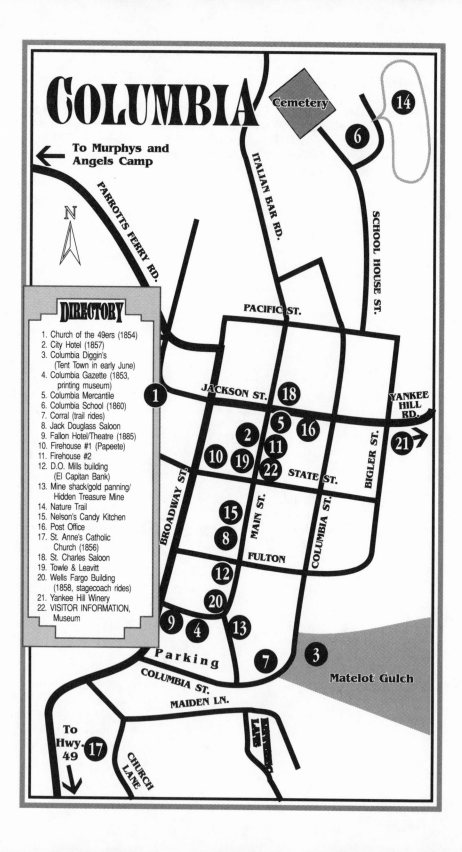

COLUMBIA

Cemetery

To Murphys and Angels Camp

N

PARROTTS FERRY RD.

ITALIAN BAR RD.

SCHOOL HOUSE ST.

PACIFIC ST.

JACKSON ST.

YANKEE HILL RD.

STATE ST.

BIGLER ST.

BROADWAY ST.

MAIN ST.

COLUMBIA ST.

FULTON

Matelot Gulch

Parking

COLUMBIA ST.

MAIDEN LN.

To Hwy 49

CHURCH LANE

DIRECTORY

1. Church of the 49ers (1854)
2. City Hotel (1857)
3. Columbia Diggin's (Tent Town in early June)
4. Columbia Gazette (1853, printing museum)
5. Columbia Mercantile
6. Columbia School (1860)
7. Corral (trail rides)
8. Jack Douglass Saloon
9. Fallon Hotel/Theatre (1885)
10. Firehouse #1 (Papeete)
11. Firehouse #2
12. D.O. Mills building (El Capitan Bank)
13. Mine shack/gold panning/ Hidden Treasure Mine
14. Nature Trail
15. Nelson's Candy Kitchen
16. Post Office
17. St. Anne's Catholic Church (1856)
18. St. Charles Saloon
19. Towle & Leavitt
20. Wells Fargo Building (1858, stagecoach rides)
21. Yankee Hill Winery
22. VISITOR INFORMATION, Museum

"Columbia...made its enormously rich deposits furnish its people with almost everything a real city could boast. The town had burned down twice, yet had sprung up again, replacing wood and canvas with fine brick buildings decorated with ironwork balconies..."

— from *Anybody's Gold* by Joseph Henry Jackson

COLUMBIA'S WELLS FARGO EXPRESS OFFICE

Chapter Seven

COLUMBIA

Life in a living museum

The night shadows dance to our lantern light as my son Dan and I follow a narrow path from our campsite into the forest. We pick our way carefully through an outcropping of quartz, cross the stage road, then pass through a thicket near the edge of town. We hear a rustling sound in the brush! Silence for a moment, then a deer explodes from the undergrowth and disappears. Startled, we trip backward, then we laugh at our "ghost" and continue on our way.

Columbia is quiet but not asleep. Lights glimmer from old wood frame homes and lusty laughter issues from the St. Charles Saloon. We step into the prim Victorian parlor of the City Hotel; I smile at the pretty hostess dressed in a lacy blouse and long black skirt.

"We're the Martins...nine o'clock dinner reservations."

She looks puzzled for a moment, then returns my smile: "You can put your lantern out. We have electric lights now."

THE WAY IT WAS ● It all started because Thaddeus and George Hildreth and their party of five got caught in the rain. They'd been prospecting for a month without a show of color in their pans. Frustrated, they set up camp in a gulch near a group of Mexican miners; rain fell during the night and added further to their miseries. The next morning, as they spread their blankets to dry, one of the party—a John Walker—did a bit of panning to kill time. It was March 27, 1850.

Gold glittered in his rusty pan!

They gathered thirty pounds of nuggets in two days and Hildreth's Diggins joined the mushrooming legions of tent cities in the Sierra foothills.

Secrets of major strikes were impossible to keep in the Mother Lode, and soon thousands swarmed over the gulch. Segregating themselves from the nearby Mexican encampment, the Yankee miners called their canvas ragtown American Camp, one of several that used that name. A Major Richard

Sullivan got himself elected *alcalde*—the Spanish term for a combination mayor, tax collector and justice of the peace. With a poetic flourish, he renamed the settlement "Columbia, Gem of the Southern Mines." Sullivan didn't stick around long; he was chased away for levying gold dust fines on both plaintiff and defendant in his court. But the name survived.

Columbia was a "dry diggins" with only seasonal creeks, so the camp alternately flourished when miners could wash for gold in rain-swollen creeks, then wilted with the summer heat. At times during its first two summers, it became a virtual ghost town.

Finally, a system of ditches and flumes brought water from the Stanislaus River and Columbia indeed became the gem of the southern Mother Lode. By the mid-1850s, it was one of the largest towns in California, with 6,000 citizens, 53 stores, 40 saloons and 159 gaming halls. And three churches.

It burned to the dirt twice and was rebuilt of sturdy brick and iron; many of these structures survive. When surface gold was exhausted, eager argonauts began digging in the dirt, then they blasted it away with powerful water jets called monitors. They undermined houses, threatened to topple poor St. Anne's Church atop Kennebec Hill and lowered much of Columbia's ground level by as much as eight feet. This is why today's visitors see great outcroppings of limestone and marble.

By the time the miners gave up in the early 1870s, $87 million worth of gold had been taken away. At today's figures, the dollar amount would top two billion. That's a lot of bullion.

THE WAY IT IS ● Columbia might have become just another sleepy former gold camp or, even worse, a themed shopping center. But in 1945, the state of California bought most of the buildings along Main and Broadway and began restoration.

After decades of preservation and reconstruction, a little show biz and occasional squabbles between residents and state officials, Columbia State Historic Park has become the most-visited attraction in the Mother Lode. It draws upwards of 400,000 mini-cam clutchers a year.

Initially, Columbia SHP functioned as a conventional town with only a few historic exhibits. However, in recent years the state's policy has shifted away from private ownership, toward a blend of preservation and tourism. The Columbia Docent Association helps bring history to life with costumed guided tours and frequent dress-up celebrations. Gift shop concessionaires, while peddling their scented soaps and postcards, are encouraged to wear period dress and market products appropriate to the era. Tasteless souvenirs and wax museums, the ruination of places like San Francisco's Fisherman's Wharf, are forbidden.

Columbia thus has become a living—and lively—museum. During summers and most any weekend, visitors can board a stagecoach destined to be robbed by a lady Black Bart, listen to street musicians fiddle along Main Street, be photographed in period costume, watch a real working blacksmith and take home a personalized horseshoe, pan for gold in Matelot Gulch where real miners worked the dirt a century and a half ago, and swagger into a saloon and order a mug of suds or a sarsparilla.

It's also a favorite haunt of Hollywood. Scenes for *High Noon*, episodes of

TV's *Paradise* and *The Young Riders* and many other horse operas have been filmed here and you'll recognize the Wells Fargo Express office from TV commercials. Photographers and students of early Western architecture find the place irresistible, with its rich collection of false-front buildings, century-old wood frame homes and brick stores with iron shutters and doors. Inside the structures, oiled wood floors, high ceilings and frilly Victorian trim convey visitors back to the Gold Rush.

With all this tourism, it's still a working town with its own Zip Code, a functioning bank and a corner grocery where we residents stop by for an occasional loaf of bread and quart of non-fat. And we grin when visitors think the century-old post office is a mock-up. ("Isn't that cute, Melissa. They've even put fake letters in those little post boxes!")

Thus, what we offer here is a rather sanitized version of the original. There are no dirt streets, no bawdy ladies, no drunks being heaved through batwing doors to land plop in muddy gutters. It's history the way tourists like it—rinsed clean and hung out to dry in a warm summer sun.

DISCOVERIES
The best attractions

We were kids in an historical candy store, trying to decide which of the town's many attractions were the best. We picked one because it offers a good overview, and the other because it taught my son Dan what school was like in the last century. In fact, it was not unlike the school his father attended a few decades ago in rural Oregon.

The William Cavalier Museum • *Main and State streets; daily 10 to 4:30.* Named in honor of the man who helped establish the park, the museum is a good starting point, providing a quick study of the Gold Rush and Columbia. Exhibits include curiosities such as a miner's washboard, just four by eight inches because only socks and neckerchiefs were washed regularly; and an 1870 teamster's knife, a forerunner of the Swiss army knife with a cutting blade, saw, corkscrew, wood drill, leather punch and horse's hoof cleaner. Other exhibits depict the steps taken by the state to restore this fine old town. Slide shows and films are shown in a small theater.

The museum is housed in Sewell Knapp's Miners Supply Store; legend says Knapp saved the place from the 1857 fire by pouring barrels of vinegar on the structure when he ran out of water.

Columbia School • *School House Street, just above the town.* Perhaps the neatest thing about this place is that it was preserved by California's school children. They contributed their paper route funds and lunch money in a 1950s restoration drive. The lower floor of this imposing red brick structure is a typical elementary classroom, complete with ink wells, flash cards and slate boards. Upstairs, the junior high school kids tried to concentrate on their ciphers and history, probably distracted by squirrels and jaybirds in the nearby trees. Their wooden desks and other typical furnishings are still in place. Built in 1860 for under $5,000 and used until 1937, it is one of California's longest surviving schoolhouses. **Columbia Cemetery**, a brambly but well-tended burial ground opposite the school, is the final resting place of many Columbia pioneers. It was moved to this spot in 1855 after gold was found in the original cemetery site closer to town.

Some of the rest

Fallon Hotel lobby • *Washington Street and Broadway.* It's a vision in Victorian elegance: floor to ceiling green velvet drapes, print wallpaper and oak chair rails, a patterned ceiling, Oriental carpets and a handsome green S-curve love seat. Since the Fallon is a functioning hotel, visitors are not encouraged to wander about the halls, although they can browse in this beautiful lobby and peek into a room that's furnished as it might have been for an 1860s miner. It's in stark contrast to the rest of the Fallon's Victorian refinement, exhibiting a simple brass bed and patchwork quilt, marble-topped wash basin and roller blinds.

Museum of the Gold Rush Press • *In the Columbia Gazette book shop near the Fallon Hotel.* Freedom of the press didn't get much respect during the Gold Rush, according to exhibits in the Gazette's nice little basement museum. Newspaper editors were cursed, beaten and sometimes gunned down for expressing their thoughts during that often violent era.

An interesting exhibit tells the tale of California's oldest printing press. Initially imported for the state's first newspaper—the *Alta Californian* in Monterey—it was sold to four other publishers to begin their journalistic efforts. Sadly, this historic press came to a violent end. It was sold by Dr. Lewis Gunn of the *Sonora Herald* to G.W. "Wash" Gore, a fiery entrepreneur

Getting ready for business, a costumed shopkeeper opens the iron shutters of one of Columbia's 19th century stores.

who used it to print the first issue of his *Columbia Star*. A dispute arose over payment for the press and it was sold in a sheriff's sale to Gunn's agents. Before they could take it back to Sonora, the enraged Gore dragged it into the street and burned it.

The museum also features a "gallery of Gold Rush journalists," with brief biographies of folks like Mark Twain and the de Young brothers, who founded San Francisco's *Dramatic Chronicle* in 1865.

Nelson's Columbia Candy Kitchen • *Main Street between Fulton and State.* Talk about a kid (of any age) in a candy store! Nelson's is not only a neat looking place with its oiled floors, print wallpaper and ceiling fans, it's also brimming with diet breakers. Third and fourth generations of the Nelson family operate it, using century-old recipes to create horehound drops, licorice whips and peppermint hard drops. The shop also offers contemporary sweets, like gummy bears and hand-dipped truffles.

It's a delightful showplace during the Christmas holidays, when the Nelsons create classic ribbon candy and other Yule delights in their windowed kitchen, in full view of passersby. Park rangers often join the gathering crowd outside and deliver a brief lecture on early-day candy making.

St. Anne's Catholic Church • *Crowning Kennebec Hill on Church Lane.* This sturdy red brick church with its impressive bell tower and flying buttresses is thought to be the oldest brick church in California, dating from 1856. No longer an active church, it is open to visitors during summer weekends, generally from about 11 to 4. At other times, visitors can stand on tippytoe and peek through the tall windows to admire the pretty white and light blue interior, white and gold trimmed altar and heavenly mural. Under the care of Sonora's St. Patrick's parish, it's frequently used for special service and is popular for weddings. An ancient cemetery tumbles downhill from the noble old structure.

Old time saloons • Three Columbia saloons survive from the original 40. The **St. Charles** and **Jack Douglass** offer wine and beer for grownups and sarsparilla for the kids, and the **What Cheer** is a comely woodpaneled establishment off the City Hotel Restaurant, offering full bar service. We particularly like the St. Charles, a good-old-boy hangout that's less touristy and more authentic, with its long walnut and brass-railed bar, mirrored back bar and hurricane lamp chandeliers. Local folks like to whoop it up there of a Saturday night. If some of the shaggy Bud drinkers look like they just came down out of the hills, they probably did.

Nuggets

Special little "Nugget" attractions are almost as numerous as real nuggets were 135 years ago.

D.O. Mills Building • *Main and Fulton streets.* Like many of Columbia's structures, this brick building is both an operating business and a visitor attraction. It houses the local branch of El Capitan National Bank, and it exhibits historic photos, graphics and the gold scales used by D.O. Mills. He started a bank here during the Gold Rush and went on to become one of early California's leading citizens.

Fallon House Ice Cream Parlor • *Adjacent to the hotel.* The aroma of freshly-baked waffle cones draws you into this old fashioned ice cream parlor. Then the selection of ice cream flavors, like strawberry cheesecake and tin roof sundae, clinches the sale.

Karen Barkerville Smith Nature Trail • *Adjacent to the old Columbia School.* This quarter-mile nature trail named in honor of a much-loved local schoolteacher winds through an oak and pine forest and along a grassy meadow. Interpretive signs, when they haven't been destroyed by vandals, point out natural attractions and early mining sites.

Papeete Fire Pumper • *In Tuolumne Engine Company No. 1 firehouse on State Street.* This little hand-drawn pumper, Columbia's first fire engine, has been restored with meticulous care, involving more than 900 man hours. Note particularly the fine red and gold piping and the provocative portrait of a lady on the side. The fire engine was built in Boston in 1852. It supposedly was intended for shipment to Tahiti—thus the unusual name—but it somehow got diverted to Columbia after a brief tenure in San Francisco. (Columbia folk affectionately call it *Pa-peet.)* The little pumper often performs during Columbia's annual Firemans' Muster and its oldstyle Fourth of July Celebration.

Wells Fargo Office • *Main and Washington streets.* This red brick building was erected in 1858 and used until 1917. Displays include period office furniture and the original Wells Fargo scales, where tens of millions of dollars worth of Columbia gold was weighed. It's now the official stop for visitors' stagecoach rides into nearby woodlands. You'll probably recognize it as a frequent architectural star of present-day Wells Fargo Bank commercials.

DIVERSIONS

Effortless fishing • *Springfield Trout Farm, 21980 Springfield Rd., Sonora, CA 95370; (209) 532-4623. Daily 10 to 6 in summer, Thursday-Monday 10 to 5 from September through May.* If your fisherman's luck is like ours—lousy—try the Springfield Trout Farm. The folks here provide fishing tackle, hook and bait, which you dangle into a trout-filled pond and wait for a strike. When you've caught sufficient (no limit or license), they'll clean and ice them and tote up the cost, from $1 for a little guy to $4.50 for a 14-incher. Or you can just buy a netful at $3.50 a pound, not a bad price for fresh trout. The farm is in a pleasant little green hollow. If you don't want to fish, you can walk about the lawns and watch the thousands of squigglers in the breeding races; there's no charge for looking.

Despite the Sonora address, the trout farm is about a mile and a half southwest of Columbia. (See On the Road Again at the end of this chapter for directions.)

Gold mine tour • *Hidden Treasure Mine, P.O. Box 28, Columbia, CA 95310; (209) 532-9693. Tours daily in summer and weekends the rest of the year; adults $6, kids and seniors $5.* What's it like in the cool, dark depths of a hardrock mine? You can sign up at the mining shack in Columbia for a tour of the Hidden Treasure Mine, which is a short drive away, above a beautiful river canyon. Dating back more than a century, the mine is still being worked. Lights have been added and the floor smoothed to accommodate visitors.

During our tour, the guide took us into one of the side drifts and swung his lamp upward. There it was: a marbled, off-white seam running the length of the ceiling. It was *La Veta Madre*—one of those elusive veins that drew legions to these hills.

"That's it," the guide said, almost solemnly, "Gold-bearing quartz."

"Wow," said my son Dan.

History had come alive. An odd little chill went through me and it wasn't the mine's 54-degree temperature.

Stage coach rides ● *Call (209) 785-2244 for details. Adults $4, kids and seniors $3.50, "shotgun seat" beside the driver $1 extra. Daily in summer, weekends in the off-season, weather permitting.* Columbia Stage Line offers rides into the nearby woods, where a bandit suddenly appears and demands that the driver "stand and deliver." It probably doesn't scare the passengers but we saw evidence at the holdup site that the horses are often startled.

The company owns several coaches, including some you'll recognize from movies or TV shows. The folks also offer horseback rides from a corral below the Miner's Shack.

Wine tasting ● Two tasting rooms just outside the park offer gratis sips and wine sales to visitors.

Gold Mine Winery, *22265 Parrotts Ferry Rd., Sonora, CA 95370; (209) 532-3089. Daily 11 to 5; MC/VISA.* A mile south on Parrotts Ferry road, the tasting room is housed in an old weathered barn of an A-frame, used by a former tenant for tours of a simulated gold mine. Grapes are grown elsewhere and wines are blended here. Note the weathered overshot water wheel behind the tasting room.

Yankee Hill Winery, *11755 Coarsegold Lane (P.O. Box 330), Columbia, CA 95310; (209) 533-2417. Daily 10 to sundown; MC/VISA.* The winery is situated on an attractive a wooded slope off Yankee Hill Road, a mile east of the park; picnic deck outside the tasting room. It's a working winery; ask for an informal peek at the small aging and production facility.

GOLD COUNTRY DINING

City Hotel Restaurant ● ∆∆∆∆ $$$ ∅∅

Main Street between Jackson and State, Columbia; (209) 532-1479. American regional; multi-course prix fixe dinners $28.50, or individual entreès $12 to $18; full bar service. Lunch Thursday-Saturday 11:30 to 2, dinner Tuesday-Sunday from 5, Sunday brunch 11 to 2. Reservations advised, essential on weekends. MC/VISA, AMEX. Begin with an historic hotel restaurant, blend in period furniture, line it with red velvet draperies, add efficient and friendly employees in period dress, stir well with excellent food and you have a memorable evening in the Gold Country.

The City Hotel Restaurant captures the opulence which prosperity brought to Columbia 135 years ago, yet the food is contemporary—an delicious. Its kitchen has earned plaudits from *Gourmet Magazine* and other serious restaurant-watchers. The prix fixe dinners feature savories such as grilled chicken breast with sweet potato gravy, *polenta* cakes and corn salsa, or one can select entreès from a constantly changing menu. An excellent wine list focuses on California, with a good selection of Gold Country labels.

An interesting note: although professionally managed, with a top-flight chef, the restaurant is staffed by students of the highly-regarded hospitality management program at nearby Columbia College.

Columbia House Restaurant • △△ $$ ∅∅

Main and State streets, Columbia; (209) 532-5134. Western American; dinners $8.50 to $14; wine and beer. Breakfast and lunch daily 8 to 3, dinner Thursday-Sunday 5 to 9. Reservations accepted for dinner. MC/VISA. Gold Rush era restaurant housed in a former saloon that started in a tent in 1850. Pleasant rural Americana look with wainscoting, print wallpaper and quilt panel wall hangings. Sturdy American fare, innovatively spiced, including charbroiled chicken, chops, steaks and pastas.

Csarda's Deli-Bakery • △ $

22758 Broadway (Parrotts Ferry Road), Columbia; (209) 532-9114. Light meals and deli items; meals $4 to $9; beer. Wednesday-Sunday 8 to 4. No credit cards. Semi-cute little place that's handy for a quick bite while exploring the park, just a block off Main Street. Remarkably versatile for a small cafe, offering deli sandwiches, croissants, bakery goods and international coffees. Shady brick patio out front.

El Sombrero • △△△ $ ∅∅

11256 State St. (between Main and Columbia), Columbia; (209) 533-9123. Mexican; dinners $7 to $10; wine and beer. Sunday-Thursday 11 to 9, Friday-Saturday 11 to 10. MC/VISA. One of the Gold Country's best inexpensive Mexican restaurants, housed in a turn-of-the-century cottage. Homey atmosphere and good food. No pre-packs; all food is prepared in-house. Typical tacos, tamales, enchiladas and such, plus Mexican steak and a remarkably tasty Chili Colorado and Chile Verde. Dinners include crisp corn and flour tortilla chips, *sopapilla* and dessert. Smoke-free dining room. Outdoor tables on a wrap-around porch.

Peppermill Restaurant • △ $$ ∅

22267 Parrotts Ferry Rd. (about a mile outside the park), Columbia; (209) 533-0272. American; dinners $8.25 to $10; beer and wine. Daily 5:30 a.m. to 8 p.m. No credit cards. Simple family restaurant serving typical American steaks, chops, chicken—even liver and onions; ample dinners including soup, salad and potatoes. Basic wood-paneled interior, Naugahyde booths and counter.

Stagecoach Inn • △△ $$

22628 Parrotts Ferry Rd. (just outside the park), Columbia; (209) 532-5816. Italian-American; dinners $8 to $14; full bar service. Lunch Monday-Friday 11 to 4:30; dinner week nights 4 to 9, Saturday 4 to 10, Sunday noon to 9. MC/VISA. Locally-popular family style place specializing in typical Italian and American fare, with servings ample enough to feed an offensive lineman. Dinners include minestrone, soup, salad, potato or rice and tapioca pudding. You can tell it's a folksy place because it lists chicken fried steak as one of its gourmet entreès. Western Naugahyde decor with simulated wainscoting and an appealing stagecoach theme with bas relief and model coaches, stained glass and paintings. Cocktail lounge and gift shop.

Is there life after dark?

Considering its lusty past, Columbia is surprisingly quiet after nightfall, although the **Jack Douglass** and **St. Charles** saloons occasionally have live musicians. The St. Charles often books lively and sometimes loud country and Western groups that bring back noisy memories of yesteryear. Street musicians, incidentally, perform frequently—generally during daylight hours on weekends.

Columbia Actors Repertory, *Fallon Theatre, P.O. Box 1849, Columbia, CA 95310; (209) 532-4644.* This highly-regarded group presents a full schedule of contemporary dramas, musicals and comedies. Many are done in concert with Columbia College. Patrons receive a bonus here—watching good theater in an historic theater dating back to 1863. It began life as a Fallon Hotel dance hall, used primarily as a social center for miners and their families. Operators even installed springs under the dance floor to give folks a little more bounce to their step. It was converted to a theater in 1886 and has functioned almost continuously since then.

LODGINGS
Historic hotels, bed & breakfast inn

The City Hotel and Fallon House, both in the historic park, are administered jointly. Combined lodging/Fallon Theatre packages are available at both. Like the City Hotel Restaurant, they are professionally managed and run largely by students of Columbia College's Hospitality Management Program.

City Hotel • ⌂⌂⌂ $$$ ØØ
Main Street between Jackson and State, (P.O. Box 1870) Columbia; (209) 532-1479. Doubles $65 to $85, singles $5 less; rates include continental breakfast. Gold Rush era rooms, all with half-baths; share showers. Major credit cards. Guests checking into the City Hotel step into 1860s. Rooms are dressed for the period, with floral wallpaper and Victorian or early American furniture, including Eastlake beds with their simple lines and high wooden headboards. Bathrooms are down the hallways; fluffy robes and wicker baskets containing bath essentials are provided to simplify the short trip. **Restaurant** reviewed above.

Fallon Hotel • ⌂⌂⌂⌂ $$$ ØØ
Washington Street at Broadway (P.O. Box 1870), Columbia CA 95310; (209) 532-1470. Doubles $55 to $85, singles $5 less, one suite for $130; rates include continental breakfast. Victorian rooms, one with full bath, others with half-baths; share showers. Major credit cards. The Fallon is most exquisite historic hotel in the Gold Country, following a $4 million renovation in 1986. Rooms are perfect mirrors of the Victorian era of the 1880s, color co-ordinated with patterned ceilings, print wallpaper and antique furnishings. Some have fireplaces (non-functioning) and balconies. The building dates from 1860, when it served as a courthouse, then a bakery and ultimately a hotel. It was "enlarged and elegantly furnished" after surviving the fire of 1867. The adjoining Fallon Theatre was added in 1886.

The Harlan House • ⌂⌂⌂ $$$ ØØ
22890 School House St. (P.O. Box 686), Columbia, CA 95310; (209) 533-4862. Doubles $75 to $80. Three rooms with private baths. Full breakfast. MC/VISA. This handsome Columbia Victorian became the county's newest B&B in early 1992 after a complete renovation by owner Samantha O'Brien. The two-story gem, considered one of Columbia's finest homes at the turn of

the century, occupies a hillside niche three blocks above the historic district. It's across the street from the venerable Columbia School. Nicely-appointed rooms feature a mix of Victorian and American antiques. Guests can relax on the shady porch or in surrounding garden patios, or perhaps pitch a horse-shoe or two. Afternoon snacks and local wines are served in the comfortable living room. Free shuttle service is provided to nearby Columbia airport.

Motels

Columbia Gem Motel ● △ $$

P.O. Box 874 (on Parrotts Ferry Road a mile from the historic park), Co-lumbia, CA 95310; (209) 532-4508. Doubles $35 to $65. MC/VISA. Twelve-unit inn with cute little cottages and motel rooms tucked among the pines; TV, in-room coffee.

Columbia Inn Motel ● △ $$

22646 Broadway (P.O. Box 298) Columbia, CA 95310; (209) 533-0446. Doubles $46 to $56, singles $32 to $34. MC/VISA. A 24-room motel with TV, room phones; small pool and hot tub. Stagecoach Inn restaurant adjacent; see listing above.

CAMPGROUNDS & RV PARKS

49er Trailer Ranch ● *P.O. Box 569 (on Italian Bar Road, half a mile from the historic park), Columbia, CA 95310; (209) 532-9898. RV and tent sites, $17.50. Reservations recommended; no credit cards.* Well-tended park in wooded setting with full hookups, flush potties, showers, cable TV, picnic ta-bles and barbecues, games and square dance center in "Fun Barn"; laundro-mat. Open all year.

Marble Quarry RV Park ● *P.O. Box 850, (a third of a mile east on Jack-son Street/Yankee Hill Road) Columbia, CA 95310; (209) 532-9539. RV and tent sites, $17 to $22. Reservations recommended; MC/VISA.* Attractive RV park in a shady grove near an old marble quarry; a short trail leads to the state historic park. Full hookups, picnic tables, flush toilets and showers; swimming pool, store, lawn play area, ping pong, volleyball, horse shoes, laundromat. Open all year.

Trail's End RV Park ● *P.O. Box 106, (two miles south on Parrotts Ferry Road), Columbia, CA 95310; (209) 533-2395. RV sites, $17. Reservations ac-cepted; no credit cards.* RV park with full hook-ups including TV, flush pot-ties and showers, snack bar; public laundromat adjacent. Open all year.

ANNUAL EVENTS

The Columbia Docent Association and other local groups will stage a celebration at the drop of a hint or a holiday. Among Columbia's annual events are:

Victorian Easter Parade on Easter Sunday, (209) 532-3401; docents dress up in old Western, Gold Rush and Victorian finery.

Firemans' Muster in early May, (209) 532-7423; exhibits and demon-strations of old-time fire fighting equipment, fire fighting "games" such as bucket brigades.

Columbia Diggins, late May to early June, (209) 532-3401; faithfully reconstructed tent town with shops, foods, music, customs and costumes of

Columbia's earliest days.

Fathers Day Fly-in, Fathers Day weekend, (209) 532-4616; aircraft exhibits, aerobatics and such at Columbia Airport.

Fourth of July Celebration on Independence Day, (209) 532-3401; old-timey festival with sack races, watermelon eating contests, greased pole climbing, patriotic parade and such.

Admission Day on weekend nearest to Sept. 9, (209) 532-3401; "formal" 1850 ceremonies around the Columbia flagpole to welcome California into the Union.

A Miner's Christmas Carol, late November to mid-December, (209) 532-4644; a miners' version of Dickens' Christmas Carol, presented at the Fallon Theatre by the Columbia Actors Repertory.

Christmas Lamplight Tour in early December, (209) 532-3401; in-costume nighttime tours of Columbia's historic attractions.

Victorian Christmas Feast in early December at the City Hotel, (209) 532-1479; elaborate banquet with a Gold Rush version of a Victorian Christmas pageant.

Miners Christmas and **Los Posadas** first and second weekends of December; (209) 532-3401; gold miners' rendition of the Nativity.

ON THE ROAD AGAIN...TO CALAVERAS COUNTY

Head south from Columbia on Parrotts Ferry, turn right onto Springfield Road (just beyond the airport turnoff) and follow it about a mile to its junction with Horseshoe Bend Road. On your right, in mid-intersection, you'll see a monument marking the site of Springfield, named for springs that once gushed from granite outcroppings in the area.

They've dried up but the boulders remain, scattered and glistening in the fields beside the road. Look among the catalpa trees to the right of the monument and you'll see Springfield's only surviving structure, a crumbling and neglected brick schoolhouse with a wooden lean-to kitchen.

Continuing on, you can drive into the nearby Springfield Trout Farm (listed above) at the apex of a 90-degree turn in the road. Or swerve around the bend onto Shaws Flat Road and go a mile to Highway 49. Cross the highway, drive half a mile and watch for a marker on the left that discusses the town of Shaw's Flat. It's at the juncture of Shaws Flat and Mount Brow roads. Opposite the monument are two tattered buildings, one fronted by one of those old-fashioned gravity feed gasoline pumps, the other the remnants of a saloon called the Mississippi House.

Only those two ruined buildings and traces of stone foundations remain; the area today is a gathering of rural homes. The monument advises that the Shaw's Flat was established in 1850, with J.D. Fair of San Francisco's Fairmont Hotel as one of its citizens. The Mississippi House bartender once used an ingenious method to pick up a little spare change, says the monument. As he took a pinch from a miner's poke to pay for drinks, he let a bit of dust drop on his boots, which he kept muddy. He later panned the boots to retrieve the gold.

Return to Highway 49 and continue your northward journey, with a pause to absorb the contents of a marker in Tuttletown. It reports that Mark Twain hung out here, and traded at the Swerer General Store built in the 1850s. The store is gone but stones from its granite walls were used to build the monument. Tuttletown today is a small residential community.

About a mile beyond, swing slightly right onto Jackass Hill Road and drive a mile to "Mark Twain's cabin." Historians like to prove their worth by disagreeing with other historians, and the cabin's authenticity is in dispute. Those who believe say it was owned by the Steve, Jim and Bill Gillis, cronies of Twain, and that the author stayed here for a time. To speculate further, he may have written the Calaveras jumping frog story here, based on a miners' tale he'd heard at Angels Camp Tavern.

The cabin, with an unusual vertical log design, has been reconstructed, not necessarily on the original site, but with the original fieldstone fireplace.

A small bonus of your detour to the cabin is a nice view of the surrounding oak foothill countryside and New Melones Reservoir shimmering in the sun. Back on the highway, Route 49 swoops down to the reservoir and crosses a bridge. At mid-point, where the Stanislaus River once flowed, we pass into Calaveras, the "Jumping Frog county" and our next chapter.

To learn more...

Columbia State Historic Park, P.O. Box 151, Columbia, CA 95310; (209) 532-4301. Visitor center in William Cavalier Museum at Main and State streets, open daily 10 to 4:30.

Columbia Docent Association, Columbia State Historic Park, P.O. Box 357, Columbia, CA 95310; (209) 532-4301

"I found Simon Wheeler dozing comfortably by the barroom stove of the dilapidated hotel in the decaying mining camp of Angels. He backed me into a corner and related the story of Jim Smiley and his frog, Daniel Webster, who was loaded with buckshot."

— from a Mark Twain Journal

Chapter Eight
ANGELS CAMP & MURPHYS
Where writers loved to tread

JUMPING FROG MONUMENT IN ANGELS CAMP

We have noted in our rambles that Highway 49 is not a main artery, despite its heralded "Golden Chain" status. We suspect that only serious students of the Gold Rush and writers of guide books make it an uninterrupted project to drive its entire length. Most visitors follow busier routes that bisect Highway 49, linking the San Joaquin Valley and coastal cities to the major tourist lures of Yosemite National Park and Lake Tahoe/Reno.

Calaveras County is isolated from main east-west arteries, sitting between above Yosemite and below Tahoe, so it is one of the least populated (38,000) and the most bucolic of the Mother Lode counties. It has no stoplights (blinking ones don't count) and only one elevator, which travels just one floor—in the Hall of Records building in San Andreas.

It's odd that the area isn't more populated, considering all that publicity generated by Mr. Twain, and by Bret Harte's writings. Since it has changed so little in the last century, the county still lures the media—in the form of movie and TV production companies. Calaveras scenes have appeared in *Little House on the Prairie,* the short-lived *Seven Brides for Seven Brothers* TV series and other television shows and films.

Angels Camp is the county's largest town, with a population pushing 3,000, but it isn't the county seat. That honor went to San Andreas in 1854. However, Angels is certainly more famous and we all know why. It gained glory as the setting for Mark Twain's first successful short story, *The Celebrated Jumping Frog of Calaveras County,* published in 1864. And it may have been the setting for Bret Harte's *Luck of Roaring Camp.*

You've probably heard the frog story but if not, we'll review it briefly. A miner named Jim Smiley boasted that he had the best jumping frog in all of the Mother Lode, a critter named Daniel Webster. A stranger in town bet him a sizable sum that he could find a frog that could out-jump old Daniel. Trouble was, the outsider didn't have a frog handy. Eager to fleece the newcomer, Smiley offered to go find him a competitor, but while he was gone on his frog hunt, the stranger filled Daniel with about a pound of buckshot. Obviously, the frog couldn't get off the starting block. The stranger collected his bet and was out of town before Smiley realized that his champion was loaded.

THE WAY IT WAS ● Historians quarrel—as usual—about who established Angels Camp. We've paired Angels and Murphys in this chapter, so we're tempted by the usually accepted tale that George Angell and brothers John and Daniel Murphy traveled to the Mother Lode together. The story says that Angell stayed in the area bearing his name and the Murphys moved on up the road a bit to establish the other settlement. However, area historians with access to original records tell us a different story:

Angels Camp was founded by one Henry P. Angel, a Rhode Islander who opened a trading post in the area in 1848. There are records of a George Angell in the area, but local history buffs insist the town was named for Henry with one "l".

Several rich placer strikes were made, and within a year more than 4,000 miners swarmed along the creeks and dry gulches. The surface gold was soon panned out and Angels Camp began to fade—even before Mark Twain arrived to give it that great publicity boost. Fortunately, underground gold was discovered, and hardrock mining kept the town going for several more decades. And therein lies one of the strangest tales of the Mother Lode. It probably isn't true, but it's fun to repeat, particularly since the lead character's name was Bennager Raspberry.

An entrepreneur with that kind of name was bound to get into the history books. Ben was a sharp trader who played on the miners' lust for luxuries. He knew that lucky argonauts would spend extravagant sums for things like champagne and caviar, so he had such items shipped around Cape Horn. He even brought in a case of brandied peaches but they spoiled en route, so he dumped them behind his store, and a couple of local hogs got juiced out of their minds.

But that isn't how Mister Raspberry (some spell it Rasberry) came to fame. He got the ramrod stuck in his breech-loading rifle one day and, in frustration, he fired into the ground to free it. The steel shaft chipped a chunk off a rock and—you can guess the rest—the fracture revealed a vein of gold.

Utica, the area's largest hardrock mining company, was organized in the 1850s (not by Mr. Raspberry) and mining continued into this century. With underground mining came hazards. In 1889, a cave-in dumped 60,000 tons of rock into the mine, killing 16 men. Today, that hole in the ground, filled and landscaped, is the city park.

Historians agree, for a change, that the Murphy brothers founded Murphys Diggins in 1848. Like Henry P. Angel, they had better luck trading than mining. John Murphy, only 23 years old, became one of the first and youngest millionaires in the Gold Country by bartering with the Mi-Wuk Indians, who would dig up the glitter to trade for practical goods. An item in the *San Andreas Independent* reveals how Murphy got rich quick:

"...An Indian had found a five-pound lump of gold for which Murphy had given him a blanket." The story further relates: "The camp of Mr. Murphy is

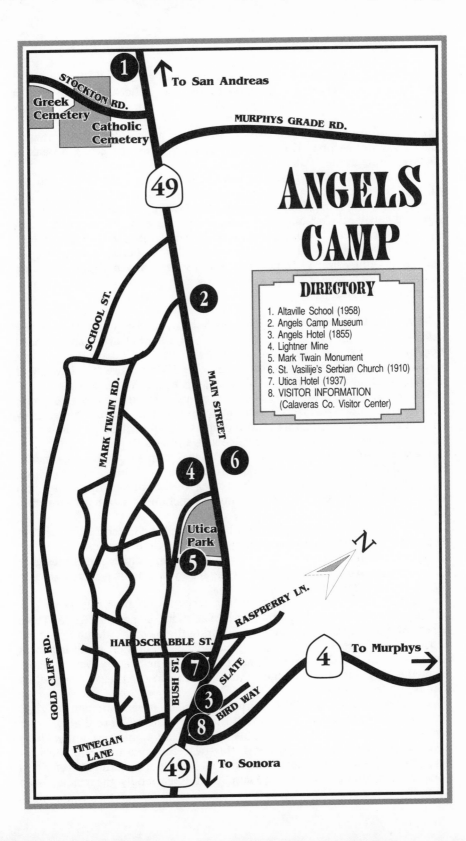

in the midst of a small tribe of wild Indians, who gather gold for him, and receive in return provisions... He knocks down two bullocks a day to furnish meat. They respect his person in part due to the fact that he has married the daughter of the chief."

The Murphys left within a year with their millions—leaving an unhappy chief's daughter behind. The camp continued to prosper, hitting a peak of 3,000 residents in the 1850s.

"The sun of Murphys' greatness has but just risen; a short time and she will take the sceptre of the mountain queen," gushed a reporter for the *San Joaquin Republican* in 1852. "The city has upwards of 500 frame houses, large and substantially built. Mr. P. Birmingham is constructing a large hotel, and it is rumored it will have mattresses and blankets void of fleas."

The sun of Murphys' greatness was dimmed by the usual decline in gold production and by fires in 1859, 1874 and 1893. It was rebuilt, however and the town today is one of the most charming and graceful of the Gold Country's smaller communities.

THE WAY IT IS • Angels Camp lies smack astraddle Highway 49, along a slope trimmed in evergreens and oaks. Its residential areas are terraced snugly into the hillside above and below Main Street. The setting is pleasant enough, although the town has lost much of its 19th century look because of new construction and re-facing of old buildings earlier in this century.

While not a grand Mother Lode monument, it's a fun place to explore, with its high sidewalks and small collection of historic structures. They house an interesting assortment of boutiques, antique shops and art galleries, which draw a goodly number of sidewalk strollers.

Naturally, there are frogs all over the place, from a statue atop a monument at the town's southern entrance to silhouettes painted on sidewalks. Angels Hotel, where Mark Twain heard the birdshot-filled frog story, still survives, although it suffers the indignity of functioning as a hardware store and auto parts shop.

Fortunately, Old Angels Camp has been spared the latter-day invasion of shopping centers and Safeway parking lots. Its neighbor to the north, Altaville, shoulders that burden of progress. Angels Camp, which sometimes goes by the presumptive name of City of Angels (Are you listening, Los Angeles?), annexed Altaville in 1972.

Although miners reportedly held frog races to kill time during Angels' earliest days, its famous frog jumping jubilee didn't begin until 1928. Town fathers decided to stage the event to celebrate the paving of Main Street. (It also gave the frogs a firm launching pad.) The celebration eventually was combined with the Calaveras County Fair and is held every May at Frogtown, the fairgrounds just to the south. Visitors can even lease competitors from rent-a-frog outlets.

Meanwhile, handsome little Murphys, its main street canopied by giant locust and elms, looks like it never left the 19th century. More than a dozen ancient buildings, weathered veterans in brick and stone, rest under these stately trees. Located off Highway 4, this peaceful town of 1,800 souls invites strolling. As we took our constitutional one quiet Autumn evening, a group of horsemen clopped along Main Street, like friendly ghost riders from the past.

The stone and brick store fronts house candy shops and antique stores, but the essence of age survives. Oldest survivor is the 1856 Peter Travers building, now home to the Old Timers Museum. Across the street, reconstructed and altered after three fires but still functioning, is the cornerstone of the town's memories—the 1856 Murphys Hotel, with its classic iron shutters and second-floor balconies. Despite its bucolic appearance, Murphys is not a backwater town. Its boutiques are smart and tasteful and in recent years it has becomethe center of Calaveras County's growing wine industry.

DISCOVERIES
The best attractions

Angels Camp Museum • *753 S. Main St. (P.O. Box 667), Angels Camp, CA 95222; (209) 736-2963. Daily 10 to 3 from April until the day before Thanksgiving; Wednesday-Sunday the rest of the year. Adults $1, kids 25 cents.* Recently reorganized and expanded, this city-run museum offers the typical pioneer collection of old rifles, period china, cattle brands and probably even a butter churn if you look carefully enough.

Many of the museum's exhibits occupy its extensive three-acre grounds: two large logging engines, an overshot water wheel, a blacksmith/carriage shop, 20-mule-team logging wagons, assorted horse-drawn farm equipment and an extensive old-timey carriage exhibit. A "rock patio" features minerals and petrified trees, and an elaborate model of the six-stamp mill that crushed ore for the nearby Carson Hill Mine. Press a button and you get a minute's worth of clanking.

At one time, more than two hundred "stamps" were running day and night in Angels. Funny thing; when the last stamp mill finally shut down, it was so quiet, nobody could sleep.

Calaveras Big Trees State Park • *P.O. Box 120 (Off Highway 4), Arnold, CA 95223; (209) 795-2334.* It's one of California's most attractive state parks—a 6,000-acre preserve of subalpine beauty, including two fine stands of sequoias. And the park indeed figures into Gold Country history.

Pioneer John Bidwell made note of the park's present-day North Grove in 1841, but A.T. Dowd, a gold seeker and hunter from Murphys, is generally credited with its discovery, in 1852. Apparently no one was impressed by Dowd's excited description of these impossibly huge trees, so he peeled the bark from one (a practice frowned upon today) and brought the pieces back.

In 1853, a promoter cut down Dowd's "Discovery Tree," carefully stripped a 150-foot section of bark and exhibited it—reassembled—from New York to London. The huge tree stump, measuring 25 feet in diameter, was used as a dance floor. Many famous personages who overnighted at Murphys Hotel were on their way to see these wondrous *sequoiadendron giganteum.*

Now, 250,000 people a year crowd into the popular North Grove, just inside the park entrance. They follow nature trails beneath the great trees and browse in an interpretive center that offers a quick study of sequoias and how they function. Far fewer people hike a mile along a brushy forest path to enjoy the breathtaking giants of the South Grove (see hiking in our Diversions department).

Old Timers Museum • *472 Main St. (Sheep Ranch Road), Murphys; (209) 728-2607. Thursday-Sunday 11 to 4 (weekends only in winter). Admis-*

sion free; donations appreciated. Built in 1856, this sturdy structure is the oldest fully intact building in Murphys. It functioned as a general store, Wells Fargo express office, then later as an auto repair garage until Ethelyn and Coke Wood turned it into a museum in 1949. A classic of Mother Lode construction, it's built of hewn stones fitted together without mortar. The museum a busy clutter of typical pioneer and Gold Rush regalia. A reconstructed blacksmith shop out back was donated by a retired smithy from Sheepranch.

The museum's most interesting feature is the ECV Wall of Comparative Ovations on the west side, an historical and often whimsical collection of bas relief plaques. They honor early Gold Country pioneers and latter-day historians, and praise the accomplishments of E Clampus Vitus, a fun-loving organization started during the Gold Rush as a parody on serious fraternal orders such as the Masons and International Order of Odd Fellows. (See Chapter 1 for more ECV details.)

The rest

Moaning Cavern • *P.O. Box 78 (off Parrotts Ferry Road), Vallecito, CA 95251; (209) 736-2708. Daily 9 to 6 in summer and 10 to 5 in winter. Forty-five minute tour, $5.75 for adults; $2.75 for children. Special rappelling entry $24.50 by reservation; age 12 and over (see box).* This is said to be the largest natural cavern in California, with a main room capable of holding the Statue of Liberty. It's essentially a vertical cave, thought to have been created by volatile gases seeping through and dissolving the area around a fissure during volcanic activity. Then its intricate formations were created through the eons as dripping water left tiny mineral deposits. Entry is gained through a series of wooden stairways, and an iron spiral staircase welded together in 1922. The walk down—and back up—requires 236 steps.

Mercer Caverns • *P.O. Box 509 (one mile north of Murphys, off Sheep Ranch Road), Murphys, CA 95247; (209) 728-2101. Daily 9 to 4:30 Memorial Day through September; weekends and school holidays 11 to 3:30 the rest of the year. Forty-five minute tour, $5 for adults and $2.50 for children.* This is another of the three major limestone cavern complexes in Calaveras County. It's more extensive than Moaning Caverns; visitors descend the equivalent of a 16-story building through several chambers. One sees a goodly assortment of stalactites, stalagmites, helicites and flowstone, plus striking formations such as snow crystal-like Aragonite and delicate thin translucent "Angels Wings." However, we felt the tour and attendant narrative were a bit too slow paced. Colored lights, presumably used to discourage algae growth, give the formations a contrived look.

Murphys Hotel • *Main Street (P.O. Box 329), Murphys, CA 95247; (209) 728-3444.* The old hostelry still functions as a hotel, restaurant and bar, and it's also a fascinating living museum. It's one of the Mother Lode's better examples of a "working hotel"—not too fancy and not too shabby. Tourists stay at the Murphys today; the famous stayed there yesterday. Mark Twain, U.S. Grant, J. Pierpont Morgan, Horatio Alger and Charles Bolton are among the names on the register. Charles who? You'll find out later. Signatures of famous guests are displayed in photocopies on the walls, along with historic photos and Gold Rush icons.

It seems that President Grant must have slept in every hotel in the Gold

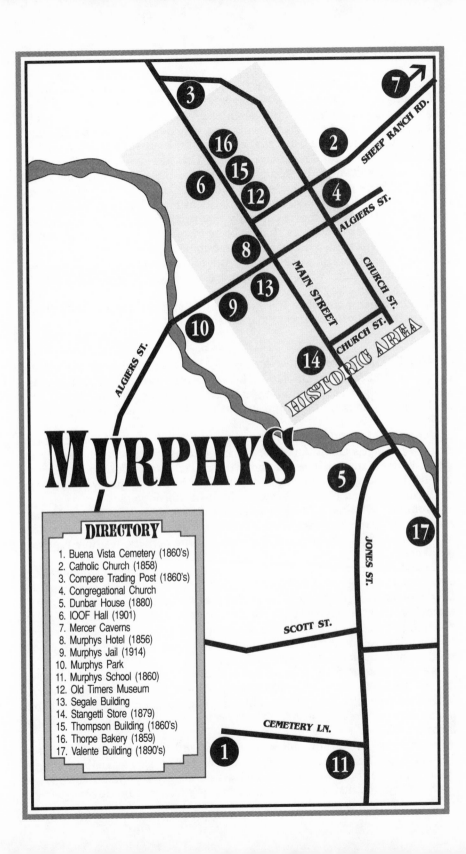

MURPHYS

DIRECTORY

1. Buena Vista Cemetery (1860's)
2. Catholic Church (1858)
3. Compere Trading Post (1860's)
4. Congregational Church
5. Dunbar House (1880)
6. IOOF Hall (1901)
7. Mercer Caverns
8. Murphys Hotel (1856)
9. Murphys Jail (1914)
10. Murphys Park
11. Murphys School (1860)
12. Old Timers Museum
13. Segale Building
14. Stangetti Store (1879)
15. Thompson Building (1860's)
16. Thorpe Bakery (1859)
17. Valente Building (1890's)

Country, and as one historian said: "He probably did, if it had a bar in it."

Murphys Town Park • *On Algiers Street, below the Murphys Hotel.* It's a pretty, if somewhat scruffy, little patch of green alongside a rushing brook. Sit beneath the shade of giant locust and elm trees, admire the charming old-timey bandstand and listen to the music of the stream.

Utica Park • *Main Street, Angels Camp.* This little park, just off Main between Angel and Altaville, occupies the site of the Utica Mine, one of the largest hardrock mines in the Mother Lode. It offers a children's play area, a few picnic tables and a cast concrete statue of Mark Twain. It was given to the town in 1945 by a movie company that produced a film of Twain's life, starring Frederick March. Is that noble concrete face Mark or Frederick? You decide. When the park was dedicated in 1954, developers added a suitable reminder of Angels' fame—a pond full of frogs. But the water kept seeping into underground mine tunnels and the croakers, not caring much for dry land, hopped away.

Several other mines once were strung out along Main Street, to the north of the park, but little remains to mark their sites.

Nuggets

Angels Camp Mercantile • *1267 S. Main St. (P.O. Box 8), Angels, Camp, CA 95222; (209) 736-4100.* This is the most versatile of Angels' many boutique and gift shops, offering antiques, giftwares, a book shop and a small cafe. It's housed in an 1860 structure with an unusual pressed tin false front.

Angels Hotel and jumping frog monument • *Corner of Main Street and Bird's Way, Angels Camp.* An historic marker across the street advises us that this is where Twain first heard about the clever rascal who won a jumping frog bet by filling his opponent's hopper full of birdshot. The two-story stone hotel with its upper balcony is one of old town's focal points.

Compere Store • *570 Main at Church Street, Murphys.* This is the best example of Murphys' several distinctive rough stone houses. Built as a store in 1858 with fieldstone walls and quarried stone corners, it's now a private residence.

Frog boutiques • If you collect things with froggy themes, Angels Camp obviously is the place. Among shops offering good croaker collections are **Country Manor** at 1252 S. Main St., **Reza Rags** at 1212 S. Main and across the street at **The Pickle Barrel** snack and gift shop, 1255 S. Main. You'll find frog key chains, tennis frogs in tennis togs, frogs doing somersaults, frogs looking terribly nonchalant, frog coffee mugs and several croakers that look suspiciously like Kermit.

Miles Metzger Fine Arts • *1619 Moose Trail (P.O. Box 444), Angels Camp, CA 95222; (209) 736-4466. Open daily 9 to 5.* Noted soapstone artists Miles Metzger welcomes visitors to his studio and shop off Highway 4, about a mile north of the Highway 4/49 intersection. You'll see a good selection of items for sale and many works in progress.

Monument at Carson Hill • *On Highway 49 about three miles south of Angels Camp.* There's not much left of Carson Hill. A bait-tackle-beer shop is the town's total business district, and a sign claims a population of 47. In 1848, so says the historical marker, California's largest gold nugget—weighing 195 pounds troy—was unearthed at the Morgan Mine near here. It was valued at $43,000 then, when gold was under $20 an ounce. Imagine its worth now...

Quyle Kilns • *3353 E. Highway 4 (four miles east of town), Murphys, CA 95247; (209) 728-3562.* Paul and Joyce Quyle's fine pottery literally comes from the good earth of the Mother Lode. They quarry their own clay, make their molds and even fashion their equipment in a busy blacksmith shop. Their operation is housed in a weathered pottery factory they built by hand. One can buy vases, cookware and other pottery pieces and even bulk clay blended by the Quyles. When they aren't too busy, they'll offer you a short course in their craft.

St. Vasilije's Serbian Church • *Main Street near Bret Harte Road, Angels Camp.* This immaculately maintained little structure is the second oldest Serbian Church in the United States, built in 1910. Note its blue modified onion dome, its gleaming white walls, unusual star window in the bell tower and the distinctive rounded altar area at the back.

Stories in Stone Earth Science Emporium • *444 Main St., Murphys; (209) 728-2404.* Housed in one of Murphys' ancient storefronts, this shop offers an interesting selection of gems, minerals and other nature-oriented giftwares.

DETOUR

Angels Camp to Copperopolis, Poker Flat and Calaveritas • *A 60-mile loop trip.* From the Altaville end of Angels Camp, turn left onto Highway 4. If we've left you in Murphys, return to Angels Camp via Murphys Grade, which follows a pretty wooded creek ravine and strikes Highway 49 in Altaville, just south of Highway 4.

Route 4 winds quickly down into the lower foothills, with their tawny moors and groves of oaks. After 12 miles, swing left onto O'Byrnes Ferry Road (County Road E-15). You're in Copperopolis, which has two claims to fame—it's the only Mother Lode town where a metal other than gold was sought, and it's near the site of the undoing of Charles Bolton.

A marker explains the obvious: the area yielded copper, not gold. A couple of saloons, stores and service stations function as modern-day Copperopolis. Just beyond are three fine looking brick buildings dating from the 1860s, when the Copper Consolidated Mining Company pulled tons from the soil. Immediately across the street are the remnants of the company's efforts: huge tailing dumps with loose talus sides that suggest volcanic cinder cones.

About five miles north of here, on the Milton to Sonora Road (which no longer exists), famous early California highwayman Charles E. Bolton, alias Black Bart, committed his last robbery. On November 3, 1883, he held up the Sonora-Milton stage as it slowed to a crawl nearing the top of Funk Hill. He dragged the strongbox to what he thought was a safe place, but he was surprised by the coach driver and a passenger as he fiddled with the lock. He managed to escape, although in his haste he left behind a handkerchief bearing the laundry mark *FXO 7.2.6.* We'll continue this story in the next chapter when we get to San Andreas, where Bolton spent some time in the clinker.

Continuing on O'Byrnes Ferry Road, you'll dip down to Tulloch Reservoir

The E Clampus Vitus "Wall of Comparative Ovations" at Murphys' Old Timers Museum offers an historical-whimsical look at the Gold Country.

and the site of a famous Mother Lode town that never existed. While Mark Twain was fiddling with a frog story in Angels Camp, Bret Harte wrote *The Outcasts of Poker Flat*, the tale of a gambler, an old boozer and a prostitute who were kicked out of a town by that name, then were faced with a terrible winter blizzard.

Harte's "Poker Flat" was set in this valley, although the settlement actually was called O'Byrnes Ferry. A cable ferry was built here in the early 1850s to get people, critters and freight across the Stanislaus River. It was replaced in 1862 by a covered bridge, which stood until the area was inundated by the reservoir behind Tulloch Dam in 1957. There is a Poker Flat today, however—a resort home area, marina, restaurant and motel along the reservoir's shoreline.

Now, retrace your route through Copperopolis, turn right onto Highway 4, then drive six miles and go left onto Pool Station Road. This parallels Highway 49 but it's prettier, winding gently through oak thatched foothills and pasturelands. You pass the large Calaveras Cement plant, which has dusted the roadside with its product, and join Highway 49 on the northern edge of San Andreas.

Turn right and go south through town, turn left onto Mountain Ranch Road, then right after about a mile onto Calaveritas Road. (You still with us?) You'll arrive shortly in Calaveritas, a tiny town tucked into a hollow along a creek bank. With its old stone fences, neat corrals and a farmhouse or two, it has the look of a Swiss farm village. But it was a busy mining camp, primarily a Mexican settlement with the usual assortment of fandango halls and saloons. It was a reputed hangout of Joaquin Murieta, but then, wasn't nearly every town in the Gold Country? For an outlaw, he certainly made himself public. The only Calaveritas Gold Rush survivor is an adobe structure built in 1852 as Luigi Costa's store.

Continuing through town, blend from Calaveritas Road onto Esmerelda Road, then turn right onto Dogtown Road and follow its twisting course back into Angels Camp.

DIVERSIONS

Gold country tours ● *Mother Lode Tours, P.O. Box 252, Murphys, CA 95247; (209) 728-1190.* Diane Campana offers an assortment of two to five-day coach tours to various Gold Country sites and to Yosemite.

Gold panning ● *Jensen's Pick & Shovel Ranch, 4977 Parrotts Ferry Rd., Vallecito; mailing address: P.O. Box 1141, Angels Camp, CA 95222; (209) 736-0287.* This ranch hosts and coaches novice gold panners for $17.50 an hour per person or $30 per family. All-day prospecting trips to nearby streams are $75 per person or $130 per couple. Folks with campers can spend the night free at the ranch.

Hiking ● *Calaveras Big Trees State Park.* Several hiking trails lure the footloose faction to this beautiful sequoia wilderness. A one-mile stride from the main area leads to the remote South Grove, where a trail loops through the giant sequoias. Other trails lead to remote sections of the Stanislaus River and up through a lava flow area.

Whitewater rafting ● *Oars, P.O. Box 67, Angels Camp, CA 95222; (800) 446-RAFT or (209) 736-4677.* This firm offers whitewater trips on several rivers in the Gold Country and throughout the west, including the grandest of all—down the Colorado River through its affiliate, Grand Canyon Dories.

Wine tasting ● Calaveras now rivals Amador and El Dorado counties as a major Gold Country wine-producing area. The wineries, like others in the foothills, are particularly noted for award-winning Zinfandel. They also produce a variety of other premium wines. A recently-formed Calaveras Wine Association offers a brochure and guide map to the wineries, clustered around Murphys. Some are open weekends only, although they will host you to sips and informal tours by appointment.

Black Sheep Vintners, *Main Street and Murphys Grade Road (P.O. Box 1851), Murphys, CA 95247; (209) 728-2157. Weekends noon to 5; MC/VISA, AMEX.* In downtown Murphys, housed in a wonderfully scruffy log and tin-roofed tasting room. A collection of sheep figurines shares the space with aging barrels of wine.

Chatom Vineyards, *1969 Highway 4, Douglas Flat (mailing address: P.O. Box 2730, Murphys, CA 95247); (209) 736-6500. Daily 11 to 4:30; most major credit cards.* Attractive new winery and tasting room is just south of Douglas Flat with a blend of French country and American railroad station decor; picnic patio.

Indian Rock Vineyard, *1154 Pennsylvania Gulch Rd. (P.O. Box 1526), Murphys, CA 95247; (209) 728-2266. Weekends 10 to 5; no credit cards.*

Pleasantly rustic tasting room is housed in an old dairy barn in a bucolic set-ting a mile east of Murphys; picnic tables beside a pond.

Kautz Vineyards at Hay Station Ranch, *Six Mile Road (P.O. Box 2263), Murphys, CA 95247; (209) 728-1251. Weekends and holidays 11 to 4:30; MC/VISA.* New winery a mile south of Murphys, with a tasting room in cool manmade caverns (although it will move later into a new winery build-ing); tree-shaded picnic area.

Milliaire Vineyard Selections, *276 Main St. (P.O. Box 1554), Mur-phys, CA 95247; (209) 728-1658. Daily 11 to 4:30; MC/VISA.* In downtown Murphys, housed in a one-time service station; winery in the former garage section and tasting room tasting room in the "office."

Stevenot Winery, *2690 San Domingo Rd. (P.O. Box 345), Murphys, CA 95247; (209) 728-3436. Daily 10 to 5; MC/VISA, DISC.* The county's senior winery, founded in 1974 by the descendant of a Gold Rush family. In a shel-tered valley with a tasting room occupying a distinctive log and sod roofed "Alaska House"; shaded picnic area adjacent.

GOLD COUNTRY DINING

Avery Hotel Dining Room • ΔΔ $$

Moran Road off Highway 4 (15 miles northeast of Murphys), Avery; (209) 795-9935. American-continental; dinners $9 to $14; full bar service. Dinner 6 to 9:30 Friday-Saturday, 6 to 8:15 Sunday, Monday, Thursday, closed Tues-day-Wednesday. Reservations accepted; MC/VISA. Cozy dining room in an 1853 hotel (now a bed and breakfast inn); dimly lit with lace and brocade curtains and a fireplace. Generous portions of steaks, chops, birds and fish, plus veal scaloppini and Cajun shrimp.

Gold Country Kitchen • Δ $

1246 Main St., Angels Camp; (209) 736-2941. Light lunches; meals $5 to $8; no alcohol. Weekdays 5 a.m. to 2 p.m., Saturday 5 to noon, closed Sunday. No credit cards. A basic breakfast and lunch place offering omelets, soup and sandwiches. There's nothing terribly clever about the menu, but the lunch-eon special of a turkey-avocado-tomato sandwich and cup of rich split pea soup is a great buy at $3.75. Oldstyle look with wainscoting, maple furniture and country crafts on the walls.

Murphys Hotel Restaurant • ΔΔΔ $$$

Main Street, Murphys; (209) 728-3444. American-continental; dinners $9 to $15; full bar service. Sunday-Thursday 7 a.m. to 8 p.m., Friday-Saturday 7 to 9. Reservations accepted, essential on weekends; MC/VISA, AMEX. Victorian dining room in an historic setting. American steaks and chops, plus conti-nental fare such as lobster fettuccine, coquilles St. Jacque, veal Marsala and calamari. Slightly scruffy dining room but generally excellent food. Oldstyle, rather dim saloon next door; it could use some sprucing up.

Nugget Restaurant • ΔΔ $$

75 Big Trees Rd., Murphys; (209) 728-2608. American; dinners $7 to $14; full bar service. Breakfast and lunch daily 6 to 11, dinner Tuesday-Thursday 4 to 8 and Friday-Saturday 4 to 10, no dinner Sunday. No credit cards; checks OK. Ample servings of good old fashioned; the hefty dinners include French bread, soup or salad, veggies, and potato or rice. Simple pine-paneled interior with Naugahyde booths and counter service.

The Peppermint Stick • ∆∆ $ ØØ

454 Main St., Murphys; (209) 728-3570. Light lunches, desserts; meals $4 to $7, no alcohol. Monday-Saturday 11 to 5, Sunday noon to 5. No credit cards. Cute ice cream parlor and lunch cafe in Murphys' former ice house. Oldstyle soda fountain chairs and tables, red and gold wallpaper and jars of candy along the walls complete the early American ice cream parlor look. The "miner's soup," served in a hollowed round loaf of sourdough bread, is intriguing and tasty. Espresso, cappuccino and cafe latté.

The Utica Mansion Restaurant • ∆∆∆∆ $$$ ØØ

1090 Utica Lane (opposite Utica Park), Angels Camp, CA 95222; (209) 736-4209. American-continental; dinners $10 to $16; wine and beer. Thursday-Monday 5:30 to 9:30, closed Tuesday-Wednesday. Reservations advised; MC/VISA. Striking Victorian dining room in the former ballroom of an immaculately restored 1882 mansion. Elegant table service, wallpapered ceiling, tulip chandeliers and Casablanca fans. Not a terribly imaginative menu, but tasty fare in ample portions: steaks, teriyaki chicken, stuffed Monterey chicken, calamari marinara, a couple of fettuccines and nightly specials. Good wine list with a Gold Country focus. (Also see Lodging listing below.)

Is there life after dark?

The Black Bart Players (728-3956 or 728-3675) present a season of comedy and drama in their theater on Algiers Street, just west of the Murphys Hotel. **The Sacramento Symphony** makes occasional county appearances, sponsored by the Calaveras County Arts Council Friends of the Symphony, P.O. Box 250, San Andreas, CA 95249; (209) 754-1774 or 728-1585.

Murphys Hotel sometimes offers live music on weekends in its dim saloon. The **Calaveras Cattle Company**, a saloon in the Altaville end of Angels Camp at 570 North Main, is a source of live Western and country music; 736-6996.

LODGINGS

Bed & breakfast inns

Cooper House Bed & Breakfast Inn • ⌂⌂⌂ $$$$ ØØ

1184 Church St. (P.O. Box 1388), Angels Camp, CA 95222; (209) 736-2145. Doubles $95, singles $85. Three units with private baths. Full breakfast. Smoking outside only. MC/VISA. The Stevenot family has renovated and furnished this Craftsman style home with family heirlooms and other antiques, which blend well with a mix of modern furnishings. Once one of Angels' most stylish homes, it was built for Dr. George P. Cooper in 1911. Works of local artists decorate the walls and the suites offer private entrances and decks or sun rooms. Guests can relax on an oldstyle veranda or back patio, and follow a path through well-tended gardens to a gazebo. Afternoon refreshments are served.

Dunbar House Bed and Breakfast Inn • ⌂⌂⌂ $$$$ ØØ

271 Jones St. (P.O. Box 1375), Murphys, CA 95247; (209) 728-2897. Doubles $95 to $105. Four units with private baths. Full breakfast. Smoking on the *porch or in the garden. No credit cards.* If you have a flash of *deja vous* when you stay in this rambling 1880 Italianate home, you probably saw it on the brief Seven Brides for Seven Brothers TV series. The grand old house, listed on the National Register of Historic Places, brims with European and early American antiques. Guests are served a buffet on arrival, and will find a free bottle of local wine in their room. Breakfasts are served in the rooms, the stylish dining room or in the well-tended garden.

Utica Mansion Inn ● △△△ $$$$ ∅∅
1090 Utica Lane (P.O. Box 1), Angels Camp, CA 95222; (209) 736-4209. Doubles $90. Three units with private baths. Full breakfast. Smoking on the veranda and in the garden only. MC/VISA. This 5,000-square-foot mansion above Utica Park houses one of the Gold Country's most elaborately coiffed inns. Restored to exacting detail, it's a splendid study in print wallpaper, linquesta, polished woodwork, English-tile fireplaces and tulip chandeliers. It's a decorator's dream in burgundies, rusts and browns, with plush burgundy carpeting. Guest rooms feature oversized beds with carved wooden headboards and Victorian furnishings. A piano, fireplace and well-stocked library draw guests into a comfortable parlor. **Restaurant** listed above.

Historic hotels and ordinary motels

Murphys Hotel and Lodge ● △△ $$$ ∅
457 Main St. (P.O. Box 329), Murphys, CA 95247; (209) 728-3444. Nine historic rooms in hotel with share baths, $55 per couple including continental breakfast; 20 motel-type units with private baths and TV, $53 per couple. No smoking in hotel rooms; smoking OK in motel rooms and hotel public areas. Major credit cards. Hotel rooms are nicely restored and stocked with antiques; particularly striking is the Victorian style Presidential Suite, where General Grant stayed. Conventional motel units are next door.

Gold Country Inn Motel ● △ $$$ ∅
P.O. Box 188 (720 S. Main St.), Angels Camp, CA 95222; (209) 736-4611. Doubles from $39. MC/VISA, AMEX. A 41-unit motel in the Altaville end of Angels Camp. TV, room phones, some waterbeds, handicapped units.

Jumping Frog Motel ● △ $$
330 Murphys Grade Rd., Angels Camp, CA 95221; (209) 736-2191. Doubles from $39. MC/VISA. Small motel half a block off Highway 49 in the northern end of Angels Camp, with TV movies in rooms and a picnic/barbecue area. Restaurants nearby.

Poker Flat Lodge ● △△ $$$$
Star Route, Box 31 (on Lake Tulloch), Copperopolis, CA 95228; (209) 785-2286 or 785-2287. Doubles from $95 in summer, $60 in the off-season. MC/VISA. Modern motel with rooms overlooking Lake Tulloch in Poker Flat resort community; marina adjacent, offering assorted water sports. TV, swimming pool; **restaurant** and lounge. MC/VISA.

CAMPGROUNDS & RV PARKS

Calaveras Big Trees State Park ● *P.O. Box 120 (four miles above Arnold on Highway 4), Arnold, CA 95223; (209) 795-2334. RV and tent sites in two campgrounds, $12 to $14 per night. Reservations via MISTIX w/$3.95 fee;*

A JOURNEY TO THE CENTER OF THE EARTH

What a wild way to enter a cave!

Rappelling is a technique used by mountain climbers to descend sheer faces and overhangs while dangling from safety ropes. But rappelling into the earth? That was something we had to try.

In addition to the more conventional—and sane—method of walking down a spiral stairway, one can enter Moaning Cavern by rappelling nearly 200 feet from the surface into the main chamber.

We'd never done rappelling, either above or below the earth, so we greeted this venture with a mix of curiosity and fear. The fear mounted when, rigged in a harness of straps and buckles and clasps, we were told to back down a sheer cliff.

"Keep your feet against the wall, and lower yourself by playing your rope through the rigging," said our guide. "Your feet should be kept high, about level with your shoulders."

Feet level with shoulders? Feeling and probably looking ridiculous, I began lowering myself into the pit. Curiosity overcame fright as I awkwardly scuttled crab-like down the wall. Then, following the guide's instructions, I reached a ledge, turned around and squirmed into a small opening "about the size of a garbage can." But this garbage can had no bottom.

As I worked through the small opening, I heard my wife laughing nervously above me. Betty, who a few months ago disliked high stairways, was following me into eternity.

I cleared the hole and then positioned myself against another wall, waiting for her to catch up. We worked down farther and suddenly we were clear of the wall, suspended in the center of the largest natural cavern in California. A rush of sensations peppered my brain: exhilaration at the freedom of dangling in space; fascination as I twisted slowly on my rope, studying the intricate cave wall formations revolving around me; and curiosity at this strange feeling, something akin to a space walk and a Matterhorn descent.

Fear? I left that on the first ledge.

---

(800) 444-7275; MC/VISA. Flush toilets, showers, picnic tables and barbecues. Nice campsites under towering evergreens. See park listing under Discoveries above. Open all year.

Golden Torch RV Park • *In Darrington, eight miles northeast of Calaveras Big Trees; mailing address P.O. Box 4248, Arnold, CA 95223; (209) 795-2820. RV and tent sites; full hookups $17, no hookups $11. Reservations accepted; no credit cards.* Wooded campground with more than 100 sites, flush potties and picnic/barbecue facilities. Showers, store, coin laundry, pool, playground, rec room. Open all year.

New Melones Reservoir • *P.O. Box 1389, Angels Camp, CA 95222; (209) 984-5248. Campsites (primarily RV), $10.* Camping at Glory Hole Recreation area just south of Angels Camp and at Tuttletown Recreation Area south of Highway 49 near Tuttletown. Flush potties and showers, no hookups. Picnic tables, barbecues, swimming, boating fishing. Campsites located in oak knolls, offering a bit of shade. Open all year.

Frogtown (Calaveras County Fairgrounds) ● *P.O. Box 96 (just south of town, half a mile off Highway 49), Angels Camp, CA 95222; (209) 736-2561. RV sites and separate tent area, $10. No credit cards.* Newly renovated campground with electric and water hookups, showers and potties. Open all year.

ANNUAL EVENTS

Jumping Frog Jubilee, third weekend in May at the Calaveras County Fairgrounds, (209) 736-2571; historic frog-jump competition, in conjunction with the Calaveras County Fair with the usual livestock shows, horse racing, food booths, carnival and such.

Music from Bear Valley, in July, (209) 753-2574; annual music festival in the Bear Valley summer/winter resort above Murphys.

Murphys Gold Rush, first weekend of October, (209) 728-3724; a street fair with arts and crafts, entertainment and beer and wine gardens.

On the road again...to San Andreas/Mok Hill

Only 11 miles separate Altaville and San Andreas, and they take you through typical oak foothill country. A monument marking the gold camp of Fourth Crossing advises that this was the fourth crossing of the Calaveras River. The place was called Formans in the 1850s and yielded rich ore deposits. It later became an important stage and freight depot, serving the mines until after the turn of the century. Nary a shred of Fourth Crossing remains.

To learn more...

Calaveras County Visitor Center, 1301 S. Main St. (P.O. Box 637), Angels Camp, CA 95222; (800) 695-3737 or (209) 736-0049. The center, at the intersection of Highways 49 and 4, is open Monday-Saturday 9 to 4:30.

"I've labored long and hard for bread,
For honor and for riches.
But upon my corns too long you've tread
You fine-haired sons of bitches."
— **poem left at a robbery by Black Bart**

Chapter Nine

SAN ANDREAS & MOK HILL

Black Bart and
Joaquin Murieta, too?

HOTEL LEGER
IN MOKELUMNE HILL

Among the Mother Lode's assortment of claim jumpers, high-graders, horse thieves and highwaymen, two bandits emerge larger than life: Black Bart and Joaquin Murieta. Both were the stuff of which legends are made. Murieta, in fact, probably was more legend than reality.

We bring them up at this point because both were linked, at least fleetingly, to the towns in this chapter. Black Bart, alias Charles Bolton alias Charles Boles, was brought to justice in San Andreas, although he got off with a pretty light sentence.

If you're ready for yet another Joaquin Murieta story, he supposedly began a Robin Hood life of crime after being driven out of San Andreas by greedy gringo miners. He later hung out in Mokelumne Hill where he made "daring personal appearances" in fandango halls, says one historian. But other chroniclers say his crime spree started after he and other Mexican miners were chased from Sonorian Camp. No way, say other history buffs. It all happened in Murphys, where American tormentors tied him to a tree, beat him, abused his wife and killed his brother. (And stole his Bible?)

THE WAY IT WAS • "In the winter of 1848, a few Mexicans encamped at the works of the Gulch about one-fourth of a mile above where the town now stands," reports an 1856 issue of the *San Andreas Independent.* Naturally, as soon as substantial gold deposits were found, Americans moved in and tried to muscle the Mexicans aside.

The Latinos moved up the gulch a bit, where their numbers increased to nearly a thousand. Americans continued arriving, too, and the two groups functioned under an uneasy truce within their respective camps. San Andreas was a tent and shanty town until 1851 when it got its first permanent building—a small adobe.

Mokelumne Hill, seven miles to the north, also began in 1848 when Colonel Jonathan D. Stevenson, late of the Mexican War, established a town

109

and named himself *alcalde*. In 1851, several major strikes were made near Mok Hill and most of San Andreas' citizens were lured to these more profitable diggins, so it shrank while Mok Hill boomed to 15,000 souls. It was briefly one of the largest towns in California. And certainly the wildest.

"A flood of gold flowed into the growing settlement," writes historian Emmett P. Joy. "Stores had to keep open all hours to serve customers clamoring to change their gold for something to eat and wear. Saloons opened their doors never to close for years."

During one period, at least one killing occurred between Saturday night and Sunday for 17 consecutive weeks. On one particularly rowdy weekend, five miners bit the dust.

It was a racially mixed community, but hardly a model of tolerance. Yankees drove a group of Frenchmen off their hill—supposedly because they'd insulted America by raising a French flag. In reality, the Americans wanted their claims. At nearby Chili Hill, another battle erupted when American miners expelled a Chilean mine owner for allegedly abusing his workers and using slave labor. Meanwhile, Joaquin Murieta and his buddy Three Fingered Jack roared in and out of town, stealing and pillaging—but probably not raping; the ladies apparently were quite fascinated by Joaquin.

Mok Hill's gold ran out—as it always does—and the town shriveled. About the same time, San Andreas began to prosper. In 1866, its citizens decided that Mok Hill should surrender its county seat. An election was held and San Andreas won, but it was contested all the way to the California Supreme Court. Mokelumne's resentment stemmed from the fact that San Andreas cast more votes than it had voters.

Black Bart's involvement with San Andreas was brief but indelible. Between 1877 and 1883, he supposedly held up 28 stage coaches (or 27 or 29; pick your historian) throughout northern California. He confronted the stage drivers on foot, wearing a flour sack for a mask and brandishing an empty shotgun. He was polite to the ladies and never hurt anyone: a perfect gentleman. By a twist of fate, his first and last hold-ups occurred at Funk Hill near Copperopolis. As noted in the last chapter, he fled the scene of his final robbery in rather a hurry, leaving behind a laundry-marked handkerchief.

Wells Fargo hired special detective Harry N. Morse, who checked a hundred laundries and traced the hankie to one Charles E. Bolton (A.K.A. Boles) of 316 Bush St., apartment 40, San Francisco. Since San Andreas was the seat of the county where the holdup occurred, local Sheriff Ben Thorn was dispatched to San Francisco to fetch him back. Boles remained in San Andreas only a few weeks. He confessed to the Funk Hill robbery but staunchly denied involvement in the other holdups.

Sentenced to six years in San Quentin north of San Francisco, he was released for good behavior after four, and vanished forever. One of history's pet rumors is that Wells Fargo officials paid him a monthly allowance to go away and stop stealing their gold shipments.

THE WAY IT IS ● You can drive right through San Andreas without realizing it's part of the Mother Lode unless you pause to peek down Main Street. A block-long stretch, perpendicular to the highway, holds most of the town's historic treasures, mixed in with early 20th century architecture.

The focal point of its history is hidden behind the staid brick and cut stone Hall of Records, which was built in 1893 and contains the county's lone elevator. It also houses the Calaveras County Museum (see Attractions below). Shielded by the hall is the older and more interesting Calaveras County Courthouse, dating from 1867. It was here that Mister Boles was jailed and tried.

Like its neighbor, Mok Hill's historic area also eludes the casual eye, since it sits on a downslope just off Highway 49. It's a more believable Gold Rush town. Mok Hill has shrunk from 15,000 rowdy miners and their families to a village of about eight square blocks. What little remains is mostly 19th century vintage. Since it lost its county seat, it escaped the progress that has changed San Andreas.

So while San Andreas is mostly modern, Mok Hill—boasting a population of 560—is content to relax with its memories. It's a mix of the carefully preserved and the scruffy, ranging from the beautifully maintained 1865 white clapboard Mok Hill Community Church to the intriguing but weathered Hotel Leger (pronounce it *Leh-zhay*). The Leger is the town's architectural and social focal point, where tourists bed down for the night and dice cups thump on the bar below.

Newest addition to Mok Hill's tourist lures is the history society museum, listed below. Small but nicely arranged, it's worth a brief visit.

DISCOVERIES
The best attractions

Calaveras County Museum and Archives ● *30 N. Main St., San Andreas, CA 95249; (209) 754-4023. Daily 10 to 4; donation 50 cents. Gift shop with extensive Gold Country book selection.* The museum covers a full spectrum of Calaveras County history, from the Mi-Wuk Indians to the Spanish, gold-seekers and later settlers.

Exhibits include a bark wikiup surrounded by Mi-Wuk crafts, a typical gold miner's camp with a simple white canvas tent and clutter of cooking utensils, rocker, pan and "possibles" bag, plus pioneer relics and historic photos.

The museum's three buildings are perhaps its best features. The facility occupies the original 1850 county offices, the 1856 Masonic and I.O.O.F. hall and the 1867 courthouse and jail. The court and several other rooms have been restored, with original furnishings that transport visitors back to San Andreas' gold- grubbing heyday.

A popular stop is the preserved jailyard and five cells where assorted bad guys, including the notorious Black Bart, awaited the consequences of their dire deeds.

California Caverns ● *Twelve miles east of San Andreas, off Mountain Ranch Road; mailing address is P.O. Box 78, Vallecito, CA 95251; (209) 736-2708. Eighty-minute tours, hourly from 10 a.m. to 5 p.m. daily from June through October; weekends only in November; closed from about December through May due to winter rain seepage. Admission $5.75 for adults; $2.75 for kids 6 to 12. Special four-hour spelunking tours for $59, by reservation (see box).*

California Caverns is the largest and most interesting of Calaveras County's three cave systems, and it played a role in Mother Lode history. A

I.O.O.F. halls were commonplace during the Gold Rush; this one in Mokelumne Hill now houses a saloon.

registered state historical landmark, this limestone grotto was discovered in 1849 when a prospector noticed a cool whiff of air emerging from a rocky formation where he was target practicing. It was opened to public tours the following year, becoming the first commercial cave tour in California. Admission was a pinch from your gold poke. The resort community of Cave City, complete with luxury hotel, grew up around the entrance and such personages as John Muir and Mark Twain toured the caverns.

Cave City is gone, but the caverns are very much intact and present-day owners offer a "Trail of Lights" tour past its extensive formations. The Jungle Room, discovered only recently and therefore protected from vandalism by the owners, offers one of the greatest collections of limestone formations you'll see anywhere. It earns its name from thousands of stalactites and other shapes hanging from the ceiling like creepers from a tropical forest canopy.

The rest

Hotel Leger and Calaveras County Courthouse • *8304 Main St., Mokelumne Hill.* Big, bold and bright yellow, this two-story structure commands your eye as you drop down off Highway 49 into Mok Hill. It was built in 1851 as Hotel de France, then reopened in 1854 by George Leger after a damaging fire. An adjacent building served as the county courthouse until San Andreas snatched the seat of government in 1866. Leger then absorbed that structure into his hotel. With its railed porch and matching wooden balcony, the old stone and brick hotel is an attractive structure. The interior, while far from posh, is being renovated in stages. When we last visited, the saloon—which could be a treasure trove of memories from this once wild and wooly town—was spartan and scruffy.

Mokelumne Hill History Society Museum • *Main and Center streets, Mokelumne Hill; (209) 286-1770. Open 11 to 3 Friday through Monday in summer, Friday through Sunday the rest of the year. Free; contributions appreciated, since the museum is self supporting.* Housed in one of Mok Hill's old storefronts, this small and tidy museum was opened in 1988, thanks mostly to the efforts of local historian Dorris Tyrrel. Photos, old documents and a few artifacts tell of the mining camp's yesterdays. The museum also offers a good selection of Gold Rush and other Western history books.

Nuggets

Adams & Co. Genuine Old West Saloon and Museum • *In the I.O.O.F Hall at the foot of Main Street, Mokelumne Hill.* More saloon than museum, this place is a kick: an odd mix of Old West and new whimsy, like a moose head sporting horn rimmed sunglasses and a trapeze artist in a burlap bag.

Black Bart exhibit • *County Courthouse, 30 N. Main St., San Andreas, CA 95249; (209) 754-4023.* Photos,
sketches and old clippings outside the cell that once hosted Black Bart. Among the exhibits are a copy of the official rap sheet describing him as "5 foot 7 inches tall, poor teeth, cleft chin and blue, deep-set eyes." That hardly sounds like one of the West's most notorious bad guys.

DETOUR

San Andreas via West Point and Rail Road Flat to Mokelumne Hill • *A 50-mile loop trip.* Main Street in San Andreas swerves to the left and becomes Gold Strike Road. Follow it for a mile or so, then turn right onto Hawver Road, which takes you eight miles through a scenic creekside wilderness area.

If you'd rather not put up with a lot of bumps, twists, turns and a seasonal stream crossing (impassable after rains), you might wish to avoid this. An easy alternate is to remain on Gold Strike; it rejoins Highway 49 and takes you Mok Hill.

Either way, turn right (east) onto Highway 26 in Mok Hill and follow it into the pines. You'll pass through Glencoe, a small gathering of summer homes and service stations, once the site of Mosquito Gulch, a Mexican mining camp. You next encounter West Point, another forest clearing. A marker advises you that it was named by Kit Carson, who paused here while searching for a route through the Sierra, and that Bret Harte lived here for a bit.

From West Point, retrace your path for a mile, and then swing left onto Rail Road Flat Road. Wilseyville, a general store and tiny cluster of homes, comes and goes in the blink of an eye. After winding up and down a hill or two, you'll arrive in Rail Road Flat, a neat old town in a high forest-rimmed meadow.

Two ancient general stores will catch your eye: a red-shingled two-story 1930 structure with its second story built over gas pumps; and the wood frame, tin roofed Haag Store, which began peddling possibles in 1867. The railroad never reached Rail Road Flat. The town earned its name from a short length of wooden track built for mule powered ore carts during its 1850s mining heyday.

Beyond Rail Road Flat, pick up Jesus Maria Road, which offers a lazy, reasonably scenic trip from the pines back down into the oaks and ultimately to Mok Hill.

MUD, MARVELOUS MUD

Two words describe the special spelunking tours offered by California Caverns near San Andreas: marvelous and muddy. Water seepage, which produces all those beautiful formations, also creates thick, chocolaty mud in several of the chambers visited by spelunkers. (The conventional tour is dry, of course.)

By the time we'd donned our gear—lighted helmet, coveralls, heavy boots and gloves—we looked ready to explore outer space instead of inner earth. For four fascinating, sticky hours we slithered and wriggled through tiny openings and down mysterious tunnels in one of the most complex cave systems in California.

We entered through a corkscrew burrow that would have given the White Rabbit fits, then we leveled out and walked along the same "Trail of Lights" course that regular visitors follow. At the awesomely beautiful Jungle Room, where the normal tour ends, we turned on our lighted hats and slithered into the blackness, covering about a mile of recently discovered caverns. Through much of the journey, thick mud tugged at our hands and tried to snatch away our boots, making noises like bubble gum popping and other sound effects I'd rather not describe.

With laconic general manager and expert spelunker John Fairchild as our guide, we survived challenges such as Push-up Passage, the Womb Room (don't ask) and the Mole Crawl. We explored beautiful grottos never seen on ordinary cave tours, and we were able to approach within inches of rare formations. At one point, we descended a rope ladder, stepped into a rubber raft and paddled silently across an underground lake. (Betty's entrance was particularly dramatic: she fell in.)

We emerged hours later, weary, curiously elated and looking like losers in a mud-wrestling match.

For details on these tours, see the California Caverns listing.

DIVERSION

Water sports of all sorts • *New Hogan Recreation Area, 1955 New Hogan Parkway (nine miles west of San Andreas off Highway 12), Valley Springs, CA 95252; (209) 772-1343; if no answer, call (209) 772-1462.* This reservoir on the Calaveras River offers boating, water skiing, fishing and swimming.

GOLD COUNTRY DINING

Black Bart Inn • ΔΔ $$

35 Main St., San Andreas; (209) 754-3808. American; dinners $10.50 to $23.50; full bar service. Dinner daily 5 to 10 p.m. (until 9 in the off-season); coffee shop 6 a.m. to 4 p.m. Major credit cards. Typical American fare most days, although the menu switches to Chinese on Tuesday and Mexican on Thursday. Early American decor with red checkered table cloth, old portraits (naturally including Black Bart's).

Nonno's Cucina Italiana • ΔΔ $$ ∅

In Hotel Leger, 8304 Main St. Mokelumne Hill; (209) 286-1401. Italian; dinners $9 to $15; full bar service. Thursday-Saturday 5 to 9; Sunday 3 to 8. MC/VISA. Nicely renovated oldstyle restaurant with print wallpaper, brass chandeliers and such. The usual fettucini, tortellini, linguine and Parmigiana, plus specials such as rosemary garlic chicken and calamari served abalone style. Good selection of Gold Country wines.

Wendells Restaurant • ΔΔΔ $$ ∅

9036 W. Center St. (at Highway 49), Mokelumne Hill; (209) 286-1338. California cuisine; dinners $11 to $17; full bar service. Breakfast and lunch weekends 9 to 4, dinner Sunday, Wednesday and Thursday 5 to 9 and Friday-Saturday 5 to 10, closed Monday-Tuesday. MC/VISA. Very appealing country style restaurant of stone, wood and brick; lots of polished wood, wainscoting, wallpaper and ceiling fans. Handsome bar adjacent to dining room. Menu items range from prime rib to veal and fresh seafood.

Is there life after dark?

Other than listening to the liars' dice cups thump at the **Hotel Leger** saloon? As a matter of fact, yes. The **Metropolitan Players** offer a season of dramas in San Andreas (754-1774) and **The Stage Door** in Hotel Leger produces onstage stuff as well (286-1401). The **Sacramento Symphony** makes occasional appearances in the area, sponsored by the Calaveras County Arts Council Friends of the Symphony, P.O. Box 250, San Andreas, CA 95249; (209) 754-1774 or 728-1585. The Leger and the **Black Bart Inn lounge** (754-3808) occasionally schedule live entertainment on Friday and Saturday nights and **Wendell's** (286-1338) features live music and comedy nights.

LODGINGS

The Robin's Nest • ⌂⌂⌂ $$$ ∅∅

P.O. Box 1408 (247 W. St. Charles St., downtown), San Andreas, CA 95249; (209) 754-1076. From $65 per couple. Three rooms, one private and *two share baths; full breakfast. No smoking. Major credit cards.* This nest is an 1895 blue-gray Queen Anne home on San Andreas' main street, which has been enlarged and renovated into an attractive, spacious B&B. Each bedroom has a turn-of-the-century travel theme—one of the more clever decorating schemes we've seen. My favorite was the Airplane Room with an old wooden prop and airplane prints on the walls. Arriving guests are offered lemonade and chocolate chip cookies. Innkeeper Jack McKibben likes to plan special theme weekends—by advance reservation—for chocoholics, mystery fans and wine buffs.

Hotel Leger • ⌂ $$$ ⊘⊘
P.O. Box 50, Mokelumne Hill, CA 95245; (209) 286-1401. Doubles $55 to $79. Some private, some shared baths. Expanded continental breakfast. MC/VISA. New owners are gradually sprucing up this venerable hotel. Its rustic rooms are furnished with antiques; while not posh, they're neat, clean and comfortable. Some have fireplaces. Outdoor pool; massage therapy by appointment. All hotel rooms are non-smoking. **Nonno's Restaurant** listed above.

Black Bart Inn • ⌂ $$
35 Main St., San Andreas, CA 95249; (209) 754-3808. Doubles from $40. Major credit cards. Modern rooms with TV; swimming pool, cocktail lounge and **restaurant** (listed above.) Part of the complex is in an old brick building fronting on San Andreas' historic district.

Bonnie's Inn • ⌂ $$$ ⊘
P.O. Box 356 (Highway 49 and 12 junction), San Andreas, CA 95249; (209) 754-3212. Cottages $55, kitchen unit $60; Major credit cards. Simply furnished but large, neat rooms with TV movies, refrigerators and antiques. Hot tub, barbecue area; in downtown San Andreas.

CAMPGROUNDS & RV PARKS

New Hogan Lake Recreation Area • *1955 New Hogan Parkway (nine miles west of San Andreas off Highway 12), Valley Springs, CA 95252; (209) 772-1343; if no answer, call (209) 772-1462. Several camping areas with RV and tent sites, no hookups, $10 from April 1 through September; $5 the rest of the year.* Flush potties, hot showers, picnic tables and barbecues, water sports. Full service marina; boating, fishing and other water sports. Open all year.

Gold Strike Mobile Village • *1925 Gold Strike Rd., San Andreas, CA 95249; (209) 754-3180. A mobile home park with 25 overnight spots for RVs. Full hookups $15, no hookups $10.* Flush potties, showers, swimming pool, laundromat. Open all year.

ANNUAL EVENT

Black Bart Days in September, old town San Andreas, (800) 695-3737; old-time Gold Rush celebration.

ON THE ROAD AGAIN...TO AMADOR COUNTY
A mere eight miles separate Mok Hill in Calaveras County from the town of Jackson, our first Amador County stop. Motoring through the usual oak thatched meadowlands, we cross the Mokelumne River and pass three his-

toric sites. Two are merely markers: the location of Big Bar gold camp and its Whaleboat Ferry; and a mile or so beyond, the locale of another town called Middle Bar. The third landmark offers something visual—stone and brick ruins of the 1850s Butte Store, the lone survivor of the town of Butte City.

To learn more...

The Calaveras County Historical Society office on the ground floor of the old county complex at 30 N. Main St., San Andreas, serves as an area visitor center; it's open weekdays 10 to 4.

Primary source of tourist information is the **Calaveras County Visitor Center,** 1301 S. Main St. (P.O. Box 637), Angels Camp, CA 95222; (800) 695-3737 or (209) 736-0049. The center, at the intersection of Highways 49 and 4 in Angels, is open Monday-Saturday 9 to 4:30.

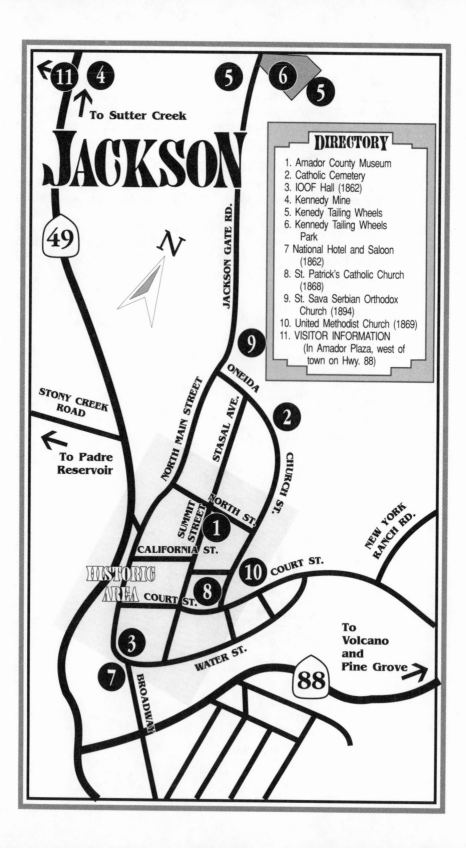

JACKSON

To Sutter Creek

STONY CREEK ROAD

To Padre Reservoir

JACKSON GATE RD.

ONEIDA

STASAL AVE.

NORTH MAIN STREET

CHURCH ST.

NORTH ST.

SUMMIT STREET

CALIFORNIA ST.

HISTORIC AREA

COURT ST.

COURT ST.

WATER ST.

BROADWAY

NEW YORK RANCH RD.

To Volcano and Pine Grove

"There were three ways to get to California, and all of them were hell."
— Frank Liddicoat, Jackson hardrock miner

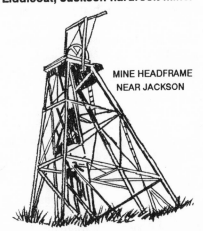
MINE HEADFRAME
NEAR JACKSON

Chapter Ten
JACKSON &
SURROUNDS
From hardrock mines
to tailing wheels

It was the largest human migration in history. Several hundred thousand hopefuls—no one knows exactly how many—rushed to California's gold fields. They either crossed the hot, hostile American desert, made the long voyage around South America or sailed to Panama and risked malaria to cross the isthmus and hopefully pick up a San Francisco-bound ship on the other side.

Frank Liddicoat, who mined in Jackson during the 1930s and is quoted in one of the Amador County Museum exhibits, knows well the risks of getting here, for he talked with families of those who made the trip. And he knows the hard work and frustration they faced once they arrived, for Frank spent many a year down in those dark mines.

Although Amador County was an important mining center, its county seat of Jackson isn't typical of the early gold camps. It didn't explode into being, but grew slowly, first as a watering hole (for stock, not thirsty miners), then as one of the earliest and most durable of the Mother Lode's hardrock mining areas. Its population has remained remarkably stable, between two and three thousand for well over a century.

Jackson outlasted most of the other camps, and its gold production continued into this century, to a time when environmental concerns began changing the ways men mined. In 1912 the state legislature ruled that mining companies could no longer pollute streams and silt up farmers' fields with their tailings. This law led to the creation of the famous Jackson Tailing Wheels, perhaps the strangest objects in the Mother Lode. These monstrous disks, 58 feet in diameter, carried tailings from Jackson's Kennedy Mine to a containment reservoir. Two of the four wheels stand today, and we shall examine them shortly.

THE WAY IT WAS ● The community began life in 1848 as a provisioning station around a freshwater spring which Mexican prospectors called *Bottileas,* supposedly because of discarded water jugs around the well. Those

119

ever-quarrelsome historians dispute this theory, however. Containers were precious commodities and it's extremely unlikely that pioneer travelers would toss them aside like spent Coke bottles. Logic suggests that it earned its name as "the place to fill one's bottles."

In 1849, the settlement was named for local miner Alden Appolas Moore Jackson. However, some historians say Alden didn't hang around long, and that it was in fact named for President Andrew Jackson.

When California became a state, this area was part of Calaveras County. An election was held to determine whether Jackson or Mokelumne Hill would function as its seat. Mok Hill won but Jackson officials claimed the election was rigged. In a heated dispute over the surrender of county records to Mok Hill, Jackson area Judge William Smith killed the county clerk, L.A. Collier, in a gunfight. When things calmed down, the records were returned to Jackson and the judge was run out of office.

Two years later, another election was held and that pesky Mok Hill won again. Weary of this foolishness, area citizens voted to create their own jurisdiction and Amador County, one of the smallest in the state, was born in 1854. Jackson barely beat out Volcano for the privilege of becoming county seat.

Hardrock mining began in 1856 when Andrew Kennedy hit a vein in a hill north of town. The Kennedy Mine operated off and on for nearly a century, finally closing in 1942 because mercury and explosives used in mining were needed to fight World War II. The Kennedy and its neighbor, the Argonaut, were at one time the deepest mines in the world, burrowing more than a mile into the earth, with miles of shafts extending out in search of those elusive quartz veins. They survived a union-breaking strike in 1891 and a disastrous Argonaut Mine fire in 1922 that suffocated 47 miners, despite a frantic cross-tunnel dig from the Kennedy Mine to rescue them.

Although Jackson wasn't one of the Mother Lode's wilder mining camps, it wasn't exactly a church camp, either. Nickel slots and "girls dormitories" survived until the 1950s. A local group generated national headlines on Valentine's Day, 1968, by dedicating a heart-shaped bronze plaque to those former ladies of the evening.

THE WAY IT IS ● Jackson's past role as a major hardrock mining center is still obvious today. Headframes of the Kennedy, Argonaut and several other mines rise from the nearby hillsides as sentinels of yesterday.

It's an attractive community occupying a forested valley, and many century-old buildings survived downtown. Particularly noteworthy is the three-story balconied National Hotel with a vague Spanish colonial look. Most of the other downtown structures have been modernized. They house a mix of antique shops, boutiques, shoe shops and insurance agencies. Highway 49 bypasses Main Street so Jackson doesn't suffer from traffic jams.

Driving or walking about Jackson's residential areas will reveal some fine old Victorians, particularly along Summit and Stasal streets. Note also two distinctive 19th century churches, St. Patrick's Catholic and the United Methodist, both around Court and Church streets. We like the wonderfully out-of-character Amador County Courthouse at Summit and Court streets. Built of brick in 1863, it's now clad in an Art Deco skin with severe geometric lines and recessed windows.

DISCOVERIES
The best attractions

Kennedy Mine Tailing Wheels ● *In Jackson Kennedy Wheels City Park, north of town on Jackson Gate Road.* They are among the most photographed and perhaps the strangest objects in all of La Veta Madre—four giant wooden wheels built in 1912 to satisfy the demands of an environmental law. Far from being typical Gold Country structures, they're a one-of-a-kind creation. They represent the closing days of the Gold Rush, an attempt by mine owners to meet demands of a more environmentally aware public.

Despite their enormity, the wheels were simple in concept. Basically, they acted as water wheels—except that they were powered by electricity and used lift buckets to elevate a slurry of tailings into high flumes and transport it to a reservoir about half a mile away.

Only two of the giant wheels remain standing. The others have crashed into ravines, scattered and broken in the underbrush, looking like crude space laboratories that fell from the sky. We first visited the wheels at night, staring in fascination at their silhouettes in the light of a full moon. They do indeed look like something from another world.

Amador County Museum ● *225 Church St. (mailing address: 108 Court St., Jackson, CA 95642); (209) 223-6386. Wednesday-Sunday 10 to 4; admission by donation. Kennedy model mine tour $1 for adults, kids under 8 free, conducted hourly on weekends from 11 to 3.* Located in a large 1859 brick home, the museum offers a quick study in the early day life of this small Gold Country county. Some rooms in this venerable mansion are furnished as they were during Jackson's heyday, with period cookware, an ancient piano and gramophone and other antiques. Recently added is a fine costume display, featuring the bustles, petticoats, lace and starched collars of the 19th century.

The museum's finest exhibit is a series of scale model mining replicas in an adjacent building: the Kennedy Mine headframe with a cutaway of the main shaft and side drifts, one of the tailing wheels and a working model of a stamp mill that actually crushes small stones. Docents conduct tours hourly on weekends, operating the models and explaining the complexity of hardrock mining.

Indian Grinding Rock State Historic Park ● *14881 Pine Grove-Volcano Rd., Pine Grove, CA 95665; (209) 296-7488. Museum open daily 10 to 5. Park fee $5 per vehicle. Camping available; see listing under Campgrounds below.* This 135-acre state park in a pleasant pine grove protects the site of the largest grinding rock (chaw'se) in America. Covering 7,700 square feet, the rock is peppered with 1,158 mortar holes and patterned with more than 350 petroglyphs. The thing is so impressive that a replica is housed at the Smithsonian Institution in Washington.

A typical Mi-Wuk village nearby features a ceremonial round house (hun'ge), tree bark dwellings (u'macha') and an Indian game field (poscoi a we'a). The park also contains a museum and cultural center with artifacts from assorted Indian tribes and books for sale. Local Indians gather here the fourth weekend of every September for "Big Time," a festival of dances, crafts demonstrations and sales of Native American arts and foods.

The rest

Daffodil Hill • *Shake Ridge Road north of Volcano; (209) 223-0608 or 296-7048.* This is a springtime attraction, generally during the last half of March, when 300,000 daffodils bloom on the Arthur and Lizzie McLaughlin ranch above Volcano. The McLaughlins have stuffed thousands of daffodil bulbs into a four-acre plot that produces a dazzling show. It's not a commercial venture, but a gratis splash of color offered by these nice folk. Visitors are welcome to come and view the daffodils without charge. To reach "The Hill," follow directional signs north from Volcano, or join us in our detour below.

Sutter Creek-Volcano Road drive • We describe this route as an "attraction" because it's one of the prettiest short drives in the Gold Country. It follows the twisting course of Sutter Creek through a narrow canyon lined with overhanging oaks and cottonwoods. The little stream begs you to pull over, clamber down the bank and unpack a picnic lunch, pick blackberries or pan for gold. (However, watch for private property signs.) A hiking trail follows the bank opposite the roadway. In the fall, this Gold Country beauty presents its own special golden show of poplars and maples.

Nuggets

The Amador Cannonball • *On the grounds of the Amador County Museum, 225 Church St., Jackson.* This realistic looking 1875 narrow gauge steam engine and tender is actually a replica. Its career began in 1950 as a TV and movie train, best known for its long role as the "Hooterville Cannonball" in the TV series, *Petticoat Junction.*

National Hotel and saloon • *#2 Water St. (at Main), Jackson, CA 95642; (209) 223-0500.* The Louisiana House originally occupied this site, built above the spring that gave Jackson its start as a community. The hotel was destroyed by fire and another rose from its ashes in 1863. Claiming to be the oldest continuously operating hotel in California (along with several others), it still rents out rooms (see lodgings listing below), and operates a restaurant and saloon. The National Saloon is a genuine Gold Rush relic with a century-old mirrored back bar, ceiling lamps with teardrop crystals and dark wainscoting and simulated red velvet wallpaper. And of course, a brass rail. Incidentally, most of Jackson's antique and curio shops are in or clustered around the hotel. A plaque at the side of the structure marks the spot of the original Bottileas Spring.

Old Abe • *Consolation Street near Charleston Street, Volcano.* This 140-year-old brass cannon has become Volcano's mascot, lovingly polished and rolled out for special events. The rest of the year, it lives in a sheltering shed, where a placard tells its story. The cannon was purchased during the Civil War by the Volcano Blues, ostensibly to control renegades but in reality to intimidate the Knights of the Golden Circle, who wanted Volcano to side with the South. The cannon was never fired in anger, which is fortunate because—according to observers of the day—it was so stuffed with powder, wadding and shot that it probably would have exploded.

St. George Hotel Saloon • *Charleston Street, Volcano.* The eclectic collection of artifacts, pictures, posters and other doodads tacked to the walls of this venerable pub will keep your eyes occupied through at least three beers. Our favorite is a picture of General George Custer with a suction cup arrow stuck to his temple. The ceiling is covered with dollar bills and calling cards, affixed by thumb tacks. Getting them up there without a ladder is surprisingly simple, but it'll cost you a dollar to learn how it's done.

St. Sava Serbian Orthodox Church • *724 North Main St., Jackson; (209) 223-2700.* This small white jewel, surrounded by a steeply terraced cemetery, was built in 1894 as the mother church of the Serbian Orthodox faith in North America. It's one of the Gold Country's most attractive houses of worship, with arched stained glass windows and the traditional Serbian starred window in a square bell tower. The charming little church is listed on the National Register of Historic Places. Although it's generally locked, if you visit between 9:30 and 10:30 before Sunday services, you may have a brief look inside the small sanctuary, with a white and gold-trimmed wood paneled altar and small but elaborate chandeliers gracing the steeply-pitched ceiling. Above the altar, golden stars are painted on a domed sky, accounting for the unusual rounded back end of the church.

Volcano General Store • *Charleston Street, Volcano.* This sturdy stone store offers the usual selection of "possibles" crowded onto floor-to-ceiling shelves, and a small five-table restaurant serving remarkably good hamburgers and other simple fare. The grill is in an old fieldstone fireplace—a neat touch.

DETOURS

Jackson to Volcano and Indian Grinding Rock State Park • *A 55-mile loop trip.* Head northeast on Highway 88 out of Jackson; you'll climb swiftly from oaks to conifers. Pine Grove, eight miles up the line, is worth a brief pause. It dates to 1855 when Albert Leonard built his Pine Grove House on the Volcano to Jackson immigrant trail.

Today, it's still a mountain retreat, with summer homes, small businesses and service stations scattered along Highway 88. A few of the older structures remain: the century-old Pine Grove Hotel on the site of Leonard's establishment, the 1879 town hall (originally the Dance and Temperance Hall) and a cemetery with plantings dating from 1860.

Another point of interest: By turning right onto Mount Zion Road, you shortly arrive at a lookout offering an impressive view of the Mother Lode foothills below and—on a rare haze-free day—the San Joaquin Valley beyond. Continuing on Route 88, you'll encounter Pioneer, which has the same small business scatter but none of the historic buildings of Pine Grove, so it will give you little cause to pause. Further along, you hit Buckhorn, smaller, more Western-rustic in architecture and therefore more appealing than Pioneer.

About six miles above Buckhorn, take a hard left onto Silver Lake Road which leads you through thick woods and thicker plots of summer homes. It's a particularly pretty drive in spring, when roadside dogwoods bloom. Fork left onto Shake Ridge Road, pass Daffodil Hill (and certainly pause, if it's springtime), then go left again onto Rams Horn Road.

You'll spiral dizzily down toward Volcano, passing through a transition zone from evergreens to oaks, enjoying roadside vistas of pastoral ranch scenes with old red barns and green pastures with white-faced cattle lowing (whatever that means).

With a mere 100 citizens and a fine collection of Gold Rush buildings, Volcano is one of the foothills' more charming mini-towns. This isn't a restored Gold Rush town like Columbia. It's a survivor, similar to Mok Hill but smaller, more remotely located and therefore more peaceful.

Established in 1848, Volcano grew quickly and led a surprisingly proper life for a gold camp. It fostered the state's first lending library, first little theater group and the first literary and debating society. Its curious name came from its unusual location in a high mountain-rimmed basin. Early settler, seeing mist rising from the basin, fancied that it resembled a volcanic crater. Of course the only thing that ever erupted in this area was an occasional Saturday night saloon brawl. Volcano's flower bloomed and faded quickly. Placer and later hydraulic mines soon played out, and within ten years, most of the population had left in search of more golden pastures.

One can explore the town's weathered remnants in an hour or two, strolling along streets with names like Clapboard, Consolation and Plug. The few surviving stone buildings house a curio store or two, including Little Shamrock Gifts of Nature in the 1853 Sin Kee store, and the Glory Hole, which sells books, giftwares and antiques and serves as the town's information center. Appropriate to Volcano's past, one of the ancient buildings has been converted into the Cobblestone Theatre, where a local drama group hits the boards.

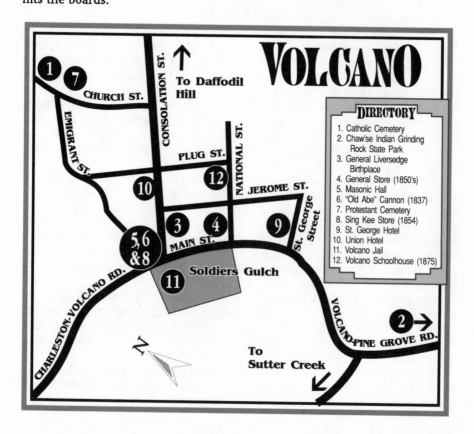

VOLCANO

DIRECTORY

1. Catholic Cemetery
2. Chaw'se Indian Grinding Rock State Park
3. General Liversedge Birthplace
4. General Store (1850's)
5. Masonic Hall
6. "Old Abe" Cannon (1837)
7. Protestant Cemetery
8. Sing Kee Store (1854)
9. St. George Hotel
10. Union Hotel
11. Volcano Jail
12. Volcano Schoolhouse (1875)

Volcano's most imposing structure is its surviving hotel—the three-story balconied St. George. It offers a fine restaurant and overnight lodgings (both reviewed below) and a wonderfully cluttered bar that we've listed in Nuggets above. One of our favorite Volcano hangouts is the general store, built in 1852 and operating continuously since then; it's discussed in more detail under Nuggets above. After exploring Volcano, continue south to Indian Grinding Rock State Park, then return to Jackson. However, instead of following Highway 88, backtrack to Volcano and follow the pretty Sutter Creek-Volcano Road we described under Discoveries above.

Jackson to Ione and Sutter Creek ● *A 40-mile loop trip.* Just north of Jackson, turn left from Highway 49 onto Hoffman Street, which becomes Stony Creek Road and winds down into brushy lowlands. You'll pass Pardee, one of several reservoirs that siphon off the Mother Lode's water to the thirsty San Joaquin Valley and Bay Area.

After ten miles or so, you hit a T-intersection; go left onto Lancha Plana-Buena Vista Road. Beyond the neatly aligned grapevines of Winterbrook Vineyards, the country assumes a New England look, with kelly green pastures, small creeks shaded by overhanging oaks, and distant wooded ridge lines. At a four-way stop, you may like to pause for a light beer at Buena Vista Saloon and Store, which is considerably more saloon than store. The only survivor of the community of Buena Vista, it's a weathered fieldstone structure built in 1860. We like this old pub, with its plank wood floor, elbow-worn bar and hunting trophies on the walls.

Continuing on Buena Vista Road, cross Highway 88 and follow signs to the former town of Bedbug. The present name is somewhat more appealing: Ione. It has the look of a Mother Lode town, with false front stores and the oldstyle Ione Hotel, supported by Doric columns.

However, this is a farming valley, and Ione was the vegetable basket for mining towns higher in the foothills. It's rather large for a farming hamlet, with 2,500 residents; not much smaller than Jackson. Iron Ivan, an 85-year-old Baldwin steam locomotive, sits in a small park beside city hall. Between 1937 and 1956, this black and silver chuffer ran on the 12-mile-long Amador Central Railroad between Ione and Martell, just north of Jackson. It was one of the shortest rail lines in America.

Beyond Ione, if you think you're seeing a red brick castle in the air, it's merely the main building of the Preston School of Industry. This Romanesque structure was built in the 1890s as the state's first reform school aimed at rehabilitating instead of punishing juvenile offenders. It was condemned in 1960, although more contemporary facilities of the school still function there, so "Preston Castle" is off limits to casual visitors. But you can get a good photo from the parking lot.

From Ione, follow Highway 124 north to its juncture with routes 16 and 49 in the town of Martell. Turn south on 49 and return to Jackson or continue on to Sutter Creek and our next chapter.

DIVERSIONS

Water sports of all sorts ● Several fake lakes in the lower toes of Amador County's foothills lure the boating set: **Camanche Reservoir North Shore**, 2000 Jackson Valley-Camanche Rd., Ione, CA 95640, (209) 763-

5121; **Lake Pardee Reservoir and Marina**, 4900 Stony Creek Rd., Ione, CA 95640, (209) 772-1472; and **Lake Amador**, 7500 Lake Amador Rd., Ione, CA 95640, (209) 274-2625. They offer the usual assortment of fishing, boating, water skiing and such.

National forest lures ● Working our way northward, we've come abreast of yet another national forest, El Dorado, with its usual packet of alpine offerings. For information, see the end of this chapter.

Gold panning vacations ● *Roaring Camp Mining Company P.O. Box 278, Pine Grove, CA 95665; (209) 296-4100. Lodgings $310 a week for one or two people.* Half-day to week-long gold prospecting vacations are offered in the summer at an old mining camp on the Mokelumne River, far down a dusty road from civilization. Prospectors cabins come with "Aladdin lamps" (no electricity), basic furnishings and shared baths. Light meals are available at a saloon and snack bar. The retreat features swimming, fishing, cookouts and other activities. The main amusement is gold panning, and the firm has 14 miles of river under lease, where guests can try their luck sloshing and swirling.

Promoters take a bit of license in hinting that this was the site of Bret Harte's *Luck of Roaring Camp.* Young Bret invented that name, along with Poker Flat. But it's a nice woodsy place offering a comfortable facsimile of a gold prospecting experience.

Wine tasting ● *Greenstone Winery, Highway 88 at Jackson Valley Road, Ione, CA 95640; (209) 274-2238. Wednesday-Sunday 10 to 4.* This attractive French country style winery crowns a slope just off Highway 88, a couple of miles below Ione.

GOLD COUNTRY DINING

The Balcony ● ∆∆ $$
164 Main St., Jackson; (209) 223-2855. Continental; dinners $14 to $16; wine and beer. Lunch Wednesday-Friday 11 to 2:30, dinner Wednesday-Saturday 5 to 9 and Sunday 4 to 8, closed Monday-Tuesday. Reservations recommended. MC/VISA. Stylish restaurant balconied over Jackson's historic Main Street, decorated with Elvis Presley memorabilia. The versatile menu wanders from stuffed sole and scampi Napoleon to roast pork grand meuniere to peppercorn steak.

Buscaglia's ● ∆∆ $$
1218 Jackson Gate Rd., Jackson; (209) 223-9992. Italian-American; moderate; full bar. Lunch Wednesday-Friday 11:30 to 2, dinner Wednesday-Saturday from 4:30 and Sunday from noon; closed Monday and Tuesday. Reservations essential on weekends; MC/VISA. One of two longtime Jackson Gate restaurants, dating from 1916. It has a modern interior with candle-lit tables, offering little hint of its historic past as a miner's boarding house. The menu is standard Italian. Our own experiences and comments by others suggest that service is attentive, portions are ample but the food is uneven. *Al dente* pastas are the best things on the menu.

Mel and Faye's Diner ● ∆ $ ∅
Highways 49 and 88, Jackson; (209) 223-0853. American graffiti; dinners $7 to $10; wine and beer. Daily 5 a.m. to 10 p.m. No credit cards. This is

where folks in Jackson goes for that quick burger, a filling breakfast and an inexpensive dinner, served in an old fashioned American diner setting. Menu wanders from steaks and "moo-burgers" to crisp salads, good fries and honest desserts. Non-smoking tables.

Mike's Inn • △△ $

1555 N. Highway 49, Martell; (209) 223-0306. Mexican-American; dinners $7 to $10; wine and beer. Monday, Wednesday and Thursday 11 to 2:30 and 4:30 to 9, Friday-Saturday 11 to 10, closed Tuesday. MC/VISA. Typical Mexican fare served in a simple and comely colonial style restaurant with iron grillwork and Spanish arches. Not historic but on the site of the 1860s Ryan's Station hotel and stage stop. Mexican dishes—enchiladas, burritos, taquitos and such—are quite tasty although the more complex items such as *carne asada* are rather unpredictable.

DIRECTORY

1. Baptist Church (1877)
2. Catholic Church (1877)
3. Heirloom (1863)
4. Hotel Ione (1910)
5. Howard Park
6. Ione Cemetery (1852)
7. "Iron Ivan" locomotive
8. Methodist-Episcopal Church (1862)
9. Preston Castle (1890)
10. Sinclair House (1863)
11. Stewart Store (1856)

Rosebud's Classic Cafe • ΔΔ $$ ∅

26 Main St., Jackson; (209) 223-2358. American; dinners $8 to $12; wine and beer. Open daily: breakfast 6 to noon, lunch noon to 5 and dinner 5 to 9 (until 10 on Friday and Saturday). MC/VISA. An honest American cafe serving palatable food at reasonable prices. Typical chicken and chops fare, plus specials such as vegetable lasagna; espresso, cappuccino and Mother Lode wines featured. The cafe has a simple diner look, with black and white vinyl floors, Gold Country photos and old fashioned coffee cans and food containers. Non-smoking area.

St. George Hotel • ΔΔΔ $$

P.O. Box 9, Volcano; (209) 296-4458. American-Continental; prix fixe dinner $10.50; full bar service. Breakfast 8:30 to noon Saturday and Sunday; single-seating dinners by advance reservation only at 7 p.m. Wednesday and Thursday and 8 p.m. Friday and Saturday; regular dinners 3 to 7 Sunday; closed Monday and Tuesday. Reservations essential. MC/VISA.

My conversation with Sara, the cook and waitress, went like this:

"Don't I get a menu?"

"No, you get chicken."

"Chicken?"

"Why yes. It's Sunday, isn't it?"

You don't get a choice at the St. George Hotel dining room; you get Sarah's excellent cooking—whatever she's decided to prepare that night. For a mere $10.95, we got half a chicken cooked in a tasty cream sherry sauce, a pound or two of spaghetti and a piping hot roll, along with the usual accompaniments. The pleasant hotel dining room has a proper yesteryear look with lace its lace curtains, paintings of old Volcano and neat white tablecloths.

Teresa's • ΔΔ $$

1235 Jackson Gate Rd., Jackson; (209) 223-1786. Italian-American; $7.50 to $12.50; full bar service. Lunch Monday-Tuesday and Friday-Saturday 11 to 2, dinner Monday-Tuesday 5 to 8:30, Friday-Saturday 5 to 9 and Sunday 2 to 8, closed Wednesday-Thursday. MC/VISA. This is the other venerable Jackson Gate Italian restaurant, in business since 1921. Note that it's open on days when neighbor Buscaglia's is closed, and visa versa. Teresa's is a former miners' boarding house divided into several small dining rooms with tulip lamps, scalloped curtains and patterned wallpaper. Generous portions of typical Italian fare which, like neighbor Buscaglia's, can range from tasty to awful. Fast, efficient and furiously noisy service; it's a jovial family place that borders on chaos during busy nights. Oldstyle smoky bar up front.

Is there life after dark?

Liveliest spot in Jackson is the **National Hotel Saloon**, offering everything from banjo and bluegrass to Dixieland on Friday and Saturday night. **Buscaglia's** at Jackson Gate offers music for dancing Fridays and Saturdays. T he **Volcano Pioneer Community Theatre** group has a season of contemporary comedy and drama at the Cobblestone Theatre in Volcano; call (209) 223-HOME or write: Volcano Pioneers Community Theatre, P.O. Box 88, Volcano, CA 95689.

LODGINGS

Bed & breakfast inns and historic hotels

Ann Marie's Country Inn • △△△ $$$$ ØØ

410 Stasal St., Jackson, CA 95642; (209) 223-1452. Doubles from $75. Five rooms, three with private and two with share baths. Full breakfast. No smoking. MC/VISA, DISC. Early American antiques create a homey rural atmosphere in this 1892 Victorian home. Each room has an Americana theme: a wedding ring quilt on the wall of the Wilson Room, where guests are invited to add their own stitches; an antique Singer sewing machine in the Sewing Room; a collection of dolls and figurines in the Doll Room and a sturdy Eastlake wooden bed in the Miner's Room. A garden cottage is warmed by a wood-burning pot-bellied stove. Arriving guests can relax on the front porch with a glass of wine.

Court Street Inn • △△△ $$$$ ØØ

215 Court St., Jackson, CA 95642; (209) 223-0416. Doubles $75 to $125, singles $65 to $115. Seven rooms, four with private baths. Full breakfast. MC/VISA. Listed on the national register of historic places, this 1870 beauty has been artfully restored and furnished with American and European antiques. Two of the individually decorated rooms and a two-bedroom cottage have fireplaces and all have TV. Rimmed by rose gardens and patios, this attractive B&B is near downtown Jackson's shops and historic sites. Guests are served *hors d'oeuvres* in the inviting parlor.

Gate House Inn • △△△ $$$$ ØØ

1330 Jackson Gate Rd., Jackson, CA 95642; (209) 223-3500. Doubles from $75. Four units in main house and a separate two-room Summerhouse, all with private baths. Full breakfast. No smoking. MC/VISA, DISC. Innkeepers Stan and Bev Smith offer an impeccably maintained B&B in this ornate yellow Queen Anne home in the Jackson Gate area. Much of the Victorian decor is original—even the wallpaper in some rooms. Intricately patterned oak parquet floors, Italian marble and oak staircase add special touches of elegance. Spacious grounds, open porches, a swimming pool and a ping pong table offer guests plenty of leisure choices. The slender Victorian sits atop a knoll, offering guests pleasant views of the Jackson Gate countryside.

The Heirloom • △△△ $$$ Ø

P.O. Box 322 (214 Shakeley Lane), Ione, CA 95640; (209) 274-4468. Doubles $53 to $85, singles $48 to $80. Six units, four private and two share baths. Full breakfast. Smoking OK in some areas. No credit cards. This "petite Colonial mansion" with plantation columns and a second story gallery was built in 1863. Main house guest rooms are color keyed to the four seasons, furnished with family heirlooms. An unusual grass-roofed rammed earth cottage provides two additional rooms, one with country style furnishings, the other with a curious blend of early American furniture and Brazilian art. Focal point of the main house is a 150-year-old rosewood piano owned by Gold Rush entertainer Lola Montez. Guests are greeted with lemonade or tea and snacks. Innkeepers Patricia Cross and Melisande Hubbs are particularly noted for their breakfast crepes and souffles.

National Hotel • △ $$
2 Water St. (at the foot of Main), Jackson, CA 95642; (209) 223-0500. Doubles from $42 with bath, $25 without. Thirty-five rooms, some private and some share baths. Smoking OK. MC/VISA. The rooms are minimally furnished, and some of the mattresses sag a bit, but you can sleep with history for a modest price. Earlier guests include Presidents Garfield and Hoover, Will Rogers and John Wayne. The original Louisiana House hotel was built on this site in 1849. After assorted burnings and rebuildings, it became the National Hotel in 1919 (see Nuggets listing above).

St. George Hotel • △△ $$ ø
P.O. Box 9 (16104 Volcano-Pine Grove Road), Volcano, CA 95689. Doubles from $39. Twenty rooms, 14 share baths, six private. Full breakfast. No smoking or pets in the main building; OK in the annex. MC/VISA. When it was built in 1862, the St. George was one of the most opulent hotels in *La Veta Madre*. It's not completely refurbished, but it's clean, tidy and wears its age well. Rooms are simply furnished and comfortable, and those in the adjacent Annex have private baths. A scattering of antiques add yesterday accents to the hotel. We particularly like the large lobby with its big, friendly fireplace. The **dining room** is listed above.

Volcano Inn • △△ $$$
P.O. Box 4 (St. George and Jerome streets), Volcano, CA 95689; (209) 296-4959. Doubles $50 to $60, singles $30 to $40. Three rooms in the main house, one private and two share baths, plus a rustic cottage with a full kitchen and bath, from $75. No credit cards. Family antiques such as a 300-year-old clock and four-poster bed accent this cozy 1946 small-town Americana home. It's nestled between towering pine trees and a cheerful creek in "downtown" Volcano. Guests can relax with a welcoming glass of wine in the New England style parlor before an intriguing "sampler" stone fireplace made of chunks of mariposite, quartz, granite and other minerals. The cottage, which has a similar fireplace, is not particularly fancy, but it's a pleasant retreat built right over the creek. An ideal family cottage or ski chalet, it sleeps up to eight.

The Wedgewood Inn • △△△ $$$$ øø
11941 Narcissus Rd., Jackson, CA 95642; (800) 933-4393 or (209) 296-4300. Doubles $80 to $110, singles $70 to $100. Five rooms plus a carriage house, all with private baths. Full breakfast. No smoking. MC/VISA, DISC. Vic and Jeannine Beltz' strikingly beautiful inn is not a careful restoration, but a new Victorian replica. It thus offers a taste of yesterday with reliable plumbing. This hideaway inn is tucked into a tucked into a secluded wooded lot off Highway 88 just east of Jackson. Rooms are individually decorated, with special touches such as stained glass, needlework and Victorian lace. Guests in the carriage house, which has a wood burning stove, can get acquainted with "Henry," a 1921 Model-T Ford that lives in an adjacent showroom. Complimentary nibbles and beverages are served in the afternoon.

Windrose Inn • △△△ $$$$ øø
1407 Jackson Gate Rd., Jackson, CA 95642; (209) 223-3650. Doubles $75 to $135. Four rooms, all with private baths. Full breakfast. Smoking on the porch or in the garden. MC/VISA. This carefully restored century-old farm-

house sits in a pretty green vale in the Jackson Gate area. A glass solarium, grape arbor, fish pond and gazebo in the carefully tended garden adds special charm to the place. Marv and Sharon Hampton have furnished the rooms with antiques while keeping them bright, cheerful and airy. Afternoon refreshments are served, and guests can relax in the solarium near the English style kitchen, on an arbor-shaded patio or loaf on a hammock beside the fish pond.

Motels

Amador Motel • △ $$

12408 Kennedy Flat Rd., Jackson, CA 95642; (209) 223-0970. Doubles $33 to $39, singles $25; MC/VISA, DISC. A 10-unit motel in the Martell area with TV and a pool. Near the junction of highways 49 and 88.

Best Western Amador Inn • △△ ∅

P.O. Box 758 (200 Highway 49 South), Jackson, CA 95642; (800) 528-1234 or (209) 223-0211. Doubles $60 to $66, kitchens $15 extra, singles $50. Major credit cards. Attractive brick-faced 119-room motel near downtown. TV, room phones; swimming pool. **Restaurant** serves 7 a.m. to 2:30 and 5 to 9:30; American fare; dinners $8 to $14; full bar service.

El Campo Casa Resort Motel • △△ $$ ∅

12548 Kennedy Flat Rd., Jackson, CA 95642; (209) 223-0100. Doubles and singles $37 to $66. Major credit cards. An older, well maintained California Mission style resort hotel on landscaped grounds near highways 49 and 88 junction in the Martell area. TV, pool, playground, barbecues.

Jackson Holiday Lodge • △△ $$

P.O. Box 1147 (highways 49 and 88), Jackson, CA 95642; (209) 223-0486. Doubles $34 to $50, singles 31 to $45, duplex housekeeping cottages $48 to $58. MC/VISA, AMEX. A 36-unit motel in the Martell area with TV movies, room phones; pool.

Linda Vista Motel • △ $$ ∅

10708 N. Highway 49, Jackson, CA 95642; (209) 223-1096. From $35 for two; MC/VISA, DISC. Small motel at the "top of the hill" northwest of Jackson; TV and room refrigerators.

Pine Acres Resort • △ $$

P.O. Box 56, Pine Grove, CA 95665; (209) 296-4650. Motel units and cabins from $34 for two; kitchenettes from $39; MC/VISA.. Basic accommodations in a wooded setting, just off Highway 88. Swimming pool, horse shoe pits, picnic and barbecue area. (See campground listing below.)

CAMPGROUNDS & RV PARKS

Indian Grinding Rock State Historic Park • *On Pine Grove-Volcano Road (P.O. Box 177), Pine Grove, CA 95665. Phone reservations by MISTIX, (800) 444-7275. Twenty-three RV or tent sites, no hookups, $14 in summer and $12 the rest of the year.* Flush toilets; picnic tables and barbecues. Oak-shaded campsites near historic Mi-Wuk village and grinding rock (see Discoveries above). Open all year.

Pine Acres Resort RV Park & Campground • *P.O. Box 56, Pine Grove, CA 95665; (209) 296-4650. Full hookups, $12; tent sites, $8.50.* Flush potties, showers, picnic tables, barbecue areas, swimming, horse shoes and other activities. Wooded setting. Open all year. Gold panning tours, and gold prospecting packages to Roaring Camp (listed above) in summer.

Camanche Reservoir North Shore ● *2000 Jackson Valley-Camanche Rd., Ione, CA 95640; (209) 763-5121. RV and tent sites in several campgrounds overlooking the lake; $11.* Flush potties, showers, laundry, grocery store, service station, water sports (some of these facilities are on the south shore). Open all year.

El Dorado National Forest ● Campgrounds are available in a variety of areas. RV and tent sites. No hookups or showers, pit toilets; most sites have barbecues or fire pits and picnic tables. For a map and list of campgrounds, send $2 to the address listed at the end of this chapter.

Pardee Reservoir ● *4900 Stony Creek Rd., Ione, CA 95640; (209) 772-1472. RV sites with hookups $15, tent and RV sites with no hookups, $11.* Flush potties, showers, marina, store, water sports. Open mid-February to mid-November.

ANNUAL EVENTS

Daffodil Hill blooms, generally in mid-March, above Volcano, (209) 223-0608 or 296-7048.

Chaw'se Native American Art Show, mid-August to late September at Indian Grinding Rock State Park in Pine Grove, (209) 296-7488 or 267-0211. Mi-Wuk arts and crafts.

Ione Melon Festival, late August in Ione; (209) 223-0350; barbecue, games and dancing.

Big Time Indian Days, late September at Indian Grinding Rock, (209) 296-7488; Mi-Wuk games, dances, crafts and foods.

ON THE ROAD AGAIN...TO SUTTER CREEK

We nudged Sutter Creek and its surroundings earlier, on one of our detours from Jackson. For the record, it's a short drive, only three miles north on Highway 49. Pause at a vista point at the hilltop above Jackson for a view of the famous Kennedy mine headframe and distant tailing wheels. A sign there will tell you what you already know, assuming you've read the first part of this chapter.

To learn more...

Amador County Chamber of Commerce, 2048 Highway 88, Suite #3 (P.O. Box 596), Jackson, CA 95642; (800) 649-4988 or (209) 223-0350. The

chamber visitors center is located in the Stockton Savings Building in Amador Plaza shopping center, less than half a mile west of Jackson on Highway 88; it's open weekdays from 9 to 5.

Amador Ranger Station, El Dorado National Forest, Star Route 3, Pioneer, CA 95666; (209) 295-4251. For a national forest map listing campsites and recreational facilities, send $2 to: Forest Supervisor, El Dorado National Forest, 100 Forni Rd., Placerville, CA 95667.

"I located the camp on Sutter Creek, and thought I should be there alone. (But) three or four traveling grog shops surrounded me. Then, of course, the gold was taken (by my men) to these places for drinking, gambling etc., and the following day they were sick and unable to work. I found that it was high time to quit this kind of business and lose no more time and money."

— John Sutter

Chapter Eleven

SUTTER CREEK & BEYOND

Northern Amador County's gold-gathering hamlets

SUTTER CREEK'S MAIN STREET

The great irony of the California Gold Rush is that it ruined the man whose lumber mill started it all. John Sutter was one of the wealthiest men in the state before his construction foreman James Marshall discovered gold in the tailrace of his Coloma mill. Sutter's wealth had come from agriculture, lumbering and land speculation. His California empire, rather loosely assembled, crumbled as his workers fled to the gold fields.

In late 1848, he gathered a group of Hawaiian servants and Indian workers and began mining along the creek where he had established a lumbering camp earlier. But Sutter was no gold miner. His men drank and gambled what little they found and he gave up in disgust.

Several camps grew up near the Amador County creek bearing Sutter's name. Among the survivors are Sutter Creek, Amador City, Drytown, Plymouth and Fiddletown. None enjoyed the flamboyant fame of places like Hangtown, Mok Hill and Columbia. Today, however, three of them—Sutter Creek, Amador and Fiddletown—are among the little jewels of the Gold Country. The county itself has gained fame in recent years for "bottled gold"; its many wineries produce some of the finest Zinfandels and other premium wines in the state.

THE WAY IT WAS • After Sutter stomped away from his namesake creek in disgust, the settlement continued to grow, but slowly. Placer mining was poor, as Sutter discovered, so the town became more of a provisioning center. Then in the early 1850s, riches were found beneath the earth and the area produced its share of millionaires, including one of California's most famous citizens.

A young merchant named Leland Stanford was given a share of Sutter Creek's Lincoln Mine as payment for one of his customer's debts. He worked the mine for months with no success and was on the verge of selling out, but his foreman, Robert Downs, talked him out of it. Shortly thereafter, they hit a big vein and Stanford's fortune was made. He sold his interest in the mine for $400,000 and went on to become a railroad baron, state senator, governor and founder of one of America's great universities.

With the advent of hardrock mining, the fortunes of Sutter Creek and neighboring Amador City, Drytown and Plymouth continued to rise. Sutter Creek's Central Eureka Mine, whose tailings can still be seen at the south end of town, proved to be one of the richest gold mines in California. And it was one of the longest-operating, finally closing down in 1958. This wealth allowed Sutter Creek to line its main street with handsome brick and stone buildings in the 1890s. These survive today to create one of the Mother Lode's most attractive towns.

Neighboring Amador City was named for Mexican rancher Jose Amador, who mined without success here in 1848. Then four former men of the cloth came along in 1851, found a rich quartz vein and the place was dubbed

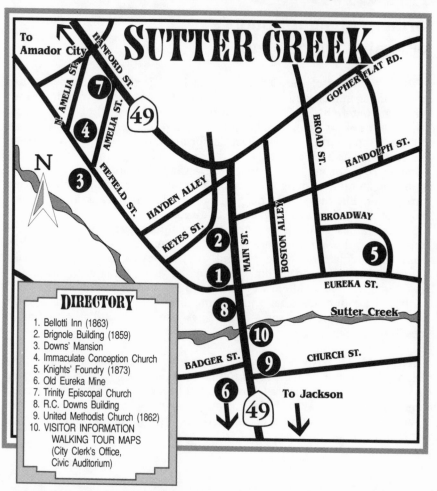

SUTTER CREEK

To Amador City

HANFORD ST.
N. AMELIA ST.
AMELIA ST.
49
FIEFIELD ST.
N
HAYDEN ALLEY
KEYES ST.
MAIN ST.
BOSTON ALLEY
BROAD ST.
GOPHER FLAT RD.
RANDOLPH ST.
BROADWAY
EUREKA ST.
Sutter Creek
BADGER ST.
CHURCH ST.
To Jackson
49

DIRECTORY

1. Bellotti Inn (1863)
2. Brignole Building (1859)
3. Downs' Mansion
4. Immaculate Conception Church
5. Knights' Foundry (1873)
6. Old Eureka Mine
7. Trinity Episcopal Church
8. R.C. Downs Building
9. United Methodist Church (1862)
10. VISITOR INFORMATION
    WALKING TOUR MAPS
    (City Clerk's Office,
    Civic Auditorium)

Minister's Gulch. (Historians put the apostrophe in the wrong place.) Like Sutter Creek, the town became immensely wealthy through deep-shaft mining; the Keystone Mine produced $24 million between 1853 and 1942.

Drytown was named for the lack of water in its creeks, not the lack of booze in its bars. The oldest town in the county, it was settled by homesteaders as early as 1845. The discovery of gold brought it into prominence in 1848, but placer diggins gave out within 11 years and fire added a final insult, leveling most of the town in 1858. It was not the beneficiary of a major deep pit mine.

Oddly, little is known about the beginnings of Amador County's northernmost city. The twin gold camps of Pokerville and Plymouth were established around 1852, and today's Plymouth more resembles a sleepy farming community than a mining town. The look isn't deceiving, for it plodded along as a minor provisioning center until the Plymouth Consolidated Mines finally brought significant wealth in the 1880s.

Meanwhile, farther up in the foothills, a group of Missouri prospectors joked that their younger members were "always fiddlin' around," which gave the woodsy gold camp of Fiddletown its colorful name. A later arrival said he couldn't find a violin in the whole town, so its founders must have had a different kind of fiddlin' in mind.

Unlike the hardrock camps of Amador County's lowlands, Fiddletown was a rich placer mining area, with the attendant explosive growth, hasty shanties and violent saloon brawls. Its population hit 10,000 by the middle 1850s, including one of the largest Chinatowns outside of San Francisco. But with no deep shaft mines to sustain it, most of Fiddletown faded back into the bushes by the 1870s.

THE WAY IT IS ● The four-block business district of Sutter Creek rivals Nevada City's Broad Street as the most appealing thoroughfare in the Mother Lode. Highway 49 traffic is pesky but it fails to distract from the appeal of these false-front stores, strutting down the high sidewalks on thin wooden columns that support their upper balconies. They run the full gamut of Gold Country architecture, from little yellow clapboards to bold brick and sturdy stone, yet the overall effect is one of 19th century uniformity.

The town rests in a wide basin, its tin roofs glinting among the trees. Highway 49 becomes a pleasant boulevard with a green planter strip as it enters Sutter Creek from the south, then it tucks in its shoulders to pass between the close-knit rows of buildings. In the neighborhoods, proud Victorians stand along narrow streets shaded by magnificent century-old trees.

Amador City is a smaller clone of Sutter Creek, occupying another scenic creek hollow. This tiny town, the smallest incorporated city in California with fewer than 300 citizens, resembles a movie set. Its one-block Gold Rush business district is a rich repository of antique stores. Highway 49 makes an S-turn through the town, leading northbound travelers straight toward the bold brick facade of the Imperial Hotel with its unusual cantilevered balcony.

The farther we go, the smaller they get. Drytown, just beyond Amador City, isn't much larger than the historical monument that tells of its past. Only a handful of stores survive to harbor ghosts of the days when this town certainly wasn't dry. A poster on the Old Well Cafe on the site of the former

Drytown Exchange Hotel talks of times passed:

"The dance floor was slicked down by bales of hay being shoved around, and the dancing lasted until 3 a.m. A collection was taken to pay the Springer and Patton Orchestra, and the revelers headed for home. Four o'clock in summer was coming daylight, and the fellows who came in from the ranches barely had time to change their clothes and get out to milk. But they had something to think about—after the ball."

They probably had hangovers, too.

Plymouth does not wear its age well. Only a few Gold Rush buildings survive, and most are rather scruffy. The two-tone green Plymouth Hotel is in urgent need of restoration and many businesses along Main Street are closed. The street is perpendicular to Highway 49 and is therefore spared its traffic, but this only makes Plymouth look even more forlorn. Marble mausoleums in the weedy cemetery above the town speak of more prosperous times.

However, Plymouth offers two major attractions. It's the gateway to the Shenandoah Valley, the Mother Lode's major wine producing area, and it's home to the Amador County Fairgrounds, site of assorted special events.

Eight miles up Fiddletown Road from Plymouth, old Fiddletown also looks a bit scruffy. However, it's more of a deliberate scruffiness of a town proud to preserve its past. This venerable village seems to be sprouting from the thicket of locust trees and evergreens that crowd the narrow roadside.

DISCOVERIES

The best attraction

Sutter Creek Walking Tour ● The Amador County Chamber of Commerce back in Jackson handles the county's promotional chores, so there's no chamber here. However, you can pick up copies of a walking tour map at the tiny city clerk's office in Sutter Creek's cavernous city auditorium and from some local merchants. It will guide you past the town's wonderful collection of Gold Rush buildings. Strolling along the high cement sidewalk— so steep in places that it abruptly breaks into short flights of steps—you can learn the vintage of every building along Main Street.

The route then takes you into residential areas, past fine old homes that look like they've been brought in from New England, or maybe San Francisco. At Hanford Street (North Highway 49) and Amador Road, note the plaque marking the main shaft of the Lincoln mine, where Stanford began his fortune. The walking tour map also pinpoints the mansion of Robert Downs, the mine foreman who talked Stanford into sticking around.

The rest

Knights Foundry ● *81 Eureka St., Sutter Creek, CA 95685; (209) 267-5543.* The only water-powered foundry in America, Knights has been operating since 1873. If this conjures visions of an old moss-covered water wheel running the factory's machinery, it isn't quite that romantic. High pressure piped-in water makes the foundry wheels spin. Castings are usually poured every Friday afternoon (so they'll have the weekend to cool), and folks can watch through the door—as long as they stay at a safe distance.

It's a fascinating process to observe. As the furnace is opened, a shower

Sutter Creek's 19th century buildings occupy one of the Gold Country's more picturesque settings in a tree-shrouded valley.

of sparks flares into the dimly lit foundry like a thousand fireflies, and a gleaming orange trickle of molten iron flows into a heavy cauldron. Suspended from a crane, the glowing bucket is guided by workmen to graphite-lined molds. The fiery liquid is poured into the molds as easily as one might pour syrup on a waffle—except this syrup would burn all the way to the basement.

Sutter Creek and Amador City antique and gift shops ● These two towns are meccas for shoppers and browsers. Even though I hate to shop, I found myself walking slow motion down their cluttered, intriguing aisles. Here are some particularly noteworthy ones.

In Sutter Creek: **Sutter Creek Fine Art** at 35 Main St., brims with artwork, mostly from contemporary Mother Lode artists; **Creekside Unusual Shops and Antiques** across the street, is a gathering of several shops under one roof; **Lizzie Ann's** at 59 Main features giftwares and an extensive assortment of collectibles; **The Squirrel's Nest** at 60 Main St., features collectible critters, gourmet kitchenware and giftwares; **Columbian Lady,** 61 Main St., a bold dark gray Colonial style building with ornate trim, offers early American antiques. A block north, the **Amador County Arts Council Gallery** at 71 Main displays works of local artists and crafts people.

In Amador City: **Country Living** in an 1960 red brick building features American country crafts; **A Tisket A-Tasket Basket Shop** needs no elaboration; **Amador Hollow** features antiques and dried flowers, as does **Amador City Antiques & Dry Flowers**; and **Barbara's Antiques & Collectibles** offers just what the name says.

Nuggets

Bellotti Inn ● *53 Main St., Sutter Creek.* We don't rave about its rooms (which are a bit basic) nor its restaurant (which is all right but not awesome). This is a nugget because of its curious mansard roof and odd marquee front, an incongruous but not unpleasant figure along Sutter Creek's row of classic Gold Rush facades. It started life as the American Exchange Hotel in 1854, then was rebuilt in 1867 and the curious mansard roof was added in 1897.

Buffalo Chips Emporium • *Highway 49, Amador City; (209) 267-0570. Light lunches and desserts daily from 9 to 5.* This old fashioned ice cream parlor and snack shop dishes up one of the best slices of hot rhubarb pie a la mode we've ever tasted. The decor is simple and fun: dozens of collector Coca-Cola trays, pictures and posters, assorted other regalia and a big old red and green jukebox. Naturally, it has a marble-topped serving counter.

Chew Kee Store • *Main street in Fiddletown. Saturday noon to 4.* This is a rarity, one of a few rammed earth adobes still surviving in California. Although thousands of adobes were built and hundreds remain, nearly all were made of adobe bricks. Chew Kee Store, built in 1850, sheltered the home, office and shop of an herbalist named Dr. Yee. It now houses a small museum, with a collection of Oriental artifacts. Hours are limited but the exterior is certainly worth a look. With walls two and a half feet thick, it was a structure ahead of its time, since rammed earth is now vogue for some energy-conscious home builders.

Fiddletown General Store • *Main Street in Fiddletown.* Looking just the way a general store should look with a wonderful melèe of merchandise, this sturdy structure claims to be the oldest continuously operating general mercantile in California. It has been peddling possibles since 1850.

Shenandoah Valley Museum • *At Sobon Estate Winery, 14430 Shenandoah Rd., Plymouth; (209) 245-6554. Daily 10 to 5.* The valley's yesterdays are preserved in this tidy museum housed in one of the old earth and stone buildings of the 1856 D'Agostini Winery. Exhibits focus on the Gold Rush, Shenandoah Valley pioneers and early wine production.

DETOUR

Plymouth to Fiddletown and the Shenandoah Valley • *A 20-mile loop trip.* We'll assume that you've puttered your way slowly northward on Highway 49, pausing in Amador City and Drytown, and you're now sitting on Main Street in Plymouth.

Head east on Main Street across Highway 49 onto Fiddletown Road. The route soon splits; remain on Fiddletown Road by taking the right fork (which is actually straight ahead). You're now passing through a pleasant pastorale of pasturelands and ancient oaks overhanging the highway.

No sign announces that you've arrived in Fiddletown, but the presence of Gold Rush buildings sleeping under a canopy of oaks and Trees of Heaven suggests that you've arrived *somewhere*. And that giant fiddle hanging from the community hall confirms your suspicion.

You can park your car and walk its entire length in a couple of minutes, or you can browse about for a couple of hours. Looking pleasantly out of place for such a funky old town is the neatly groomed Fiddletown Ostrom-McLean Park with a tennis court, basketball court, lawn area, kids playground and picnic tables. The Chew Kee Store we described in Nuggets is adjacent to the park.

A couple of wagons are parked along the road, as if the teams have just been unhitched and trotted into the livery stable. Up American Flat Road, an old white school house with green trim sits among the trees. Its bell is intact and a pot-bellied stove still sits inside, awaiting students that don't come anymore. Across the street, a cemetery climbs a steep, wooded slope. Back in front of Fiddletown General Store, several residents sit in the sun, enjoying a beer and one another's lies.

After poking about this wonderfully seedy old place, go left onto Tyler Road at the east end of town, cross a bridge, take an immediate left, drive a couple of blocks and then fork right onto Ostrom Road.

You soon top a rise and see a vineyard, a clue to your next destination, the winelands of Shenandoah Valley. Although our driving route doesn't take you past all the area's many wineries, you can pick up a proper map at the first winery you encounter. Or, contact the Amador Vintners Association listed at the end of this chapter.

Our route continues through a pleasant oak thicket, interrupted here and there by meadows and more vinelands. After less than three miles, you'll hit a stop sign at Plymouth-Shenandoah Road. Turn right and drive a few blocks to Sobon Estate Winery. Although the valley is relatively new as a major wine producing area, this facility has been here since the Gold Rush, founded in 1856 as D'Agostini Winery. Its ancient wine cellar now houses

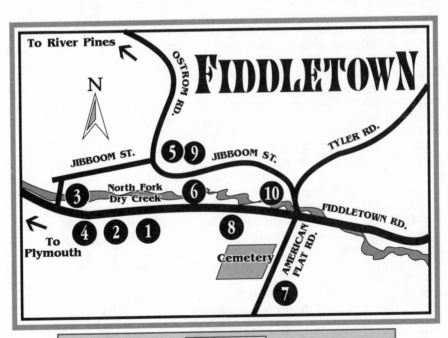

DIRECTORY

1. Atkison Store
2. Blacksmith Shop
3. Chew Kee Store/Museum (1850's)
4. Chinese gambling hall (1850s)
5. Farnham House (1850's)
6. Fiddletown Community Hall
7. Fiddletown School (1863)
8. General Store (1850's)
9. Head House (1865)
10. Schallhorne Building (1870)

the Shenandoah Valley Museum, which we listed above in Nuggets.

From Sobon Estate, continue east on E-16 to River Pines, a tiny town on the edge of the Sierra pine belt. It offers a general store, service station and a few homes nestled among the conifers. You can complete a loop by veering right onto Omo Ranch Road, left onto Fairplay Road and left again onto Mount Aukum Road. This returns you to Plymouth-Shenandoah Road to finish your circuit. There's nothing scenically awesome on this loop, but the mix of oak and pine groves and occasional meadows are pleasant. Three wineries, listed in the next chapter because they're in El Dorado County, are off Fairplay.

Driving back toward Plymouth, if you've armed yourself with an Amador County Wine Country map, you can sip the products of several local vintners. Most are off Steiner Road and Bell Road. A marker at the junction of Steiner advises you that the valley was settled in 1852; pioneers mined for gold, grew livestock, and planted orchards and some of the state's first vineyards.

DIVERSION

Wine tasting • With so many vintners in the Shenandoah Valley, we're tempted to call this area the Napa Valley of the Mother Lode. However, these are small operations and their tasting rooms are rarely crowded. Some are little more than small family vineyards with a few acres of grapes; others are state-of-the-art, modest-sized operations.

The Sierra Foothills Winery Association and the Amador Vintners Association publish guides to all the wineries, listing locations and tasting room hours. They're available at chambers of commerce and wineries. Association addresses are listed at the end of this chapter.

Amador Foothill Winery, *12500 Steiner Rd., Plymouth, CA 95669; (209) 245-6307. Weekends and most holidays noon to 5; MC/VISA.* State-of-the art facility in a glossy white passive solar structure, with tasting counter on a gallery above the main winery; view picnic area among the vineyards.

Karly Winery, *11076 Bell Rd., Plymouth, CA 95669; (209) 245- 3922. Daily noon to 4; MC/VISA, AMEX.* Combined tasting room and kitchen, noted for fine wines and for tasty nibbles offered to visitors, bunkered into a slope surrounded by vines; small picnic area.

Kenworthy Vineyards, *10120 Shenandoah Rd. (P.O. Box 361), Plymouth, CA 95669; (209) 245-3198. Weekends 10 to 5; MC/VISA.* Modern winery in a weathered wooden barn, with a small tasting room, set in a rustic farmyard; picnic area.

Montevina Winery, *20680 Shenandoah School Rd., Plymouth, CA 95669; (209) 245-6942. Daily 11 to 4; MC/VISA.* Nice Spanish-California complex with a cathedral ceiling tasting room; winery is owned by Napa Valley's Sutter Home; landscaped picnic area.

Santino Winery, *12225 Steiner Rd., Plymouth, CA 95669; (209) 245- 6979. Daily noon to 4:30; MC/VISA.* Spanish California style tasting room in a hollow surrounded by vineyards; guided tours by appointment, for a fee; shaded picnic area.

Shenandoah Vineyards, *12300 Steiner Rd., Plymouth, CA 95669; (209) 245-3698. Daily 10 to 5; MC/VISA.* Modern fieldstone winery on a hill above the vineyards; with a log beam tasting room and art gallery adjacent; small picnic area.

Sobon Estate, *14430 Shenandoah Rd. (mailing address: 12300 Steiner Rd.), Plymouth, CA 95669; (209) 245-6554. Daily 10 to 5; MC/VISA.* Once the historic D'Agostini Winery, purchased by owners of Shenandoah Vineyards; tasting room and deli in one of the ancient winery structures, Shenandoah Valley Museum (see Nuggets) in another; shaded picnic area.

Charles Spinetta Winery and Wildlife Gallery, *12557 Steiner Rd., Plymouth, CA 95669; (209) 245-3384. Tuesday-Sunday 10 to 5; MC/VISA.* Unusual combination of tasting room and wildlife art gallery, with prints of famous artists on sale; also a frame shop; large shaded picnic area.

Story Vineyard, *10525 Bell Rd., Plymouth, CA 95669; (209) 245-6208. Weekends 11 to 5; no credit cards.* Small winery with rustic tasting room perched on the rim of Consumnes River Canyon; valley view picnic area.

GOLD COUNTRY DINING

Bar-T-Bar • ΔΔ $$
Highway 49 (just south of town), Plymouth; (209) 245-3729. Western, primarily barbecue; dinners $8 to $13; full bar service. Daily 11 a.m. to 9 p.m (to 9:30 Friday and Saturday). MC/VISA A likable roadhouse that dishes up hearty fare at modest prices; dinners include soup and salad, potatoes or rice and hot bread. American country decor with warm wood paneling, ceiling fans and maple furnishings.

Bellotti Inn • ΔΔ $$$ Ø
53 Main St., Sutter Creek; (209) 267-5211. Italian-American; dinners $14 to $16; full bar service. Sunday-Monday and Wednesday-Thursday 11:30 to 9, Friday-Saturday 11:30 to 10, closed Tuesday. Reservations accepted; MC/VISA. Gold Rush style restaurant in an historic hotel (see Nuggets above) with attractive although spartan 19th century decor. Usual pastas plus specials such as breast of chicken Parmesan, calamari steak and some American steak and prime rib dishes. Huge dinners, including soup and salad, pasta and ice cream. Past dining experiences have been uneven, ranging from outstanding to awful. Non-smoking tables available.

Imperial Hotel Restaurant • ΔΔΔ $$$
Main Street, Amador City; (209) 267-9172. Continental; dinners $11.50 to $17.50, full bar service. Nightly 5 to 9, Sunday brunch 10 to 2. Reservations accepted; major credit cards. Smart new restaurant in an 1879 brick Gold Country classic. High backed fabric chairs, ceiling fans and white nappery in the stylish little dining room. Menu items include filet Diane, pork loin in rhubarb sauce, bleu cheese chicken, prawn and scallop scampi and several low fat/low cholesterol entrées. Attractive oldstyle saloon adjacent to dining room.

Old Well Cafe • Δ $
15947 Highway 49, Drytown; (209) 245-6467. American, dinners $6.50 to $10, wine and beer. Daily 7 a.m. to 8 p.m. No credit cards. Basic family cafe with Naugahyde and vinyl decor. Menu includes such yesterday staples as chicken fried steak and liver and onions. Certainly not gourmet, but good, honest food for the price.

Pelargonium • ΔΔΔ $$$ ∅∅
#1 Hanford St. (Highway 49 North), Sutter Creek; (209) 267-5008. Contemporary cuisine; dinners $13 to $19; wine and beer. Dinner Monday-Friday 5:30 to 9, closed Sunday. Reservations accepted. No credit cards. This eye-appealing restaurant in a Victorian house is all gussied up in geranium wallpaper and Americana frills. The food presentations are pretty as well, with artfully-assembled entrées and cute little patterns in soups and salads. Locally popular place, offering a daily-changing menu with enrèes such as gallantine of chicken, pork loin, crepes Florentine and red snapper almondine.

Sutter Creek Palace • ΔΔΔΔ $$$ ∅
76 Main St., Sutter Creek; (209) 267-9852. American; dinners $11 to $15; full bar service. Lunch Friday-Wednesday 11:30 to 3, dinner Friday-Tuesday 5 to 9, closed Wednesday night and all day Thursday. Reservations suggested on weekends; MC/VISA. Sutter Creek's most attractive restaurant; a study in Victorian elegance, housed in an 1896 building that began life, appropriately, as a restaurant and saloon. With stained glass panels and polished woods, little has changed, except in the menu, which is decidedly modern. Entreès include tournedos of beef, calamari almondine, wine country scallops and such. Remarkably consistent food and prompt, friendly service; one of our favorite Gold Country restaurants. Non-smoking tables.

Is there life after dark?

There is if you like theater. **The Claypipers,** one of the Mother Lode's oldest and best known melodrama groups, offers presentations of "villainy, skullduggery, love, honor and virtue triumphant" from mid-May through mid-September at the Piper Playhouse in Drytown. Appropriately, the show place is a converted 19th century dance hall. For ticket information, call (209) 245-3812. **Sutter Creek Palace** puts a pianist in the pub on Friday and Saturday night. Otherwise, most folks head south to Jackson or north to Placerville for cocktail lounge entertainment.

LODGINGS

Bed & breakfast inns and an historic hotel

The Culbert House Inn • ⌂⌂⌂ $$$$ ∅∅
10811 Water St. (P.O. Box 54), Amador City, CA 95601; (209) 267-0750. Doubles $80 to $195, singles $75 to $100. Three rooms with private baths. Full breakfast. No smoking. MC/VISA. Located near the Shenandoah Valley wine country, this 1860s country estate with a plantation style porch is a pretty vision in French country style antiques. Brass, wicker and blue and white French *etoile* fabrics offer cheerful touches to the stylishly done rooms. Guests are served snacks and beverages before the fire in late afternoon, often with a tasting of local wines. The Culbert House was built in the 1860s by an engineer for the nearby Keystone Mine, then purchased and expanded by Charles Culbert, prominent citizen, county clerk and owner of 30,000 acres.

The Foxes • ⌂⌂⌂ $$$$ ∅∅
77 Main St. (P.O. Box 159), Sutter Creek, CA 95685; (209) 267-5882. Doubles from $95. Six rooms, all with private baths. Full breakfasts. No smok-

ing. MC/VISA, DISC. This foxy bed and breakfast, occupying a beautiful 19th century home, sitting in a nicely landscaped garden off Sutter Creek's Main Street, is the Gold Country's most elegant, impeccably appointed inn. Pete and Min Fox and have created a 19th century vision of opulence in this 1857 Greek Revival home. Each room is color coordinated from wallpaper to drapes to chair coverings; half-canopied beds and massive armoires complete a vision of old European elegance. And good grief, the foxes! Everywhere you look, hundreds of little foxes—in figurines, old prints, Jim Beam jugs, throw pillows, antique clock frames and carvings. In the Fox Room, you're greeted with a realistic stuffed fox, all curled up and keeping your pillow warm; a stream of foxes chase around the room on a wallpaper frieze.

Gold Quartz Inn ● ⌂⌂⌂ $$$$ ØØ

15 Bryson Dr., Sutter Creek, CA 95685; (800) 752-8738 or (209) 267-9155. Doubles $75 to $125. Twenty-four rooms, all with TV and private baths. Full breakfast. Smoking on porch only. MC/VISA, AMEX. This is one of the Gold Country's most appealing inns—brand new and modern, with a "Victorian farmhouse" look that's right at home in Sutter Creek. Rooms are large with distinctive color coordinated Victorian decor, yet they feature modern touches such as tucked-away TV sets, phones, individually controlled heat and hair dryers. Other amenities include afternoon tea, complimentary beverages, a courtesy laundry and concierge services. The inn is equipped with an elevator and full facilities for the handicapped.

Hanford House ● ⌂⌂⌂ $$$ ØØ

P.O. Box 847 (61 Hanford St.), Sutter Creek, CA 95685; (209) 267-0747. Doubles $60 to $85 Sunday-Thursday and $75 to $110 weekends and holidays. Nine rooms, all with private baths. Continental breakfast. No smoking. MC/VISA, DISC. Jim and Lucille Jacobus have expanded a 1920 Spanish stucco cottage into a stately two-story brick mansion. The exterior brick has an almost severe look, but a handsome inn dwells within. It's an appealing blend of today and yesterday, with country furnishings accented by early California antiques and several Spanish mission era pieces. The bedrooms have coordinated drapes and bedspreads, with pine armoires and headboards to carry out the simple refinement of the country theme. Where the Foxes have foxes, Jim and Lucille have bears—perched on bedspreads, smiling down from shelves, occupying chairs. More whimsy: the "guest register" is on the walls and ceilings of the dining room. Two walls are full and signatures are now working across the ceiling. Incidentally, the Hanford House offers full wheelchair access.

Imperial Hotel ● ⌂⌂⌂ $$$ Ø

Main Street (P.O. Box 195), Amador City, CA 95601; (209) 267-9172. Doubles $75 to $90. Six rooms with private baths. Expanded continental breakfast. No smoking in rooms; smoking OK in common areas. Major credit cards. Closed for decades, this oldstyle two-story brick hotel at the end of Amador's main street re-opened as a hotel and restaurant in 1988. Individually decorated upstairs rooms are bright and sunny, set with a mix of antique and modern furniture. The old fashioned bar has been carefully restored by new owners Bruce Sherrill and Dale Martin, and the **restaurant** (listed above) has been earning good notices.

Indian Creek • ⌂⌂ $$$ ØØ

21950 Highway 49, Plymouth, CA 95669; (800) 24-CREEK or (209) 245-4648. Doubles $45 to $95, singles $40 to $90. Four rooms, two private and two share baths. Continental breakfast. No smoking. MC/VISA, DISC. This large log home was built in 1932 by a Hollywood producer and was known locally as the John Wayne House because the Duke supposedly partied here. It's an impressive structure reminiscent of some of the grand national park lodges, with cathedral ceilings, a two-story quartz fireplace and wood floors. Guest rooms off a second floor balcony are furnished with an mix of early American pine and European antiques with Southwestern and Oriental accents. The inn is tucked into a wooded glen three miles north of Plymouth.

Mine House Inn • ⌂⌂ $$$

14125 Highway 49 (P.O. Box 245), Amador City, CA 95601; (209) 267-5900. Doubles $55 to $65, singles $50 to $60. Eight rooms, all with private baths. Continental breakfast. Smoking OK. No credit cards. This 1880 office building for the Keystone Mine has been cleverly converted into a comfortable inn, nicely furnished with Gold Rush era antiques. Owners Peter and Ann Marie Daubenspeck have shown considerable ingenuity in retaining the original appearance of the rooms while transforming them to B&B units. In the Mill Grinding Room, for instance, shaft supports for machinery that pulverized ore for assaying are still in place. The massive vault door and heavy safe are part of the Vault Room, and the Directors Room retains its 13-foot ceiling, and a fireplace that marks the luxury enjoyed by mine owners. A swimming pool is open from May to October.

Sutter Creek Inn • ⌂⌂ $$$ ØØ

P.O. Box 385 (75 Main St.), Sutter Creek, CA 95685; (209) 262-5606. Doubles from $55. Nineteen units, all with private baths. Full breakfast. Smoking and non-smoking rooms. No credit cards. Despite its many units, there's no feeling of congestion in this huge 1859 country estate. Guests can seek out a quiet nook in the large garden, relax on the lawn or browse through a magazine in the living room. The rooms—many with fireplaces—are located in the Greek Revival main house and in several outbuildings on the extensive grounds. Furnishings are a mix of European and American antiques. The Roosevelts and Salingers have been entertained at this large country estate. Today's guests are served afternoon drinks and snacks.

Motels

Old Well Motel • ⌂ $$

Highway 49 (P.O. Box 187), Drytown, CA 95699; (209) 245-6467. Doubles from $32 to $40; MC/VISA. Rustic cabin type rooms with TV; swimming pool, picnic grounds, gold panning in nearby creek.

Shenandoah Inn • ⌂⌂ $$$

17674 Village Dr. (on Highway 49), Plymouth, CA 95669; (800) 542-4549 or (209) 245-3888. Doubles $55 to $65, singles $50 to $55. Major credit cards. Attractive Spanish-style 47-room inn located on a knoll just outside of Plymouth. Large rooms with Southwestern decor, TV movies and phones. Landscaped grounds with pool and spa. Situated on the edge of the Shenandoah Valley wine country.

CAMPGROUNDS & RV PARKS

49er Trailer Village • *Highway 49 and Empire Street (P.O. Box 191), Plymouth, CA 95669; (209) 245-6981. More than 300 RV sites with full hookups, $20 to $25. Reservations accepted; MC/VISA* A full-scale RV resort with flush potties, showers, cable TV hookups, barbecue areas and general store. Other facilities include two pools, pool hall, rec hall, horse shoe pits, volleyball, fish pond and even a beauty parlor, deli and ice cream parlor.

Amador County Fairgrounds • *Plymouth, CA 95669; (209) 245-6921. RV and tent sites, $10 with water and electrical hookups.* Well-kept fairgrounds with two camping areas. Flush potties and showers.

ANNUAL EVENTS

Amador County Wine Festival, late June at the Amador County Fairgrounds, Plymouth, (209) 245-6921; wine tasting and barbecue.

Amador County Fair, late July at the county fairgrounds in Plymouth, (209) 245-6921; displays, food booths, livestock shows, rodeo and such.

Gold Country Jubilee, mid-September at the county fairgrounds, Plymouth, (209) 223-0350; fiddling contest, gold panning and such.

Celebrate the Harvest, early October; open house at Amador County wineries, with grape stomping, barbecues, barrel tastings and such.

ON THE ROAD AGAIN...TO PLACERVILLE

Although we're nearing El Dorado County where it all began, there is curiously little hint of Gold Rush activity on the 22-mile stretch of Highway 49 between Plymouth and old Hangtown—Placerville, if you prefer. However, it's a nice woodsy drive, particularly when you cross the Consumnes River as you enter El Dorado County. The creek-sized Consumnes follows the winding highway for a bit, offering inviting views of its meandering stream bed sheltered by oaks and cottonwoods. It's particularly beautiful in the fall, rivaling the pretty Volcano-to-Sutter Creek route along Sutter Creek.

After hitting a stop sign at the former gold camp of El Dorado, turn right to stay with Highway 49, then descend quickly into the once rowdy mining town that was named for an omelet. Or was it the other way around?

To learn more...

Sutter Creek Business & Professional Association, P.O. Box 600, Sutter Creek, CA 95685. This group produces the walking tour map mentioned above. For details call the city offices at (209) 267-5647.

Amador County Chamber of Commerce, 2048 Highway 88, Suite #3 (P.O. Box 596), Jackson, CA 95642; (800) 649-4988 or (209) 223-0350. Its office is midway between Jackson and Sutter Creek in the Stockton Savings Building in Amador Plaza shopping center, about half a mile west of Highway 49; open weekdays from 9 to 5.

Sierra Foothills Winery Association, P.O. Box 425, Somerset, CA 95684. Send for a free brochure listing wineries of the Shenandoah Valley and other Gold Country regions. A self-addressed, stamped business sized envelope would be appreciated.

Amador Vintners Association, P.O. Box 718, Plymouth, CA 95669; publishes an area winery brochure, available at the chamber and wineries.

"Hangtown gals are plump and rosy,
 Hair in ringlets, mighty cozy."
— **Placerville mining camp song**

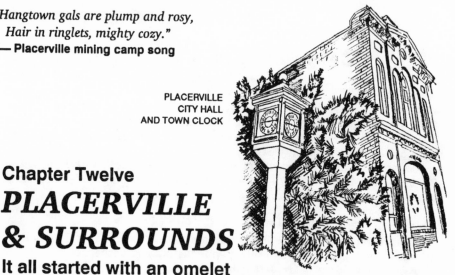

PLACERVILLE
CITY HALL
AND TOWN CLOCK

Chapter Twelve
PLACERVILLE & SURROUNDS
It all started with an omelet

Placerville didn't really begin as an omelet, but eggs do figure in its history.

Its original name, like several other gold camps, was Dry Diggins. Then it was changed to Hangtown, since the local vigilance committee was inclined to mete out pine tree justice to claim-jumpers, bushwhackers and other socially unacceptable folks.

The town gave its name to a curiously Californian concoction called Hangtown Fry, essentially an oyster and bacon omelet. Naturally, historians disagree about its origin. Some say a newly wealthy miner walked into a restaurant and asked for the most expensive meal in the place. Canned oysters, they say, had to be shipped from Boston, bacon was rare and eggs were more scarce than hen's teeth, so the cook blended these expensive items for the free-spending miner.

A more logical theory suggests the opposite—that chickens were fairly portable so eggs soon arrived in the gold camps, and of course, San Francisco Bay was full of oysters. Bacon was available because it would keep without refrigeration. So Hangtown Fry may have been created because those were the only ingredients a local chef could find. Whatever its origin, the omelet is still served in a few Placerville restaurants (see box) and it's popular in San Francisco. Oysters have long since fled the polluted San Francisco Bay, however, and are now bussed in from Tomales Inlet to the north.

But enough of this. Let's explore the home of Hangtown Fry.

THE WAY IT WAS ● Since James Marshall's gold discovery was just nine miles to the north in Coloma, it didn't take long for argonauts to find nuggets in areas nearby. More than 30 mining camps sprung up within two years—places with names like Bottle Hill, Georgia Slide and Murderer's Bar. Only a few of these survived the Gold Rush, including Placerville, Georgetown, Diamond Springs, Shingle Springs and El Dorado.

Three gents named Daylor, Sheldon and McCoon clawed nearly $20,000 in gold out of a dry gulch in 1848, and dubbed the place Dry Diggins. More miners, fandango ladies and bartenders soon followed and a tent city sprang up within weeks. Obviously, a lot of unsavory character followed too, because hanging became a regularly scheduled event. Three men were set to swinging on the same day for allegedly stealing a Frenchman's gold. A bit later, "Irish Dick" Crone did an air dance for unsportsmanlike conduct during a poker game: he knifed one of the players. It didn't take long for Dry Diggins to earn its new name.

However, the morbid title didn't last. By 1854, Hangtown had become California's third largest city, after Sacramento and San Francisco (Los Angeles was a distant fifteenth). Civic pride dictated a more socially acceptable name. Placerville was born.

The booming town launched several remarkable careers. J.M. Studebaker built wheelbarrows and peddled them to miners in the 1850s, then he left for South Bend, Indiana, to establish the firm that eventually became the Studebaker car company. Phillip Armour tried his hand as a ditching contractor, decided that was too much work and opened a meat market in Placerville, the seedling for the Armour packing industry. Mark Hopkins and Collis P. Huntington operated stores here, and moved on to become Sacramento merchants and then railroad barons.

Horace Greeley and Mark Twain numbered among the town's early visitors. Greeley's painful bounce over Placerville Road on Hank Monk's Concord stagecoach provided fodder for Twain's book, *Roughing It.*

Placerville didn't die when the diggins went dry. The Pony Express galloped through here during its brief tenure (see box), and Placerville Road served as the main freight route to the Comstock silver mines in Nevada. After the turn of the century, the road became U.S. Route 50, one of America's first transcontinental highways.

THE WAY IT IS ● Since Highway 50 brings the world to and through Placerville, the town's outer edges are strictly modern, and the place is experiencing something of a growth surge. However, several Gold Rush buildings survive in the downtown area, tucked into a narrow forested valley. Locals like to call it "Old Hangtown." Among its more appealing early day structures are the slender brick city hall, built as a firehouse in 1860; the Placerville Historical Museum in an old brick and fieldstone structure; and the iron shuttered Cary House hotel and shopping complex.

Many of the other storefronts have been modernized during the past half century, providing an architectural museum that, like Jackson, ranges from Art Deco to Fifties post modern to Eighties Chic.

A focal point on Main Street—unfortunately—is a dummy dangling from a beam above Hangman's Tree bar. The tree that gave Hangtown its name once stood here. The dummy wears a curiously benign expression, considering its predicament.

Although their ancestors forsook the town's rowdier name, many modern folks seem to prefer "Hangtown" to "Placerville." Everything from real estate offices to pizza parlors bear the more earthy title.

Incidentally, if you dutifully follow Highway 49 through Placerville, you'll miss Old Hangtown since it's a bit to the east. To find Placerville's roots, turn right off Highway 49 onto Main Street in the downtown area just before it crosses Highway 50.

DISCOVERIES
The best attractions

Gold Bug Park and Mine • *Bedford Avenue a mile north of downtown Placerville; (916) 642-5232.* The only city-owned gold mine in the nation, the Gold Bug gives visitors a firsthand view of the excitement and drudgery of hardrock mining. The 61-acre park is in the midst of a major renovation and improvement project that hopefully will be finished by the time this book reaches your hands. The old stamp mill, one of a few still on its original site, should be stamping noisily away at the behest of visitors, and do-

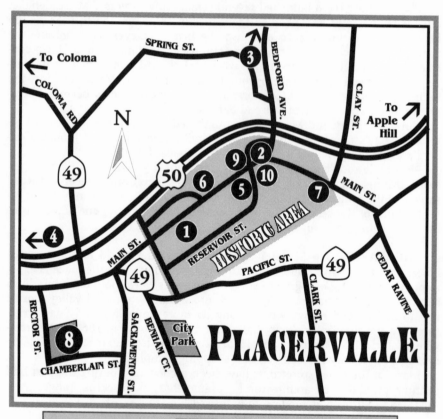

DIRECTORY

1. Cary House (1860)
2. City Hall/County Courthouse
3. Gold Bug Mine and Park
4. El Dorado Co. Historical
   Museum (at the Fairgrounds)
5. Fountain-Tallman Soda
   Works Museum (1852)
6. Hanging tree site
7. Pearson Soda Works (1854)
8. Placerville Cemetery
9. Plaza and bell tower (1865)
10. VISITOR INFORMATION
    (El Dorado Co. Chamber of
    Commerce)

cents will take tourists into the dim, cool interior of the Gold Bug, one of 250 mines that once pock-marked the park.

The quartz vein that lured eager miners still can be seen. The shaft was started in 1888 as the Hattie Mine, and was renamed the Gold Bug by new owners, who operated it from 1926 until it was closed at the onset of World War II. Other park facilities include picnic and barbecue areas and hiking trails.

El Dorado County Museum ● *100 Placerville Dr. (county fairgrounds entrance west of town), Placerville; (916) 621-5865. Wednesday-Saturday 10 to 4 and Sunday 1 to 4; admission free.* This large museum building with a rough-hewn "great hall" look is a treasure house of Gold Country yesterdays. Among its exhibits are the nine-foot, 25-pound skis worn by "Snowshoe" Thompson, a legendary character who carried 80-pound mail sacks between Placerville and Carson City in the 1850s; one of John Studebaker's wheelbarrows and a finely appointed cream colored Concord stagecoach.

The museum grounds contains all manner of equipment and vehicles used during the latter half of the 19th century. Bas relief metal tableaux on a rock wall trace the area's history from native Americans and gold panners to the Pony Express and steam trains.

Apple Hill ● *Visitor center at 4123 Carson Rd. (P.O. Box 494), Camino, CA 95709; (916) 622-9595.* Nowhere in the Mother Lode are scenic landscapes and diet-wrecking delicacies so nicely packaged as in Apple Hill. The climate and soil of a hilly area northeast of Placerville is ideal for apple cultivation. A group of growers got together several years ago to form the Apple Hill Growers Association, offering direct-to- consumer sales.

The growers have advanced considerably beyond the simple peddling of freshly-plucked pippins. Many of the farms have developed into large-scale tourist attractions, with picnic areas, mini lakes, bakeries and cafes offering apple specialties. This area also is home to many of El Dorado County's wineries.

Apple Hill is rich in scenery as well as calories, especially in the fall. It offers a mix of orderly orchards, evergreen groves and occasional Christmas tree farms. Clusters of cottonwoods and poplars provide dazzling bursts of autumn flame, joined by the rusts and yellows of vineyards. Many farm buildings are painted bright red, set against this backdrop of green and gold, with a cobalt autumn sky beyond.

The area's popularity creates occasional traffic jams, mostly on fall weekends when thousands come to admire the scenery and enjoy the crisp crunch of newly ripened apples. If you plan an autumn visit, call in sick one day and schedule your trip for a weekday.

The rest

Cary House ● *300 Main St., Placerville.* This three-story vine-entwined brick classic was built in the late 1850s to replace the Raffles Hotel, which went up in smoke in 1856. Now meticulously restored, it houses several newly decorated rooms (see Lodgings below), professional offices and upscale shops. The most striking feature is the beautifully appointed hotel lobby with its Tiffany lamps, white wrought iron and polished wood. Take time to browse through the lobby's Cary Shoppe.

A small shopping complex, complete with gurgling fountain, is built around a brick patio beside the Cary House. Snacks are available from two take-outs: **Hangtown Deli**, featuring assorted sandwiches and other light lunches; and **Gelato d'Oro**, specializing in Italian ice creams and a tasty line of cappuccino and espresso. Once you secure your goodies, you can retire to an umbrella-shaded patio table.

El Dorado County Historical Society Museum • *In the Fountain-Tallman Soda Works building, 524 Main St., Placerville; (916) 626-0773. Friday-Sunday noon to 4; admission by donation.* This small, nicely-maintained museum offers just what you'd expect—flatirons, high-button shoes and other early-day memorabilia. It also features a soda water machine and an upstairs roomful of Victorian furniture donated by Stella Ralston Tracy, niece of San Francisco millionaire William Ralston. Perhaps the most interesting item is the building itself—a brick and fieldstone structure looking as rough and gnarled as a prospector's hands.

Placerville to Pollock Pines Pony Express Route • The much heralded but short-lived Pony Express galloped through here from 1860 to 1861. Several monuments mark its hurried course. Eastbound riders, starting in Sacramento, followed Main Street through Placerville, then Carson Road and the Pony Express Trail (essentially a Highway 50 frontage road) through Pollock Pines, thence over Carson Pass to Carson City and beyond.

"Here, on April 4, 1860, the first east-bound pony rider William (Sam) Hamilton, changed horses, added one express letter to his *mochila* and sped away for Sportsman Hall." Thus reads a plaque at Main and Sacramento streets in Placerville. Another marker sits in front of the present Sportsman Hall in Pollock Pines, a Western style cafe on the site of the original way station. The restaurant's knotty pine and rough-hewn beam interior houses a scattering of exhibits concerning the Pony Express, Gold Rush and other early Western lore.

Nuggets

Bennett Sculpture Studio and Foundry • *4505 Greenstone Rd., Placerville, CA 95667; (916) 626-8044. Tours daily 10 a.m. to 5 p.m. by appointment.* Learn how fine bronze sculptures are made on a 45-minute tour of this large complex on the outskirts of Placerville. It's one of the few galleries that executes every step of the "lost wax" casting process in one place. Visitors will see artists making clay designs, from which molds are cast. These are used to form wax figures, which are covered with an "investment" coating, then melted, leaving an empty shell for the bronze casting.

Georgetown Hotel • *In Georgetown, 12 miles north of Placerville on Highway 193.* This two-story 1850s wooden hotel is the focal point of an out-of-the-way hamlet perched high on the Georgetown Divide northeast of Placerville (see Detours below). The hotel's saloon oozes Gold Rush atmosphere; it's a study in rough cut stone, flocked wallpaper and polished woods. Settle onto a barstool, have a drink, admire yourself in the handsome back bar mirror, then study its wonderful clutter: trophy heads, cowboy boots hanging from the ceiling and a scatter of farming, ranching and blacksmithing implements. A rough-cut stone fireplace dominates one wall.

Placerville City Hall • *Main and Bedford streets.* This narrow, two-story stone and brick structure was built in 1860 for the local fire department,

Confidence Engine Company #1. The brigade had been established in 1857 as the Mountaineer Engine Company. When the fire laddies bought a used engine called the "Confidence" from a Sacramento brigade, they couldn't remove the engraved name from the rig. So they did the logical thing—they named their company after the engine. The structure has served as City Hall since 1902.

Placerville Soda Works building (Pearson Soda Works) • *Main and Clay streets.* This stone relic rivals City Hall for its homey Mother Lode look. It was built in stages—a curious mix of fieldstone, rectangular blocks and odds and ends rubble. The first story was erected in 1859 by John McFarland Pearson to produce fizz-water and syrup flavors. Forty years later, his sons added another floor to expand the business; it perches atop the original like an architectural afterthought. The wonderfully homely relic cries out to be a museum or boutique, but it was vacant and up for lease when we last passed through.

Steel bell tower • *Main and Center streets on the town plaza.* A warning tower has occupied this spot since 1865 to advise folks of fires and other disasters. This version was built in 1898 after a wooden one burned down. Its stern, ungainly features are dressed with patriotic bunting around the Fourth of July, and with Christmas lights in winter.

DETOURS

Placerville via Pollock Pines through Apple Hill • *A 35-mile loop trip.* From downtown, head south on Highway 49, following its twisting course up to Pleasant Valley Road. Turn left and go east through Diamond Springs, one of the area's many gold boom camps that went bust.

Most of the town has been modernized into a Placerville suburb, although a few antique shops function in 19th century buildings. The old I.O.O.F. Hall, a pleasant vision in dressed stone and brick, looks down on the town from a nearby hill.

Pleasant Valley Road takes you into pine and fir country, and changes its name to Sly Park Road, which skirts Jenkinson Lake. The reservoir's Sly Park offers camping, picnicking and sundry water sports. Continue climbing into ever thickening evergreen thickets, then veer left and cross under Highway 50 freeway to Pollock Pines. A left turn onto Pony Express Trail takes you the length of this woodsy town. You shortly encounter the noted Sportsman Hall, which is worth a visit and maybe a lunch stop (See Discoveries above and Dining below.)

Pony Express Trail merges into Carson Road, placing you on the rim of Apple Hill. Unless it's a bumper-to-bumper October Sunday, plunge randomly into this pretty area, following winding roads at will and whim, enjoying the scenery and the apple goodies.

From here, you can follow Carson Road back to Placerville and ready yourself for Detour #2.

Placerville to Georgetown to Coloma • *A 25-mile route.* From downtown Placerville, cross Highway 50 and follow Route 49 through a hilly residential area for about a mile, then take a right fork onto Highway 193. The route twists down into the beautiful, forested canyon of the South Fork of the American River and crosses the stream at Chili Bar, a popular put-in for

THOSE SWIFT PHANTOMS OF THE DESERT

Few images have captured the fancy of history buffs, and Hollywood, like the Pony Express. It's a glamorous vision alive in our imagination: swift young riders galloping their mounts through the Western wilds, mail sacks slapping against saddles, riders' hair and horses' mane flying in the wind, hostile savages in hot pursuit.

Mark Twain described them as "swift phantoms of the desert who swept across the landscape like the belated fragment of a storm."

Movies, and more currently television, have distorted the story, however. Although the imaginary *Young Riders* encounter more difficulties and setbacks than Indiana Jones on a treasure hunt, the real riders emerged remarkably unscathed. Only one died at the hands of Indians and just one mail sack was lost.

These were indeed brave young men—and temperate as well, forbidden by their employer to touch alcohol or tobacco. Like today's jockeys, they had to be light weight so their horses could move swiftly. It was their skill, daring and speed that spared them the mishaps portrayed by filmmakers.

Created to hurry the mail between the East coast and growing California, the Pony Express was short-lived, a quick victim of progress. It was started by Messrs. William H. Russell, Alexander Majors and William B. Waddell in 1860. A year and a half later, the company was put out of business by the transcontinental telegraph. Majors, the chief financier, lost more than a million dollars even though the mail rate was $5 per half ounce.

The first rider left St. Joseph, Missouri, on April 3, 1860. Ten days, a dozen riders and 75 ponies later, the mail pouch arrived in San Francisco. John Butterfield's Overland Mail stagecoaches, following a circuitous southern route, required three weeks for such a crossing.

The young pony riders streaked from way station to way station, across the midwestern plains and the Great Basin, up the steep eastern escarpment of the Sierra Nevada, down through Pollock Pines and Placerville, then across the Central Valley to Sacramento. The final leg to San Francisco was accomplished by river steamer.

"The greatest excitement prevailed," a San Francisco newspaper said of the first rider's arrival. "After which, the various parties participating in the celebration adjourned, pleased with themselves and the rest of mankind and the Pony Express in particular. All took a drink at their own expense."

river runners. Some current and former mining activity is visible on a cliff face across the stream.

Climb steeply out of the valley, passing attractive little Finnon Lake, captured behind a small concrete dam, then pause in the tumbled-down town of Kelsey to explore a bit of history. It was here that James Marshall settled after the furor of his gold discovery quieted, and after his own efforts yielded little additional gold. He ran a blacksmith shop here until he died—a poverty-ridden recluse—at the age of 73 in 1885. A badly-done imitation of his original shop, built several decades ago as a tourist gimmick, is deteriorating in a pine grove just off the highway on the edge of town.

Continuing on, you arrive in Georgetown, one of the Gold Country's hidden delights. It's a weathered hamlet nestled in a high mountain valley, out of the main stream, content to bask in its memories. Although it was an early gold camp, it has the look of a slightly scruffy New England community. Its wide, tree-shaded streets are lined with wood frame buildings instead of the typical brick and iron- shuttered structures.

An interesting exception is the 1859 I.O.O.F. Hall, with a brick lower floor and wooden upper one; it's at the corner of Main Street and Highway 193.

Georgetown blossomed as a tent and shanty city after George Phipps and his friends discovered gold in 1849. A fire leveled the town in 1852, started by a photographer's flash powder. It was rebuilt with unusually wide streets to serve as firebreaks against future blazes. The town claims a population of 1,150 with a business district comprised mostly of saloons. We counted three during our last visit.

After poking about this old town, head south on Main Street, cross Highway 193 and turn immediately left onto Marshall Road. It spirals down through a thick evergreen forest that's particularly beautiful in the fall, marbled with the golden glow of oak and sycamore. Pausing on a ridge above a wide valley, you can see the ribbon of the American River and the small town where all this business began—Coloma.

DIVERSIONS

High country hiking and the like ● *Three former offices of El Dorado National Forest have been consolidated into a single, nicely appointed visitor center, east of Placerville in Camino, just off Highway 50 freeway; open daily 7 to 6 in the summer and 8 to 5 the rest of the year.* The center offers exhibits of forestland activities, the usual national forest recreation and visitor map for $2, plus leaflets on hiking, camping, cross-country skiing, river running and the like.

Water sports ● *Sly Park Recreation Area, c/o El Dorado Irrigation District, P.O. Box 577, Pollock Pines, CA 95726; (916) 644-2545. Day use fee $3.50 per vehicle, boat launch $2.50.* This recreation area on Jenkinson Lake offers fishing, swimming boating, hiking and camping (see campground listing below). Contact the El Dorado Irrigation District for a brochure.

Wine tasting ● El Dorado County rivals neighboring Amador in the number of its wineries and certainly in the quality of its wines. Wineries are a bit more widespread here, with a few focused in Apple Hill and others south of Camino along Mount Aukum and Fairplay roads. The El Dorado Winery Association's brochure will steer you from one to another. Get one free at wineries, the chamber of commerce or by contacting the association at P.O. Box 1614, Placerville, CA 95667; (916) 622-8094.

Boeger Winery, *1709 Carson Rd., Placerville, CA 95667; (916) 622-8094. Daily 10 to 5; MC/VISA.* Interesting tasting room in a rough-cut stone and log structure that housed an earlier winery dating back to 1870; old-style ranch yard with shaded picnic tables.

Fitzpatrick Winery and Lodge, *7740 Fairplay Rd., Somerset, CA 95684; (209) 245-3248. Weekends 11 to 5; MC/VISA.* Unusual combined winery and inn with the tasting room in a large chalet-style log lodge; high on a slope with an impressive valley view; picnic deck.

Gerwer Winery, *8221 Stoney Creek Rd., Somerset, CA 95684; (209) 245-3467. Weekends 11 to 5; MC/VISA.* Winery and tasting room tucked into a wooded glen, well off the highway; specialty foods as well as wines sampled; lawn picnic area.

Granite Springs Winery, *6060 Granite Springs Rd., Somerset, CA 95684; (916) 621-1933 or (209) 245-6395. Weekends 11 to 5.* Simple bungalow tasting room near the ranch-style winery, tucked against a hillside in a wooded hollow; shaded picnic areas near a pond.

Latcham Vineyards, *2860 Omo Ranch Rd., Somerset; mailing address: P.O. Box 134, Mount Aukum, CA 95656; (209) 626-3697. Weekends 11 to 5; MC/VISA.* Winery and tasting room in a weathered barn in a pleasant old farmyard rimmed by vineyards; shaded picnic areas.

Lava Cap Winery, *2221 Fruitridge Rd., Placerville, CA 95667; (800) 475-0175 or (916) 621-0175. Daily 11 to 5 Labor Day through Thanksgiving weekend, closed Tuesdays and Thursdays the rest of the year; MC/VISA.* Housed in a "modern barn" among its own vineyards in the heart of Apple Hill; pleasant redwood paneled tasting room; picnic deck.

Madrona Vineyards, *High Hill Rd. (P.O. Box 454), Camino, CA 95709; (916) 644-5948. Daily 11 to 5 Memorial Day through December, weekends only the rest of the year; MC/VISA.* Tucked into a shady retreat beneath cinnamon-barked trees that inspired its name; vineyards and Apple Hill orchards just beyond; picnic tables in the wooded glen.

Sierra Vista Winery, *4560 Cabernet Way, Placerville, CA 95667; (916) 622-7221. Weekends 11 to 5; most major credit cards.* Dramatically perched on a high ridge with views of the Crystal range of the Sierra Nevada; one of California's loftiest wineries at 2,900 feet; picnic area with a great view.

Windwalker Farm, *7360 Perry Creek Rd., Somerset, CA 95684; (209) 245-4054. Weekends 11 to 5; MC/VISA.* A blend of winery and Arabian horse ranch; tasting room in a distinctive Pennsylvania Dutch structure; shaded picnic deck nearby.

GOLD COUNTRY DINING

Cafè Sarah's ● △△ $ ∅∅
301 Main St., Placerville; (916) 621-4680. Country American; meals $3 to $7; wine and beer. Daily 8 a.m. to 2 p.m. No credit cards. Pleasing early American-style cafe in a 19th century building with a white embossed tin ceiling, maple chairs, potted palms in wicker baskets and modern art. Breakfasts and light lunches of burgers, sandwiches and elaborate salads.

Carriage Room Restaurant at Smith Flat House ● △△△ $$ ∅
2021 Smith Flat Rd. in historic Smith Flat; (916) 621-0667 or 622-0471. American; dinners $9 to $17; full bar service. Lunch daily 11 to 2 daily, dinner Sunday-Thursday 5 to 9 and Friday-Saturday 5 to 10. Reservations accepted. MC/VISA, DIN. Generous portions of pioneer history come with the menu of steak, chicken, chops and pasta. The 1850 structure was a hotel, restaurant, wagon and stage stop, dance hall, Pony Express stop, post office and general store. A mine shaft leads from the old fashioned saloon to the Blue Lead Channel, which yielded $18 million in gold.

Boots & Saddles Steakhouse • ∆∆ $$$

In the Diamond Springs Hotel at 245 Pleasant Valley Rd., Placerville; (916) 626-3926. American; dinners $9 to $13; full bar service. Monday-Thursday 5 to 9, Friday-Saturday 11 to 9, Sunday brunch 9 to 2 then dinner until 10. No credit cards; personal checks accepted. Cute oldstyle restaurant with a Western theme, housed in a red and white gingerbread trim hotel. The busy, down-home menu features steak, shrimp, scampi, barbecued chicken, ribs and prime rib.

La Casa Grande • ∆∆ $$

251 Main St., Placerville; (916) 626-5454. Mexican-American; dinners $7 to $13; full bar service. Sunday-Thursday 11 to 9:45, Friday-Saturday 11 to 10:45. MC/VISA. Attractive restaurant in a remodeled 1856 Old Hangtown structure with brick arches, pressed tin ceiling, brass chandeliers and Mother Lode paintings. Although the look is Gold Rush, the menu is mostly Mexican, with the usual smashed beans and rice things plus *cerdo al horno en mole* (roast pork basted in Spanish sauce) and *lengua de Fiestas* (beef tongue); also very American liver and onions, top sirloin and seafood.

THE ULTIMATE OMELET

One mustn't pass through Placerville without sampling that curious culinary creation called Hangtown Fry—that is, if one's palate is keyed to a blend of scrambled eggs, fried oysters and bacon.

We prefer the version served by **Soup n' Such** in the heart of old town Placerville. The folks there enliven it with salsa, useful if you aren't that wild about oysters (which we aren't). Their Hangtown Fry goes for $5.50, including toast. It's served all day (until 4 p.m.), in case you aren't emotionally prepared to start your morning with oysters (which we aren't).

To make your own historic omelet, try this recipe from the Placerville Junior League's *California Cookbook*.

1/2 pound bacon	1/4 cup heavy cream
6 to 8 oysters	1/4 cup chopped parsley
2 eggs, beaten	1/4 cup grated Parmesan cheese
10 to 12 soda crackers	salt and pepper
6 eggs	2 sprigs parsley

Fry bacon crisp and set aside. Remove all but 6 tablespoons of grease from skillet. Dip oysters in 2 beaten eggs, then in cracker crumbs, and fry them in bacon grease over medium heat, one minute per side. Beat 6 eggs with cream, chopped parsley and grated cheese in a mixing bowl; season with salt and pepper. Pour mixture over oysters in skillet, reduce heat to low and scramble eggs, lifting oysters so mixture surrounds them. When eggs are semi-firm but still moist, transfer omelet to a broiler to brown lightly. Serve on heated platter with bacon strips and sprigs of parsley. Serves six.

It sounds like cholesterol city. *Bon apetit!*

Mama D Carlo's • ∆∆∆ $$
482 Main St., Placerville; (916) 626-1612. Italian-American; dinners $6 to $15; wine and beer. Monday-Thursday 11:30 to 9, Friday 11:30 to 10, Saturday 3 to 10, closed Sunday. Reservations accepted. No credit cards. Locally popular spot, recently expanded to double its dining room; pleasant wood-paneled interior with an early American look. Menu ranges from scallop and scampi sautè through the usual cacciatores, Parmesans and pastas to American steaks. Consistently good fare in generous portions.

Martha's Restaurant and Ice Cream Parlor • ∆ $
6326 Highway 193, Georgetown; (916) 333-4632. American, dinners $6 to $11; wine and beer. Weekdays 11 to 9, weekends 9 to 9. MC/VISA. Simple but almost cute family cafe with maple furniture, knotty pine wainscoting and vinyl. Mostly light lunches and sodas fountain treats, plus a few dinner items such as calamari Diablo and halibut.

Powell Bros Steamer Company • ∆∆ $$
425 Main St., Placerville; (916) 626-1091. Seafood; dinners $10 to $12; full bar service. Daily 11 a.m. to 10 p.m. MC/VISA. Old Hangtown cafe with a Fisherman's Wharf decor, featuring a good assortment of shellfish, seafood stews, fish and an occasional pasta. One of the few full-scale seafood restaurants in the Mother Lode; fun and lively place with generally fresh fare. Foothill wines featured.

Soup 'n Such • ∆ $
423 Main St., Placerville; (916) 626-3483. American; meals $3 to $7; no alcohol. Monday-Saturday 7 to 4, Sunday 8 to 3. No credit cards. Typical family diner, spartan but appealing with high ceilings, drop lamps and booths. Features Hangtown Fry (box on previous page), plus breakfast, a soup and salad bar, tuna or turkey melt, ribeye steak and assorted sandwiches.

Sportsman Hall • ∆∆ $$ ∅
5620 Pony Express Trail, Pollock Pines; (916) 644-2474. American; meals $7 to $30; no alcohol but it can be brought in. Monday-Thursday 5:30 a.m. to 9 p.m., Friday-Saturday 5:30 to 10 and Sunday 6 to 9. MC/VISA, AMEX. Western-style knotty-pine restaurant that's a virtual museum of early-day paraphernalia; on the site of an original Pony Express way station. Typical American fare in hearty portions—steaks, chicken and chops, plus salmon and prime rib specials.

Is there life after dark?

Theatre El Dorado offers assorted dramas and comedies in the Discovery Playhouse at the El Dorado County Fairgrounds; call (916) 626-5193.

Live listening and/or dancing music issues from these establishments: Western and rock 'n' roll at the **Diamond Springs Hotel**, 245 Pleasant Valley Rd., Diamond Springs, (916) 626-3926; popular music and rock on weekends at the **Smith Flat House,** 2021 Smith Flat Rd., Smith Flat, (916) 626-9003; assorted live music at the **Georgetown Hotel bar** in Georgetown, generally Friday and Saturday night and Sunday afternoon, (916) 333-4373; and Sunday jazz from 1 to 5 p.m. at **Powell Bros Steamer Company**, 425 Main St., Placerville, (916) 626-1091.

LODGINGS

Bed & breakfast inns and historic hotels

The American River Inn • ⌂⌂⌂ $$$ Ø
Main and Orleans streets, (P.O. Box 43) Georgetown, CA 95634; (800) 245-6566 or (916) 333-4499. Doubles from $73; some private and some share baths. Full breakfasts. Smoking in designated areas. MC/VISA, AMEX. The 49ers never had it this good. A former miners' boarding house built in 1863, the American River Inn has been fashioned into an stylish B&B with perks such as a spa, swimming pool, aviary and landscaped gardens. Naturally, the rooms are furnished in antiques. In fact, an antique and gift shop on the premises is sometimes pressed into service as a room. Guests gather in the parlor to sip local wines, nibble goodies and listen to the tinklings of a piano. More active ones can indulge in croquet, ping pong, putt or drive a few golf balls or check out a bicycle.

The Chichester House • ⌂⌂⌂ $$$$ ØØ
800 Spring St., Placerville, CA 95667; (800) 831-4008 or (916) 626-1882. Doubles from $60. Three units with half baths, tub and shower down the hall. No smoking. MC/VISA, DISC. Beautifully ornate wood fretwork highlights Doreen and Bill Thornhill's nicely refurbished Victorian. Built in 1892, the house is an elaborate blend of Queen Anne and Italianate style. Rooms are tastefully color coordinated and furnished with American antiques. Closets have been converted into half baths with pottie and sink; one features a 1930s Pullman train car sink. Country crafts, a doll collection and vintage photos add pleasing touches of Americana to this nicely-appointed inn.

Combellack-Blair House • ⌂⌂⌂ $$$$ ØØ
3059 Cedar Ravine, Placerville, CA 95667; (916) 622-3764. Doubles $89 to $99. Two units with a private baths. Full breakfast. Smoking on front porch only. MC/VISA. A Queen Anne classic, this is one of the most attractive of Placerville's many Victorian homes. The ornate exterior is a jewel of 19th century architecture. Built in 1895, this pink and mauve house perches on a hill like an elaborately coiffed Southern belle surveying her domain. Rooms are done in a Victorian motif with lots of lace and antiques. Guests can relax by a pond, on the oldstyle porch swing or stroll a couple of blocks to town.

Georgetown Hotel • ⌂⌂ $$
Main Street, Georgetown, CA 95634; (916) 333-4373. Ten units with share baths, $45 per couple; a suite with private bath, $55. Smoking OK. MC/VISA. Although a bit weathered on the outside, this 1896 hotel has undergone considerable interior face-lifting. It's not elegant but reasonably orderly and clean, with rooms furnished in early American style. When we last visited, the semi-cute little **restaurant** beyond the bar was serving only weekend dinners, with ribs, beef and chicken entreès at $7.95 each. It may have become a more ambitious operation by the time you get there. Great oldstyle saloon.

River Rock Inn • ⌂⌂ $$$ ØØ
1756 Georgetown Drive (three miles northeast at Chili Bar), Placerville, CA 95667; (916) 622-7640. Doubles $70 to $90. Four rooms, some with private

and some with half baths. Full breakfast. No smoking. No credit cards. The most striking thing about this inn is its location, at streamside in the scenic American River Canyon. The home is ranch style, nicely decorated with a mix of early American and contemporary furnishings. A deck invites guests to enjoy views of the river and surrounding forests. The emphasis seems to be on privacy here; half a dozen signs on the approach to the River Rock stress that this is private property. Guests greeted with ice tea and snacks.

Cary House Hotel ● ⌂⌂⌂ $$ ∅
300 Main St., Placerville, CA 95667; (916) 622-4271. Doubles from $43. Twenty units, all with private baths. Non-smoking rooms available. MC/VISA. We've already nominated this handsome 1857 hotel with its tastefully appointed lobby gift shop as one of Placerville's special attractions. A carved stairway bannister and warm wooden wainscoting add to this picture of 19th century hotel finery. The carefully refurbished rooms are stylishly furnished with country oak, patchwork quilts and ruffley print curtains. The lobby is an immaculate rendering of 19th century finery, with polished woods, beveled glass and chandeliers.

Motels

Best Western Placerville Inn ● ⌂⌂⌂ $$$ ∅
6850 Greenleaf Dr. (Missouri Flat off ramp), Placerville, CA 95667; (800) 528-1234 or (916) 622-9100. Doubles $64 to $75, singles $59 to $69, suites from $135. Major credit cards. A 105-unit motel with large, pleasant rooms; TV movies, room phones. Pool and spa. **Brawley's Restaurant** serves from 5:30 a.m. to 11 p.m., 24 hours on Friday-Saturday; American; dinners from $9 to $15; full bar service; non-smoking section.

Days Inn ● ⌂⌂ $$ ∅
1332 Broadway, Placerville, CA 95667; (916) 622-3124. Doubles from $50. Major credit cards. Clean, prim and well-maintained motel just east of downtown. TV movies, room phones; non-smoking rooms.

Gold Trail Motor Lodge ● ⌂ $$ ∅
1970 Broadway, Placerville, CA 95667; (916) 622-2906. Doubles $46 to $51, singles $41 to $46; Major credit cards. Small 32- room motel with pleasantly landscaped grounds; TV, pool; non- smoking rooms.

Mother Lode Motel ● ⌂ $$ ∅
1940 Broadway, Placerville, CA 95667; (916) 622-0895. Doubles $39 to $51, singles $39 to $43. MC/VISA, AMEX. A 21-unit motel with TV movies, some room refrigerators; pool; non-smoking rooms

CAMPGROUNDS & RV PARKS

El Dorado National Forest ● More than 30 campgrounds are available in the national forest. RV and tent sites. No hookups or showers, pit toilets at most(flush toilets at Big Meadows, Wench Creek and Yellowjacket. Most sites have barbecues or fire pits and picnic tables.

Sly Park Campground and Recreation Area ● *c/o El Dorado Irrigation District, P.O. Box 577 (2890 Mosquito Rd.), Placerville, CA 95667; (916) 644-2545. Wooded campground on Jenkinson Lake, with 185 RV and tent sites; no hookups; $9.* Pit potties, water but no showers; picnic tables, fire rings and barbecues. Fishing, swimming, boating, hiking. General store and gas station across the road.

El Dorado County Fairgrounds • *100 Placerville Drive, Placerville; (916) 621-5860. RV sites only, $10 with hookups.* Clean, well-kept fairgrounds with water and electric hookups; flush toilets and showers.

ANNUAL EVENTS

Pony Express re-ride, Fourth of July, Placerville, (916) 621-5885; riders gallop east, following Pony Express route.

Wagon Train, mid-July, Highway 50 Association, P.O. Box 454, Placerville, CA 95667; annual two-week wagon train trek from Carson City to Folsom, following early wagon and Pony Express route.

El Dorado County Fair, August at fairgrounds in Placerville, (916) 621-5860; booths, rodeo, parades and the usual fair fare.

Apple Hill Harvest, September-November, (916) 622-9595; apple specialty foods, apple bake-off, music, crafts and such.

On the road again...to the beginning of the Gold Gush

A winding, forest-rimmed nine-mile drive takes you from Placerville to Coloma on Highway 49. A pleasant alternate is via Georgetown, described in a Detour above.

To learn more...

Apple Hill Growers, Visitor center at 4123 Carson Rd. (P.O. Box 494), Camino, CA 95709; (916) 622-9595.

El Dorado County Chamber of Commerce, 542 Main St., Placerville, CA 95667; (916) 621-5885. Chamber office, located in one of old town's 19th century cut stone and brick buildings, is open weekdays 8 to 5.

El Dorado National Forest, Forest Supervisor, 100 Forni Rd., Placerville, CA 95667; (916) 622-5061. Send $2 for a national forest visitor map.

El Dorado Winery Association, P.O. Box 1614, Placerville, CA 95667; (916) 622-8094. Ask for a free El Dorado County winery tour guide.

El Dorado County Ranch Marketing Guide, The guide lists farms and ranches that sell direct to consumers. For a copy, send two first class stamps to the El Dorado County Chamber of Commerce.

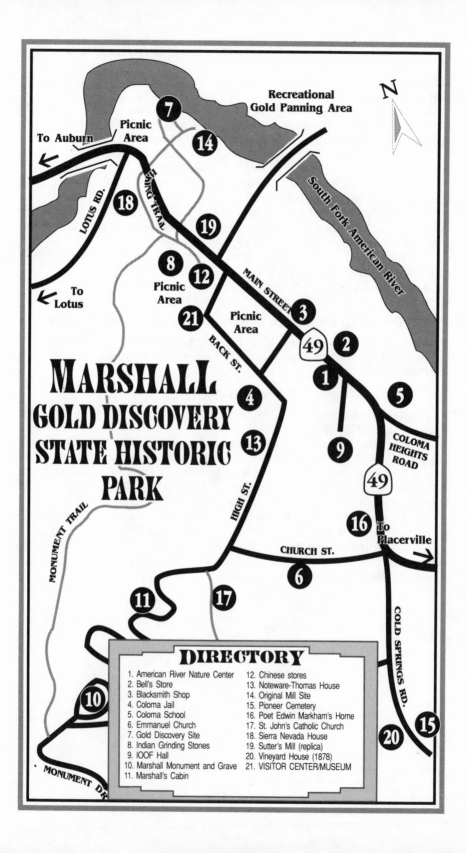

MARSHALL GOLD DISCOVERY STATE HISTORIC PARK

Recreational Gold Panning Area

To Auburn

Picnic Area

To Lotus

Picnic Area

Picnic Area

Picnic Area

South Fork American River

LOTUS RD.

EWING TRAIL

MAIN STREET

BACK ST.

HIGH ST.

MONUMENT TRAIL

COLOMA HEIGHTS ROAD

CHURCH ST.

To Placerville

COLD SPRINGS RD.

MONUMENT DR.

DIRECTORY

1. American River Nature Center
2. Bell's Store
3. Blacksmith Shop
4. Coloma Jail
5. Coloma School
6. Emmanuel Church
7. Gold Discovery Site
8. Indian Grinding Stones
9. IOOF Hall
10. Marshall Monument and Grave
11. Marshall's Cabin
12. Chinese stores
13. Noteware-Thomas House
14. Original Mill Site
15. Pioneer Cemetery
16. Poet Edwin Markham's Home
17. St. John's Catholic Church
18. Sierra Nevada House
19. Sutter's Mill (replica)
20. Vineyard House (1878)
21. VISITOR CENTER/MUSEUM

"Probably no man ever went to his grave so misunderstood, so misjudged, so misrepresented...as James W. Marshall."

— Margaret A. Kelly, a friend of Marshall's

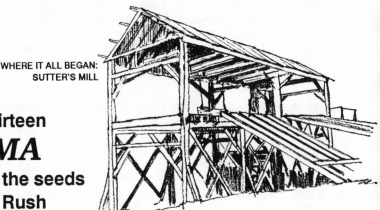

WHERE IT ALL BEGAN:
SUTTER'S MILL

Chapter Thirteen
COLOMA
Unearthing the seeds of the Gold Rush

What an improbable pair!

Johann Augustus Suter was a suave, free-wheeling entrepreneur from Switzerland. Fleeing debtors' prison and abandoning his family, he arrived in California via Hawaii in 1839 and received permission from Mexican officials to establish a colony in California's great heartland. Selecting a likely spot at the junction of the Sacramento and American rivers, he began building New Helvetia. And he Americanized his name to John Sutter.

James Wilson Marshall was a wandering carpenter, probably more idealistic than clever. He contracted with Sutter to build a water-powered sawmill on the South Fork of the American River, in the foothills 30 miles to the east. Sutter, who habitually operated on a shoestring and occasionally wrote rubber checks, provided Marshall with a crew. He agreed to give him 25 percent of the mill's output for supervising its construction and operating it.

The rest, as they say, is history.

But Marshall didn't pull a big, glittering nugget from the tailrace of the mill that chilly January morning in 1848. He found two tiny particles, the first one "about half the size and of the shape of a pea," worth maybe fifty cents. He hammered them flat with a river rock to test their malleability, suspected they were gold, and stuck them in his hat brim.

Of course, even a little gold brings gleams to men's eyes. Four days later, after detecting more yellow flakes in the mill channel, he rode through the rain to Sutter's Fort to share his discovery with his boss. The two agreed to keep it a secret until the mill was completed. But, as the 25 million of us who have since been lured to California know, the secret leaked out.

THE WAY IT WAS ● When Marshall arrived in this forested valley, it was inhabited only by a small tribe of Indians called Culloomas. Most Native Americans had no concept of land ownership. Thus, the Culloomas weren't disturbed when the newcomer staked out a chunk of river bottom and began building a curious looking wood frame contraption. In fact, several of them went to work for him, in exchange for trade goods.

The mill's function was simple. Water was diverted from the river through a millrace—a ditch, really—where it would drive a water wheel which in turn would power a long saw blade above. Lumber would then be floated downstream to Sutter's settlement near present-day Sacramento. (John Bidwell, another early Californian, called the idea of rafting lumber through the canyons of the American River a "wild scheme" that only a man like Marshall would entertain.)

Ironically, neither Sutter nor Marshall fared well in the rush that followed the mill ditch gold discovery. Sutter lost his workers and his loosely assembled empire, and he was unsuccessful in his own attempts to prospect for gold.

Marshall wound up a muttering, alcoholic eccentric, claiming mystical gold-finding powers. He ended his days puttering around his blacksmith shop in nearby Kelsey, and selling his autograph for pennies. Sympathetic legislators appropriated a small state pension for him in 1872. But they declined to renew it when he appeared before that august body in 1878 to plead his case—and a brandy bottle dropped from his pocket. Both men died broke, Sutter in 1880 and Marshall five years later.

The discovery that altered America's history stirred little excitement initially. Only a few men came to the mill site during 1848, and the first of the Mother Lode's gold camps began life slowly. Then the world began to believe, and Coloma's population ballooned to 5,000 by 1850.

The town's fame was spurred by people like Sam Brannan, an opportunistic Mormon and friend of Sutter's. He supposedly gathered a handful of nuggets in a quinine bottle, then ran (or rode horseback, depending on your historian) down San Francisco's Montgomery Street, shouting: "Gold! Gold from the American River!" However, he first bought up every pick and shovel he could find. He then lit out for the discovery site and made a quick fortune selling them for $50 apiece. Coloma thus set the pace for the rampaging inflation that marked the first years of the Gold Rush.

But the town's bloom wilted quickly. While neighboring Auburn and Placerville became major mining camps, Coloma's placer gold soon ran out and it was labeled "the dullest mining town in the whole country" in 1851.

It lost its county seat to Placerville in 1856 and, like Marshall, it puttered along for the next several decades, neglected and overlooked by history. It survived as a sleepy farming community until people began recalling its significance. Tourism probably began around 1890, after a statue of Marshall was erected on a hillside above the town.

The statue is still there today, pointing a stiff bronze finger at the gold discovery site below. Its right hand clutches a huge nugget, bigger than anything Marshall ever found. Like a badly posed photo, the statue stares off into space, not looking at the spot that brought this ordinary man his accidental fame.

THE WAY IT IS ● Coloma today is a curiosity, part quiet village, part historic park. Fewer than 200 residents occupy a few wood frame homes tucked among the trees, while other structures house early-day exhibits. More than two-thirds of the town is encompassed by the 275-acre Marshall Gold Discovery State Historic Park, established in 1942.

The town lacks the orderly rows of narrow brick or wooden buildings typical of Columbia, Jamestown and Sutter Creek. Its historic survivors are scattered, separated by manicured lawns, parking lots and picnic areas. Most of the buildings, original and reconstructed, stand alongside Highway 49, beneath a canopy of locust, persimmon and catalpa trees. Nearby, the American River glimmers in the Sierra sun. Protected from development by the park service, the town is unmarred by garish neon and Golden Arches. Coloma thus enjoys one of the most attractive settings in the Mother Lode.

It's a busy place in summer, when tourists jockey for parking spaces, swarm around the reconstructed Sutter's Mill like curious ants and spread their Kentucky Fried Chicken lunches on picnic tables. The river is bright with orange rafts and sleek kayaks, for its modest rapids here are popular with individual and organized river runners.

In the off-season, there's a tranquility, a whisper of history about this place that exists nowhere else in *La Veta Madre*. We prefer Coloma in the fall, when gold is found in the slender leaves of the locust and Trees of Heaven, when the river that created California flows crisp, clean and cold.

We like to walk along its banks, studying the green and beige ridge of distant hills, still largely unsettled, looking the way they must have looked to Jim Marshall. We stand in silence, listening to the soft cadence of the stream. "Gold," it sighs, "gold in the American River."

DISCOVERIES
The best attractions

Sutter's Mill ● *Just off Highway 49 in Coloma.* It's easy to believe that this simple structure, looking like an oversized shed without walls, was built nearly a century and a half ago, with its hand-hewn beams and simple mortise-and-tenon joints (basically, a square peg in a square hole). But it isn't that old, of course.

The state park service, El Dorado County Historical Society and volunteer citizens of Coloma got together in the 1960s, researched old records and created a faithful replica of the original sawmill. Two important sources were Marshall's own sketches and an early photograph. Latter-day builders even used hand adzes and other early tools to give the mill its final touch of rough realism. The duplicate was dedicated on Discovery Day, January 24, 1968. It sits farther up the bank than the original mill, so it really wouldn't work because the millrace is high and dry. It does operate, however, by electricity. Park rangers saw a few boards for tourists on most weekends, particularly during the summer.

The original mill was nearly completed when Marshall found his fateful yellow flakes. He made his men promise to finish it before they ran off to seek gold, and they did. The mill ran briefly and furiously, working around the clock to saw the boards that became Coloma's first houses. But the workers couldn't keep their minds on such mundane work, with all that excitement around, and it was abandoned after a few months.

The sawmill fell to ruin, and a flood washed most of its remains downstream. Folks digging in the area in 1924 found some of its foundation posts, and they're on exhibit in the park museum. The original mill site is under water because the river shifted its course; a bankside monument marks the general area.

Marshall Gold Discovery State Historic Park Museum • *Across Highway 49 from the mill; (916) 622-3470. Open daily 10:30 to 4 except Thanksgiving, Christmas and New Year's Day. Day use fee $5 per carload (includes other park exhibits).* State and national parks, freed from commercial concerns, generally do an excellent job reassembling and recording history, and the Marshall museum is certainly no exception.

Graphics, artifacts, mini-dioramas and a scale model of the mill tell the oft-told story of The Discovery. Other exhibits concern the Cullooma Indians, the town that grew up around the discovery site then quickly shrank, life in the mining camps and the Gold Rush in general. Historic films and slide shows are shown in an adjacent auditorium.

American River Nature Center • *8913 Highway 49 (P.O. Box 562), Coloma, CA 95613; (916) 621-1224. Wednesday-Saturday 10 to 4, Sunday noon to 4.* While the rangers of Marshall Gold Discovery State Historic park interpret the area's human history, the non-profit American River Land Trust's Nature Center is concerned with the natural history of this river corridor. Dioramas and other exhibits focus on the area's flora and fauna and a small gift shop sells things with wildlife themes. Still in its formative stages when we last visited, the facility is shaping up as the Gold Country's finest natural history center. Exhibits were scheduled for completion in mid-1992. The center also sponsors a variety of programs, ranging from stargazing to nature hikes to photography workshops. The center is housed in the 1886 clapboard Kane House.

The rest

Marshall Monument • *On a hill overlooking the discovery site.* Four years after Marshall's death, the California Legislature appropriated $9,000 for this monument, which was cast in San Francisco and dedicated with much flourish in May, 1890. It stands over Marshall's grave, on a hill above a pretty thicket.

When Marshall died in Kelsey, his friends iced him down, brought him back to Coloma for a wake and buried him on this hill overlooking the spot that brought him fame and failure. A reconstruction of a rough board cabin he occupied before moving to Kelsey is a short downhill hike away, near the 1858 St. Joseph's Catholic Church.

The village of Lotus • *About a mile north, then a mile west on Lotus Road.* This tiny town offers a funky old general store and an antique shop, housed in Gold Rush era buildings. Timbers inside the 1855 Adam Lohry's General Store, on the right near an antique shop a block or so beyond the general store, may have been sawed at Sutter's Mill. The town originally was named Marshall (for obvious reasons) then it was changed to Uniontown. Prowl through the old Uniontown cemetery and you'll find headstones dating back to Marshall's day.

Nuggets

Mormon Cabin • *Opposite Sutter's Mill.* This is a nugget primarily because of the story behind it. It's a faithful replica of a workers' cabin with a plank table and benches, crude wooden bunks and tools hung from wall pegs. It was built for several of Marshall's workers, members of the Mormon Battalion that had come West to help liberate California from Mexico. They

Like a poorly posed photo, James Marshall's statue points stiffly toward the place where he accidentally discovered gold.

saw no combat, found jobs at Sutter's Fort, then came to Coloma with Marshall.

Originally, the workers occupied one wing of a double log cabin. The other wing housed Peter Wimmer, who supervised the Indian construction crew that built the tailrace, and his wife, the camp cook. The Mormons kept feuding with Mrs. Wimmer, insisting that they weren't getting their fair share of the grub. After a dispute in December, 1847, they asked Marshall to let them build another cabin where they could do their own cooking. By coincidence, they moved into their new home just one day before Marshall's epic discovery in the tailrace.

Chinese stores • *Adjacent to the museum, across Highway 49 from Sutter's Mill.* Built around 1860, these two stone buildings have been turned into mini-museums. Man Lee Store focuses on gold mining, with exhibits concerning ore processing, dredging and stamp mills. Wah Hop Store and Bank offers a fine example of a Chinese general store. Its contents include a rough table set for dinner with rice bowls and teacups, a makeshift desk where sales were transacted, and banks of drawers containing herbs and animal parts used for preparing potions. Pictures of ancestors, gone before and properly glorified, hang from the rough stone walls of a simple family altar. Both structures were built around 1859 by one Jonas Wilder, then leased to Chinese merchants.

Vineyard House Saloon • *Cold Springs Road.* There's a certain indefinable ambiance that makes a great bar, and whatever it is, the Vineyard House Saloon has it. It's a cozy old place, all brick and stone and weathered wood, occupying the former wine cellar of the Vineyard House Inn (see dining and lodging sections below). One can join the noisy camaraderie at the old fashioned bar, or retreat to a dimly lit side room for quiet moments with someone special.

DIVERSIONS

Hot air ballooning ● *c/o Coloma Country Inn, P.O. Box 502, Coloma, CA 95613; (916) 622-6919.* You can float blissfully above history on hot air balloon flights operating daily from Coloma, weather permitting.

River running ● As we mentioned earlier, the American River is just bouncy enough here to attract a lot of amateur rubber rafters and kayakers, and it's a major launching point for more extensive voyages through the wilder American River Canyon beyond. Amateurs like to play in the splashy mile-and-a-half run between Coloma and Camp Lotus; it can get crowded on summer weekends. Several campgrounds offer put-in or take-out spots.

A more challenging stretch extends from Chili Bar, off Highway 193 above Placerville, 20 miles through Coloma and Lotus to Salmon Falls bridge, south of Pilot Hill, near Auburn. Or one can take half this route by putting in at Coloma. With names like Meatgrinder and Satan's Cesspool, these are serious rapids to be tackled only by skilled boatmen. These commercial operators in the area can get you through wet but unscathed:

A Whitewater Connection, 7170 Hwy. 49, Coloma, CA 95613, 622-6446; **Adventure Connection**, P.O. Box 475, Coloma, CA 95613, 626-7385; **American River Recreation**, 6770 Marshall Grade Rd., Coloma, CA 95613, 622-6802; **California River Trips**, P.O. Box 460, Lotus, CA 95651, 626-8006; **Chili Bar Whitewater Tours**, 1669 Chili Bar Ct., Placerville, CA 95667, 622-6632; **Gold Country River Runners**, 431 Coloma Heights Rd., Coloma, CA 95613, 626-7326; **Mother Lode River Trips**, P.O. Box 456, Coloma, CA 95613, 626-4187; **Outdoors Unlimited**, P.O. Box 854, Lotus, CA 95615, 626-7668; **River Runners Inc.**, P.O. Box 433, Coloma, CA 95613, 622-5110; **Wilderness Adventures**, (800) 323-7238.

GOLD COUNTRY DINING

Coloma Club Cafe ● ∆∆ $$

Highway 49 at Marshall road, just east of Coloma; (916) 626-6390. American; dinners $7 to $10.50; full bar. Daily 6:30 a.m. to 9 p.m. AMEX. Western-style cafe, newly renovated with a pioneer town facade; bright airy dining room. Varied menu, ranging from Stroganoff to lasagna to steaks, chicken and chops. Hearty full-course dinners include soup or salad and garlic bread. Pleasing scatter of cowboy and mining regalia in adjoining bar.

The Vineyard House ● ∆∆∆ $$$ ∅

Cold Springs Road, Coloma; (916) 622-2217. American-continental; dinners $11 to $17; full bar service. Friday-Saturday 5 to 10, Sunday 3 to 8:30 (hours may be expanded later). Reservations accepted. MC/VISA, AMEX. An eye-appealing restaurant in an 1878 Victorian inn with plate rails, hurricane lamps, bentwood chairs and big oval rag rugs. Busy menu, ranging from papaya chicken and shrimp dijon to beef stroganoff and New York steak. After several rocky years, food and service have improved under new management, and the American folk setting is delightful. Dinner theater specials offered in combination with the adjacent Old Coloma Theatre.

Is there life after dark?

The **Old Coloma Theatre** (626-5282) offers oldstyle melodramas (Are there any other kind?) on Friday and Saturday nights at 8 from May through September in a properly rustic theater off Cold Springs Road. The dramatists obviously have a sense of humor; they call themselves the **Coloma Crescent Players** and they use an outhouse for a logo.

The **Coloma Club** (626-6390) features live music on Friday and Saturday nights, and the new management at the **Vineyard House saloon** (622-2217) may bring in entertainment. The recently re-opened **Sierra Nevada House** (621-1649) offers live music Friday, Saturday and Sunday.

LODGINGS

Coloma Country Inn ● ⌂⌂ $$$$ ØØ

P.O. Box 502 (345 High St.), Coloma, CA 95613; (916) 622- 6919. Doubles $89 with private bath, $79 with shared bath. Combination lodging-hot air balloon package $195 per person. Six units; full breakfast. No smoking. Checks accepted, no credit cards. This 1856 yellow and white trimmed Victorian just above the historic park is nestled among green lawns and shady trees. A handsome old structure with bargeboard trim and a wrap-around porch, it has been carefully restored by innkeepers Cindi and Alan Ehrgott. Alan is a hot air balloonist; he'll provide guests with an aerial view of the valley where gold was discovered. The inn's interior decor is a mix of American country and Victorian furniture, accented by a large collection of antique quilts. A prim little gazebo, popular for weddings, graces the five and a half acre grounds. Evening amenities include wine or brandy with snacks.

Sierra Nevada House ● ⌂⌂ $$$

Highway 49 at Lotus Road (P.O. Box 496), Coloma, CA 95613; (916) 621-1649. Doubles $65 to $75, singles $55 to $65. No credit cards. Six rooms with private baths. No credit cards. This 1850 wood and stone hotel and way station offers simple, neat and clean rooms with early American decor. The six rooms are off a second floor wrap-around balcony and one even has its own personal ghost, Isabella, who caught her husband in a tryst here a century or so ago. Light snacks and ice cream goodies are served from an oldstyle ice cream parlor on the first floor. A Western style saloon is adjacent, featuring live music on weekends. Occasional barbecue lunches and dinners are served at a cozy patio out front.

The Vineyard House ● ⌂⌂ $$$ ØØ

P.O. Box 176 (Cold Springs Road), Coloma, CA 95613; (916) 622-2217. Doubles from $70. Seven units with share bath. No smoking. MC/VISA, AMEX. The 1878 Vineyard House earns its name from its builders, who produced wines in the area. This venerable country inn contains a restaurant (discussed above), a great bar (one of our Nuggets) and seven hotel rooms. Rooms are nicely appointed and color-coordinated with lots of Victorian touches and antique furniture. One room with pleated fabric walls is particularly attractive. This is a folksy country place where life moves at a leisurely pace, particularly in the morning, since there's only one bathroom for the seven units!

CAMPGROUNDS & RV PARKS

Although there are no state park campsites at Coloma, several private campgrounds operate in the area. All are on the river, affording handy put-in and/or take-outs for rafters. They're quite busy with river runners on weekends, so make reservations well in advance.

American River Resort • *P.O. Box 427 (Highway 49), Coloma, CA 95613; (916) 622-6700. RV and tent sites, from $12. Reservations accepted.* Water and electric hookups, flush potties, showers, picnic tables and barbecues. Swimming pool, kids' fish pond, water sports. Closed in winter.

Camp Lotus • *P.O. Box 578, Lotus, CA 95651; (916) 622-8672. RV and tent sites from $10. Reservations accepted.* Riverside campground with water and electric hookups; flush potties, showers, barbecues and picnic tables. Fishing, swimming, water sports, horse shoes, volleyball; small store. A popular staging spot for river runners, it can get crowded on summer weekends. Closed in winter.

Coloma Resort • *6921 Mount Murphy Rd. (P.O. Box 516), Coloma, CA 95613; (916) 621-2267. RV and tent sites, $20 to $22.50. Reservations accepted; MC/VISA, AMEX.* Nicely landscaped campground across the river from the park, with water and electric hookups, flush potties, showers, picnic tables and barbecues. Shaded riverfront campsites; convenience store, fishing, swimming, water sports. Closed in winter.

ON THE ROAD AGAIN...TO AUBURN

Highway 49 crosses the American River just beyond Coloma, and curves gently through the wooded countryside. At Pilot Hill, note the old three-story Bayley House, built in 1862 to serve travelers on the Central Pacific Railroad that was supposed to pass within half a mile. The railway was re-routed and Acandor A. Bayley lost his shirt on the project. This also was the site of California's first grange hall, Pilot Hill Grange #1, organized in 1870.

Continuing on, you'll pass through the town of Cool, once a stage stop and now a pleasant looking hamlet with a few Western-style shops. Beyond Cool, you approach one of the most spectacular settings along the entire length of Highway 49—the dual canyons of the north and middle forks of the American River. The route winds dizzily down a thousand feet and crosses a low bridge into Placer County at the junction of the two streams. Pausing at a turnout, you can see both canyons cleaving the forested hills, their twin whitewater courses glittering in the afternoon sun. It's a popular area for swimming, rock-sunning and gold panning.

You'll see evidence of the hand of man a few thousand feet upstream: a spectacularly high bridge, leaping the north fork canyon, 730 feet above the water. Called the Foresthill Bridge, this slender span is graceful but ominous. It was built to cross a reservoir behind the proposed Auburn Dam, which would bury both chasms and turn their swift currents into skinny, lifeless fingers of flat water. The on-again, off-again scheme has been on the back burner for years.

To learn more...

Marshall Gold Discovery State Historic Park, P.O. Box 265, Coloma, CA 95613; (916) 622-3470.

"Rose and got breckfast. At 11 attended preaching under a live oak by a Congregational Minister from New Bedford. Went to work. Made a small show. All of us got much less than an ounce. It is verry much like work. Potatoes $1 a piece, onions the same. At night the Wolves and Kiotas give us plenty of music."
— letter home by Auburn 49er Hiram Pierce

OLD TOWN AUBURN AND
PLACER COUNTY COURTHOUSE

Chapter Fourteen
AUBURN & SURROUNDS
Seeking history in a Sacramento suburb

Auburn was a pleasant surprise. Working through the stoplights of its extensive sprawl, knowing that it sat astraddle busy Interstate 80, we expected to find little more than an extended suburb of Sacramento.

Then we discovered Old Town, a gathering of rough stone and tidy brick buildings tucked into the irregular contours of a slope above Auburn Ravine. Although it's surrounded by a modern community and I-80 is so close that freight trucks rattle its shingles, Old Town Auburn is one of the Mother Lode's best preserved historic areas. It is, in fact, a national historical landmark.

THE WAY IT WAS ● Auburn Ravine was a seasonal creek rich in placer gold, just 20 miles north of the Marshall site at Coloma, so its discovery is no surprise. However, the man who put Auburn on the Gold Country map came from another direction.

French immigrant Claude Chana arrived at Sutter's Fort in 1846 and began working alongside James Marshall as a cooper. Marshall went on to build his mill on the American River and Chana took up farming near present-day Sacramento. When word of the discovery reached him, he dropped his plow and headed for the Coloma diggins.

En route, he and his party camped in a small ravine, ran a few pans, found gold and went no further. That was on May 16, 1848, less than four months after Marshall's discovery. The typical tent camp sprang up and Auburn became one of the Mother Lode's first mining towns.

Fire destroyed the original shanty town in 1855, and it was rebuilt of more substantial stuff higher up the ravine, where Old Town Auburn stands today. Its name probably came from Auburn, New York, since former mem-

169

bers of a New York regiment, sent West to help snatch California from the Mexicans, were among its first gold seekers.

The placer yields soon ran out, but Auburn's position at the confluence of the north and middle forks of the American River made it an important trading center. The town's future was assured in the early 1860s. Engineer Theodore Judah decided that the best route for the transcontinental railroad was via Auburn through Donner Pass.

Auburn wasn't a typically raucous gold camp, although a couple of incidents did mar its otherwise conservative upbringing.

The area's Maidu Indians were never particularly hostile to the miners swarming over their tribal lands. However, they had a penchant for petty theft, helping themselves to tools, liquor and an occasional mule. So in 1849, several Auburn men formed a vigilante group called the California Blades and set about to rid the area of its Native Americans. They succeeded in brutal fashion, destroying an entire Indian village near present-day Colfax and killing two more Indians at another camp. When the Maidu retaliated by staging a robbery at a mining camp, the Blades killed 20 more braves and hung their scalps in front of way stations between Colfax and Auburn.

One of the Gold Country's first and busiest stagecoach robbers was a dashing young man from Quebec named Rattlesnake Dick Barter. He began his life of crime after being accused of stealing a suit in the nearby mining camp of Rattlesnake Bar (thus his nickname). After being tried and acquitted in Auburn, he moved on to Shasta County, got into more trouble, then began his career as a highwayman. For seven years, he held up assorted stagecoaches from Shasta County to Auburn, formed two different outlaw gangs, went to jail and escaped several times.

In 1859, he and a fellow gang member were attacked by a pursuing sheriff's posse. After a quick exchange of gunfire, the posse withdrew and the two outlaws fled into the night. Dick's body was found the next morning a mile from the battle scene. He'd been shot twice through the body, obviously by the deputies, and once through the head, most likely a *coupe de grace* administered by himself or his outlaw buddy because he was bleeding to death. A note clutched in a gloved hand read: "Rattlesnake Dick dies; but never surrenders..." Richard Barter had not yet celebrated his 27th birthday.

THE WAY IT IS • The largest town in the Gold Country with a population topping 10,000, Auburn sits atop a bluff above the north fork of the American River, and it sprawls over a good share of the nearby countryside.

The Southern Pacific Railway chugs along the same route that was blazed through here by the Central Pacific more than a century ago. Thus, nearby Roseville has the largest freight staging yard west of Chicago. Interstate 80 slices through the middle of town on its dash from San Francisco to New York, spawning clusters of service stations and motels in Auburn's eastern suburbs. Lake Tahoe and Reno-bound vacationers keep them busy in summer and winter. North of town, historic Highway 49 becomes a busy four-lane boulevard lined with shopping centers.

Auburn's focal point is the bold Greco-Roman Placer County Courthouse, a domed wedding cake of a structure perched atop a hill, looking down on the shingle and tin roofs of Old Town. Another curiosity is a tall, skinny fire station that looks more like a fanciful ice cream parlor, with red and white

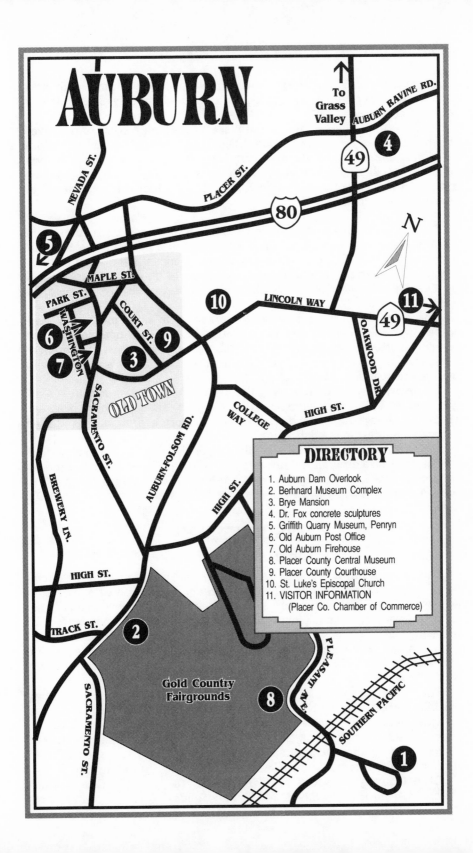

AUBURN

To Grass Valley

AUBURN RAVINE RD.

NEVADA ST.

PLACER ST.

49

4

80

N

5

MAPLE ST.

PARK ST.

WASHINGTON

COURT ST.

LINCOLN WAY

10

11

49

6

9

OAKWOOD DR.

7

3

OLD TOWN

SACRAMENTO ST.

COLLEGE WAY

HIGH ST.

AUBURN-FOLSOM RD.

BREWERY LN.

HIGH ST.

DIRECTORY

1. Auburn Dam Overlook
2. Berhnard Museum Complex
3. Brye Mansion
4. Dr. Fox concrete sculptures
5. Griffith Quarry Museum, Penryn
6. Old Auburn Post Office
7. Old Auburn Firehouse
8. Placer County Central Museum
9. Placer County Courthouse
10. St. Luke's Episcopal Church
11. VISITOR INFORMATION
    (Placer Co. Chamber of Commerce)

HIGH ST.

TRACK ST.

2

SACRAMENTO ST.

Gold Country Fairgrounds

8

PLEASANT AVE.

SOUTHERN PACIFIC

1

stripes and a witch's hat tower. Between these two architectural landmarks, 20 or more 19th century stone, brick and clapboard buildings line an irregular maze of streets.

If you're into antiques, this is the place. More than a score of these yesterday boutiques are scattered about Old Town. All are housed in historic buildings, along with a handful of restaurants and a gift shop or two. Auburn's excellent Placer County Museum sits in the Gold Country Fairgrounds a few blocks from Old Town, and beyond that you'll encounter an abandoned overlook.

A what?

In the 1970s, conservationists lost a battle to prevent construction of the giant Auburn Dam that would back water 25 miles or so up the beautiful canyons of the north and middle forks of the American River. What environmentalists couldn't stop, Mother Nature did. In 1975, an earthquake shook up Oroville, 60 miles to the north, and a fault was discovered near the Auburn dam site.

The pluggers of rivers reluctantly parked their earth movers. A landscaped overlook where visitors could watch them work is now deserted; an occasional weed pokes through the asphalt parking lot. Below, the American River carefully threads its way through the cuts and gouges and eroded dirt piles of the abandoned dam site.

However, some folk, embracing the attitude of "Build it, dam it!" (a slogan seen on T-shirts and bumper stickers a few years back), have been agitating to renew the project. The recent California drought has further generated interest in the dam thing.

Incidentally, if you're faithfully following Highway 49 from Coloma, don't stay on the route through Auburn or you'll miss Old Town. To find this worthy spot, follow Lincoln Way (which 49 intersects) westward through downtown Auburn. It takes you past the landmark Courthouse and down into Old Town.

DISCOVERIES
The best attractions

Old Town Auburn Walking Tour ● *Brochure available free at the Chamber of Commerce, 601 Lincoln Way (Elm Avenue) in the restored Auburn railway depot.* As we mentioned earlier, this area has been designated a national historical area. You can explore each and every nook and cranny on foot by following the chamber's walking tour brochure. The hike begins at a Paul Bunyan-sized concrete statue of Claude Chana, hunched over his gold pan, and wanders for half a dozen blocks through the pleasing crazy-quilt pattern of Old Town.

The route takes you past that wonderfully silly looking firehouse; along old Main Street with its hand-hewn stone curbs and embedded rings used for tying horses; up Commercial Street past Lawyer's Row, once a group of attorney's offices and now a cluster of antique shops; past the remnants of Chinatown with three surviving stores; and, if you're up to a short hike, to the beautifully-restored County Courthouse crowning the nearby hill.

Gold Country Museum ● *1273 High St. (at the Gold Country Fairgrounds), Auburn; (916) 889-4134. Tuesday-Sunday 10 to 4, closed Mondays* *and holidays; adults $1, kids 6 to 16 and adults 65 and over, 50 cents.* Built of rough stone and logs as a WPA project in the early 1940s, the museum offers a quick and fairly complete study of gold mining in early Placer County.

Exhibits include a walk-through model mine tunnel with displays of the various types of gold found in the area, an interesting collection of other minerals and crystals unearthed by miners in their quest for gold, a loaded ore cart, the usual model stamp mill and various items of mining equipment. Among other displays are the re-creation of an assayer's office with its clutter of mortars and pestles, retorts and crucibles; artifacts from Auburn's former Chinese community; Maidu Indian relics and the usual pioneer regalia.

Our favorite exhibit is a beautifully detailed scale model of the Placer County Courthouse, done in leaded stained glass.

Placer County Courthouse and Museum ● *101 Maple St., Auburn; (916) 889-6500. Call for hours.* This imposing yellow brick structure was re-opened in early 1991 after extensive remodeling and re-dedicated as the county courthouse. It was built in 1894 from local materials: granite from Rocklin, bricks made in Auburn and slate from nearby El Dorado County.

With its impressive capitol dome and four-sided matched entrances topped by Greek pediments, is one of the most photographed structures in the Gold Country. Illuminated at night, it stands like a beacon above the rolling hills of old Auburn. Courts occupy the upper floors and the new Placer County Museum is being housed in several ground floor rooms.

We say "is being" because the project was still underway at press time. Initial exhibits were to be opened in mid-1992 and from the plans we observed, the museum will be a delight. Visitors will see meticulously restored sheriff's and county clerk's offices with much of the original furniture and a main exhibit room tracing Auburn's history from the Maidu Indians to the present through a series of skillfully done dioramas. A 1920 store front with period window dressings will change with the season and a special exhibit traces the history of local transportation including, of course, the Transcontinental Railroad.

Even if you hit Auburn before the museum is completed, put the Courthouse on your must-see list. The carefully-restored structure is a pleasing blend of 18th century and Art Deco, with terrazzo floors, polished woods and marble stairways. It's open during normal county business hours.

The rest

Bernhard Museum Complex ● *291 Auburn-Folsom Rd. near High Street; (916) 889-4156. Tuesday-Friday 11 to 3 and weekends noon to 4, closed Mondays and holidays. Adults $1, kids 6 to 16 and seniors 65 and older, 50 cents.* The facility is essentially an annex of the Placer County Museum and one ticket is good for both places. It began life in 1851 as the Traveler's Rest Hotel, then was purchased by early viticulturist Bernhardus (Benjamin) Bernhard in 1868 to serve as his spacious residence.

Guided tours take visitors through its rooms, furnished in the style of a late 19th century middle class home. Also part of the complex are the old Bernhard winery and wine processing building, featuring wine making and cooperage exhibits.

Doctor Fox sculptures ● *391 Auburn Ravine Rd., Auburn; (916) 885-2769.* Kenneth H. Fox is an Auburn dentist who creates monumental con-

This concrete monument to the Chinese of the Gold Rush, done by local dentist-sculptor Kenneth H. Fox, stands before the Auburn Chamber of Commerce in the town's former railroad station.

crete sculptures in his spare time (including Claude and his gold pan at Old Town). His main collection of statues, some as much as 40 feet high, occupy the grounds of his dental office and the public is free to browse. They depict voluptuous Indian maidens and other figures done in a rough, textured finish with remarkably detailed facial features. Since most are nudes, certain other features are remarkably detailed, too. Another guidebook calls them "X-rated," but that's silly. They're no more naughty than Michelangelo's "David."

Dutch Flat Museum ● *Main Street, Dutch Flat; (916) 389-2774. Noon to 4 Wednesdays and weekends in summer only, other times by appointment; admission free.* This charming little museum in the nearby town of Dutch Flat is housed in an older miner's cabin, with furnishings typical of the 1860s and a display of photos of the town during its Gold Rush prime.

Foresthill Divide Museum ● *24601 Harrison St., Foresthill; (916) 367-3988. Open weekends from 11 to 3; admission free.* Situated in Leroy Botts Memorial Park, this small-town museum relates the history of the Foresthill area, with exhibits focusing on local geology, the Gold Rush, early settlers and logging, including a scale model of the Foresthill Logging Company.

Griffith Quarry Museum and Park • *Taylor and Rock Springs roads (six miles southwest of Auburn), Penryn; (916) 663-1837. Park open daily from sunrise to sunset, museum open weekends from noon to 4; admission free.* A century-old granite quarry has been fashioned into a 23-acre park with three miles of nature trails and picnic facilities. A small museum in the quarry's former office building offers displays concerning the granite industry and the history of Penryn and Loomis Basin.

Nuggets

Antique row • *Commercial Street between Sacramento and Maple, Old Town.* Nearly 30 antique galleries are stuffed into the historic buildings of Lawyer's Row in this one-block section of Old Town. It's a paradise for collectors of the historic, the odd and the funky.

Auburn Railway Station (chamber of commerce) • *601 Lincoln Way at Elm; (916) 885-5616.* Refurbished in 1991 to provide quarters for the chamber of commerce, the old railway station is well worth a stop, even if you aren't seeking visitor information. The 19th century structure has been carefully restored. Nearby, a prim little park has been built around yet another of Dr. Fox's monumental concrete sculptures; this one honors the Chinese contribution to the Gold Rush. A few yesterday rail cars are adjacent.

Gold Rush mural • *858 High St., Auburn.* A large mural—perhaps the largest in the Gold Country—covers the facade of this low-rise building, depicting assorted gold mining scenes. Highway 49 becomes High Street in downtown Auburn, so watch for it on your right as you follow the historic route north from Coloma.

Old Auburn Post Office • *Lincoln Way at Commercial Street, Old Town.* Dating from 1853, this venerable facility is California's oldest continually operating post office and one of the oldest in the entire West. With oiled wooden floors and iron doors, it's part of a row of buildings that escaped the 1855 fire. The entire block, in fact, is one of the oldest commercial complexes in the state.

Old Fire House • *Between Washington Street and Lincoln Way in Old Town.* This red and white striped confection of a firehouse was constructed in 1893 for the Auburn Hook and Ladder Company. The company itself was organized in 1852 as the first volunteer fire brigade west of Boston. The original bell is still in place, beneath the witch's hat roof, and it tolls at 8, noon and 5. The fire brigade fought the disastrous blaze of 1855, but it fought in vain. The entire town burned in less time than it takes to cook a Sunday dinner.

Shanghai Bar • *289 Washington St., Old Town.* This wonderfully scruffy pub is Auburn's oldest drinking establishment. What's more, it's a virtual museum of odds and ends and gold rush relics and game trophies. Note the pressed tin ceiling and a rear wall papered with old Chinese newspapers.

DETOUR

Auburn to Foresthill and Dutch Flat • *A 75-mile loop trip.* This scenic ridge route leads to the former mining camps of Foresthill and Michigan

Bar, high in the conifer foothills of the Sierra Nevada.

To begin, follow Lincoln Way north from Old Auburn (paralleling Interstate 80), then turn right onto Foresthill Road about 1.5 miles out of town. You'll soon shed Auburn's suburbs and cross that spectacularly high Foresthill Bridge mentioned in the last chapter. In fact, my son Dan and I crossed on foot, for the bridge-builders added pedestrian paths to both sides.

We succumbed to the temptation to launch a couple of paper airplanes at mid span, and watched them spiral lazily and gracefully down to the ribbon of water, 730 feet below. Yes, that's probably considered littering, and we certainly *do not* recommend it. But do you know that those fragile little gliders stayed airborne for more than five minutes?

Foresthill road follows the North Fork of the American River canyon for several miles, then runs along a forest-cloaked ridge, offering splendid mountain views in both directions. After 15 miles, it enters the alpine community of Foresthill. Gold was discovered here in 1850 and its famous Jenny Lind Mine produced more than $10 million dollars worth before it played out in the 1880s.

Little remains of the original Forest Hill gold camp, although modern Foresthill (now one word) is a pleasant place. Its main street widens into a broad boulevard and its shops, stores and service stations are shaded by pine groves. The town's most prominent landmark is a huge American Forest Products lumber mill that fills the air with the scent of newly cut timber.

From here, drive northeast, following signs to Michigan Bluff, an end-of-the-road mountain town clinging to the downslope of a steep hillside. The settlement was started in the early 1850s as Michigan City a bit farther down the slope. Relentless hydraulic mining eroded its foundations and threatened to send it to the bottom of the gully, so it was moved farther up the bluff. Today, it's a small gathering of old tin roofed homes occupied by a few seekers of solitude. It has no business district, so do not arrive in need of gasoline, food or drink.

Retrace your winding route back to Foresthill, then follow the equally twisting Yankee Jims Road west to the town of that name. Yankee Jim was an Australian who had no luck panning for gold so he took up horse-thieving. He was chased from the camp that bears his name and, ironically, rich placer deposits were found soon after he left. Yankee Jims briefly was the richest and largest gold camp in Placer County; today it's a small collection of weather-abused shacks. Continue west, over a boulder-strewn crossing of the North Fork of the American River, then rejoin Interstate 80 and head north toward Dutch Flat.

Incidentally, Yankee Jims Road is a twisting dirt route that spirals down into the American River Canyon, with an equally serpentine climb back out. Those reluctant to subject their vehicles or their nerves to this roller-coaster roadway might prefer retrace their route down Foresthill Road to Auburn, then drive north on I-80 to Dutch Flat.

Snuggled deep in the piney woods, Dutch Flat is one of La Veta Madre's most charming villages. This tiny town of three hundred folks is a virtual outdoor museum of 19th century wooden and brick buildings, for it is one of the few Gold Rush towns that never suffered a major fire. Among its noteworthy survivors are an 1852 I.O.O.F. Hall, a Masonic Hall dating from 1856, an ancient Episcopal Church and the two-story Dutch Flat Hotel, built

THE TRACKS THAT TIED AMERICA TOGETHER

If you're a devotee of choo choo history, you can trace the route of America's first transcontinental railroad as it passes through Placer County en route to its switchback climb over the Sierra Nevada near Donner Summit.

Five state historical landmarks chart its progress: at the Southern Pacific Depot in Roseville, in downtown Rocklin, at Newcastle's Southern Pacific Depot, on a slope below the SP depot in Auburn and beside the Red Caboose Museum in Colfax.

California, America's fastest growing state in the 1850s, was a virtual island, isolated from the rest of the country by a thousand miles of mountains, desert and prairie. Only the iron horse would be capable of securely tying the two halves of the new nation together. Thus, even as the Pony Express galloped through Placerville, engineer Theodore Judah planned a cross-country railroad through Auburn. That, along with a telegraph line following much of its route, soon would put the ponies out of business.

Judah campaigned tirelessly for an Atlantic-Pacific railroad for a decade, making several trips to Washington to try and win federal aid. Rebuffed by Congress, he took his idea in 1861 to four Sacramento merchants, Leland Stanford, Charles Crocker, Collis P. Huntington and Mark Hopkins. The group formed the Central Pacific Rail Road of California, issued $8.5 million in shares and set about to link the nation together.

The federal government, occupied with the Civil War, did not participate financially, although it offered tax breaks and granted huge chunks of land that ultimately made the railroad owners rich.

Construction began on January 8, 1863. From the West, a predominately Chinese crew, which became known as Crocker's pets, hacked the Central Pacific through the precipitous Sierra. Union Pacific workers, mostly Irish, laid tracks across the Great Plains, coming from the East. They converged at Promontory, Utah, in May, 1869. There, Central Pacific president Stanford, slightly pickled from partying, swung and missed a couple of times before driving one of several Golden Spikes.

The Chinese and Irish got no thanks. In fact the Asians were brushed aside and not even allowed in the historic photos of the joining of the rails. The Big Four—Stanford, Crocker, Huntington and Hopkins—went on to become the wealthiest and most influential men of 19th century California.

in 1852. An assortment of simple tin-roofed homes and a few opulent Victorians are scattered among the pines.

A German named Joseph Dorenbach found gold in the gravels hereabouts in 1851. The "Dutch" name probably was a warping of the German word *Deutsch*. The town prospered as a placer and hydraulic mining center until the 1880s. It might still be thriving today had not both the railroad and the highway missed it, passing a couple of miles to the east. We like it as it is, a pleasant yesterday village dozing comfortably among the tall pines.

After prowling Dutch Flat's streets and admiring its Gold Rush architectural survivors, return to I-80 for the quick downhill run to Auburn.

DIVERSIONS

High country hiking, boating, swimming and such • Tahoe National Forest occupies a curious checkerboard pattern northeast of Auburn, intermixed with private landholdings. Assorted lakes—some private and some in the national forest—offer boating, swimming and fishing. Hiking trails and high country camps lure outdoor types. To learn all about it, check the addresses at the end of this chapter.

Hot air ballooning • *Big Sky Balloons, P.O. Box 5665, Auburn, CA 95604; (800) BIG-SKYE or (916) 885-6717.* The firm will take you into the ethers above Auburn, and it also offers a combination package that includes a balloon ride, a night in a bed and breakfast and a whitewater raft trip.

Farm and ranch shopping • *The 49er Fruit Trail and Christmas Tree Lane, P.O. Box 317, Newcastle, CA 95658.* The organization coordinates direct-from-the-grower shopping for fruit, veggies, nuts and Christmas trees from Auburn and Roseville to Grass Valley and Nevada City. Send for a free guide at the address above. The folks would appreciate a return- addressed, stamped, legal-sized envelope.

Rivers and mountains • *Auburn State Recreation Area, P.O. Box 3266, Auburn, CA 95604; (916) 885-4527 or 988-0205.* Canyons of the north and middle forks of the American River are popular for gold panning, swimming, picnicking and hiking. Much of this area, immediately east of town, is contained in the Auburn State Recreation Area, which maintains a network of hiking trails in the river canyons and surrounding mountains.

Several stretches of the American River offer challenges for white water rafting. Skilled river folks and some commercial operators run a 14-mile stretch from Eucre Bar near Alta to a point near Colfax on the north fork, and a 25-mile section from Oxbow Bend above Foresthill to the Highway 49 bridge near Auburn on the middle fork. Both offer splendid wilderness scenery and **serious** rapids, so they should be attempted only with proper preparation and equipment. Tahoe National Forest and Auburn State Recreation Area rangers have information, or consult the *California White Water* book.

GOLD COUNTRY DINING

Note: All Auburn restaurants are smoke-free, by city ordinance.

Butterworth's • △△△△ $$$ ØØ

1522 Lincoln Way at Court Street (above old town), Auburn; (916) 885-0249. Continental; dinners $13 to $22; wine and beer. Lunch 11:30 to 2 and dinner 5 to 9 Monday-Saturday; Sunday brunch from 10 to 2 then dinner from 3 to 9. Reservations recommended; MC/VISA, AMEX. Auburn's most eye-appealing restaurant, housed in an 1887 Victorian mansion. Several small dining areas give the place a feeling of intimacy; they're nicely appointed, with crystal chandeliers, print wallpaper and lace curtains. The fare, such as beef Wellington, tournedos Mecina, chicken with cider herbs and prawns with lime and cilantro, is as appealing as the decor.

Cafe Delicias • ∆ $ Ø
1591 Lincoln Way in Old Auburn; (916) 885-2050. Mexican; meals $5 to $10; wine and beer. Daily 11 a.m. to 9 p.m. MC/VISA, DC, CB. Pleasantly funky Mexican cafe in the heart of Old Town with the usual smashed beans and rice dishes, plus specialties such as *carne asada, taquitos rancheros* and *flautas Juarez.* Generally tasty fare preceded by crisp tortilla chips with a zesty sauce. Housed in an 1852 brick survivor of the great fire, the restaurant is decorated with the expected brightly colored Latin posters and other South of the Border regalia. It's one of four Cafes Delicias in the area.

The Headquarter House • ∆∆∆ $$$ ØØ
14500 Musso Rd. (Bell Road off I-80), Auburn; (916) 878-1906. American-Continental; dinners $15 to $25; full bar service. Lunch Wednesday-Saturday 11:30 to 3, dinner Wednesday-Thursday 5 to 9:30 and Friday-Saturday 5 to 11, Sunday brunch 10:30 to 2 and dinner 4:30 to 9:30. Reservations suggested on weekends; major credit cards. Appealing country style restaurant with open beam ceilings, distressed wood paneling, oak tables and framed hunting scenes. Situated among the pines in the ranch headquarters of the Dunipace Angus Ranch. Menu is a mix of European and American fare.

Lou La Bonte's • ∆∆ $$ ØØ
13460 Lincoln Way (off I-80 at Foresthill exit), Auburn; (916) 885-7755. American-Continental; dinners $9 to $15; full bar service. Daily 6:30 a.m. to 10:30 p.m. (to 11 Friday and Saturday). Reservations suggested on weekends; MC/VISA, AMEX, DC. A noisy, friendly local institution, in business since 1946; offering shrimp Gregory and steak Diane from across the Atlantic, plus the usual American steaks, chickens and chops. Ample servings but a very uneven kitchen; several dining experiences suggest that the place thrives mostly on its past reputation. Simple decor with high ceilings, picture windows and an brick fireplace.

Mary Belle's • ∆∆ $ ØØ
1590 Lincoln Way, Old Town Auburn; (916) 885-3598. American; meals $4 to $7; no alcohol. Monday-Saturday 7 a.m. to 3 p.m., Sunday 8 to 3. MC/VISA, AMEX. Cute little cafe/antique parlor with bentwood chairs, simulated marble topped tables and lace curtains. It's filled with a happy clutter of early American antiques. Basic American breakfast-lunch menu featuring hamburgers and other sandwiches, liver and onions, fried prawns and such.

Shanghai Restaurant • ∆∆∆ $$ ØØ
289 Washington St., Old Town Auburn; (916) 823-2613. Cantonese; dinners $7 to $14; full bar service. Daily 11:30 to 9:30. Major credit cards. Longtime local favorite that has been dishing up good Cantonese fare since 1906. Typical Cantonese menu featuring and subtly seasoned veggies, fresh and lightly cooked fish. Housed in the former American Hotel in Old Town, with a mix of early Gold Rush and Oriental decor; cozy dining alcoves beneath 16-foot embossed metal ceilings. Patio in the rear. One of the Gold Country's better Asian restaurants. Adjacent bar listed above in Nuggets.

Is there life after dark?
Lou La Bonte's at 13460 Lincoln Way (885-7755) offers dinner theater Friday and Saturday nights, and live entertainment happens Friday and Sat-

urday nights in the **Harris' Restaurant** bar at 13480 Lincoln Way (885-3090). **The Shanghai,** 289 Washington St., (885-9446) books bands and combos on Fridays and Saturdays. **Headquarter House** restaurant off the I-80 Bell Road exit (878-1906) features live music nightly in the cocktail lounge.

LODGINGS
Bed & breakfast inns

Powers Mansion Inn • ⌂⌂⌂ $$$$
164 Cleveland Ave., Auburn, CA 95603; (916) 885-1166. Doubles from $75. Fifteen units, all with private baths. Full breakfast. Major credit cards. At the turn of the century, Gold Rush millionaire Harold T. Powers built Auburn's largest and most stylish Victorian mansion. It is now one of Auburn's most stylish bed and breakfast inns. The rooms are color coordinated, with period furnishings and old fashion yet modern bathrooms. "Poofy satin comforters atop big brass beds, windows covered with lace, private baths with lots of brass and porcelain," boasts the brochure, and our visit confirmed all this. The mansion is in downtown Auburn, about a mile from Old Town.

Victorian Manor • ⌂⌂⌂ $$$ ØØ
P.O. Box 959 (482 Main St.), Newcastle, CA 95658; (916) 663-3009. Doubles from $45. Four units with one private and three share baths. Continental breakfast. Smoking on the veranda. MC/VISA, AMEX. Innkeepers Cordy and Ed Sander have done a fine job in preserving the Victorian opulence of this 1900 Eastlake country home, with finely crafted ceiling medallions, cornices and other detail work. It's furnished in 19th century antiques, accented by lace and print wallpaper. Mrs. Sander often compliments this elegance by wearing one of her Victorian gowns. She also has a large collection of dolls dressed in 1930s finery. Guests can wander among huge camellias, 50-year-old orange trees and century-old Japanese maples in the spacious grounds, or sit and sip refreshments on the old fashioned veranda.

The Victorian Hill House • ⌂⌂⌂ $$$ ØØ
P.O. Box 9097 (195 Park St.), Auburn, CA 95604 (916) 885-5879. Doubles $65 to $85. Four rooms, three with shared baths and one with private bath. Full breakfasts. No smoking. MC/VISA. One of Auburn's oldest Victorians, this white clapboard house with green trim sits on a landscaped slope above Old Town. Each of the guest rooms has a predominant color theme; they're filled with antiques and assorted yesterday frills. Guests can relax in a pleasant garden and enjoy the view of Old Auburn below or take a dip in a pool or relax in a gazebo hot tub.

Motels

Auburn Inn • ⌂⌂⌂ $$$ Ø
1875 Auburn Ravine Rd. (Foresthill exit from I-80), Auburn, CA 95603; (800) 272-1444 (California only) or (916) 885-1800. Doubles $54 to $62, singles $48 to $56. Major credit cards. Attractive 85-unit motel with TV, room phones; some suites. Pool, spa, coin laundry; handicapped units. **Restaurant** adjacent.

Best Western Golden Key ● △△ $$ ∅
13450 Lincoln Way, Auburn, CA 95603; (800) 528-1234 or (916) 885-8611. Doubles $40 to $50, singles $38 to $44. Major credit cards. Nice 68-room motel with TV movies, room phones. Extensive landscaped grounds; year-around indoor pool. Off I-80 via Foresthill.

Country Squire Inn ● △△ $$ ∅
13480 Lincoln Way, Auburn, CA 95603; (800) 252-0077 or (916) 885-7025. Doubles $39 to $52, singles $34 to $38. Major credit cards. An 80-unit motel with TV, room phones; pool and spa. **Restaurant** serves American fare; dinners $8 to $12; Monday-Thursday 11 a.m. to 10 p.m., Friday-Saturday 7 a.m. to 11 p.m. and Sunday 7 to 10. Foresthill exit off I-80.

Elmwood Motel ● △△ $$
588 High St. (at Elm), Auburn, CA 95603; (916) 885-5186. Doubles $35 to $41; MC/VISA. Tidy little motel in downtown Auburn; cable TV, pool.

Foothills Motel ● △△ $$
13431 Bowman Rd., Auburn, CA 95603; (916) 885-8444. Doubles $36 to $40; MC/VISA. Cable TV, pool and spa; spacious grounds, near "motel row" off I-80 Foresthill exit.

CAMPGROUNDS & RV PARKS

Auburn KOA Kampground ● *3550 KOA Way (3.5 miles north, just off Highway 49), Auburn, CA 95603; (916) 885-0990. RV sites with full hookup $21, tent sites $15. Reservations accepted; MC/VISA.* Flush potties, showers, swimming pool and spa; store, playground, coin laundry, fish pond and rec room. Tree-shaded grounds. Open all year.

Bear River Park ● *Plum Tree Road, c/o Placer County Parks Division, 11476 C Ave., Auburn, CA 95603; (916) 889-7750. Thirty sites for tents or small self-contained RVs, $6.* Pit toilets, no hookups or showers. Picnic tables and barbecues; fishing, hiking and swimming. Open all year, but no potable water available in winter.

Gold Country Fairgrounds ● *P.O. Box 5527 (1273 High St.), Auburn, CA 95604; (916) 885-6281. RVs and trailers only, $10.* Water and electric hookups, flush potties and showers, a few picnic tables. Open all year.

Tahoe National Forest ● Several campgrounds are scattered among the forestlands, most with pit potties, barbecues and picnic tables, and no showers. For details, see addresses below.

ANNUAL EVENTS

Wild West Stampede, April at the Gold Country Fairgrounds, Auburn, (916) 885-6281; rodeo and horse show.

Firemen's Muster, late June at the Gold Country Fairgrounds, (916) 885-6281; firefighting demonstrations, games and equipment exhibits.

Gold Country Fair, early September at the Gold Country Fairgrounds, (916) 885-6281; the usual county fair fare with parades, livestock shows, exhibits, food booths and such.

Auburn Air Fair, early October at Auburn Municipal Airport, (916) 885-5863; aerobatics and aircraft displays.

Heritage Fair, mid-October in Old Town, (916) 885-5616; annual salute to Auburn's yesterday with exhibits, costumes, food booths crafts and such.

ON THE ROAD AGAIN...TO GRASS VALLEY

Are you sure this isn't Hayward? Highway 49 passes through the most commercially developed area along its entire length as it moves north out of Auburn. But soon the suburbs begin to thin, then they disappear.

During most of our drive along the route of the 49ers, pine and fir forests have been just above us, easily reached by short side trips but rarely along the highway itself. Now, as we approach Grass Valley, we climb higher into the flanks of the Sierra Nevada, up among the conifers. We are nearing the most scenic part of our long and fascinating trek along the Golden Chain.

To learn more...

Auburn Chamber of Commerce, 601 Lincoln Way, Auburn, CA 95603; (916) 885-5616. Housed in the handsomely restored Auburn railway depot at Lincoln and Elm, it's open weekdays 9 to 5.

Auburn State Recreation Area, P.O. Box 3266, Auburn, CA 95604; (916) 885-4527 or 988-0205. Your source for recreation information about the American River canyons.

Placer County Visitor Information Center, 661 Newcastle Rd. (P.O. Box 746), Newcastle, CA 95658; (916) 663-2061. Located off I-80 at the Newcastle exit three miles south of Auburn, it's open Wednesday-Sunday 9 to 4. When it's closed, visitors can pluck brochures from self-service racks.

Tahoe National Forest, Foresthill Ranger District office, 22830 Foresthill Rd., Foresthill; (916) 376-2224. Headquarters is at Highway 49 and Coyote Street, Nevada City, CA 95959; (916) 265-4531. These folks will provide you with the usual national forest recreational and campsite map for the usual two dollars.

"She still retained a slender, graceful figure. She had heavy black hair and the most brilliant flashing eyes I ever beheld. But ordinarily she was such a slattern that she was frankly disgusting. When attired in a low-necked gown as was her usual custom, even her liberal use of powder failed to conceal the fact that she stood much in need of a good application of soap."
— A Grass Valley neighbor's description of Lola Montez

EMPIRE MINE OFFICE IN GRASS VALLEY

Chapter Fifteen

GRASS VALLEY & SURROUNDS

Lola, Lotta and a lot of gold

Two events put Grass Valley on the map, and neither bore the slightest relationship to the other. In 1850, gold seeker George McKnight tripped over a small quartz outcropping while chasing a cow in the moonlight. He noticed a glimmer in the offending fragment and determined that it was gold. Four years later, after Grass Valley had swelled to a bustling mining town of 20,000, a flamboyant floozy named Lola Montez abandoned a sagging theatrical tour and bought a small home here.

Whatever Lola wanted, she didn't get in Grass Valley. She left after two years, after briefly tutoring future superstar Lotta Crabtree. On the other hand, George McKnight's discovery, that most of the Sierra's gold lay in quartz veins beneath the soil, kept the town thriving for well over a century.

Forget your images of bewhiskered argonauts squatting beside cold streams, swirling gravel in their pans and maybe dancing excitedly to the assayer's office with a nugget in hand. The new "prospectors" were entrepreneurs who convinced New York and San Francisco businessmen to invest money in complex mining operations.

The Gold Rush came of age in Nevada County and in doing so, it lost is youthful glamour and its virginity. It became big business. Grim-faced miners burrowed two miles into the earth to earn a few dollars a day, spent their paychecks at the company store and made the mine owners and investors rich.

THE WAY IT WAS ● The George McKnight story sounds rather fanciful, but history books repeat it so consistently that we're tempted to believe it. Some documents identify him as "Knight," but that's an error attributable to a little twist of history. McKnight was Irish, and the good Britons of Cornwall—Grass Valley's largest ethnic group—were troubled that one of the lads from Erin should get all that glory. So in recording the town's history, the Cornish sort of accidentally dropped the "Mc" from his name.

A few settlers preceded the argonauts to this area, coming over from Truckee in the late 1840s and pasturing their cattle in the rich grasslands that gave this pretty valley its name. Men with gold pans arrived in 1848 and their camp, called Boston Ravine, yielded a fair amount of placer glitter. However, it was McKnight's cow pasture stumble that created the Grass Valley which historians define today: the richest single town in the richest county of the Gold Country. In fact, one-fifth of California's total gold output came from Nevada County.

Initially, small-time miners pooled their energies and resources to dig into the earth, but it soon became apparent that big money was needed to burrow after the elusive veins. Large mining companies were formed, turning places like Grass Valley into company towns. A stable labor force was needed and company bosses discovered that the best men for the job were Cornish miners, experienced at digging for copper and tin in their native Cornwall, England.

Impressed by their skill, mine owners would ask if there were more where they came from. The Cornish men usually had a "Cousin Jack" or some such relative back in England, eager to leave because the Cornwall mining industry was in a slump. The endearing nickname stuck, and owners willingly put up the money to bring another Cousin Jack over from England.

Largest of the corporate mines—one of the largest in the country, in fact—was the Empire Mine. It operated from 1850 until 1956 and produced *5.8 million ounces* of gold. Tote that up on your calculator at today's prices! The Eureka, now a state park which we'll shortly explore, may have been the richest single gold mine in America. In fact, it yielded more glitter than the entire Yukon Gold Rush.

Grass Valley suffered one of the Gold Country's worst fires when flames digested 300 structures in 1855. Following the usual pattern, replacements were built of sturdier stuff, and many of these structures still house businesses in the downtown area. Some historians suggest that it was this particular fire that led to the Gold Country's distinctive architectural style of narrow brick and stone buildings with iron doors and shutters.

And where does Lola Montez come in? About a year before the fire, actually.

She was an Irish-Spanish lass, born Maria Dolores Eliza Rosanna Gilbert in Limerick, Ireland. With her silky black hair and flashing dark eyes, she gained fame as an exotic dancer and actress. Critics say she wasn't much of a dancer but she must have done something well, for she became the toast of Europe. She married and shed three husbands, and was the mistress to such gentlemen as Franz Lizst, Alexander Dumas, Nicholas I of Russia and King Louis I of Bavaria.

Lola launched an American tour in 1852 and landed in San Francisco. But jaded locals soon tired of her famous spider dance, in which she jiggled and wiggled and squirmed while imaginary spiders dropped from her scanty costume. Seeking a less sophisticated audience, she went on tour of the Gold Country. The miners weren't wild about spiders either, so she canceled her

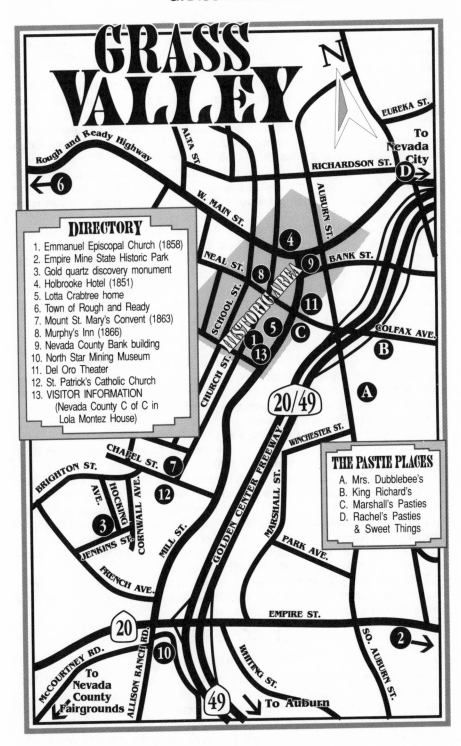

GRASS VALLEY

N

To Nevada City

DIRECTORY

1. Emmanuel Episcopal Church (1858)
2. Empire Mine State Historic Park
3. Gold quartz discovery monument
4. Holbrooke Hotel (1851)
5. Lotta Crabtree home
6. Town of Rough and Ready
7. Mount St. Mary's Convent (1863)
8. Murphy's Inn (1866)
9. Nevada County Bank building
10. North Star Mining Museum
11. Del Oro Theater
12. St. Patrick's Catholic Church
13. VISITOR INFORMATION
      (Nevada County C of C in
       Lola Montez House)

THE PASTIE PLACES

A. Mrs. Dubblebee's
B. King Richard's
C. Marshall's Pasties
D. Rachel's Pasties
   & Sweet Things

To Nevada County Fairgrounds

To Auburn

tour and bought a small home in Grass Valley. She moved in with her current husband, journalist Patrick Purdy Hill, plus a pet bear and a monkey. She soon sent Patrick packing after accusing him of shooting her bear. He later died of a broken heart, complicated by whisky.

Flitting about like a grand dame, shopping at the local supermarket in low-cut velvet gowns and probably flirting with a few husbands, she scandalized the town.

She also served briefly as a tutor to six-year-old Lotta Crabtree, who's mother owned a boarding house up the street. She taught Lotta to dance and sing and grin and bounce her Shirley Temple curls. The precocious youngster supposedly debuted in nearby Rough and Ready, dancing to the beat of a blacksmith's anvil. After a year, Lotta moved with her family to Rabbit Creek (now La Porte), 50 miles north, so Lola presumably lost track of her protegè.

Before another year had passed, Ms. Montez grew tired of small town life and launched a tour to Australia, which also flopped. Her health failed and she died a recluse in New York in 1863 at the age of 43. Even as she departed this vale, young Lotta emerged as the darling of the Gold Camps and later the toast of the nation. Reportedly the first American entertainer—and possibly the first woman—to become a millionaire, she lived to the cheerful old age of 77. She left most of her $4 million estate to charity.

THE WAY IT IS ● Grass Valley never went through the boom and bust trials of most gold camps. Its longtime stability is evident in its prosperous looking neighborhoods, carefully restored Victorians and busy business districts. Several Gold Rush relics survive in the old downtown area along Main and Mill streets, although many wear twentieth century facades.

Currently popular as a bedroom community for the nearby Auburn-Interstate 80 corridor, Grass Valley is one of the fastest-growing communities on Highway 49. It rivals Placerville as the second largest town in the Gold Country, with a population topping 8,000.

Another product of prosperity, unfortunately, is the Golden Center Freeway that connects Grass Valley and next door Nevada City while slicing both towns right down the middle. Residents hurrying from their Grass Valley offices to their medallions of veal at a Nevada City restaurant probably appreciate the convenience. However, the freeway is an aesthetic abomination. It begins about a mile south of Grass Valley then suddenly quits on the northern edge of Nevada City, covering maybe six miles.

Even with its silly freeway, Grass Valley is in a pleasing setting, with pine-covered ridges along the eastern flank of the town. The hilly green vale that fostered its name extends to the west.

DISCOVERIES
The best attractions

Empire Mine State Historic Park ● *10791 E. Empire St., Grass Valley, CA 95945; (916) 273-8522. Daily 10 to 5 in summer; call for off-season hours. Adults $2, kids $1. Tours daily in the summer; weekends only in the off-season.* Superlatives flow easily when one describes the Empire Mine. It was one of the oldest, richest and largest hardrock mines in America. More than

360 miles of underground passages were dug, fanning out from the main shaft, which had an incline depth of more than two miles. Its vertical drop was over 5,000 feet, well below sea level.

You see very little of this at the park, since tours enter only a short section of the mine. However, its extensive above-ground facilities are probably more fascinating than the unseen mole maze below.

Here one grasps the reality that mining became big business in Nevada County. Although some of the outbuildings have been torn down, many remain to form an extensive complex of huge industrial sheds and almost castle-like fieldstone buildings that housed offices and labs. One gets the impression that the Empire was built to last, and it did—for 106 years.

The most striking feature of the complex is the boldly massive "cottage" of mine owner William Bourn, Jr., constructed of stone from mine tailings. Although it was built as a part-time residence, it's a lavish mansion set on several beautifully landscaped acres. (Another of the Bourn family homes is the opulent Filoli Mansion in Woodside south of San Francisco, familiar to TV fans as the home in *Dynasty*.)

A museum occupying the former company stable and groom's residence offers an excellent study of mines, mining and the Gold Rush. Placards, graphics and models explain in detail the complex business of scouring Mother Earth for her most sought-after metal. The mine headframe was disassembled a few years ago for safety reasons. Another frame, belonging to the Rowe Mine across the street, is intact.

North Star Mining Museum and Pelton Wheel Exhibit • *Allison Ranch Road at Mill Street, Grass Valley, CA 95945; (916) 273-4255. Daily except Monday 11 to 5 from late spring through early fall; closed the rest of the year. Admission by donation.* The powerhouse building of the defunct North Star Mine serves as an intriguing exhibit center for the county historical museum. Its excellent display of gold mining equipment includes a working Cornish pump developed by Cornwall miners to lift water through several levels of a mine, making deep pit mining possible.

The star of the North Star exhibit is the world's largest Pelton Wheel, 30 feet in diameter. It was built in 1895 to run air compressors that powered the mine. Essentially a turbine water wheel, this device was invented in 1878 in nearby Camptonville by one Lester Pelton. For decades it was the primary source of power to operate California's mining machinery.

Instead of the employing the familiar water-catching troughs, the Pelton Wheel is powered by aiming a high pressure stream of water at small metal cups, seamed in the middle and attached to the wheel's rim. The rounded cups with their center dividers act as deflectors, sending the wheel spinning at high speeds while keeping the water from sloshing into adjoining cups, which would slow it down. Got that? Anyway, it's much more efficient than conventional water wheels. Some say it was the forerunner of the water turbine that generates the electricity by which you may be reading this book.

The rest

Mount Saint Mary's Convent, Chapel, Cemetery and Grass Valley Museum at Old Mount St. Mary's Academy • *South Church and Chapel streets, Grass Valley, CA 95945; (916) 272-8818. Grounds open daily; Grass Valley Museum open Tuesday-Sunday 10 to 3 in summer, Tuesday-Friday the* *rest of the year. Free admission; donations accepted.*. This pleasantly landscaped complex surrounded by eight-foot brick walls was built in from 1863 to 1865. It includes the former Holy Angels Orphanage, St. Mary's Convent, St. Joseph's Chapel, a parochial elementary school and cemetery, all sheltered within a peaceful garden.

The second floor of the convent and chapel houses the Grass Valley Museum. Exhibits include pioneer memorabilia, paintings by some of the nuns, an intriguing collection of 75 glass slippers (Cinderella would have a ball), tapestries and a lace collection featuring a bedspread which consumed 2,000 hours in the stitching. Several rooms of the convent and orphanage, including a classroom, parlor, music room and doctor's office are furnished as they were in the 19th century. A thrift shop occupies the first floor.

Even without the museum exhibits, Mount St. Mary's is worthy of a visit. The cool green lawns, fountains, palm trees and formal rose gardens offer a peaceful retreat.

Holbrooke Hotel ● *212 W. Main St., Grass Valley*. With its green on green decor, second story balcony and lathe-turned columns, the Holbrooke has a luxuriant Southern Colonial look. Inside, the lobby is nicely restored, a vision of polished woods, marble and stained glass. During Grass Valley's golden heyday, Presidents Grant, Garfield, Harrison and Cleveland and other luminaries such as Mark Twain stayed here.

A state historical landmark, the Holbrooke was built in 1862. It later fell to disrepair and was purchased in 1972 by a group of local citizens led by resident Arletta Douglas. They labored for years on its restoration. Presently operating under new owners, it's listed below underDining and Lodging.

Nuggets

Downtown architecture ● Grass Valley's downtown area is rather an architectural museum, with century-old storefronts converted to everything from Art Deco to Frugal Fifties. The **Nevada County Bank** building at 131 Mill Street is a curious anomaly among the rest: a bit of Greek architecture, complete with the classic pediment and a beehive dome supported by four fluted columns. It looks like a misplaced Monticello. Another architectural gem is **Del Oro Theater**, a marvelous Art Deco movie palace with a distinctive squared and fluted tower, at Mill and Neal streets.

Gold Quartz Discovery Marker ● *Jenkins Street at Hocking Avenue, Grass Valley*. A neat little park has been built around this state historical monument commemorating the beginning of serious hardrock mining in California. You've already read about George McKnight tripping over a piece of gold-bearing quartz while chasing an itinerant cow through the moonlight. This also marks the site of the Gold Hill Mine, whose owners pursued that vein of quartz and got $4 million for their efforts. Historians never did say what happened to the cow.

Lola Montez Home ● *248 Mill St., Grass Valley*. This shake-roofed wooden sided bungalow is a reproduction of the original, and it now houses the Nevada County Chamber of Commerce. It's not a museum in the normal sense, although a few of Lola's artifacts occupy one room. And since the chamber is a fount of Nevada County information, we'd certainly recommend a visit.

A false-front blacksmith shop is one of the few remaining yesterday structures in the once-rowdy gold camp of Rough and Ready, near Grass Valley.

Lotta Crabtree Home ● *Two doors from Lola's at 238 Mill St.* Lotta's former residence is a square, homely two-story green building containing three apartments. No sign or monument marks its significance. It's privately owned, so you'll have to stay on the sidewalk to scrutinize this former miners' boarding house that nurtured America's first millionaire sweetheart.

DETOUR

Grass Valley to Rough and Ready and Bridgeport ● *A 40-mile loop trip.* To reach Rough and Ready, with is curious history and curiouser name, head west on its namesake highway. You'll drop down out of the pine zone and arrive after about six miles. A feisty village that seceded from the Union, then defied the U.S. Postal Service a century later, it's certainly worth a visit—even though few of its early-day buildings survive.

The town was established in 1849 by gold seeker A.A. Townsend. He'd fought under "Old Rough and Ready" Zachary Taylor in the Mexican War, so he named the gold camp in his honor. Like their namesake, the citizens of Rough and Ready were an irascible lot. After the federal government levied a tax on all mining claims, Rough and Ready voted to secede from the Union rather than pay it. The rebellion didn't last long. When it came time for the annual Fourth of July celebration, the townsfolk grinned sheepishly and ran Old Glory up the flagpole.

Things were relatively peaceful for a century, then in 1948 when a new post office was built, the government wouldn't let the town use the "Rough and Ready" postmark. Too long, said the bureaucrats (and probably too peculiar). This time, the citizens wouldn't relent, and their curious postmark was granted.

After exploring the town, continue west, blend onto Highway 20, then turn north onto Pleasant Valley Road. You'll drive past oak and pine forests mixed with cattle ranches and blackberry brambles. At Bridgeport, stop to stroll across the shingle-sided covered bridge, built in 1862. Supposedly the longest single-span structure of this type in the West, it reaches 230 feet across the south fork of the Yuba River. The gently moving stream below is a popular swimming area in summer.

Continuing on Pleasant Valley Road, pause at French Corral, site of the world's first long distance telephone. In 1877, the Milton Mining Company formed the Ridge Telephone Company to connect its operation in French Corral with French Lake, 58 miles away. A California historical marker and a couple of buildings with sagging roofs and peeling paint are all that survive to remind us of that historic accomplishment.

The route then climbs back into pine and fir forests and delivers you to Highway 49. Hang a right and return to Grass Valley by way of Nevada City.

DIVERSIONS

Gold panning • *Contact Holiday Lodge, 1221 E. Main St., Grass Valley, CA 95945; (916) 273-4406.* Doss Thornton's gold panning trips are the least expensive we've encountered: $10 per adult or $5 per child for all-day outings. They depart around 9:30 a.m. from the Holiday Lodge and adjourn to a creekside spot, where you learn the techniques of panning, and hopefully take home some color.

"Your chances of getting rich with a gold pan are about as good as winning the California Lottery," says Thornton. "But panning is fun...and a great way to see the Gold Country scenery."

Nevada County history tour • *Same contacts as above.* Starting in Grass Valley, these tours take visitors to Nevada City to explore its Gold Rush buildings and museums, then back to Grass Valley to see its historic sites. Stops include Mount St. Mary's, the North Star Mine Museum and Empire Mine State Historic Park.

GOLD COUNTRY DINING

Arletta Douglas Room of the Holbrooke Hotel • △△△ $$$ ØØ

212 W. Main St., Grass Valley; (916) 272-1989. American regional-Continental; dinners $14 to $18; full bar service. Lunch weekdays 11 to 2, dinner Monday-Thursday 5:30 to 9 and Friday-Saturday 5:30 to 9:30, Sunday brunch 10 to 1:30. Reservations suggested on weekends; MC/VISA, AMEX. Strikingly handsome Victorian dining room with print wallpaper, hunter green carpet, crystal chandeliers and candle-lit table. The generally excellent fare includes such creations as wild mushroom chicken, blackened prime rib, rack of lamb and blackened sea scallops. Named for the woman who championed restoration of the Holbrooke, it's Grass Valley's most attractive dining parlor.

THE CORNISH MINERS AND THEIR PASTIES

The men of Cornwall were the backbone of the Grass Valley mining industry. They brought with them not only the expertise needed to burrow far into the earth, but their own distinctive lifestyles and food. In the late 1800s, 85 percent of Grass Valley's population was Cornish and their trim little houses gave the town the look of an English village.

Their most enduring—and tastiest—legacy is the Cornish pastie (pronounced *pah'-stee*), a meat pie they carried with them into the mines. To quote from the Nevada County Chamber of Commerce's *History of the Cornish in Grass Valley:* "In the early days, light in the mines was furnished by candle or oil lamp attached to a spike and driven into the wall of the tunnel. Above the light was a large hook. From this, the miner hung his tin cup for brewing tea, and the pastie was placed on top of the cup to warm for the midday meal."

Still popular in Grass Valley, pasties are made with a variety of meats—even fish—mixed with potatoes, onions, parsley, cubed turnips and other veggies. Modern pastie-makers have tampered with tradition by producing spicy Mexican-style and dessert versions, which would undoubtedly startle those old gentlemen of Cornwall. A pastie Olè? I say!

Pasties are sold in several local markets and cafes, although most are made by four specialty firms. We never fail to lunch on these wonderful little pies when we visit Grass Valley, and we usually bring a few home. (They can be frozen.) Pasties from the "Big Four" companies are all tasty. Our favorites come from Mrs. Dubblebee's, founded by William H. Brooks, a remarkable gentleman who ran the firm until his death in 1989, two weeks short of his 102nd birthday!

Mrs. Dubblebee's ● *251-C South Auburn, Grass Valley; (916) 272-7700. Weekdays 10 to 6 and weekends 10 to 5:30.* This country style pastie bakery and cafe occupies a cheerful old white clapboard house. One can take the meat pies home or enjoy them with drinks and dessert at tables inside and on the front porch.

King Richard's ● *217 Colfax Ave., Grass Valley; (916) 273-0286. Monday-Friday 9 to 6, Saturday 11 to 5, Sunday noon to 5.* Richard's functions in conjunction with **Antonio's Mexican Deli,** thus offering both pasties and Mexican fare. Naturally, Richard offers a spicy Mexican pastie. A few tables are available.

Marshall's Pasties ● *203 Mill St., Grass Valley; (916) 272-2844. Daily 9:30 to 6.* Marshall's occupies a tiny stall in downtown Grass Valley, offering meat, fowl, vegetarian and apple pasties. One can get a cup of coffee or tea and adjourn to a snug upstairs dining room with a balcony overlooking old town.

Rachel's Pasties and Sweet Things ● *568 E. Main St., Grass Valley; (916) 273-2973. Weekdays 6:30 a.m. to 6 p.m., Saturday 10 to 6, closed Sunday.* The newest of the pastie pack, this is a charming early American style cafe in a bright yellow Victorian. In addition to assorted pasties, Rachel offers breakfast fare and bakery items.

Empire House • ΔΔΔ $$$ ∅
535 Mill St., Grass Valley; (916) 273-8272. German-Swiss; dinners $10 to $16; full bar service. Lunch Tuesday-Friday 11:30 to 2, dinner Tuesday-Thursday 5 to 9, Friday-Saturday 5 to 10 and Sunday 4:30 to 9:30. Reservations accepted; MC/VISA, AMEX. Tasty European fare served by a locally popular Swiss-German chef in a stylish 19th century dining room. It's housed in a stately brick structure at the lower end of Boston Ravine where a public house has stood since 1851. Fare includes a range of German and Swiss dishes, plus American steaks and chops.

The Owl Tavern • ΔΔ $$
134 Mill St., Grass Valley; (916) 273-0526. American; dinners $8 to $12; full bar service. Lunch 11 to 2:30 Monday-Saturday and noon to 3 Sunday; dinner 5 to 10 Monday-Thursday, 5 to 11 Friday-Saturday and 4 to 9 Sunday and holidays. Reservations suggested on weekends. MC/VISA, AMEX, CB. Pleasingly rustic Gold Rush theme dining room with exposed beam ceilings, brick walls and tables made from the support members of old mine shafts. Typical American fare, generally well prepared, including the usual range of steaks, broiled chicken and center cut pork chops. Minestrone soup is a specialty.

Peppers • ΔΔΔ $$$ ∅
151 Mill St., Grass Valley; (916) 272-7780. Mexican Californian; dinners $7 to $13; wine and beer. Lunch weekdays 11:30 to 3, dinner Monday-Saturday 5 to 10 and Sunday 4 to 9. Reservations suggested. MC/VISA. Creative Mexican-Southwestern fare served in a pleasing cellar restaurant in downtown's 1854 Union Building. Mexican doo-dads brighten the brick-walled interior. Among the taste dishes are chicken molé, prawns *Guillermo* (stuffed with cheese and pepper and dipped in blue corn batter) and *carne la chica* (strips of steak sautéed with chilies, onions and bell peppers).

Tofanelli's • ΔΔΔ $ ∅∅
302 W. Main St., Grass Valley; (916) 273-9927. Light lunches and dinners with daily specials; dinners $6 to $12; wine and beer. Weekdays 7 a.m. to 8:30 p.m., Saturday 8 to 2 and Sunday 9 to 2 Sunday. MC/VISA. Cute oldstyle cafe with remarkably inexpensive and tasty dinners, such as garlic grilled snapper, fresh catfish and chicken Florentine for $9, including soup or salad, potato or rice and veggie. Also luncheon specials such as raspberry chicken or Caesar salad. Simple, pleasing decor: embossed tin ceilings, exposed brick walls, wainscoting and Boston ferns. Just possibly the best inexpensive restaurant in the Gold Country, and it's smoke-free.

Is there life after dark?

Nevada County offers more cultural functions and night life than any other area of the Gold Country. Here's a partial list of Grass Valley's share. Others are in the next chapter.

Community Players, P.O. Box 935, Grass Valley, CA 95945; (916) 273-2730. Active for more than 25 years, this group presents musicals in the amphitheater of the Nevada County Fairgrounds in Grass Valley.

Gold Country Productions, 127A Bank St., Grass Valley, CA 95945; (916) 273-2730. This group produces comedies and dramas in the Studio Theatre in downtown Grass Valley.

Music in the Mountains, P.O. Box 1451, Nevada City, CA 95959 (916) 265-6124. This organization offers a year-around series of concerts, celebrity concert series, opera galas, music forums and other things musical. Most performances are held in St. Joseph's Chapel, Church and Chapel streets in Grass Valley.

LODGINGS
Bed & breakfast inns

Golden Ore House ● ⌂ $$$ ∅∅
448 S. Auburn St., Grass Valley, CA 95945; (916) 272-6872. Doubles $70 to $82. Six units with three private baths and three share. Full breakfast. No smoking. MC/VISA. Built in 1904, this Colonial style home been nicely refurbished, accented with natural wood trim, lace curtains and antique furnishings. The term "casual elegance" seems appropriate here: warm and cozy, yet airy and cheerful. Skylights brighten the upstairs rooms, and a tree pops through an upper deck, giving the impression of living in a stylishly furnished tree house.

Murphy's Inn ● ⌂⌂ $$$$ ∅∅
318 Neal St., Grass Valley, CA 95945; (916) 273-6873. Doubles $74 to $123. Eight rooms, all with private baths; full breakfasts. No smoking. MC/VISA, AMEX. Built in 1866 for North Star Mine owner Edward Coleman, this Early American style home with bold, squared lines and cheerful ivy-enlaced porch has been carefully restored and opulently furnished. Innkeepers Marc and Rose Murphy have spared no detail in returning its oversized rooms to their Victorian elegance, with floral wallpaper, lace curtains, canopied brass beds and American or European antiques. Breakfasts feature such goodies as Belgian waffles and coddled eggs.

Annie Horan's Bed & Breakfast ● ⌂⌂ $$$ ∅∅
415 W. Main St., Grass Valley, CA 95945; (916) 272-2418. Doubles $55 to $95. Four units, all with private baths; from $50 per couple. Continental breakfast. No smoking. MC/VISA. This slender, gingerbread-trimmed home is one of Grass Valley's more appealing Victorians, constructed in 1874 by builder/investor James L. Horan for his wife. His builder's background is evident in the detailed craftsmanship of the exterior. The interior has been carefully restored and furnished in the typical Victorian manner, with lots of wood, brass and lace, and antiques from America, Europe and the Orient. Arriving guests can enjoy cocktails in the parlor or on the front porch.

Swan-Levine House ● ⌂ $$$ ∅∅
328 S. Church St., Grass Valley, CA 95945; (916) 272-1873. Doubles $55 to $85. Four units, all with private baths. Full breakfast. Pets negotiable; no smoking. MC/VISA, AMEX. Long on warmth and friendliness if a bit short on elegance, the Swan-Levine House is a wonderfully cluttered blend of home and art gallery. Both innkeepers Howard Levine and his wife Margaret (Peggy) Swan Levine are artists, and they've stuffed their big, busy house with sculptures, pottery and prints. For a small fee, they'll take guests into their studio (a former carriage house) and show them how to make etchings or lithographs. The home is nearly as interesting as its occupants. It was built in 1880, remodeled to a Queen Anne in 1895 with typical turrets and

cupolas, then converted into a small hospital that served Grass Valley from 1906 until 1968.

Motels and historic hotels

Alta Sierra Resort Motel ● ⌂ $$$

135 Tammy Way (at the Alta Sierra Country Club), Grass Valley, CA 95949; (916) 273-9102. Doubles $64 to $85, singles $45 to $58; MC/VISA. Resort style motel with rustic decor at Alta Sierra Country Club with a TV, pool, golf and tennis. **Restaurant** adjacent.

Best Western Gold Country Inn ● ⌂ $$ ∅

11972 Sutton Way (Brunswick exit from freeway), Grass Valley, CA 95945; (916) 273-1393. Doubles $46 to $54, singles $44 to $48, kitchen units $4 to $7 extra. Nicely-kept 84-unit motel between Grass Valley and Nevada City; TV, room phones, pool and spa.

Coach n' Four ● ⌂ $$ ∅

628 S. Auburn St., Grass Valley, CA 95945; (916) 273-8009. Doubles from $42; MC/VISA, AMEX. A choice of small, rather simple rooms or larger, more elaborate units. TV movies, room phones and refrigerators.

Golden Chain Resort Motel ● ⌂ $$$ ∅

13363 Highway 49 (two miles south), Grass Valley, CA 95949; (916) 273-7279. Doubles $54 to $68, singles $44 to $54. Major credit cards. Well-maintained 21-unit motel with TV, room phones. Picnic area and putting green on spacious wooded grounds.

The Holbrooke Hotel ● ⌂⌂ $$$$

212 W. Main St., Grass Valley, CA 95945; (916) 272-1989. Doubles and singles $70 to $104, one suite $120 to $145. Seventeen units, plus 11 in the adjacent Purcell House, all with private baths. Continental breakfast. Smoking OK. MC/VISA, AMEX. Nicely restored hotel with Gold Rush-Victorian theme; rooms feature color coordinated print wallpaper, draperies and comforters, brass beds (some canopied) and gleaming antiques. Many are named for famous people who once stayed at the hotel or lived in Grass Valley, from the exquisite Ulysses S. Grant presidential suite to the Lotta Crabtree and Mark Twain rooms. Some of the units have fireplaces and private verandas. **Arletta Douglas dining room** listed above.

The Purcell House, a sturdy Gold Rush home behind the Holbrooke at 119 N. Church St., also has been restored as a Victorian style inn and functions as an annex to the hotel.

Holiday Lodge ● ⌂ $$ ∅

1221 E. Main St. (Idaho-Maryland freeway exit), Grass Valley, CA 95945; (916) 273-4406. Doubles $42 to $48, singles $36 to $40. Major credit cards. Cable TV, pool that's enclosed in winter, spa, sauna. Gold panning and historical guided tours. Between Grass Valley and Nevada City.

Manzanita Inn ● ⌂ $$ ∅

12390 Rough & Ready Highway (2.5 miles west of town), Grass Valley, CA 95945; (916) 273-8433. Singles and doubles $44 to $56. Major credit cards. Very attractive motel with newly renovated units; TV, room phones. Pleasant wooded setting with playground, picnic tables and barbecue areas.

CAMPGROUNDS & RV PARKS

Greenhorn Campground at Rollins Lake • *State Highway 174 (11 miles southeast), Grass Valley, CA 95945; (916) 272-6100. RV and tent sites, $17 with hookups, $14 without.* Four camping areas at the lake recreation area with toilets, solar showers, picnic tables and barbecues. Boating, fishing and swimming in Rollins Lake. Open all year.

Nevada County Fairgrounds • *Off McCourtney Road (P.O. Box 2687), Grass Valley, CA 95945; (916) 273-6217. RV and trailer sites, $12.* Flush potties, showers, some picnic tables. Open most of the year, except during major events at the fairgrounds.

ANNUAL EVENTS

Living History Days, mid-April, mid-September and mid-October at Empire Mine State Historic Park, (916) 273-8522; re-creation of early mining days, with costumed docents and rangers.

Rough and Ready Chili Cookoff, April in downtown Rough and Ready, (916) 432-3725.

Bluegrass Festival, June at Nevada County Fairgrounds, Grass Valley, (209) 464-5324; gathering of bluegrass and country musicians.

Nevada County Fair, mid-August at Nevada County Fairgrounds, (916) 273-6217; livestock show, exhibits, food booths and such.

Golden Empire Fly-in, early July at Nevada County Airpark, (916) 273-3046; aerial demonstrations and aircraft displays.

Cornish Christmas, early December in Grass Valley, (916) 272- 8315; English-theme Yule celebration sponsored by the Grass Valley Downtown Association.

ON THE ROAD AGAIN...TO NEVADA CITY

Well, good grief, we're only going four miles, and that by freeway. As we approach Nevada City, note those beautifully restored Victorians on the steep hillside to the right; they appear to be rising right out of the trees.

To learn more...

Nevada County Chamber of Commerce, 248 Mill St., Grass Valley, CA 94945; (916) 273-4667 or toll free (800) 655-4667 in California only. Office open weekdays 8:30 to 5 and Saturdays 10 to 3.

Rough & Ready Chamber of Commerce, P.O. Box 801, Rough & Ready, CA 95975; (916) 273-2163.

Nevada City Ranger District, Tahoe National Forest, 12012 Sutton Way, Grass Valley, CA 94945; (916) 273-1371.

Nevada County Arts Council, 408 Broad St., Nevada City, CA 95959; (916) 265-3178. Contact the council for details on the area's various cultural attractions, or pick up its material at the chamber of commerce.

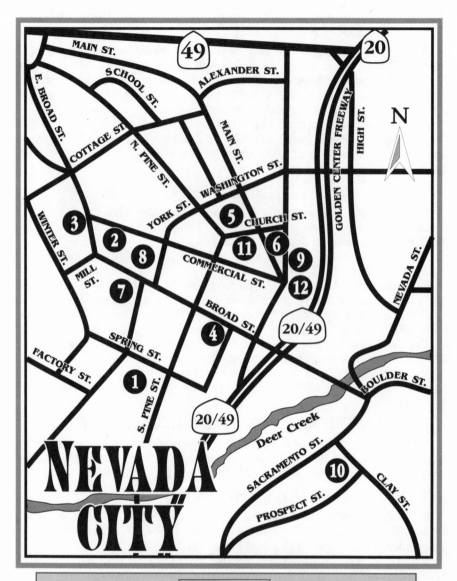

NEVADA CITY

N

DIRECTORY

1. Miner's Foundry (1856)
2. Firehouse #2
3. Methodist Church
4. Hational Hotel (1854)
5. Nevada County Courthouse (1939)
6. Nevada County Historical Museum
   (In Firehouse #1   1861)
7. Nevada Theatre (1865)

8. New York Hotel (1857)
9. Ott's Assay Office (1859)
10. The Red Castle
11. Searles Library
12. VISITOR INFORMATION
    (Nevada City Chamber of Commerce,
    South Yuba Canal Building)

"American Hill was covered with tents and brush houses, a few had put up cabins. At night the tents shone through the pines like great transparencies, and the sound of laughter, shouting, fiddling and singing startled those old primeval solitudes strangely. It was a wild, wonderful scene."

— argonaut Ben Avery's description
of Nevada City in 1849

FIREHOUSE AND MUSEUM
IN NEVADA CITY

Chapter Sixteen
NEVADA CITY & SURROUNDS
The Victorian gem
of the Gold Country

It is a pleasing blend of Victoriana and the Old West, dropped among pine-clad hills; a prosperous and carefully preserved town built in a creek-side hollow and radiating into the nearby slopes. Nevada City rivals Jamestown for its Gold Rush ambiance. However Jimtown is funky and rustic, while Nevada is dressy and elegant.

Easily the most artistic of the Sierra foothill communities, Nevada City shelters a sizable colony of writers, musicians and artists. More than a dozen drama and musical groups thrive between here and neighboring Grass Valley. It isn't surprising that this town takes its tourism more seriously than any other in the Gold Country. Glossy black surreys clip-clop along its streets, hauling camera clutchers past historic buildings now brimming with boutiques. Fine old Victorians hang out neatly lettered bed and breakfast signs.

On a summer weekend, it can be a crowded, almost hectic place where visitors vie for parking space and cue up at gift shop cash registers. On a quiet winter evening, it's a Charles Dickens vision of flickering gaslights, frosty window panes and gentle voices of good cheer issuing from Friar Tuck's pub.

THE WAY IT WAS ● Like Rome and San Francisco, Nevada City was built on seven hills (give or take a few) with names like Piety, Lost, Nabob, Prospect and Buckeye. However, seven wasn't a lucky digit for the mining camp, since that was the number of times fire roared through the town.

The settlement began in the typical fashion, with gold seekers hurrying up from Coloma in 1848. One of those was James Marshall himself, but he found nothing and soon left. The following year, three prospectors discovered rich placer diggins in Deer Creek (which still trickles through downtown) and promptly erected a log cabin. Others hurried to the camp, which went through an assortment of names: Deer Creek Dry Diggins, American Hill, then Caldwell's Upper Store in honor of the first place of business. After the harsh winter of 1850, residents named it *Nevada,* Spanish for snow-covered. Fourteen years later, the state of Nevada was admitted to the Union and the citizens reluctantly added "City" to the name to keep their mail from going astray.

Argonauts worked the creek bottom, then straggled wearily to their cabins in the surrounding hills, leaving trails that formed the town's peculiar street pattern, like twisted spokes from a hub. Despite its incessant fires, the town was bustling with 10,000 residents by 1856; it was briefly the third largest city in California. When Nevada County was formed, it became the seat of government.

Most of the area's creeks were seasonal and the lack of summer sluicing water was a problem. In 1852, a Frenchman named Chabot got smart and fabricated a canvas hose to bring water to his mining operation. The next year, Nevada City miner Edward Matteson got even smarter and attached a metal nozzle to a hose to direct his water wherever he wanted it. This led to the development of hydraulic mining, a violent and destructive procedure in which high pressure "monitors" were aimed at hillsides to blast away the earth and wash the gold bearing gravels into waiting sluices.

By bringing water from high mountain streams and reservoirs via ditches and flumes, then funneling it into increasingly smaller pipes, they could create a tremendous jet of water. One of the world's largest hydraulic mining operations was the Malakoff Diggins just north of here. We visit it later in this chapter.

Meanwhile, Nevada City's placer yield ebbed. Then in 1859, a miner from the Washoe hills in the future state of Nevada came to town looking for an assay office to have some blue mud checked out. The pesky stuff had been clogging the Nevada miners' sluice boxes and rockers. Assayer J.J. Ott examined it. The "mud" was a rich mixture of silver sulfide and gold! The state that took Nevada City's name also got most of its citizens as thousands rushed to the mines of the Comstock Lode.

However, sustained by the growth of neighboring Grass Valley and some of its own hardrock mines, Nevada City survived nicely to become the jewel of the Gold Country. Even though it was soon dwarfed by its fast growing neighbor, it managed to hold onto the county seat. It is today less than a fourth as large as Grass Valley.

THE WAY IT IS ● Silhouettes created by man and nature blend nicely in Nevada City—a mix of slender white church spires and lofty pines; of Victorian roof lines and big, fluffy sugar maples. In the fall, the look suggests New England instead of old California.

The beautifully preserved business district is centered along parallel streets, Broad and Commercial, near the original diggins. Downtown is one of the few reasonably level places in the area. Its keystone is the National

Hotel, a dignified four-storied edifice in green painted brick with white balconies and lathe-turned columns. Built in 1856, it's one of an assortment of Gold Rush hotels claiming to be the oldest in the state. It was here, incidentally, that several water barons met to form the company that became Pacific Gas and Electric.

The brick and stone storefronts of Broad and Commercial streets shelter the most concentrated collection of boutiques and restaurants in the Gold Country. From here, streets fan out and tilt upward; they're shaded by century old maples and lined with grand Victorians, comfortable and sturdy turn-of-the-century bungalows and a few latecomers of the 40s and 50s. Looking pleasantly out of place are the classic Art Deco county courthouse and city hall.

The freeway, indifferent to history's aesthetic, has slashed through the town's right flank like a clumsy surgeon, leaving a lot of stub-end streets. Fortunately, it left the historic district relatively undisturbed.

DISCOVERIES
The best attraction

Malakoff Diggins State Historic Park • *23579 N. Bloomfield Rd., Nevada City, CA 95959; (916) 265-2740. Interpretive center open daily in the summer from 10 to 5; shorter hours in the off-season. Camping; see listing below.*

It looks like the surface of the moon after a flash flood, or perhaps the fantastically eroded cliffs of Utah's canyonlands. We're standing on the brink of a huge amphitheater of manmade erosion called Malakoff Ravine, below San Juan Ridge. More than a century ago, monitors of the world's largest hydraulic mining operation ripped apart the hillside to reach gravel beds of a prehistoric river. The fluted cliffs are dramatically beautiful, but their erosion raised havoc with rivers downstream and led to America's first major environmental confrontation.

Malakoff Diggins State Historic Park encompasses the old mining town of North Bloomfield, once headquarters for the North Bloomfield Gravel Mining Company. Established in 1866, the firm built its own reservoirs, ditches and tunnels to funnel water into the monitors to blast away the hillsides. Their power was incredible. One 10-inch nozzle could hurl water into the cliffs at the rate of 16,000 gallons per minute, nearly a million gallons an hour! At the peak of Malakoff's operations, eight such monitors were in use.

However, the runoff silted up the Yuba River, ruined farmers' fields, caused a major flood in Marysville in 1875 and even turned San Francisco Bay to a murky brown. For years, lowlanders fought to have hydraulic mining stopped. Finally, in 1884, Judge Lorenzo Sawyer handed down America's first major environmental ruling, that a mining company could not dump its tailings into a stream. Malakoff Diggins went out of business and North Bloomfield went to sleep.

Today, it's a pleasant village of restored clapboard homes and white picket fences. It is essentially a state park town, with exhibits in the old livery stable, barber shop, saloon and drug store. Other buildings house park employees.

Cummins Hall, once the town meeting center with a saloon in front, is the park's interpretive center, offering an excellent study of hydraulic mining. One exhibit is particularly impressive: a 500 pound block of gold (obviously simulated), representing the typical yield from the monthly cleanup of the Bloomfield company's sluices. The museum also offers a working miniature of a hydraulic mining operation, but it didn't function very well when we pushed the button. A two-year-old boy could generate more water pressure.

Nevada County Historical Society Museum in Firehouse #1 ● *214 Main St., Nevada City; (916) 265-5468. Daily 11 to 4 (closed Wednesdays from November 1 to April 1). Donations appreciated.* The slender old building is one of the most gingerbready wedding cake Victorians in the Gold Country. It's gleaming white filigree balconies seem to be sagging a bit, although the building is properly shored up. Inside are displays of life in a 19th century gold camp, including antique guns, needlework, George Mathis sketches of Gold Country scenes, Maidu Indian artifacts and the usual pioneer relics.

Particularly interesting are an authentically reassembled Chinese joss house with a complete altar, brought over from Grass Valley's Chinatown, and memorabilia from the ill-fated Donner party that was decimated after it was trapped in a Sierra snowstorm in the winter of 1846.

We were intrigued by the title of a book in one of the display cases. It's a pity that we couldn't reach in and thumb through its pages: *The Arts of Beauty, or Secrets of a Lady's Toilet; With Hints to Gentlemen on the Art of Fascinating.* The author? Madame Lola Montez.

Nevada City Walking Tour ● *Brochures available from the chamber of commerce at 132 Main Street; (916) 265-2692.* This free brochure guides you through the outdoor architectural museum of downtown Nevada City. Much of the area has been declared a national historic landmark, with eight buildings listed on the National Register of Historic Places and 18 designated as state or local landmarks.

The rest

Miners Foundry Cultural Center ● *In the former Miners Foundry at 325 Spring St., Nevada City, CA 95959; (916) 265-5040. Weekdays 9 to 5, open at other times for special activities.* The former American Victorian Museum has closed its doors, to be replaced by a lively cultural center, sponsoring concerts, dances and live theater. It's interesting to stroll through this cavernous creation with its pressed tin ceilings, iron doors and shutters, and stone and brick walls. It resembles a medieval castle that came in under budget. The center usually exhibits something of interest from local artists, and there are a few odds and ends left over from the American Victorian Museum. Built in 1865, the foundry produced much of the equipment used in the early mines, including the first Pelton Wheel.

Nevada City Winery ● *321 Spring St., Nevada City, CA 95959; (916) 265-9463 or 265-6470. Wine tasting daily noon to 5; MC/VISA.* This is one of the Gold Country's more appealing wineries, housed in weathered, tin-sided the former garage of Miner's Foundry. The tasting room is cantilevered over the winery, where Zinfandels, Chardonnays and other good juices of the grape sleep in oak and stainless steel vats. The ancient structure with its

The Pelton wheel, whose split-bucket design provided power to the mines, was invented by gold-rusher Lester Pelton; this one stands before the visitor center in Nevada City.

pleasantly musty smells exudes the ambience of a fine old French wine cellar.

Searls Historical Library • *214 Church St., Nevada City; (916) 265-5910. Monday-Saturday 1 to 4; free admission.* This venerable structure houses the restored offices of attorney Niles Searls, who became chief justice of the California Supreme Court. It also features a library brimming with books, photos and manuscripts concerning early-day Nevada County. Staff members will help serious history buffs research the material.

Nuggets

Carriage House vehicle display • *In Pioneer Park, Nimrod and Nile Streets (east of the freeway), Nevada City. Call (916) 265-4739 for hours.* An old logging truck, stagecoach, beer wagon and fire rigs are on display in this carriage shed in the city park.

Nevada Theatre • *401 Broad St., Nevada City.* Historians say this is the oldest currently operating theater in California, opened on September 9, 1865. The likes of Mark Twain and Jack London have appeared here. Today, the comely brick and stone structure presents the offerings of the Foothill Theatre Company (see After Dark listing below) and it hosts film festivals, recitals and other functions.

Never Come, Never Go Railroad • *Railroad Avenue, south of Sacramento street, east side of freeway.* Engine #5 of Nevada County's 1880 narrow gauge railroad, which has started in many films, is on display alongside

Railroad Avenue. The curious name of the railroad, which twisted through the surrounding mountains, was a commentary on its reliability.

The Red Castle • *109 Prospect St., Nevada City.* This elaborate three-story mansion is the boldest and most ornate of several Victorians clinging to the steep slopes of a forested hill opposite downtown Nevada City, just east of the freeway. It is said to be one of only two surviving houses on the West Coast with the elaborate gingerbread trim of the Gothic Revival style. (See Lodging listings below.)

Sierra Mountain Coffee Roasters • *316 Commercial St., Nevada City;* (916) 265-5282. The aroma of international coffees drew us into this place. It's a charming little shop with a large, gleaming antique coffee bean roaster as its focal point. One can buy assorted coffee blends or enjoy pastries with espresso, cappuccino, cafe au lait and such.

South Yuba Canal Building • *Now the Nevada City Chamber of Commerce office, 132 Main St., Nevada City.* If you're a northern Californian, think of this place each time you pay your utility bill. The South Yuba Canal Company was formed in the 1850s to provide water for hydraulic mining. It later went into the utility business and became a forerunner of Pacific Gas and Electric, the world's largest utility company. Next door is the assay office where assayer J.J. Ott's findings started the stampede to Nevada's Comstock Lode.

DETOURS

Nevada City to Malakoff Diggins • *A 46-mile round trip.* There are two ways to reach Malakoff Diggins, one longer, faster and straighter; the other shorter, twistier and slower. Take both, and you've completed a scenic round trip. (During wet weather, we recommend using only the first route, via Tyler Foote Crossing, since it's mostly paved.)

Head north out of Nevada City and take a left to stay on Highway 49 (the straight-ahead route is Highway 20). You'll climb into and through thick stands of evergreens, then spiral down to a handsomely rugged crossing of the South Yuba River. Giant boulders and deep pools attract legions of summer swimmers.

Eleven miles from Nevada City, a sign indicating Malakoff Diggins directs you to the right, up Tyler Foote Crossing Road. It's narrow, but paved, passing through more of that lush, green conifer forest. At a fork in the road, just beyond the sleepy little town of North Columbia, take the left (upper) branch onto Cruzon Grade. You're on blacktop until the last four or five miles, when dirt and gravel take you into the diggins.

The route out, North Bloomfield-Graniteville Road, is twisting, dusty and beautiful. It's blacktop within the state park, then switches to dirt as it winds down into a primeval forest. You'll enjoy one of the Gold Country's more spectacular vistas as you cross a rocky, 50-foot canyon of the South Yuba River. This is the edge of the South Yuba Recreation Area, (see Diversions below). Eventually, and perhaps reluctantly, you'll rejoin Highway 49, just above Nevada City.

Nevada City to Washington, Emigrant Gap and Colfax • *We'll call this our "super loop," covering about 75 miles and a good part of Nevada County's forest and river scenery.*

This time, as you head north out of Nevada City, continue straight on Highway 20, climbing steeply and swiftly into more of that forest primeval. After 13 miles, turn left onto Washington Road, winding down to the remote mining town of Washington, hunkered at the bottom of a gorge. It's an appealing place, with a surviving hotel and restaurant, and a few businesses, all housed in yesterday buildings.

Returning to Highway 20, pause at the Omega Overlook atop a high crest to scan the distant, overlapping ridges of Tahoe National Forest. Below, you may be able to make out the tailings of the Alpha and Omega mines, which once yielded millions to gold grubbers, and some scars of hydraulic mining. Continuing north, you'll bridge another spectacular, boulder-strewn river crossing, this one on the Bear River that divides Nevada and Placer counties. You'll hit Interstate 80 at Emigrant Gap, where a state historical monument informs you that the first California-bound wagon trains topped a nearby ridge in 1845. They lowered their wagons by ropes into Bear Valley to complete the one of the first successful crossings of the Sierra Nevada.

You will get down a lot faster, taking I-80 south to its junction with Highway 174 at Colfax. Once an important provisioning center for the transcontinental railroad, Colfax still has the look of an old train town. Several Gold Rush buildings survive along Main Street, fronting on a large railyard. The town's traditional rust red with white trim railroad station is now a machine shop and auto parts store. The Red Caboose Museum (346-8549), housed in a weathered old caboose, contains a few artifacts of 19th century railroading. Call before you go, for its hours are erratic. Nearby, the Heart Federal Savings office occupies a nicely restored green turn-of-the-century Southern Pacific passenger coach.

After exploring the town's railroading past, head north on Highway 174, crossing the Bear River below Rollins Lake. In Chicago Park, you might pause for a late-afternoon dessert snack at Happy Apple Kitchen (see Dining listing below). Then drive through a mix of timber and country homes, back to Grass Valley and Nevada City.

DIVERSIONS

Bicycle outings ● *Sierra Adventure Company, Nevada City; (916) 265-9240.* The firm rents bikes for $15 a day or $5 an hour, and offers conducted bicycle tours past Victorian homes and mining sites.

Carriage rides ● *Nevada City Carriage Company, 17790 Cooper Rd., Nevada City, CA 95959; (916) 265-8778 or 265-5348. Daily 11 a.m. to 10 p.m. in summer and 11 to 5 in the fall, shorter hours the rest of the year.* Percheron draft horses clip-clop along Nevada City's yesterday streets, toting tourists-laden carriages past historic buildings.

Gold panning ● Amateur gold-seekers can dip their pans in the streams at several places near Nevada City. Areas not on private property or within mining claims include the Keleher and Golden Quarts picnic areas on the Yuba River upstream from the town of Washington, in Malakoff Diggins State Historic Park and at several places in the South Yuba Recreation Area. Local Forest Service offices can provide specifics.

Hiking, horseback riding and rock-hopping ● *The South Yuba Recreation Area. For a map/guide, contact: Bureau of Land Management, Folsom Dis-*

trict, 63 Natoma St., Folsom, CA 95630; (916) 985-4474. The South Yuba Trail extends for six miles through a rugged canyon of the South Yuba River. The area offers camping, picnicking, fishing and swimming. Explorers can see old mining sites and an assortment of forest critters. The trailhead is eight miles northeast of Nevada City on North Bloomfield County road.

Water sports ● Streams above and a reservoir below Nevada City offer an abundance of water recreation.

Flat Lake Recreation Area, *18848 State Highway 20 (at Scotts Flat Lake), Nevada City, CA 95959; (916) 265-8861. Day use fee $4 per vehicle; boat launch fee $4.* This reservoir in a pine forest offers sailing, motor boating, fishing, swimming and a bait and tackle shop, store and saloon. It's about nine miles east of Nevada City. (Also see campground listing.)

The Yuba River has several popular swimming areas, most notably at the South Yuba crossing on Highway 49 north of Nevada City, and in the South Yuba Recreation Area (see above). It's considered too rocky, shallow and fast for boating, other than short stretches, and is used mostly for tubing.

Wine tasting ● *See Nevada City Winery listing under Nuggets.*

GOLD COUNTRY DINING

The Apple Fare ● ∆∆ $

307 Broad St., Nevada City; (916) 265-5458. American; meals $4 to $7; wine and beer. Breakfast Monday-Saturday 7:30 to 11, Sunday 7:30 to noon; lunch Sunday-Friday 11 to 5 and Saturday 11 to 6. MC/VISA. Charming little breakfast and lunch cafe in one of Broad Street's venerable brick-front buildings. Apple print wallpaper, pink checked tablecloths and wainscoting hung with hand-made wreaths accent the American country look. Interesting soups and sandwiches, plus dessert specialties such as lemon cheese pie, deep dish apple pie and pastries.

Cirino's Bar and Grill ● ∆∆∆ $$$

309 Broad St., Nevada City; (916) 265-2246. Italian; dinners $10 to $14; full bar service. Lunch daily 11 to 4, dinner Sunday-Thursday 5 to 9 and Friday-Saturday 5 to 10. MC/VISA, AMEX. Upbeat, locally popular bistro with 19th century decor, ceiling fans and chandeliers, wall-papered walls with early-day photos; the sort of lively, oldstyle place you'd expect to find in San Francisco. Menu runs the Italian gamut from veal parmagiana and scaloppini to picata and scampi, plus a goodly pasta assortment. Consistently tasty food in generous portions.

Country Rose ● ∆∆∆ $$$ ØØ

300 Commercial St., Nevada City; (916) 265-6248. Continental; dinners $14 to $18; wine and beer. Wednesday-Monday 5 to 9 p.m. (to 10 Friday and Saturday), closed Tuesday. Reservations suggested on weekends; MC/VISA. Stylish Country French cafe housed in one of Nevada City's old brick buildings, with high ceilings, lace curtains, candle-lit tables and early American decor. Diners can adjourn to a pretty ivy-trimmed garden during favorable weather. Small but versatile menu focuses on seafood with continental touches, including salmon canard, orange roughie, sturgeon fettucini plus several French entrèes.

Friar Tuck's • △△△△ $$ ∅

111 N. Pine St., Nevada City; (916) 265-9093. American-Continental; moderate to moderately expensive; wine and beer. Wednesday-Thursday 6 to 10, Friday 6 to 10:30, Saturday 5:30 to 10:30, Sunday 5 to 9:30; closed Monday and Tuesday. Reservations suggested; major credit cards. One of the Gold Country's coziest and most cheerful restaurants, with brick walls, heavy ceiling beams, hanging plants and refectory booths. It's also the area's only full-scale wine bar, offering a variety of vintages by the vial. Diners have a choice of a dim, quiet back room or a more lively area adjacent to the wine bar, where they can dine to the rhythm of live music, usually guitarists or folk singers. Memorable menu items include mussels with brandy sauce, steak *Diablo* with green peppercorns and assorted fondues.

Happy Apple Kitchen • △△ $

Highway 174, Chicago Park; (916) 273-2822. Lunch and take-home desserts; meals $4 to $8; no alcohol. Monday-Saturday 9:30 to 4, closed Sunday. No credit cards. Very cute little place with wood paneling, lime green window shades and crackling fireplace; locally famous for delicious desserts: pies, cupcakes, cakes, sundaes and other delicacies made from apples (as well as pumpkin, mince, boysenberry and pecan pies). It's also a popular lunch spot, offering burgers, sandwiches, chicken and big salads.

Mayo Restaurant • △△△ $$$

Cleveland Street (across from the post office), Camptonville; (916) 288-3237. Continental; dinners $10 to $18; full bar service. Lunch Monday-Saturday 11:30 to 3, "country lunch" Sunday 11 to 3, dinner Wednesday-Saturday from 5. Reservations suggested on weekends; MC/VISA. Inviting marriage of the Gold Rush West and creative continental fare, in a slender brick 1908 saloon; rough wood plank ceiling, tulip glass chandeliers and refectory type booths. Operated by the former owner of Jack's in Nevada City; popular with locals who like to make the trek to this old forest-shrouded mining camp. Because of the saloon atmosphere, age limit is 21.

Michael's Garden Restaurant • △△△ $$$ ∅∅

216 Main St., Nevada City, (916) 265-6660. Continental; dinners $12 to $15; wine and beer. Monday-Saturday 5:30 p.m. to 9 p.m. Reservations accepted. MC/VISA. Stylish restaurant divided into several small, nicely appointed rooms of a converted home. In summer, one also can nosh in a landscaped garden. Subdued floral print wallpaper, white tablecloths and lavender silk flowers create a pleasant dining atmosphere. Tasty fare such as poached salmon with basil cream sauce, scallops in garlic cream, calamari stir fry and for dessert, whipped chocolate with raspberry purèe.

Peter Selaya's • △△△△ $$ ∅∅

320 Broad St., Nevada City, (916) 265-5697. California cuisine; dinners $10 to $16; wine and beer. Tuesday-Thursday 6 to 9 p.m., Friday-Saturday 6 to 9:30, Sunday 5 to 9, closed Monday. Reservations suggested. MC/VISA, AMEX. Both a culinary and visual treat; one of the Gold Country's better restaurants. Menu ranges from fresh salmon with mustard caper *aioli* and Scallops Rockefeller to roast duck with garlic and Zinfandel wine sauce to a gourmet vegetarian dish with vegetables and cashew-stuffed mushrooms in a baked pastry. Gold Rush style dining room with lace curtains, antique furnishings, exposed brick walls and beam ceilings cleverly fashioned to resemble a mine shaft.

Posh Nosh Restaurant • ∆∆∆ $$$ ∅

318 Broad St., Nevada City, (916) 265-6064. Pasta and continental; dinners $11 to $17; wine and beer. Breakfast Wednesday-Sunday 8 to 11, lunch daily 11 to 4, dinner Thursday-Saturday 5 to 9:30. MC/VISA, AMEX. Nice little place with a cozy oldstyle wine cellar look, accented by modern art. The busy menu wanders from pasta and "overstuffed sandwiches" to steak. Eggs Benedict, Belgian waffles and assorted omelets start the Posh Nosh day, and scampi, chicken with brie, flambè prawns and apple brandy chicken end it.

Is there life after dark?

This town that does many things well also has the most varied after-hours entertainment in the Gold Country.

For the culturally inclined, Nevada City offers a community theater, a concert group and dance guild.

Foothill Theatre Company, P.O. Box 1812, Nevada City, CA 95959; (916) 265-TKTS. Box office open Monday-Friday noon to 5. The group presents a season of comedies, dramas and light musicals at the historic Nevada Theatre, starting in the spring.

Miners Foundry Cultural Center, *325 Spring St., Nevada City, CA 95959; (916) 265-5040.* It hosts an assortment of recitals, dances, concerts and plays.

Music in the Mountains, 401 Spring St., #101 (P.O. Box 1451), Nevada City, CA 95959; (916) 272-4725. Performances sponsored by this group range from the classics to cabaret shows in Nevada City and Grass Valley. Its major function is the Summer Festival in June, featuring northern California's top 40 musicians and the 80-voice Festival Chorus.

Nevada County Dance Guild, P.O. Box 1917, Nevada City, CA 95959; (916) 292-3844. The guild's two major events are a spring performance in the Nevada Theatre and a Grecian Garden Party and Fantasy Evening in Nevada City's historic Marsh-Christie House in August.

Twin Cities Concert Association, P.O. Box 205, Nevada City, CA 95959; (916) 265-3517. Concerts at 4 p.m. Sundays. The group presents chamber music concerts featuring local and guest artists, opening at the Nevada City Band Shell in late September, and continuing through winter into spring at the Miners Foundry.

And now to the clubs and pubs. **Stacks Restaurant & Theatre Company** at 203 York Street (800-339-LIVE or 916-265-6363) presents plays, generally comedies, at its dinner-theater on Friday and Saturday nights. It's also open for lunch Monday through Saturday and for regular dinner Thursday.

Friar Tuck's at 111 Pine Street (265-9093) features singers, guitarists and other musicians most nights, and the venerable **National Hotel,** 211 Broad St. (265-4551), offers Friday and Saturday night entertainment. One of the town's livelier pubs is **McGee,** a good old Irish purveyor of spirits at 315 Broad Street (265-3205). **Mad Dogs & Englishmen Pub** at 211 Spring Street behind the National Hotel (265-8173) offers live entertainment and, of course, darts.

LODGINGS

Bed & breakfast inns

Flume's End Bed & Breakfast • ⌂⌂⌂ $$$$ ØØ

317 S. Pine St., Nevada City, CA 95959; (916) 265-9665. Doubles $75 to $125. Five rooms, plus a cottage with fireplace, all with private baths and decks; two units with tub spas. Full breakfast. Smoking on outside decks and grounds only. This mid-19th century Victorian is tucked into a striking setting: on a hillside with a creek splashing through the back yard. The landscaped grounds slope down to three wooded acres, where a flume once carried water to the mines. Guests can relax beside a fireplace in a sitting room cantilevered over the creek falls. The green and white-trimmed home has the multi-pitched roof typical of Victorians, with a distinctive stained glass window in the front. It's tastefully furnished in "Country French," with lots of lace, ruffles and flowered wallpaper. The structure was built in 1854 as a stamp mill, became a residence at the turn of the century and then a brothel, complete with secret passageways.

Grandmere's Bed & Breakfast • ⌂⌂⌂ $$$$$ ØØ

449 Broad St., Nevada City, CA 95959; (916) 265-4660. Rooms $95 to $145. Seven units, all with private baths. Buffet breakfast. No smoking. MC/VISA. The former home of U.S. Senator A.A. Sargent, one of Nevada City's most influential citizens, Grandmere's is an elegant example of Colonial Revival architecture with a marble entry, Corinthian columns and black wrought iron trim. Its present owners have restored it with meticulous care, and even a little whimsy. One of the units has a pioneer log bed complete with old fashioned quilt and dust ruffle. However, the overall impression is one of refinement befitting the former owner, who authored the bill that eventually gave women the right to vote. Built in 1861, the house is listed on the National Register of Historic Places.

The Parsonage • ⌂⌂⌂ $$$$ ØØ

427 Broad St., Nevada City, CA 95959; (916) 265-9478. Doubles $75 to $90. Three units with private baths. Continental breakfast. No smoking. MC/VISA. Built in 1865 as the parsonage for the next-door Methodist Church, this typical early American home has the appropriately simple, almost austere look of a minister's house, with simple roof lines and clapboard siding. Inside, it's considerably more cheerful, even bordering on luxurious, with print wallpaper and bright new paint to set off its museum quality antique furnishings. Some of the antiques made "the crossing" in the 1850s with the hostess Deborah Dane's pioneer forbearers. Many pieces have been in the family since the 1600s.

Piety Hill Inn • ⌂⌂⌂ $$$$ ØØ

523 Sacramento St., Nevada City, CA 95959; (916) 265-2245. Doubles from $75. Eight units with private baths. Continental breakfast. Smoking in garden only. MC/VISA. This unusual B&B began life as a 1930s motel. It's now a fetching complex of light blue stucco cottages with white and red trim. Each is individually decorated with Victorian, Early American or Art Deco furnishings. They feature TV, wet bars, refrigerators, coffee and tea. The former motel office is now a comfortable parlor where guests can sit before a large fireplace and sip wine or sparkling cider. The nicely landscaped grounds offer a whirlpool spa, lawn chairs, croquet court and dart games.

The Red Castle Inn • ⌂⌂⌂ $$$$ ∅∅

109 Prospect St., Nevada City, CA 95959; (916) 265-5135. Doubles $70 to $110. Eight units; six private baths and two share. Full buffet breakfast. No smoking. MC/VISA, AMEX. Described by an architectural critic as "one of the finest examples of domestic Gothic in the state," the Red Castle is a familiar landmark to all who live in and pass through Nevada City. Built by a wealthy mine owner in 1860, the four-story red brick mansion, rich with gingerbread trim, rises imperiously from a forested hillside. The home is opulently attired, with Victorian antiques and wicker baskets filled with silk flowers. Spotlighted palms and other plants create a striking light-and-shadow effect. There's also room for humor, such as carved wooden hands that extend from the walls and serve as towel holders. Rooms have city or forest views, and a winding pathway takes guests through a terraced formal garden, past a reflection pool and continues down to the town below.

Motels and historic hotels

National Hotel • ⌂ $$

211 Broad St., Nevada City, CA 95959; (916) 265-4551. Forty-three units, from $43 with share bath and $63 with private bath. MC/VISA, AMEX. Although not elegantly done, the National offers comfortable, clean rooms, many furnished with antiques. Some units are quite spacious, with balconies overlooking the town. One can certainly sense the essence of history here, strolling the old hallways lined with pressed tin, or sinking into a century-old love seat.

Northern Queen Motel • ⌂⌂ $$$ ∅

400 Railroad Ave. (Sacramento Avenue exit from Highway 20), Nevada City, CA 95959; (916) 265-5824. Doubles and singles $43 to $51, cottages $75, chalets $85. Major credit cards. A 75-unit motel with TV, room phones, refrigerators; cottages with wood-burning stoves; chalets with full kitchens. Pool and spa. No-smoking rooms. **Restaurant** serves 7 to 3 and 5:30 to 9; American fare; dinners $8 to $17; wine and beer; non-smoking tables.

CAMPGROUNDS & RV PARKS

Malakoff Diggins State Historic Park • *23579 N. Bloomfield Rd., Nevada City, CA 94959; (916) 265-2740. Tent and RV sites, $14 in summer, lower in the off-season.* No hookups or showers; pit toilets. Picnic tables and barbecues, swimming, fishing, small store. Located in a pine grove near the park interpretive center. Open all year.

River Rest Campground • *General Delivery, Washington, CA 95896; (916) 265-4306. RV and tent sites, water and electric hookups, from $12.50.* Flush potties, showers, picnic tables and barbecues. Swimming, fishing and tubing in nearby Yuba River; horse shoes, hiking, small store. Reservations accepted; open all year.

Scotts Flat Lake Recreation Area • *18848 State Highway 20 (nine miles east), Nevada City, CA 95959; (916) 265-5302. RV and tent sites, no hookups, $14 to $17 in summer, $12 in the off-season, $4 extra for boat. Reservations accepted.* Flush potties, showers, coffee shop and store, bait and tackle shop, playground, water sports. Open all year.

Tahoe National Forest • The forest naturally has its usual assortment of campgrounds, most with tent and RV sites, barbecues and picnic tables; no hookups or showers; pit potties. Contact the national forest headquarters at the address below.

ANNUAL EVENTS

Malakoff Homecoming, June at Malakoff Diggins State Historic Park, (916) 265-2740; historic celebration with costumes, displays and crafts.

Picnic Pops Sunday Concert, Summer Sundays at Pioneer Park in Nevada City, (916) 432-2590.

Fall Wine Tasting and Grape Stomp, late September at Miners Foundry, Nevada City, (916) 265-5040.

Victorian Christmas, early to mid-December, (916) 265-2692; decorated shops and carolers downtown, special events at Miners Foundry.

ON THE ROAD AGAIN...TO DOWNIEVILLE

There's a pleasant irony here. Driving north the final leg of our long adventure on Highway 49, we leave one of the busiest areas of the Gold Country and approach the most remote.

If you followed our first Detour, you've been this way before, en route to Malakoff Diggins. Continue now along Highway 49, climbing ever higher into the conifers. You soon encounter North San Juan, a gold camp populated by thousands when the great monitors were tearing at the nearby San Juan Ridge. Only a handful of citizens, a few weathered buildings and one saloon remain. A few miles beyond, a highway sign invites you to turn right into Camptonville. This gathering of old wooden homes offers little of visitor interest—except a monument to Lester Pelton, inventor of the wheel of the same name, and the popular Mayo Restaurant (listed above).

The highway from Camptonville to Downieville and beyond to Sierra City is the most attractive stretch in the Gold Country—perhaps in California—with its narrow canyons, rocky river crossings and steep, forest-clad hills. The route traces the twisting, rock-strewn course of the North Fork of the Yuba River. For miles, it never leaves your sight—an inviting stream that cascades over giant boulders, glimmers like scattered diamonds through gravel beds and pauses in deep pools. Hardwoods lean over the rippling water; thick stands of conifers cloak the steep walls of the canyon that rises hundreds of feet above. Picnic sites and campgrounds hug the river bank, inviting travelers to pause.

To learn more...

Nevada City Chamber of Commerce, 132 Main St., Nevada City, CA 95959; (916) 265-2692. The office, in the old South Yuba Canal building, is open weekdays 9 to 5 and Saturdays 11 to 4.

Nevada County Arts Council, 408 Broad St., Nevada City, CA 95959; (916) 265-3178. Contact the council for details on the area's various cultural attractions, or pick up its material at the chamber of commerce.

Tahoe National Forest, Highway 49 at Coyote Street, Nevada City, CA 95959; (916) 265-4531. Send $2 for a national forest recreation map, or stop by the office.

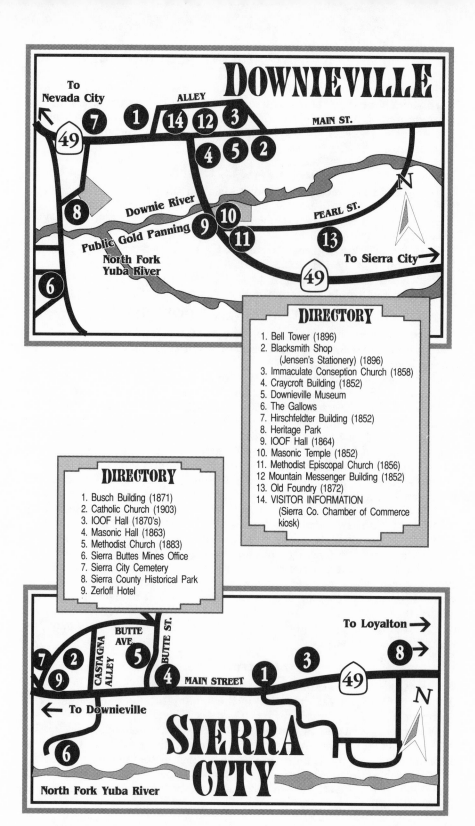

DOWNIEVILLE

To Nevada City

ALLEY

MAIN ST.

Downie River

Public Gold Panning

North Fork Yuba River

PEARL ST.

To Sierra City

N

DIRECTORY

1. Bell Tower (1896)
2. Blacksmith Shop
   (Jensen's Stationery) (1896)
3. Immaculate Conseption Church (1858)
4. Craycroft Building (1852)
5. Downieville Museum
6. The Gallows
7. Hirschfeldter Building (1852)
8. Heritage Park
9. IOOF Hall (1864)
10. Masonic Temple (1852)
11. Methodist Episcopal Church (1856)
12 Mountain Messenger Building (1852)
13. Old Foundry (1872)
14. VISITOR INFORMATION
    (Sierra Co. Chamber of Commerce
    kiosk)

DIRECTORY

1. Busch Building (1871)
2. Catholic Church (1903)
3. IOOF Hall (1870's)
4. Masonic Hall (1863)
5. Methodist Church (1883)
6. Sierra Buttes Mines Office
7. Sierra City Cemetery
8. Sierra County Historical Park
9. Zerloff Hotel

BUTTE AVE.

BUTTE ST.

CASTAGNA ALLEY

To Loyalton

MAIN STREET

To Downieville

SIERRA CITY

North Fork Yuba River

N

"There was only one street in the town; indeed, the mountain at whose base it stood was so steep that there was not room for more than one street between it and the river. There were several very good hotels, and two or three French restaurants; the other houses in the town were nearly all stores, the mining population living in tents and cabins, all up and down the river." — **description of early Downieville from *Three Years in California* by J.D. Borthwick, 1857**

KENTUCKY MINE
STAMP MILL IN
SIERRA CITY

Chapter Seventeen

SIERRA COUNTY

Tin roofs on a sleepy Sunday

The sun rises late in the narrow river canyon that shelters Downieville, particularly on a Sunday in November, when winter is reaching its cold fingers toward this cozy little town. Smoke curling from rough fieldstone chimneys and restless yard dogs pawing at back doors tell us that the village is awakening.

Frost has brushed the bare limbs of apple trees that occupy many of the yards. Ice formed in roadside puddles crunches underfoot as we stroll through a quiet residential area. The homes are simple and sturdy, like the people who live in this remote mountain town.

A bell tolls from the old Methodist Church and, as if on cue, a silver halo of sunlight silhouettes a fringe of trees on the far ridge. First light catches the mist rising from the river, then dances off tin roofs tucked into the forest. A car moves out of a driveway and climbs a hill toward the church, trailing the frosty breath of its exhaust. From somewhere, a chain saw sputters, then growls to life.

A new week has begun in the most beautiful and peaceful corner of the Gold Country.

THE WAY IT WAS ● Those historians, who'll make up a good story if they can't find one, say that William Downie offered his fellow citizens a pan of gold if they would re-name this remote gold camp called The Forks in his honor. (One version says he offered to throw the gold in the street, presumably launching a Gold Rush version of "scramble".) The yarn is a little hard to believe, since Downie was Scottish. An even better story suggests that when Downie's group first explored the area, they caught a salmon, boiled it and found gold in the bottom of the pot.

211

It is true that in November of 1849, Downie led a mixed group including several blacks (there were black gold seekers, although history has generally ignored them), an Indian and a Hawaiian up a rough trail along the North Yuba River. At the junction of the Yuba and a smaller stream, they found rich placer pickins and dubbed the area The Forks. Eventually, Downie— with or without his golden bribe—got both the town and the smaller river named for him.

Problem was, they arrived in November, so they had to struggle through an alpine winter and slosh around in cold water to pan for gold. At nearly 3,000 feet, Downieville is well into the Sierra snow zone. Also, since the area was on the outer rim of the Gold Country, reached only by a rough riverside trail, provisions were hard to come by and terribly expensive when they finally got there. However, the miners were panning around $200 a day, so they could afford $50 for a wool shirt.

By 1851, Downieville was a brawling town of 3,000 gold seekers and camp followers. It also was the scene of the first hanging of a woman in California. A Mexican, known only in history books Juanita, allegedly stabbed a Scottish miner who had kicked her door down in a drunken brawl the night before. He'd stopped by the next morning to apologize and got punctured for his efforts. In a fit of racism, a mob hung her from a bridge and eventually drove the hapless Mexicans out of town.

Some of Downieville's settlers pushed on upstream, and at the foot of the castle-like spires of the Sierra Buttes, founded the town of Sierra City around 1850. The base of the buttes proved to be rich in gold-bearing quartz and it was soon honeycombed with hardrock mines.

Three times, in 1852, 1888 and 1889, snow avalanches swept down on Sierra City, killing dozens of settlers and burying their homes and stores. Most of today's structures date from the 1870s: stone and brick buildings sturdy enough to survive the snow attacks.

THE WAY IT IS ● Content to be far from society's madding mainstream, Downieville is right where the 49ers left it, at the junction of the Yuba and Downie rivers. It's much the way it was more than a century ago, only considerably smaller. Brick and stone buildings have survived the decades, standing behind tree-lined sidewalks. Utility lines were buried a few years ago, giving the town a pleasingly uncluttered look.

An occasional boutique and gold shop, such as the **Ruffled Goose** and **Sieler's Gold**, occupy Main Street's ancient brick and stone buildings. Above the town, tin-roofed homes are terraced into the wooded valley walls. Most folks here let the forest do their landscaping; lawns would be too steep to mow anyway.

The governmental center of Sierra County, it's is one of the smallest county seats in America, numbering about 325 citizens. The county's business is conducted in a post-Art Deco 1940s courthouse across the river from downtown, in one of the few semi-level spots in the area.

A genteel version of the gold rush is still alive in Downieville. The rivers that flow through town are open to public panning and about 50 ounces of glitter are taken out of there by visitors each year. One contemporary 49er found a six-ounce nugget a few years back.

Sierra City occupies one of the most dramatic natural settings in California, sandwiched between the craggy granite palisades of the Sierra Buttes and the Yuba River. The appealing little town is 15 or so miles up Highway 49 from Downieville and more than a thousand feet higher. It is, in fact, the highest town on the Golden Chain, at 4,187 feet. The look is similar to Downieville's, although it's slightly smaller, with a venerable business district tucked along the edges of the river and a few homes cantilevered into steep slopes above.

A network of dirt roads probes the steep flanks of the Sierra Buttes, branching from the junction of Butte Street and Butte Avenue. They are **very** steep and rough, to be attempted only by the driver with a steady hand and stout heart.

Behind the Sierra Buttes, reached by paved highway north of Sierra City, is the Gold Lakes area. This chain of alpine jewels attracts boaters, fly-casters, campers and folks like us who simply like the beauty of natural lakes surrounded by green forests. Beyond the chain of lakes, in neighboring Plumas County, is Plumas-Eureka State Park, with a fine assortment of hardrock mining exhibits.

DISCOVERIES
The best attractions

Sierra County Historical Park and Museum ● *P.O. Box 260 (a mile north of town off Highway 49), Sierra City, CA 96125; (916) 862-1310. Wednesday-Sunday 10 to 5 from Memorial Day through September; weekends only in October, weather permitting; closed the rest of the year. Group tours by appointment. Guided stamp mill tour $4, kids $2; museum admission $1; kids 12 and under, free with an adult.*

The citizens of Sierra County have turned the old Kentucky Mine into one of the Gold Country's best historic parks. Forty-five minute tours through this virtually intact stamp mill give visitors a quick and complete study of a typical hardrock mining operation. They begin at the mine portal in the flanks of the Sierra Buttes, where folks see a working Pelton Wheel and an air compressor that powered drills used to place dynamite charges in the granite walls.

Guides then lead the tour across a high ore cart trestle and down through the various levels of the mine's huge processing mill. Visitors view the jaw crusher that broke the dynamited quartz into smaller rocks, the stamps that pulverized them to powder, and the broad amalgam tables where mercury was used to extract the gold. Although the mill is now silent, most of its machinery is intact.

Elsewhere in this historic park, which occupies a pine-shaded slope, one can prowl through a scattering of mining equipment and visit a museum filled with Sierra County memorabilia, old photos and ore samples. An amphitheater in a pleasant wooded setting hosts the Kentucky Mine Concert Series during July and August.

One of the many mines bored into the steep granite slopes of the Sierra Buttes, the Kentucky dates from the 1853 and was worked off an on for exactly a century. The last owners sold it to Sierra County and its historical society in the 1970s. Opened to the public in 1977, it is supported solely by museum revenue.

Plumas-Eureka State Park ● *310 Johnsville Rd., Blairsden, CA 96103; (916) 836-2380. Visitor center/museum open daily 8 to 4:30 in summer; shorter hours the rest of the year. Free admission, donations accepted.*

Another fine example of hardrock mining has been preserved at Plumas-Eureka State Park, within a beautiful 6,749-acre regrion of evergreen forests, glacier-shaped peaks and gemlike lakes. Elevations range from four to eight thousand feet, so this is definitely snow country, although the roads are kept plowed and the park is open all year. It offers an aging stamp mill, a display of mining equipment and a museum. The mill is undergoing restoration as funds become available; it was closed to visitors when we visited. A good graphics display explains how it works.

Skiing made history here, too. The first organized ski races in the Western Hemisphere were held in nearby Onion Valley in 1861, and the museum displays some of the early downhill equipment, including a pair of Snowshoe Thompson's 25-pound wooden skis. The museum, housed in the former miners' bunk house, offers the usual array of mining displays, plus an unusual wildlife exhibit of specimens freeze-dried for preservation, an improvement over taxidermy. Those critters looked real enough to bite.

Several outbuildings, housing a stable, blacksmith shop and utility shed, are open in summer. Nearby, within the state park but mostly privately owned, are the wood frame buildings of the old mining town of Johnsville. Most are painted a matching red with white trim, a pleasant affect.

The rest

Sierra County Museum ● *Main Street, Downieville, CA 95936. Open from Memorial Day to mid-October: 10 a.m. to 5 p.m. daily in summer; weekends only at the beginning and end of the season. Admission free, donations accepted.* The most interesting thing about this little museum is the building in which it resides—an 1852 mortarless schist structure with a brick front. It once housed a Chinese store and gambling den. The museum offers the typical collection of pioneer artifacts, mining equipment and the usual stamp mill model. It's certainly worth a brief visit, although its exhibits are in a bit of a jumble and could use some reorganization.

Sierra Valley Museum ● *In Loyalton City Park, Loyalton, CA 96118; call the city hall for info, at (916) 993-6750. Wednesday-Sunday 1 to 5. Free admission, donations accepted.* Loyalton is a pleasant farm town in the Sierra Valley, an agricultural basin on the northern end of Highway 49, beyond Sierra City. Its museum, although not professionally done, is a charming little exhibit center, assembled by Loyalton's citizens to preserve their yesterdays. Displays include 19th century clothing and housewares, wooden skis and I.O.O.F. vestments from an early Loyalton temple. Particularly interesting is an exhibit of Depression glass—see-through dishes that were produced cheaply during the 1930s.

Nuggets

Craycroft Building ● *Highway 49, Downieville.* This sturdy stone structure, built in 1852, once housed the longest bar in California, with more than 70 feet of elbow bending room. Now it's home to a pair of businesses, **Yoho Gold and 49er Grocery** and **Downieville Bakery,** a rustic and aromatic coffee-and-snack stop popular with locals.

The Gallows • *Beside the Sierra County Courthouse, Downieville.* The thought is rather gruesome, but this is the only original gallows in California that was actually used (the others being reconstructions or mock-ups). It was used only once, on November 22, 1885, and once was enough for its hapless patron, 20-year-old James O'Neill. It looks capable of doing in more bad guys since trap door, hardware and release lever are still intact. An organization called Friends of the Gallows (no, we're not joking) worked to get the structure restored several years ago.

Gold Exhibit • *Sierra County Courthouse, Downieville.* This is a literal nugget, more or less. Visitors to the county courthouse can view replicas of glittering nuggets taken from the Ruby Mine, one of the richest in the area. The original nuggets came not from the Gold Rush era, however; they were mined in the 1930s.

Lion's Memorial Park • *Near the forks in the river, downtown Downieville.* This small, pleasant riverside park offers a collection of rusting mining equipment, including a large steam boiler, monitor hose, stamp mill, Pelton Wheel and the usual ore cart full of quartz chunks. A marker says this is where poor Juanita was hanged from a bridge for carving up a miner. A trail leads to a public gold panning area at riverside.

Post office mural • *Highway 49, Sierra City.* This appears to be a typically modern post office structure, but look closely at its fieldstone wall. The side of an ore cart and other mining equipment have been embedded as a rustic and rusty bas relief sculpture. A portion of the rock wall above the cart is made of quartz to create the appearance of a load of ore. Clever!

DETOURS

Downieville to Alleghany • *A 60-mile loop trip.* Head south about five miles from Downieville on Highway 49, turn left onto Mountain House Road and you'll shortly reach Goodyear's Bar. It's an old mining camp with a handful of rustic buildings.

Follow dusty Mountain House as it pirouettes steeply down to a pretty little creek, then struggles back up the other side of a steep mountain cleft. After what seems to be an eternity of bumps and turns, you'll emerge into civilization at the town of Forest. Civilization? Forest is a scruffy mountain retreat with a handful of wood frame buildings; most are painted dull brown to complete the town's drab look.

A bit farther along, pick up Ridge Road, turn left and wind down to Alleghany. It's a weathered gathering of 30 or so buildings clinging to a steep forested slope. Some guidebooks describe it as a ghost town. However, Alleghany is very much alive and properly scruffy for a remote mining hamlet, with a few hundred residents and several stray dogs.

You have several choices for the return to Downieville; all are quite scenic. Foote Crossing Road drops to the bottom of the ravine below Alleghany, then winds dizzily upward, notched into a steep valley wall and not recommended for the faint of heart. Ridge Road, paved all the way, follows the gentle curves of a high ridge line, then joins Highway 49 above North San Juan. A good compromise is Henness Pass Road, which follows a former immigrant trail between the Comstock Lode and Marysville. The route is prettier than the smooth Ridge Road and less precipitous than the spectacular

The Sierra Buttes, rising dramatically above Sierra City in the upper reaches of the Gold Country, were riddled with mine shafts during the Gold Rush.

cliff-clinging Foote Crossing Road. Pick up Highway 49 in Camptonville for a repeat run through the boldly handsome canyon of the Yuba River to Downieville.

Sierra City to Eureka-Plumas State Park ● *A 50-mile round trip.* This is one of the most scenic routes in this scenic area, from Sierra City north into the Gold Lakes region.

Driving north on Highway 49, turn left onto Gold Lakes Road near Bassetts, once a stage station and hotel, and now a general store. From Bassetts, you follow a steep, smooth highway into the lakes district.

You'll likely want to pause and explore the many little gems that glimmer in this mountain basin. Our favorite is Sardine Lake, whose placid surface reflects the ragged granite spires of the Sierra Buttes. Many of the Gold Lakes, including Sardine, offer pine-shaded resorts and small marinas. Several Forest Service campgrounds also dot the region.

This area looks more like the Great North Woods than the Sierra, with these tiny gems gleaming through protective rings of evergreens, and boggy meadows where you almost expected to see a moose solemnly chewing marsh grass.

The route takes you ever higher, into a granite wilderness near the tree line. You cross a lofty, rocky divide into Plumas County and wind down to the deliberately neat town of Graeagle on Highway 89. It's a planned resort community, with chalet type homes carefully inserted into evergreen forests.

From properly planned Graeagle, follow County Road A-14 to Plumas-Eureka State Park. Pass back through Graeagle, then detour briefly down Highway 89 past the tiny village of Clio and into the cool green grasslands of the Mohawk Valley. Finally, retrace your route to Graeagle, pick up Gold Lake Road and return to Sierra City.

Gold Lakes Road is closed by snow in winter, so the only approach to Plumas-Eureka State Park is via Highway 89 from Quincy to the west or Truckee to the east.

DIVERSIONS

Doing the outdoor thing ● Since you're in the prettiest, most rugged and lake-sprinkled part of the Gold Country, diversions here focus on fishing, camping, hiking and backpacking. It's all in Tahoe National Forest; pick up the details at the forest headquarters at Highway 49 and Coyote Street in Nevada City. Offices also are located in Camptonville and Sierraville. (Addresses at the end of this chapter.)

Gold panning ● This is one of the best areas in the Sierra foothills to do a bit of gold-seeking. We aren't suggesting that gold is plentiful here; only that the region offers are many places to dip your pan. Downieville has set aside public panning areas near the forks of the Yuba and Downie rivers. Also, several streamside resorts and motels offer panning as well.

Gold-panning is permitted at any point along the two rivers within Tahoe National Forest, unless they're marked by claims. Campgrounds and picnic areas are best, since they're reserved for public panning.

Small gold dredges are active in this area, so we'll assume that there's a bit of glitter to be gotten.

GOLD COUNTRY DINING

The best

Cirino's at the Forks ● ∆∆∆ $$

Main Street, Downieville; (916) 289-3479. Italian; dinners $7.50 to $16; full bar service. Lunch daily 11:30 to 2, dinner 5 to 9. MC/VISA, AMEX. Italian fare served in a Western atmosphere: knotty pine, wagon wheel chandeliers and cowboy artifacts on the walls. Some tables overlooking the river; lunch served on a riverside patio during proper weather. Operated by the owners of Nevada City's Cirino, it features tasty parmigiana, scaloppine, shrimp linguine, pastas and such.

The rest

Country Cookin' Cafe ● ∆ $

Highway 49, Loyalton; (916) 993-1162. American; meals $5 to $9; wine and beer. Monday-Saturday 6 a.m. to 3 p.m., Sunday 8 to 3. No credit cards but checks accepted. Charming little family cafe specializing in huge breakfasts of steak and eggs, pancakes or omelets and hearty hamburgers. The simple fake brick and wallpaper decor is enhanced by offerings of Sierra County artists, which are for sale.

Coyoteville Cafe ● ∆ $

Highway 49, just south of Downieville; (916) 289-3624. American; dinners $6 to $10; wine and beer. Daily 7 a.m. to 9 p.m.; until 7 in winter. MC/VISA. Basic country cafe with good, basic food: generous omelets for breakfast, Downieville's best hamburger lunches and simple things like deep fried clams or shrimp, steak, pork chops or chicken for dinner.

Downieville Diner ● ∆∆ $

Main Street, Downieville; (916) 289-3616. American; dinners $6.25 to $9; wine and beer. Daily 7 to 7; closes at 4 in the off- season. MC/VISA. Typical rural American fare such as chicken fried steak, Southern fried chicken and roast beef, served in a simple American country setting in an 1860 Gold Rush building. One of the area's better dining buys; ample dinners include soup, salad and potatoes.

Sierra Buttes Inn • △△ $$

Highway 49, Sierra City; (916) 862-1300. American; dinners $9 to $13; full bar service. Breakfast and lunch Friday-Monday 8 to 2 Friday, dinner daily 5 to 9. MC/VISA. Pleasantly rustic family cafe with the usual steaks, chicken, chops, chicken fried steak and barbecued ribs. A salad bar is cleverly installed on a bed of ice in an old-fashioned clawfoot bathtub. The restaurant is housed in a century-old wood frame hotel with the requisite ceiling fans and wooden floors.

LODGINGS
Bed & breakfast inns

Bush & Heringlake Country Inn • △△△ $$$ ∅

P.O. Box 68 (Highway 49), Sierra City, CA 96125; (916) 862- 1501. Doubles $75 to $110. Four rooms with private baths. Continental breakfast. No-smoking rooms. This sturdy brick 1871 Wells Fargo Express and general store has been fashioned into an attractive inn. Owner Carlo J. Giuffre Jr., has retained the wide plank floors and cedar walls, added modern touches such as private baths and oversized beds, and decorated the place early American furniture. Particularly posh is the Phoenix Room, named for a local mine, with its own fireplace and spa. The inn is located in downtown Sierra City. Its stylish dining room, **Carlo's Ristorante** serves Italian fare.

Sierra Shangri-La • △△△ $$$ ∅

P.O. Box 285 (Highway 49 three miles north of town), Downieville, CA 95936; (916) 289-3455. Doubles $49 to $88, four-person units $93 to $110. Eight housekeeping cottages and three bed & breakfast units in the main building, all with private baths. No smoking in B&B units. MC/VISA. If we were looking for a place to unwind, Sierra Shangri-La would be high on our list. Picture a cozy, rustic cottage with a pot-bellied stove, perched on the brink of a swift-flowing stream, surrounded by an emerald forest. Shangri-La offers eight such cottages, tucked into a bend of the Yuba River at the base of Jim Crow Canyon. Some of the units are perched right over the stream; others are in a cool forest glen. Guests have been known to reel in fat trout from their own decks. The cottages have kitchenettes, decks and barbecue areas. The three B&B units in the main building have no kitchens, so their occupants are served a continental breakfast.

White Sulfur Springs Ranch • △△△ $$$ ∅∅

P.O. Box 136 (Highway 89), Clio, CA 96106; (916) 836-2387. Doubles from $70. Six units with two cottages, one private and five share baths. Continental breakfast. No smoking. MC/VISA, DISC. Once a stage stop hotel, this nicely restored white clapboard 1852 country ranch home is surrounded by green pasturelands. Print wallpaper and early American antiques in the guest rooms create a feeling of rural refinement. An old fashioned porch and upper balconies offer sweeping views of the Mohawk Valley, a forest-rimmed meadow surrounded by Sierra Nevada foothills. Guests can browse through a relic-filled attic that functions as a museum of early Americana, and take a dip in an Olympic sized swimming pool fed by mineral springs.

Kenton Mine Lodge • ⌂ $$

P.O. Box 942 (#3 Foote Crossing Rd.), Alleghany, CA 95910; (800) 634-2002 or (916) 287-3212. Nine rooms in an old miners boarding house with breakfast, $29.95 per person; with two meals, from $37.50 per person; seven family cabins with private baths and cooking facilities (no meals included) from $27.50 per person. Some share, some private baths. Smoking OK. MC/VISA. The Kenton is far from elegant, although it is intriguing: a hideaway resort in a deep forest canyon, fashioned from an old mining complex. Rooms are simply attired, some with hand-made furnishings crafted by early miners. Guests can peer into the mine tunnel and follow an ore cart track to a stamp mill, where they can explore various levels of the gold processing operation. Also, one can pan for gold in Kanaka Creek that gurgles through the property, play volleyball or croquet on a large lawn area, barbecue a hamburger, sleep in the sun, hike in the woods or lounge around the bar in the big old cookhouse (where meals are served family style). The Kenton Mine was started in 1860 and mining continued until 1939; most of the surviving buildings date from the thirties.

Motels

There's quite a scatter of small motels and mini-resorts in and around Downieville and Sierra City, most along the Yuba River. Many offer lower rates in winter.

The Buttes Resort • ⌂⌂ $$

P.O. Box 124, Sierra City, CA 96125; (916) 862-1170. Housekeeping units; $42 to $45, a two-room family unit $65. MC/VISA. Attractive little resort in a woodsy setting beside the Yuba River, on the edge of Sierra City. Cable TV, pool, deck overlooking the river.

Coyoteville Cabins • ⌂⌂ $$$

P.O. Box 553 (on Highway 49 south of town), Downieville, CA 95936; (916) 289-3624. Seven housekeeping cabins with kitchens, $40 per couple; MC/VISA. These rustic but kind of cute little units are terraced into a steep ravine above the highway, alongside cascading Coyote Creek.

Downieville Motor Inn • ⌂ $$

Highway 49, Downieville, CA 95936; (916) 289-3243. Doubles from $35, kitchenette from $50 (three-day minimum); MC/VISA. Small motel with simply-furnished, comfortable rooms; TV. On the edge of town.

Dyer's Resort Motel • ⌂⌂ $$$

P.O. Box 406, Downieville, CA 95936; (916) 289-3308. Doubles $54 to $59, housekeeping units $69 to $125; MC/VISA. Tidy little resort is on the river, a short walk from Downieville's historic area. Comfortable and well-maintained rooms; cable TV, swimming pool.

Herrington's Sierra Pines • ⌂⌂⌂ $$$

P.O. Box 235 (Highway 49 just south of town), Sierra City, CA 96125; (916) 862-1151. Doubles and singles $49 to $65, cottage with kitchen and fireplace, $75; MC/VISA. Nicely-appointed 20-unit motel in wooded riverside location with a trout pond. TV movies, balconies, many with view of Sierra Buttes and river. **Restaurant** serves 8 to 11 a.m. and 5 to 9 p.m.; American; dinners $8 to $20; full bar service; non-smoking tables.

Sierra Buttes Inn ● △ $$
P.O. Box 320, Sierra City, CA 96125; (916) 862-1300. Doubles from $39 with private baths, from $25 with share baths. MC/VISA. It ain't fancy, but the rooms in this century old clapboard, tin roofed hotel in downtown Sierra City are clean and neat. **Restaurant** reviewed above.

Sierra Chalet Motel ● △ $$
P.O. Box 123, Sierra City, CA 96125; (916) 862-1110. Doubles $40, kitchen units $48; MC/VISA. Basic but clean rooms with TV and queen beds; two beds in kitchen units.

CAMPGROUNDS & RV PARKS

Tahoe National Forest ● Several national forest campgrounds are alongside the Yuba River—as appealing an area as you'd ever want to pitch a pup tent or park an RV. A particularly appealing one, away from highway traffic, is Wild Plum on Haypress Creek just above Sierra City. Others are in the higher hinterlands, particularly the Gold Lakes area. Check the end of this chapter for office locations.

Sierra Skies RV Park ● *Sierra City, CA 96125; (916) 862-1166. Thirty RV sites, $15; reservations accepted.* Full hookups, flush potties and showers. Lawn areas and horse shoe pits; coin laundry at store across the road. On the north fork of the Yuba River, near Sierra City. Open May through October.

Willow Creek Campground ● *17548 Highway 49 (two and a half miles north), Camptonville, CA 95922; (916) 288-3456. Thirty-eight RV sites from $8 to $12. Reservations accepted.* Water, electrical hookups, flush potties and shower. Picnic areas, fishing; river nearby. Open all year.

ANNUAL EVENTS

All Over Town Sale, Memorial Day Weekend and Labor Day Weekend, Sierra City; town-wide yard sale, plus craft exhibit and food booths.

Kentucky Mine Concert Series, nine summer Friday evenings at Sierra County Historical Park, P.O. Box 368, Sierra City, CA 96125, (916) 862-1310; outdoor concerts ranging from swing and classic to blues and country.

Miners Day Weekend and **Clampers Day Weekend,** on August weekends in Downieville, (916) 289-3560; historic Gold Rush celebrations with exhibits, food booths and such.

On the road again...to the last link in the golden chain

We gas up Ickybod in Sierra City and head north, feeling relieved and a little sad that our trek is nearing its end. We continue climbing into the high and handsome mountains and finally top out at Yuba Pass. At 6,701 feet, it's the loftiest point on Highway 49.

Just over the ridge, we swing into a turnout and are greeted by a startling view: a wide, flat valley far below that looks like a chunk of Nebraska dropped into the middle of the Sierra Nevada. We're staring down at Sierra Valley, created when a primeval lake soaked into the ground, leaving its fertile and flat bed behind. Discovered by mountain man James T. Beckwourth in 1851, the valley played an important role in providing beef, vegetables, hay and lumber to the Gold Rush towns and to the Comstock Lode over the ridge in Nevada.

"Many of the beef and crop exports were produced by Italian Swiss, who readily adapted their knowledge of mountain agriculture to this high valley," reads a placard at the overlook. Their descendants are still down there, still farming this bucolic enclave.

We descend to the valley floor. On closer inspection, it looks even more like Nebraska, with weathered old barns, wide pasturelands and a pair of farm villages. However, the bold mountain perimeter tells us that we're still in lumpy northern California.

The road passes through sleepy little Sierraville, then follows the valley's outer rim to Loyalton, a hamlet of wide streets, weathered buildings and about a thousand people. Signs direct us to a city park with barbecues, tennis courts, a kiddie playground and the Sierra Valley Museum.

Continuing across the valley, we see the inevitable sign ahead of us: "Highway 49—end." Our route bumps into State Highway 70 at Vinton, a tiny crossroad with the requisite general store/service station and a couple of old frame buildings.

We explore what little there is to explore, put away our pencils and head for home. It has been a long, intriguing trip. The Golden Chain that began with a flourish in Oakhurst, three hundred and ten miles ago, ends with a contented sigh in Vinton.

To learn more...

Sierra County Chamber of Commerce, P.O. Box 222, Downieville, CA 95936; (916) 289-3560. The chamber operates an information booth in Downieville, open from Memorial Day to mid-October: 10 a.m. to 5 p.m. daily in summer; weekends only at the beginning and end of the season.

Tahoe National Forest, Two offices are in the area: Downieville Ranger District, Star Route, Box 1, Camptonville, CA 95922; (916) 288-3231 and Sierraville Ranger District, Sierraville, CA 96126; (916) 994-3401. For a forest service map send $2 to: Tahoe National Forest Headquarters, Highway 49 at Coyote Street, Nevada City, CA 95959.

HISTORIC SACRAMENTO

N

I STREET BRIDGE 5
9 7
OLD SACRAMENTO
STATE HISTORIC PARK
12
River
Sacramento
TOWER BRIDGE
FRONT ST.
11
2nd ST.
1
3rd ST.
4th ST.
5th ST.
CAPITOL MALL
6th ST.
7th ST.
8th ST.
9th ST.
N ST.
3
6
O ST.
4
P ST.
Q ST.
R ST.
S ST.
T ST.
U ST.
V ST.
W ST.
10th ST.
11th ST.
12th ST.
South Side
Park
5

D ST.
E ST.
F ST.
G ST.
H ST.
I ST.
J ST.
160
K STREET MALL
L ST.
5
Capitol
Park
8
160
13th ST.
14th ST.
15th ST.
16th ST.
17th ST.
18th ST.
19th ST.
160
160
C ST.
160
2
80
BROADWAY
10
X ST.

DIRECTORY

1. Crocker Art Museum
2. Governor's Mansion
3. Stanford Mansion
4. State Archives
5. State Capitol
6. State Library
7. State Railroad Museum
8. Sutters Fort/State Indian Museum
9. Sacramento History Center
10. Sacramento Zoo/Discovery Park
11. Towe Ford Museum
12. Delta King

> *"I subjugated all the Indians in the Sacramento Valley. I had frequent fights with them...and had frequently to punish them for stealing cattle. At this time, I had the power of life and death over both the Indians and the white people."*
> — **John A. Sutter, reminiscing in 1876**

Chapter Eighteen
HISTORIC SACRAMENTO
Where the Gold Rush really began

SACRAMENTO'S FIRST CAPITOL IN 1854

This is not intended to be a comprehensive chapter on Sacramento, for that interesting city of nearly half a million people deserves a book on its own. Rather, we intend to touch on its historic attractions. For indeed, this is where the Great California Gold Rush really began.

THE WAY IT WAS ● We've already met Johann Augustus Suter, the flamboyant Swiss-German opportunist who Americanized his name to John Sutter and set into motion—accidentally—events leading to the Gold Rush.

California's golden history, then, is really the history of Sutter. He was born in 1803 in Kandern, the Duchy of Haden, Germany, near the Swiss border. Married in 1826, he later opened a dry goods and drapery shop in Switzerland. Not much of a businessman, he was forced to flee to avoid debtor's prison, leaving his wife and five children in his wake.

He began an erratic journey to California, gathering followers as he went. After stops in New York, Missouri, New Mexico, Kansas, British Columbia, Hawaii and Alaska, he landed on the West Coast in 1839 and presented himself to Mexican California Governor Juan B. Alvarado. He convinced Juan that he was a gentlemen of stature, and he laid out a grand plan—to cultivate and settle the great Central Valley. Aware of the need to further colonize California, the governor gave him permission to start a settlement. He granted Sutter Mexican citizenship and later awarded him 47,827 acres.

In 1840, even before he had received his land patent, Sutter began constructing his adobe "fort" on a bluff above the confluence of the American and Sacramento Rivers. He dubbed it "New Helvetia" (Switzerland). Through a blend of gifts, kindness and threats, he subjugated the local Indians, conning them into doing most of the work.

Gregarious, generous, cunning and a genial host, Sutter became a central figure in early California. New Helvetia was a popular way station and refuge, where travelers were fed, sheltered and even clothed by the generous Sutter. He sent a rescue team for the ill-fated Donner Party in 1847, and invited the survivors to recuperate at his fort. He hosted the likes of John C. Frèmont (who didn't trust him), Kit Carson and pioneer John Bidwell.

Bidwell wrote: "Sutter has surpassed in many respects any man I have ever known. He spoke several languages and was courteous and princely in manner. He listened respectfully to others, and made everyone his friend."

Sutter created California's first factories and was its first major employer, with as many as 450 on his payroll—a mix of sailors, Kanakas (Hawaiians), Mexican cowboys and Indians. The fort, with its tannery, carpentry shops, bakery, distillery and kitchens, became the state's first shopping center.

It was inevitable that he become entangled politically as America worked to snatch California from Mexico. He became unwilling host to a sputtering Mariano Guadalupe Vallejo, northern California's Mexican governor-general, who had been captured by a group of Yankees during Sonoma's Bear Flag Revolt in 1846. Although Sutter sympathized with Americans and saw that their conquest of California was inevitable, he owed his fortunes, his vast holdings—and at least a certain amount of allegiance—to his Mexican hosts.

When the 1848 Treaty of Guadalupe Hidalgo granted California to the United States, Sutter decided he'd rather switch than fight; he allied himself with the Americans. He might have remained in his pivotal role as early California's leading citizen had he not sent itinerant carpenter James Marshall into the nearby hills to build a sawmill.

As mentioned earlier, the Gold Rush ruined Sutter. Settlers squatted on his land and, in a final insult, the new California legislature ruled in the squatters' favor, essentially stripping him of his vast holdings. Disgusted and financially ruined, he spent his last years in Washington, D.C., trying to recover some shred of his holdings. He died of heart failure on June 18, 1880.

Even as Sutter's fortunes declined, Sacramento thrived—as the gateway to the gold fields, the head of navigation on the Sacramento River and the stopping point for the Pony Express and transcontinental railroad. After several false starts, it became California's capital in 1854.

Ironically, Sutter's fort languished while the new Sacramento flourished. Sutter's own son, John Augustus, Jr.—left in charge while Sutter was in the Gold Country trying to save his empire—decided that the new community should be built along the riverfront, a mile away.

THE WAY IT IS • Ignore those disparaging remarks about "Sacratomato" (inspired by a catsup company which, unfortunately, uses Sacramento as its brand name). California's capital is an attractive, thriving city with wide, tree-lined streets, prosperous suburbs and—for the visitor—an abundance of attractions. Much of its American River corridor is preserved in pretty parklands. The Sacramento River front, where Sutter Junior decreed that the new city should be built, is now California's largest state historic park.

Sacramento is an easy city to navigate, since it's laid out like a giant waffle, with numbered streets running east to west and lettered ones north to south. A true California hub, it is served by major east-west and north-south freeways and by a busy airport.

DISCOVERIES
The historic attractions

Although Sacramento is logically arranged, it *is* large, so we'll take you on a driving tour of its major historic attractions, beginning where the city began. From whatever direction you're approaching, get on Business I-80 and watch for an off-ramp sign directing you to Sutter's Fort, at 28th and L streets.

Sutter's Fort State Historic Park • *2701 L St., Sacramento, CA 95814; (916) 445-4422. Daily 10 to 5. Adults $2, kids 6 to 17, $1.* This large off-white quadrangle is a faithful reconstruction of the original. The fort had deteriorated to a single scruffy building by the late 1850s, as settlers carried off its lumber and adobe bricks to build the new California. It was purchased by the Native Sons of the Golden West in 1890 and became a state historic park in 1947.

Although the fort is surrounded by homes and commercial districts of busy Sacramento, it's buffered by a four-block-square park shaded by mature trees. Once inside the sheltering walls, the visitor can picture life as it was during Sutter's day. The tannery, blacksmith shop, cooperage, candelry and other shops have been re-created. Docents and rangers bring them to life with talks and demonstrations during "living history days" conducted several times a year. At other times, you can clap a "magic wand" to your ear and follow a numbered course, listing to the sounds of yesterday.

The interpretive museum just to the right of the entry gate is the fort's best feature. Here, through excellent dioramas, artifacts and graphics, you will learn much about this remarkable who shaped a good deal of California's early history.

State Indian Museum • *2618 K Street, Sacramento, CA 95814; (916) 445-4209. Daily 10 to 5. Adults $2, kids 6 to 17, $1. Located on the northwestern corner of the Sutter's Fort park at 26th and K streets.* The best Indian museum in California, this facility presents an accurate, realistic and sympathetic portrait of the peoples who were displaced, first by the Spanish and then by the American argonauts.

Nicely done exhibits are thematic, with artifacts and graphics detailing the Native Californians' crafts, food preparation, weapons, social and spiritual lives. Displays convey the visitor from pre-Columbian days through Spanish and American settlement to the present as California Indians work to preserve their heritage. Films and slide shows portray their lives yesterday and today. "Think of the museum as a bridge across time, not just a storehouse of objects," says one of the film narrators.

One leaves this place with a sobering statistic. Two hundred years ago, 300,000 Indians lived in California. Within 50 years, at the peak of the Gold Rush, the population had been reduced to 30,000.

From the fort-Indian museum complex, follow one-way K Street West. Within a mile, you'll brush the side of your next stop.

California State Capitol • *Tenth Street at Capitol Mall; (916) 324-0333. Weekdays 7 to 6, weekends 10 to 5; docent tours on the hour, 9:30 to 4.* California's seat of government since 1869, the capitol still gleams from its six-year, $68 million restoration, completed in 1981. A study in turn-of-the-century grandeur, it's the most exquisite capitol building in America. It's even more beautiful than the Nation's Capitol, of which it is a copy.

Guided tours will take you down marbled corridors, beneath gleaming chandeliers, up monumental stairways and past state offices with their great polished wood doors. Or, you can wander about on your own, rubbing shoulders with those who ponder various ways to spend our taxes. Everything you see here—except our legislators, of course—is a feast for the eyes. Admire the gold leaf, scrollwork, *fleur de lys* and filigree of the most meticulous restoration of a public building ever accomplished.

You should end your visit with a stop at the Capitol Museum in the basement. There, exhibits will tell you more about California's seat of government than you probably ever wanted to know. The museum offers a nice little book and gift shop as well. You might like to plan lunch in the Capitol Restaurant, a cafeteria-style cafe which, like the rest of the place, is a study in turn-of-the-century finery.

After doing the capitol, you may want to explore the lush green expanses of its surrounding park, covering ten city blocks. You can pick up a walking tour of the grounds and other government buildings at the Capitol Museum.

Then bid goodbye to the park squirrels who—like many capitol visitors— are seeking something for nothing, and continue on to Old Sacramento. You could walk the eight-block stretch west along Capitol Mall, but then, who would feed your parking meter? It's probably best to return to K Street, drive west and follow directional signs. Several 90-degree turns will get you to Old Sacramento's parking garages. You can find street parking on weekdays.

Old Sacramento • *Between Second and Front streets, along the Sacramento River, next to I-5. Two visitor centers offer information and guide maps: Sacramento Visitor Information Center near the Delta King at 1104 Front Street, (916) 442-7644; and the Old Sacramento Merchants Association Visitor Center at 917 Front St., next to the Eagle Theater, (916) 443-7815. At the Sacramento History Center, California Railroad Museum or Central Pacific Passenger Station, you can purchase combination tickets good for admission to six historic sites in Sacramento. Walking tours of Old Sacramento are conducted daily at 9:30 and 11, departing from the front of the railroad museum.*

Once a rundown waterfront area, Old Sacramento has experienced a remarkable transformation in the past two decades. It's now a wonderful gathering of restored brick, stone and masonry buildings, cobbled streets and raised wooden sidewalks. It offers the city's largest collection of museums, boutiques, curio shops and restaurants. What the historic park lacks in authenticity (We've found no record of a Carl's Jr., Subway or sushi restaurant during the Gold Rush) it makes up for with its many attractions. Here's a list of some of the best:

California State Railroad Museum, *Second and I streets; (916) 448-4466. Daily 10 to 5 (last entry at 4:30); adults $5, kids 6 to 17, $2.* We're tempted to call this one of the finest historical museums in the state; it is certainly the best railroad museum anywhere. This is the cornerstone to Old Sacramento—appropriate since it was the railroads that knitted California to the rest of the Union. Later, these same railroads spread the state's rich agricultural and industrial bounty across America.

This is a monumental museum, a stunning collection of full-sized trains in larger than life settings. You see the original Central Pacific Engine #1, poised to enter a Sierra Nevada tunnel hacked out by Chinese laborers; Lucius Beebee's luxurious Gold Coast private railway car; and a full-scale Spanish Colonial California railway station straight out of the 1920s. You walk the narrow corridor of a Pullman coach as it hurries through the night, feeling its gentle sway, hearing the rhythmic click of the rails and watching signals flash by at the crossings. In one of the most impressive museums exhibits anywhere, you see the gleaming red, black, brass and gold 1873 Empire locomotive displayed in a hall of mirrors, creating a stunning kaleidoscopic effect.

Sacramento History Museum, *Front and I streets; (916) 449-2057. Tuesday-Sunday 10 to 5, closed Monday. Adults $2.50, kids 6 to 17, $1.* Housed in a brick 1854 waterworks building, this large, nicely-done museum effectively captures Sacramento's yesterdays, from John Sutter's arrival through the discovery of Gold to the turn of the century and beyond.

Visitors see full-sized mock-ups of the 18th century *Sacramento Bee* (still publishing), a gold miner's cabin, exhibits focusing on the city's various ethnic groups and a time line with graphics, artifacts and old posters. Our favorite display focuses on California agriculture, with old fruit box labels, farm equipment, an early kitchen set up for home canning and a conveyer belt that parades cans of Blue Diamond almonds throughout the exhibit.

Central Pacific Passenger Station and **Freight Depot,** *Front Street between K and I streets. Daily 10 to 5; admission included with State Railroad Museum.* Got to catch a train? This is a faithful reproduction of the wooden passenger station that served Sacramento during the 1870s.

"Magic wand" audio tours take visitors through the ticket office, into a waiting room reserved for ladies, and to train-side where a steam locomotive chuffs quietly, waiting to begin its trip east. Through your wand, voices tell you what train travel was like back in those days. The Silver Palace Refreshment Saloon is a replica of a train station diner, serving real food (listed below). A recent addition to the complex is the Central Pacific Freight Depot, with a collection of freight cars and stacks of cargo ready for shipping.

The Delta King riverboat, *at the foot of K Street; (916) 444-KING or (800) 825-KING.* Two grand riverboats, the *Delta King* and *Delta Queen*, ran passengers between San Francisco and Sacramento from 1927 until 1940. The Queen eventually found a new life on the Mississippi but the King languished and crumbled at dockside for generations. Then in the late 1980s, it was rescued by a private firm, returned to its original glossy elegance and berthed at Old Sacramento.

The King offers staterooms done in the style of the Roaring Twenties, the Pilot House restaurant, two cocktail lounges and a cute little below-decks theater that hosts plays and musicales. Visitors are free to walk about the riverboat's primly restored decks, peek into the theater and, of course, have dinner or drinks in the two lounges.

Citizen Soldier Museum, *1119 Second St.; (916) 442-2883. Tuesday-Sunday 10 to 5, closed Monday. Adults $2.25, seniors $1.50, kids 6 to 17, $1.* Sponsored by the California National Guard Historical Society, it traces the history of the state's part-time soldiers from the days of the Spanish through 19th century home militia companies to the present-day National Guard. It ends with an Operation Desert Storm scene, with a called-up California guardsman sharing a tent with an Arab soldier; an Arabic-lettered can of

Coke adds a nice touch. Exhibits include uniforms, weapons, medals, company banners and such.

Huntington and Hopkins Hardware, *Front and I streets. Daily 10 to 5.* This brickfront structure is part working hardware store and part exhibit center. Docents or park interpretive specialists will talk about hardware stores of yesterday, or sell you a scythe, gold pan or oil lamp.

Wells Fargo Museum, *1000 Second St.; (916) 440-4263. Daily 10 to 5.* This small museum offers artifacts of Wells Fargo's early days as the Gold Rush's largest express company. Exhibits include a strongbox, gold scales, bank drafts, a model stage coach and a display concerning Black Bart. It also has an automatic teller machine, in case you have a cash card, and you've spent too generously in Old Sacramento's dozens of shops.

Old Eagle Theatre, *925 Front St.; (916) 323-7234. Open weekends 10 to 4.* This is a reproduction of Sacramento's first theater, which brought entertainment to argonauts from 1849 until 1851. A 14-minute slide show, presented on the hour, focuses on Sacramento's history. A local theater group presents contemporary plays here on weekends.

Other Sacramento attractions

While not linked to the Gold Rush, these other lures in California's capital city are certainly worth your consideration.

Crocker Art Museum • *Third and O streets; (916) 449-5423. Tuesday-Sunday 10 to 5 (until 9 Thursdays). Adults $2.50, kids $1.* This is the oldest art museum in the West, started in 1873 and currently housed in a restored Victorian. Exhibits range from European masters and Asian art to works of California artists and photographers.

Governor's Mansion • *Sixteenth and H streets; (916) 324-0539. Guided tours on the hour from 10 to 4. Adults $1, kids $1.* This beautifully restored Victorian was home to 13 California governors, from 1877 to 1967. It has been returned to its 19th century elegance with crystal chandeliers, polished woods, Italian marble fireplaces and French mirrors.

Leland Stanford Mansion • *802 N St.; (916) 324-0575. Tours generally on Tuesdays and Thursdays at 12:15 and Saturdays at 12:15 and 1:30; schedules vary so call first.* Folks who take these tours will see a museum in the making. This brick Victorian, home to railroad baron and governor Leland Stanford from 1861 until the turn of the century, is being restored as California's newest historic park. **McClellan Aviation Museum** • *McClellan Air Force Base, North Highlands; (916) 643-3192. Monday-Saturday 9 to 3; free. Entry through Gate Three.* Indoor and outdoor displays trace the history of military aviation, with a goodly collection of planes, uniforms and such.

Silver Wings Aviation Museum • *Mather Air Force Base, Rancho Cordova; (916) 364-2177. Weekdays 10 to 4, weekends noon to 4; free.* This flight museum offers a large gathering of both military and civilian aircraft, from rag-wing World War I fighters to modern jets.

Towe Ford Museum of California • *220 Front St.; (916) 442-6802. Daily 10 to 6. Adults $5; teens 14 to 18, $2.50; kids 5 to 13, $1.* Is there a Ford in your future or, more appropriately, in your past? The Towe Museum exhibits the world's largest antique Ford collection, with 175 cars and trucks, starting with the earliest Tin Lizzies.

OLD SACRAMENTO DINING

California Fats Pacific Grill and Wok • ΔΔΔ $$$ ∅

1015 Front St.; (916) 441-7966. California-Oriental; dinners $10 to $16; full bar service. Lunch Monday-Saturday 11:30 to 2, midday menu 2 to 5, Sunday brunch 10:30 to 2, dinner nightly 5:30 to 10. Reservations accepted; MC/VISA, AMEX. Intriguing *nouveau* machine shop decor with neon piping, open beams, assorted blue and red shapes and a 30-foot waterfall. Creative menu is a mix of California and Pacific Rim fare, with goodies such as honey-glazed duck, immigrant's beef, and catfish with tomato and onions.

Fanny Annie's • ΔΔ $

1023 Second St.; (916) 441-0505. Light snacks; meals $4 to $6; full bar service. Monday-Saturday 11:30 a.m. to 2 a.m., Sunday 11:30 to midnight. MC/VISA. Lively, cheerful oldstyle saloon decorated with an explosion of 19th century doo-dads: wagon wheels, moonshiner jugs, carousel horses and whatever; most of it hangs from the ceiling. Drinking establishment, with a limited menu featuring burgers, chicken fingers, buffalo wings and such.

Firehouse • ΔΔΔΔ $$$$ ∅∅

1112 Second St.; (916) 442-4772. Continental; dinners $18 to $35; full bar service. Lunch weekdays 11:30 to 2:15, dinner Monday-Saturday 5:30 to 10:15. Reservations accepted. MC/VISA, AMEX. Old Sacramento's most elegant restaurant, with a posh New Orleans decor, inserted into an 1853 brick firehouse. Attractive courtyard for warm weather dining. Small, creative Continental menu features grilled swordfish, mango chicken, fettucini and such. Coat and tie preferred for dinner.

Fat City Bar & Cafe • ΔΔΔ $$$ ∅

1001 Front St.; (916) 446-6768. American-continental; dinners $11 to $15; full bar service. Lunch weekdays 11:30 to 2:30, brunch weekends 10:30 to 2:30, dinner Sunday-Thursday 5:30 to 10 and Friday-Saturday 5:30 to 11, early bird dinners weekdays from 4. Reservations for groups only. MC/VISA, AMEX. Exceptionally appealing 19th century style restaurant and bar with polished woods, Tiffany style fixtures and leaded glass. Versatile menu ranges from fish to pepper steak, garlic sirloin, pork chops and some pasta dishes. The cocktail lounge is Old Sacramento's most attractive, with a century-old mahogany, brass and glass back bar and Victorian couches.

Fulton's Prime Rib • ΔΔΔ $$$ ∅

900 Second St.; (916) 444-9641. American; dinners $16 to $25; full bar service. Lunch daily 11 to 3, dinner Monday-Thursday 5 to 10, Friday-Saturday 5 to 11 and Sunday 4 to 9:30. Reservations accepted. Major credit cards. Warm, wood-paneled restaurant with a cozy, clubby feel; sunken patio for warm-weather dining. Prime rib, of course, along with fresh seafood, roast chicken, scampi and steaks.

Pilot House Restaurant • ΔΔΔ $$$ ∅

Aboard The Delta King; (800) 825-KING or (916) 444-KING. California nouveau; dinners $16 to $30; full bar service. Lunch 11:30 to 2, Sunday brunch 10 to 2, dinner 5 to 10. Reservations accepted. Major credit cards. Small, stylish wood paneled dining room with brocaded chairs, wall sconces, brass trim and other subtly elegant nautical touches. The small menu features creative California and American regional fare.

Silver Palace Cafe • △△ $

In the Central Pacific Railway station at Front and I streets; (916) 448-0151. American diner style menu; meals $4 to $6; wine and beer. Daily 10 to 5, lunch served 11 to 4. No credit cards; checks accepted. Typical 19th century diner with oiled wooden floors, wooden counter and bentwood chairs. Early California specials such as miner's stew and dog breath chili, plus assorted sandwiches and salads.

Spirit of Sacramento cruise boat • △△ $$$ ØØ

On the waterfront at 1207 Front St.; (916) 552-2933. California nouveau; dinner cruises $15 to $17.50 per person plus dinners at $13 to $20, lunch cruises $20 including meal, Sunday brunch cruises $25 with meal; full bar service. Lunch cruises depart at 11, dinner cruises at 7:30. Reservations essential; office hours 7:30 a.m. to 5 p.m. daily. MC/VISA. While the *Delta King* is anchored at dockside, the *Spirit of Sacramento* paddlewheeler chugs up and down the river with its dining guests. Like the *Delta*, it has been handsomely refurbished with teakwood, polished brass and beveled glass.

LODGING

The capital city offers thousands of rooms in scores of hotels and motels, but only one in Old Sacramento.

The Delta King • △△△ $$$$ Ø

1000 Front St., Sacramento, CA 95814; (916) 444-KING or (800) 825-KING. Doubles $85 to $400, singles $75 to $350. Major credit cards. Restored riverboat staterooms with mahogany wainscoting, print wallpaper, oversized brass beds, TVs tucked into armoires, wall sconces and wicker furniture. Small baths modernized with tile bath and showers. Captain's suite is a study in nautical elegance, with opulent decor and a private deck.

Is there life after dark?

Laughs Unlimited comedy showroom at Second and Firehouse Alley (446-5905) features stand-up humor Tuesday-Thursday and Sunday at 8 p.m. and Friday-Saturday at 8 and 10:30. **Fannie Annie's,** 1023 Second St. (441-0505) offers DJ dancing nightly and the **Spirit of Sacramento** provides live music with its Friday and Saturday night dinner cruises. **The Delta King** riverboat theater (444-KING) hosts plays and musicales, while its **Delta Lounge** features a pianist nightly and vocalist Tuesday-Saturday and its **Paddlewheel Saloon** offers 50s to 70s DJ dancing.

To learn more...

Sacramento Convention & Visitors Bureau, 1421 K St., Sacramento, CA 95814; (916) 449-6711. The bureau's Old Sacramento information center at 1104 Front Street (442-7644) is open daily 9 to 5 daily.

Old Sacramento Citizens & Merchants Association, 917 Front St., Sacramento, CA 95814; (916) 443-7815 or 443-0677. The visitors' bureau near the Eagle Theater is open weekdays 10 to 5.

> *"For a golden decade the mines had poured their riches down into the State of California and through San Francisco's Golden Gate to the rest of the world. Some six hundred millions of dollars had been lifted from stream-beds, washed from dry diggings to which water had been painfully brought, crushed from the hard quartz, sluiced down from the hills by giant nozzles."*
>
> **— from *Anybody's Gold* by Joseph Henry Jackson**

THE END OF AN ERA:
TAILING WHEEL
NEAR JACKSON

Chapter Nineteen

AFTERTHOUGHTS

The very best and a Gold Rush glossary

THE WAY IT WAS • As we've established in the preceding 230 pages, Marshall's discovery at Sutter's Mill was the single most significant event in California's history. The rush for gold launched a wave of immigration that catapulted the Golden State into statehood. That flood tide of folks continues, and today it is the most populous state in the Union.

What would California be like, some have asked, if Marshall hadn't found those flakes? Would it have remained for several more decades a genteel land of cattle ranches and Latin charm? After all, it had been Mexican territory until the United States snatched it away in the late 1840s.

"Americans were filtering in, more every year, but they were scattered and there were not enough of them to affect the Californian way of living," writes historian Joseph Henry Jackson in *Anybody's Gold.* "Many of them married into old families, settled into ranch life and found it good."

However, even if Marshall were myopic and hadn't noticed that gleam in the tailrace, or if he didn't know gold flakes from corn flakes, someone was bound to stumble across it before too long. Gold was abundant in the Sierra Nevada foothills. So Marshall's discovery merely started in motion an event that was bound to occur.

And what an event it was! More people moved across the country between 1849 and 1859 than in any decade before or since. The Gold Rush not only started a stampede of Americans across America, it attracted fortune hunters from all over the globe.

The Chinese of Chinese Camp, the Mexicans of Sonora, the Gauls of Frenchman's Gulch, the Cornish of Grass Valley, Sutter's Hawaiians, the

Blacks who followed William Downie—all gave California a rich ethnic mix that flourishes to this day.

THE WAY IT IS • Gold comes from granite, and granite doesn't grow grain. The irony of the Gold Country is that, with a few exceptions, it's now one of the least populated areas of California. Certainly, it is one of the state's most beautiful regions, but one can't eat scenery.

When the gold played out, many of the argonauts adjourned to the valleys and the coast, where crops could be planted and fish could be caught. The Sierra Nevada streams were beautiful but not navigable, and large cities need reliable supply routes. Thus San Francisco and the river-navigable towns of Sacramento and Stockton became the new state's population centers. Hundreds of gold camps dissolved into the foothill foliage and others survive as shadows of their former glory.

It was this abandonment, boom followed by bust, that created the Gold Country we enjoy today. More than any other place in California, perhaps in America, *La Veta Madre* is a rich repository of yesterday. Nowhere else can one find such a collection of 19th century architecture, historical monuments, mining ruins and fine museums, all set amidst the Sierra foothill scenery.

Unfortunately, there is trouble in this beautiful land. While some communities are earnestly concerned about preserving their past, others seem more preoccupied with shopping centers and tract homes. The problem is aggravated by a recent growth surge as San Francisco Bay Areans and burned-out Los Angelenos are attracted by the Gold Country's scenery, laid-back lifestyle and inespensive housing.

Consider, for instance, this comment from one of those throw-away tourist newspapers published in Mariposa: "It is not...gold mining and pioneering memorabilia which pillar the community today. Rather, it is the expanding motel market, new homes, and small shopping malls that make up the town's revenue."

That same mentality led to the dissection of Grass Valley and Nevada City by a freeway, the drowning of Bagby and Jacksonville by fake lakes and the excess modernization of many fine old business districts.

Fortunately, that attitude has taken a dramatic turn since the first edition of this guide was published. Mariposa is again focusing on downtown preservation and the area has been declared a national historic district. Sonora has done wondrous things with its old town area while trying valiantly to solve its traffic problems. Auburn has returned its courts to its impeccablely refurbished 1894 County Courthouse.

We are witnessing a cultural revolution in reverse, as everyone from Nevada City shopkeepers to Native Americans of the Wassama Roundhouse turn to the past, working to preserve the heritage of this land.

So be not alarmed, potential Gold Country visitors. There is even more to discover in *La Veta Madre*.

After spending these 200 or so pages seeking the best of the Gold Country, let's have a bit of fun and select the Ten Best of the best. We'll pick our favorite, followed by the other nine in alphabetical order. Thus, we have no losers in **The Best of the Gold Country**—only winners and runners-up.

THE TEN BEST ATTRACTIONS

1. Sierra County Historical Park • *Sierra City (Chapter 17)*. This is a dark horse winner since other historic sites, particularly the state parks, are more elaborate, and several Gold Country museums are more professionally done. However, this offers the ideal mix of attractions: an intact mine and stamp mill that gives visitors a complete picture of hardrock mining, plus an interesting museum, and an amphitheater that hosts a summer concert series, all in a pretty hillside forest setting.

2. California State Mining and Mineral Museum • *Mariposa (Chapter 3)*. The state mineral museum, with its mock-up mine, excellent historical exhibits and glittering displays of gold and other minerals, is the newest and one of the finest of the Gold Country's exhibit centers.

3. Chaw'se Indian Grinding Rock State Historic Park • *Pine Grove (Chapter 10)*. Here, you learn how the original Mother Lode residents, the Native Americans, lived before outsiders ruined their culture.

4. Empire Mine State Historic Park • *Grass Valley (Chapter 15)*. This fine museum offers a vivid portrayal of mining as a big business, with many of the original structures intact.

5. Kennedy Mine Tailing Wheels • *Jackson (Chapter 10)*. The most fascinating structures in the Gold Country, these giant wheels symbolize the closing days of the Gold Rush.

6. Malakoff Diggins State Historic Park • *North Bloomfield (Chapter 16)*. The park, set in an attractive pine forest, offers a fascinating view of controversial hydraulic mining—and its scars.

7. Mariposa County History Center • *Mariposa (Chapter 3)*. It's the best of the county-sponsored history centers, and one of the Sierra foothills' finer museums.

8. Plumas-Eureka State Park • *Blairsden (Chapter 17)*. This is one of the Gold Country's most attractive parks, preserving the remnants of a large mining operation and an old mining town high among the Sierra pines.

9. Railtown 1897 State Historic Park • *Jamestown (Chapter 5)*. Here, we learn of the vital role that railroads played in the development of the Sierra Foothills after the Gold Rush.

10. Sutter's Mill • *Coloma (Chapter 13)*. This realistic reproduction of the mill that started it all is the focal point of Marshall Gold Discovery State Historic Park.

THE TEN BEST RESTAURANTS

1. City Hotel Restaurant • *Columbia (Chapter 7)*. This blend of excellent food, historic setting and a friendly, efficient staff earns our vote as the Gold Country's best place to pick up a fork.

2. Butterworth's • *Auburn (Chapter 14)*. Fine European dining in a handsome Victorian gives Butterworth's a spot on our list.

3. Erna's Elderberry House • *Oakhurst (Chapter 2)*. That Mediterranean villa elegance and imaginative prix fixe menu gains it a nomination.

4. Friar Tuck's • *Nevada City (Chapter 16)*. With its great wine bar ambiance and tasty American food, it's one of our favorite restaurants, not only in the Gold Country, but in California.

5. Hemingway's • *Sonora (Chapter 6)*. A pleasant blend of European decor in a ranch setting, with fine French cuisine wins Hemingway's a Ten Best spot.

6. Peter Seleya's • *Nevada City (Chapter 16)*. The next generation has taken over Seleya's and taken the California *nouveau* menu to new culinary heights.

7. Ristorante LaTorre • *Sonora (Chapter 6)*. This stylish new second-floor restaurant is a study in Gold Rush refinement, with an interesting Italian-continental menu.

8. Sutter Creek Palace • *Sutter Creek (Chapter 11)*. The Palace offers a bit of Gold Rush opulence with its excellent American cooking.

9. Tofanelli's • *Grass Valley (Chapter 15)* This cute little cafe earns a Ten Best spot because of its remarkably tasty *and* inexpensive fare, served in a pleasant yesterday setting.

10. Utica Mansion Restaurant • *Angels Camp (Chapter 8)*. This faultlessly restored Victorian mansion shelters one of the Mother Lode's most appealing dining retreats.

THE TEN BEST B&Bs

1. The Foxes • *Sutter Creek (Chapter 11)*. Many of the area's bed & breakfast inns are in refurbished Victorian homes, and The Foxes is the best of the lot. Impeccable restoration, exquisite Victorian furnishings and hostess Min Fox's delightful fox collection guarantee a memorable stay.

2. Château du Sureau • *Oakhurst (Chapter 2)*. This is an opulent new French country style chateau furnished with the finest European antiques, fabrics and artworks.

3. Chichester House • *Placerville (Chapter 12)*. Fine interior woodwork and attractive antiques highlight this beautifully finished Victorian.

4. Gold Quartz Inn • *Sutter Creek (Chapter 11)*. This is a stylish new inn with an elegant "Victorian farmhouse" look, coupled with modern conveniences.

5. Grandmere's Bed & Breakfast • *Nevada City (Chapter 16)*. This stately Colonial Revival home is one of the Gold Country's more opulent B&Bs.

6. Meadow Creek Ranch Bed and Breakfast Inn • *Mariposa (Chapter 3)*. We like the relaxed rural setting of this nicely furnished inn, housed in an old ranch house and stage stop.

7. The Red Castle Inn • *Nevada City (Chapter 16)*. A rare example of Gothic Revival architecture, this gingerbread classic is a Gold Rush landmark.

8. Wedgewood Inn • *Jackson (Chapter 10)*. You'll bask in 19th century charm, although this is brand new, a striking replica of an elegant Victorian home.

9. Windrose Inn • *Jackson (Chapter 10)*. Pretty gardens and a solarium add special charm to this restored century-old farmhouse.

10. Utica Mansion Inn • *Angels Camp (Chapter 8)*. This stunningly restored Victorian mansion is one of the Gold Country's most elaborately coiffed lodgings.

THE FIVE BEST HOTELS

Face it, folks, there are only about ten surviving hotels in the Gold Country, and some are rather worn around the edges. The five listed below have been carefully restored.

1. The best state-restored hotel: THE FALLON • *Columbia (Chapter 7)*. In a rare gesture of extravagance, the usually snug-budgeted State of California spent generously several years ago to re-create a vision in 1880s opulence.

1. The best privately-restored hotel: THE HOLBROOKE • *Grass Valley (Chapter 15)*. History-conscious citizens preserved a piece of history and re-created a masterpiece in this opulent hostelry.

3. The City Hotel • *Columbia (Chapter 7)*. This is a dual winner: the Gold Country's finest restaurant and an authentic restoration of an 1860s hostelry.

4. Jamestown Hotel • *Jamestown (Chapter 5)*. This small hotel mirrors its Gold Rush past with its lavish Victorian dress, yet its underpinnings are modern.

5. Murphys Hotel • *Murphys (Chapter 8)*. History echoes through the hallways of this venerable hostelry, where the likes of Mark Twain, J. Pierpont Morgan and Ulysses S. Grant rested their heads.

A GOLD RUSH GLOSSARY
What did they mean by that?

You hope a new business venture "pans out" so you can "strike it rich." Then you can "lay claim" to your share of the profits and get some money in your "poke." Meanwhile, with all your funds invested, you need a "grubstake" to get by in a "pinch." These are among the many expressions added to our language during the California Gold Rush.

What follows is a glossary of terms used in mining, yesterday and today:

Amalgamation — The process of using mercury, which combines with gold and silver, to separate it from pulverized ore. The mercury is thus the "amalgam."

Aqua regia — A mixture of nitric acid and hydrochloric acid, which dissolves gold and platinum; used in ore processing.

Argonaut — A seeker of gold, specifically a 49er. The term originated with Jason who sailed his ship, the *Argo*, in a *nautical* search for the Golden Fleece.

Arrastra — A mule-powered millstone for crushing gold ore, used by Mexican miners; similar to a horizontal flour mill.

Audit — Mine entrance that's horizontal or inclined.

Bar — Not a saloon, but a reference to a sand or gravel bar in a river.

Bullion — gold or silver that's been processed and melted into bars or bricks.

Celestials — A name for Chinese miners; a reference to the Celestial Empire. Victims of vicious discrimination, they were the source of many negative expressions, such as "He doesn't have a Chinaman's chance," and "He'll work for China wages."

Color — traces of gold in a pan, usually referring to flakes or dust.

Cousin Jack — Cornish miners' nickname. They were such good miners that an employer would pay to have a relative—a "cousin Jack"—brought over from England.

Coyote hole — A shaft or tunnel—usually about man sized—that yields gold. "Coyoting" was the practice of digging these shallow holes.

Diggins — a claim being worked; mining camps often were called "diggins."

Drift — A horizontal shaft leading from the main bore in a mine.

Dust — Fine gold flakes, often used as legal tender during the Gold Rush. A "pinch" was the amount of dust held between the thumb and forefinger, usually worth a dollar in trade. (Some bartenders would covertly press buckshot or a small pebble between their thumb and forefinger to make a greater indention and thus get a larger pinch from the miner's poke.)

El Dorado or Eldorado — Spanish for a land of wealth; a term often applied to California. *Dorado* means gilded or golden.

Fandango hall — Mexican saloon, named for a popular and rather wild dance.

Flat — A level area or basin, often applied to mining camps, such as Big Oak Flat.

Fools' gold — Pyrite, which never fools a real miner, since it's flaky and brittle and bears little resemblance to soft, malleable gold.

Glory hole — an excavation, usually shallow, that yields a lot of gold.

"Going to see the elephant" — An expression to describe the adventure of heading for the California goldfields.

Grubstake — Sufficient food and supplies to keep a prospector going. Some investors would "grubstake" a miner in exchange for a percentage of the gold he found.

Headframe — Tall framework above a vertical mine shaft, used for lowering men and equipment and bringing out the ore. Also called a gallows frame.

Hydraulicking — A mining technique using a powerful jet of water to remove surface material and reach gold deposits underneath. The loose material was then directed into a sluice to separate the gold.

Lode — An underground vein bearing gold or other valuable metal.

Long tom — A long sluice with riffles in the bottom to separate gold from sand and gravel. Material from hydraulic mining would be passed through a "tom."

Monitor — Metal nozzle attached to a length of hose, used to direct a powerful jet of water for hydraulic mining.

Mother lode or Motherlode — The main gold vein, from Spanish *Veta Madre*.

Ore — Rock containing metal in sufficient quantity to make it worth mining.

Overburden — Dirt, rock and other material covering gold-bearing veins or gravel; the stuff removed by hydraulicking.

Paydirt — Ore, sand or gravel that's rich in gold or other precious metal.

Placer — A sand or gravel deposit containing gold, usually eroded from the hills or deposited by a river.

Placer mining — Basically, mining on the surface, as opposed to hardrock or deep-pit mining. Panning and sluicing are placer mining techniques.

Pocket — An area of sand or gravel that's rich in gold, or a gold-bearing vein in a hardrock mine.

Poke — A small pouch, usually leather, in which the miners carried their gold dust. A pinch from a poke would buy a shot of whisky.

Retort — High-temperature furnace used for refining gold.

Rocker — A wooden box with rockers and a ribbed bottom, used to separate gold from sand and gravel; also called a cradle, which it resembled.

Sluice — An inclined flume with a ribbed bottom used, like the rocker, to separate gold. A long tom was simply a long sluice.

Sniping — Reworking an abandoned claim, often practiced by the Chinese of the Gold Rush; they sometimes found more gold than the original miners.

Stamps — Metal battering rams, lifted and dropped by rotating cams, to crush ore for gold or silver extraction; the mechanical heart of a stamp mill.

Strike — A presumably profitable discovery of gold or silver.

Tailings — Waste material left over after ore is processed; also material removed from a mine during tunneling.

Tailing dump — Mound of waste material at the entrance to a mine.

Worked out — An underground mine or placer mining claim that no longer yields gold or silver.

INDEX